PLAYS BY RENAISSANCE AND RESTORATION DRAMATISTS
General Editor: Graham Storey

VOLUMES IN THIS SERIES

PUBLISHED

The plays of Cyril Tourneur, edited by George Parfitt: *The Revenger's Tragedy; The Atheist's Tragedy*

The selected plays of Philip Massinger, edited by Colin Gibson: *The Duke of Milan; The Roman Actor; A New Way to Pay Old Debts; The City Madam*

The selected plays of Thomas Middleton, edited by David L. Frost: *A Mad World, My Masters; A Chaste Maid in Cheapside; Women Beware Women; The Changeling* (with William Rowley)

The plays of William Wycherley, edited by Peter Holland: *Love in a Wood; The Gentleman Dancing-Master; The Country-Wife; The Plain Dealer*

The plays of George Etherege, edited by Michael Cordner: *The Man of Mode; She Would if She Could; The Comical Revenge*

FORTHCOMING

The selected plays of John Webster, edited by Jonathan Dollimore and Alan Sinfield: *The White Devil; The Devil's Law Case; The Duchess of Malfi*

The selected plays of Ben Jonson, edited by Johanna Procter: *Sejanus; Epicoene*, or *The Silent Woman; Volpone; The Alchemist; Bartholomew Fair*

The selected plays of John Marston, edited by M. D. Jackson and Michael Neil: *Antonio and Mellida; Antonio's Revenge; The Malcontent; The Dutch Courtezan; Sophonisba*

The selected plays of John Ford, edited by Colin Gibson: *'Tis Pity She's a Whore; The Broken Heart; Perkin Warbeck*

THE COMEDIES OF WILLIAM CONGREVE

The Old Batchelour

The Double Dealer

Love for Love

The Way of the World

EDITED BY
ANTHONY G. HENDERSON

CAMBRIDGE UNIVERSITY PRESS
CAMBRIDGE
LONDON NEW YORK NEW ROCHELLE
MELBOURNE SYDNEY

Published by the Press Syndicate of the University of Cambridge
The Pitt Building, Trumpington Street, Cambridge CB2 1RP
32 East 57th Street, New York, NY 10022, USA
296 Beaconsfield Parade, Middle Park, Melbourne 3206, Australia

First published 1982

Printed in Great Britain at the University Press, Cambridge

Library of Congress catalogue card number: 82–1182

British Library Cataloguing in publication data

Congreve, William, *1607 – 1729*
The comedies of William Congreve. – (Plays by
Renaissance and Restoration dramatists)
I. Title II. Henderson, Anthony G. III. Series
822′.4 PR3362

ISBN 0 521 24747 0 hard covers
ISBN 0 521 28932 7 paperback

CONTENTS

PREFACE TO THE SERIES

This series provides the best plays (in some cases, the complete plays) of the major English Renaissance and Restoration dramatists, in fully-annotated, modern-spelling texts, soundly edited by scholars in the field.

The introductory matter in each volume is factual and historical rather than critical: it includes, where appropriate, a brief biography of the playwright, a list of his works with dates of plays' first performances, the reasons for the volume editor's choice of plays, a short critical bibliography and a note on the texts used. An introductory note to each play then gives the source material, a short stage-history, and details of the individual editions of that play.

Short notes at the foot of the page are designed to gloss the text or enlarge on its literary, historical or social allusions. Editors have added substantial explanatory notes and have commented on textual variants.

The volumes are intended for anyone interested in English drama in two of its richest periods, but they will prove especially useful to students at all levels who want to enjoy and explore the best work of these dramatists.

Graham Storey

INTRODUCTION

Nineteen-year-old Will Congreve must have been delighted with London when he arrived there late in 1689. Although born in remote Yorkshire, in January 1670, and raised in Ireland, where his father was an officer in the British military garrison, he was not handicapped by his provincial background. His father's family were Staffordshire gentry who had a number of influential connections in the capital. Also, Lieutenant Congreve had provided his son with the best education available in Ireland, at Kilkenny School and at Trinity College, Dublin, where he was a good classical scholar, and where, beyond the college walls, he discovered the life of the theatre. Dublin's fondness for plays was second only to London's; the famous theatre in Smock Alley offered the latest comedies of Etherege, Wycherley, and Shadwell, and the eager student supplemented his attendance with wide reading in dramatic theory and practice. Disturbances connected with the Revolution of 1688 eventually closed the college, however, and cost Congreve's father his commission. In order to seek a new post, the family left Ireland for London, where their son was enrolled as a law student in the Middle Temple. Life at the Inns of Court was popular with young gentlemen casting about for a career, and Congreve apparently never intended seriously to follow the law. The three or four years he spent there may account for the numerous legal references in his plays, and did help ease his introduction to his real love, the London world of letters. He quickly became one of the circle of authors and wits who met at Will's coffee house to take their punch and tobacco with England's greatest living author, John Dryden, and, naturally, the restless student soon felt the urge to publish something of his own. Early in 1692, he brought out a short novel, *Incognita: or Love and Duty Reconcil'd,* with a fashionably romantic plot of separated young lovers and mistaken identities. He also turned out songs and pseudo-Pindaric odes, and kept up his studies with translations of classical authors. First recognition came from Dryden himself, who selected Congreve's version of the eleventh satire of Juvenal for his complete edition of the translated satires of Juvenal and Persius. The following year, 1693, Dryden included three of Congreve's odes and two of his short translations of Homer in his *Examen Poeticum,* and expressed the hope that his young colleague would go on to translate all of Homer. Congreve had other ambitions, however; Dryden was presented instead with the manuscript of a comedy, *The Old Batchelour,* which Congreve had been working on privately for several years.

Although its characters and situations are scarcely original, Congreve's first comedy struck all who read it with the craftsmanship and sparkle of its writing. After minor cuts and emendations by Dryden and his friends, the play opened at Drury Lane in April 1693. Its reception endorsed Dryden's opinion of it as the best first play he had ever seen,* and the Earl of Burlington reported to Congreve's father that even 'persons of Quality' had to be turned away from the theatre for lack of room.† Congreve worked closely with his actors, and showed particular skill in writing parts to fit their individual talents. In Anne Bracegirdle, for example, he found both the ideal interpreter of all his heroines, and an extraordinary woman to whom he was devoted throughout his active years in the theatre.

Congreve soon attempted to cap the success of his *Old Batchelour* with a second comedy, *The Double Dealer,* produced towards the close of the same year. He had reason to expect an even greater triumph; his new play offered a much tighter plot construction than *The Old Batchelour,* a more penetrating satirical dissection of human foibles, and, in the character of Lady Touchwood, a woman of stature approaching heroic tragedy. The audience was unprepared for such a darkening of the dramatist's view of society, however, and was disappointed, even though astute critics–Dryden, Swift, and Addison among them–quickly supported the play, and the author himself published a heated defence of it in the dedication to the first quarto.

Although Congreve yielded few points to critics of his *Double Dealer,* at this point in his career he was particularly sensitive to the taste of the town, and eager to satisfy it without compromising his craft. Approximately one year after the comparative failure of his second offering, he was ready with a third play, *Love for Love.* In its prologue, the author promised ingredients to please every taste: amusing, diversified characters, a well-constructed plot, and strokes of satire

* See John C. Hodges, ed., *William Congreve, Letters and Documents* (New York, 1964) p. 151.

† Quoted in *The Complete Plays of William Congreve,* ed. Herbert Davis (University of Chicago Press, 1967) p. 4.

in the great tradition of his predecessor Wycherley, yet softened and generalized for 'polite' ears. Its production was delayed by the revolt of the players at Drury Lane, led by Betterton, who set up a rival theatre in a converted tennis court in Lincoln's Inn Fields. Congreve naturally followed his beloved Anne Bracegirdle to the new house, and, on 30 April 1695, *Love for Love* opened to great applause.

Congreve, at twenty-five, was now at the peak of his reputation. Two of his three comedies were repeatedly revived, and although his income from them was not large, his loyalty to the Whig government manifest in a number of poems celebrating its achievements, and his cultivation of influential politicians and lords, now brought some return. He was appointed a commissioner for licensing hackney coaches, a near-sinecure which left him free to fulfil a contract with his company to provide them with one play a year, his health permitting. Clearly, Congreve's audience looked for more comedies from him. He appeared to encourage this hope soon after the publication of *Love for Love* in a long letter to the critic John Dennis, agreeing with Dennis that 'there is more of *Humour* in our English Writers, than in any of the other Comick Poets, Ancient or Modern', and discussing at length the proper presentation of character in comedy.* Before he put these theories into further practice, however, he set out to conquer another, loftier genre – tragedy, an ambition he had admitted to associates ever since his first success in the theatre. His friends were concerned at the news; Swift, in verses written to Congreve as early as 1693, expressed their misgivings at such an abandoning of his proven genius for comedy.† Undaunted, in February 1697, Congreve allowed Betterton's company to mount his tragedy, *The Mourning Bride,* a skilful revival of the exotic settings and declamatory rhetoric of the almost-defunct heroic drama, recalling the atmosphere of gloom and violence of Jacobean tragedy, and anticipating the libretti of Italian opera enormously popular in London early in the next century. Swift's fears were groundless; the audience loved Congreve's extended pageant of woe. It was the author's most popular and profitable play in his time, and now is forgotten entirely, save for the opening line, 'Musick

* Hodges, *Letters and Documents,* p. 176.

† *The Poems of Jonathan Swift,* ed. Sir Harold Williams (Oxford, the Clarendon Press, 1937) I, p. 47.

has Charms to sooth a savage Breast', and a condensed version of the conclusion to act three:

Heav'n has no Rage, like Love to Hatred turn'd,
Nor Hell a Fury, like a Woman scorn'd.††

Congreve had been nettled by the cool reception of *The Double Dealer,* but in the spring of 1698 he faced a storm of hostile criticism which shook the stage more profoundly than any controversy since the events leading up to the closing of the theatres in 1642. Jeremy Collier, a nonjuring Tory clergyman, published *A Short View of the Immorality and Profaneness of the English Stage,* concentrating on Dryden, Vanbrugh, and Congreve as examples of modern licentiousness in the arts. The Jacobite Collier in fact resented Congreve's support of King William and the Protestant succession, and political hostility underlay his moral objections. Certainly, many of his charges are wildly intemperate, but there is no doubt that he reflected changing public taste. We need only compare any of Congreve's work of the 1690s with his friend Richard Steele's successful comedy of 1722, *The Conscious Lovers,* to mark the later emphasis on bourgeois respectability, 'soft' emotions, and explicit moralizing. It is often assumed that Congreve, hating controversy, withdrew from the theatre as a direct result of Collier's attack. On the contrary, he first struck back vigorously with *Amendments of Mr Collier's False and Imperfect Citations,* etc., and went on immediately to write his finest comedy, *The Way of the World,* produced in March 1700. The loyal Dryden, now in the last year of his life, summed up his first impressions: 'Congreve's new play has had but moderate success, though it deserves much better.'* However, its author showed no sign of disappointment; he knew that he had given his best. Nevertheless, he wrote no more comedies, and may have sensed that *The Way of the World* was to be the last of its kind. Like Rossini, who retired at thirty-seven after dazzling success as an opera composer, he devoted most of the rest of his life to leisure. He did retain some ties with the theatre, however. In 1701, he contributed a masque, *The Judgment of Paris,* which, set to music in a competition by four leading composers, provided elegant entertainment at the Queen's Theatre. In 1704, he collaborated with Vanbrugh and Walsh, contributing one act of an adaptation of Molière's *Monsieur de Pourceaugnac* to a

†† Quoted from *Complete Plays,* ed. Davis, pp. 326, 361.
* John Dryden, *Works,* ed. Scott-Saintsbury (London, 1893) XVIII, p. 177.

three-act farce, *Squire Trelooby.* He remained interested in play production, and served for a short time in 1705 as a director of the new Haymarket Theatre. In 1710, he published his complete *Works,* incorporating a new entertainment, *Semele,* destined to be set magnificently by Handel thirty-four years later. With his retirement his income from the theatre dropped, and he was grateful for the small income from a new post as a commissioner of wines, secured for him by his friends in the political and literary Kit-Cat Club, and retained by him even after the fall of the Whig government in 1710. In fact, in an age of violent political animosities, Congreve was remarkable for his tact, and his ability to maintain friends in every camp. Tories like Swift and Pope valued him no less than Whig literati, Addison, Garth, Vanbrugh, or Steele, and he was close even to such notoriously prickly characters as Lady Mary Wortley Montagu and the critic John Dennis. Pope paid Congreve the supreme compliment of dedicating his translation of the *Iliad* to him. In 1714, with the return of the Whigs, a lucrative post as Secretary to the Island of Jamaica finally removed the author's financial worries, and he spent the rest of his life in comfort among friends, in particular Henrietta, younger Duchess of Marlborough, who replaced Anne Bracegirdle in his affections. She accompanied the famous bachelor playwright, now corpulent and gouty in the best Augustan tradition on frequent excursions to Bath to take the waters, was with him when he died, in January 1729, and supervised his impressive burial in Westminster Abbey.

Congreve has been reasonably well served by biographers. In 1730, the ever-abominable Edmund Curll published despite protests an alluring *Memoirs of the Life, Writings, and Amours of William Congreve, Esq.,* but it delivers little more than harmless gossip, and snippets from the author's writings. Dr Johnson, in his chapter on Congreve in *Lives of the English Poets,* overcomes his Tory bias to reach a characteristically judicious appreciation of the plays, but claims that Congreve in private life was 'deficient in candour,' implying that he concealed aspects of his Irish background. Early in the next century, Hazlitt's *Lectures on the English Comic Writers* praised the plays as brilliant depictions of an artificial society, but the Victorians, in a typical misunderstanding of Augustan modes of living, had scant use for Congreve as man and playwright. Macaulay was able to appreciate Congreve's epigrammatic brilliance, but dismissed his life as a conflict between the desire to be a great writer and to be a man of fashion.* Edmund Gosse helped restore the reputation of the plays, with his *Life of William Congreve,* first published in 1888, but found their author's life relatively barren in information and interest. D. Crane Taylor's biography of 1931 furnishes more material, but has been superseded by *William Congreve, the Man,* by John C. Hodges (MLA General Series, New York, 1941), who has published a number of articles on his subject, and edited an important collection of Congreviana, *William Congreve, Letters and Documents* (New York, 1964). Those who still find Congreve unappealing as a man may consult Kathleen M. Lynch, *A Congreve Gallery* (Harvard, 1951), for a study of his numerous friendships. Important information on the reputation and performance history of the plays appears in Emmett Avery's *Congreve's Plays on the Eighteenth-Century Stage* (MLA Monograph Series, New York, 1951). Some useful critical studies are by Bonamy Dobrée, *Restoration Comedy* (Oxford, 1924); Kathleen M. Lynch, *The Social Mode of Restoration Comedy* (New York, 1926); T. H. Fujimura, *The Restoration Comedy of Wit* (Princeton, 1952); and N. N. Holland, *The First Modern Comedies* (Cambridge, Mass., 1959). Readers should also be prepared to come to terms with L. C. Knights' attack on the genre, 'Restoration Comedy: the Reality and the Myth,' published together with a reply by F. W. Bateson in a useful collection, *Restoration Drama: Modern Essays in Criticism,* edited by J. Loftis (New York, 1966).

Congreve's plays appeared in quarto soon after performance, and for several years thereafter in a series of increasingly altered and corrupt versions. In 1710, their author published his complete *Works,* with the wording of the plays slightly changed from the original quartos, scene divisions altered, and all traces of bawdy and profanity removed to suit new conceptions of gentility. By 1730, five editions of the *Works* had appeared, and there were many more during the century, including the attractively printed and illustrated Baskerville edition of 1761. The modern, one-volume edition by F. W. Bateson (London, 1930), is based on the *Works.* Montague Summers returned to the first quartos in his *Complete Works*, furnished with copious, useful notes, for the Nonesuch Press (London, 1923), and Bonamy Dobrée followed with an edition for World's Classics in

* T. B. Macaulay, *Works* (Albany Edition, London, 1898) IX, pp. 370-393.

To Mr. CONGREVE

The Danger's great in these censorious days,
When Criticks are so rife, to venture Praise;
When the infectious and ill-natured Brood
Behold, and damn the Work, because 'tis good;
And with a proud, ungenerous Spight would try
To pass an Ostracism on Poetry.
But you, my Friend, your Worth does safely bear
Above their Spleen; you have no cause for fear;
Like a well-metled Hawk, you took your flight
Quite out of reach, and almost out of sight.
As the strong Sun, in a fair Summer's day,
You rise, and drive the Mists and Clouds away,
The Owls and Bats, and all the Birds of Prey.
Each Line of yours, like polisht Steel's so hard,
In Beauty safe, it wants no other guard.
Nature herself's beholden to your Dress,
Which tho' still like, much fairer you express.
Some vainly striving Honour to obtain,
Leave to their Heirs the Traffick of their Brain;
Like *China* under Ground, the ripening Ware,
In a long time, perhaps grows worth our Care.
But you now reap the Fame, so well you've sown;
The Planter tastes his Fruit to ripeness grown.
As a fair Orange-tree at once is seen,
Big with what's ripe, yet springing still with Green;
So at one time my worthy Friend appears,
With all the sap of Youth, and weight of Years.
Accept my pious Love, as forward Zeal,
Which tho' it ruins me I can't conceal:
Expos'd to Censure for my weak Applause,
I'm pleas'd to suffer in so just a Cause:
And tho' my Offering may unworthy prove,
Take as a Friend the Wishes of my Love.

J. MARSH.°

To Mr. *CONGREVE*, on his PLAY, called, The *OLD BATCHELOUR*

Wit, like true Gold, refin'd from all Allay,
Immortal is, and never can decay:

° Grandson of Jeremy Taylor and son of the Archbishop of Dublin. A friend from Congreve's youth in Ireland.

1 *Allay*: base metal.

'Tis in all Times and Languages the same;
Nor can an ill Translation quench the Flame:
For, tho' the Form and Fashion don't remain,
Th' intrinsick value still it will retain.
Then let each studied Scene be writ with Art;
And Judgment sweat to form the labour'd Part:
Each Character be just, and Nature seem;
Without th' Ingredient, Wit, 'tis all but Phlegm:
For that's the Soul, which all the Mass must move,
And wake our Passions into Grief, or Love.
But you, too Bounteous, sow your Wit so thick,
We are surpriz'd, and know not where to pick:
And while our Clapping does you Justice do,
Our selves we injure, and lose something new.
What may'nt we then, great Youth, of thee presage,
Whose Art and Wit so much transcend thy Age?
How wilt thou shine at thy Meridian height?
Who, at thy rising, give so vast a Light.
When *DRYDEN* dying, shall the World deceive,
Whom we Immortal, as his Works, believe;
Thou shalt succeed, the Glory of the Stage,
Adorn and entertain the coming Age.

*BEVIL HIGGONS.**

PROLOGUE Intended for The *OLD BATCHELOUR*. Written by the Lord *FALKLAND**

Most Authors on the Stage at first appear
Like Widows-Bridegrooms, full of doubt and fear:
They judge from the experience of the Dame,
How hard a Task it is to quench her Flame:
And who falls short of furnishing a course,
Up to his brawny Predecessors force:
With utmost rage from her Embraces thrown,
Remains convicted, as an empty Drone.
Thus often, to his Shame, a pert Beginner
Proves in the end, a miserable Sinner.
As for our Youngster, I am apt to doubt him,
With all the vigour of his Youth above him:

* (1670-1735): Jacobite playwright, historian, and coffee-house wit.

* Anthony Carye, fifth Viscount Falkland, a prominent political figure briefly imprisoned in 1693. Early editions of the play withheld his name; the Prologue was first published as 'sent to the author by an unknown hand.'

1925 and 1928. A recent volume of the plays, edited by Herbert Davis (Chicago, 1967), has been particularly useful to me in preparing this edition. Davis bases his text on the earliest versions, collated with later quartos and with the *Works* of 1710, but with many errors in punctuation, stage directions, etc., allowed to stand. Those interested in variant readings may consult the appendix to his edition. I have tried to preserve the elegant appearance of the Restoration texts, keeping some of the old spellings and the original capitals and italics, correcting only obvious inconsistencies. In a few cases, stage directions have been introduced or changed in position. In matters of punctuation, I have had little patience with the vagaries of seventeenth-century typesetters, and modernized wherever clarity demanded, retaining, however, many of the quartos' frequent dashes to help convey the rapid give-and-take of the dialogue.

I wish to thank a most distinguished colleague, Brian Vickers, for his invaluable help in launching this volume, and both him and his wife Ilse Renate Vickers for their boundless hospitality and friendship since my student days at Trinity College, Cambridge.

Anthony G. Henderson

THE OLD BATCHELOUR

Introduction

Congreve's precocious first play, *The Old Batchelour,* was first performed at the Theatre Royal, Drury Lane, in March 1693. It had been accepted for production late the preceding year, but was delayed by the death of three members of the company, one of them the popular actor William Mountford, murdered for rescuing his beautiful colleague Anne Bracegirdle from abduction by a nobleman. Despite the necessary substitutions, the company provided a splendid cast, headed by the pre-eminent Thomas Betterton in the role of Heartwell, the surly old batchelor. Audience and author were delighted, and the play had the exceptional initial run of fourteen days, filling the twelve-hundred-seat theatre night after night. Three quarto editions of the play sold out within a month; the *Gentleman's Journal* spoke for the town in declaring the play as charming to read as to see on the stage.*

In the published dedication to *The Old Batchelour,* Congreve claimed to have first written the play almost four years earlier, probably in the spring and summer of 1689 at home in Staffordshire, but, as Colley Cibber noted, he was always a careful craftsman who frequently revised his work. Also, he was shrewd enough to seek professional advice in London. An older colleague, the playwright Thomas Southerne, carried the manuscript to Dryden, who was much impressed by the material and suggested minor changes to shape the material according to the 'fashionable cutt of the town.'*

Dr Johnson summed up *The Old Batchelour* as 'one of those comedies which may be made by a mind vigorous and acute, and furnished with comick charac-

Gentleman's Journal (February, 1693) p. 61.

Note by Thomas Southerne, quoted in John C. Hodges, *William Congreve: The Man* (MLA General Series XI, New York, 1941) p. 40.

ters by the perusal of other poets.'† Congreve had indeed borrowed widely from his readings in classical, Jacobean, French, and Restoration drama. The most obvious hints came from Jonson, whose comedies were rarely performed but well-known in print, and from the still-living and still-popular Wycherley. Heartwell and Belinda are gentler versions of Manley and Olivia in Wycherley's *The Plain Dealer,* and Sharper suggests Wycherley's Freeman. Bellmour takes something from Horner in *The Country Wife,* and both he and Vainlove can hold their own with the rakes of Etherege and Sedley. Captain Bluffe has an ancient lineage, descended from the *Miles Gloriosus* of Plautus, and Jonson's Bobadill in *Every Man in His Humour.* Even the names of the characters acknowledge the old tradition of the Jonsonian comedy of humours, with each person representing a dominant human characteristic, and the plot takes them through a familiar succession of disguises and discoveries. Congreve's characters and situations, in fact, had been the common stock of playwrights for generations; what delighted his audience was his presentation of this material, transformed into something fresh and original by language alternating between stylized gracefulness and abrupt colloquialism, dissecting the paradoxes of man-in-society with a poised comic tone itself supremely paradoxical.

Although we have scant information concerning the daily offerings of the London theatres at this time, it seems probable that *The Old Batchelour* was given frequently in the period before 1700, when Congreve produced his last comedy. Thereafter, for many years it was one of the classics of the repertory, performed three hundred times in the eighteenth century, although often in a condensed form, and purged of the 'indelicate' expressions lending spice to the 1693 quarto. The last century has seen a few performances, notably in 1925 at the Regent Theatre in London, as part of a complete Congreve cycle, but *The Old Batchelour* remains Congreve's least-known and least-published play.

Samuel Johnson, *Lives of the English Poets,* ed. G. B. Hill (Oxford: The Clarendon Press, 1905) II, p. 215.

THE

Old Batchelour,

A

COMEDY.

As it is ACTED at the

Theatre Royal,

BY

Their MAJESTIES Servants.

Written by Mr. *Congreve.*

Quem tulit ad Scenam ventoso gloria Curru,
Exanimat lentus Spectator; sedulus inflat.
Sic leve, sic parvum est, animum quod laudis avarum
Subruit, aut reficit——*

Horat. Epist. I. Lib. II.

LONDON,

Printed for *Peter Buck*, at the Sign of the *Temple* near the *Temple-gate* in *Fleet-street*, 1693.

* O you! whom Vanity's light bark conveys
On Fame's mad voyage by the wind of praise,
With a shifting gale your course you ply,
For ever sunk too low, or born too high!
Who pants for glory finds but short repose,
A breath revives him, or a breath o'erthrows.

(Pope's *Imitation*, II. 296 ff.)

To the Right Honourable, Charles *Lord* Clifford *of* Lanesborough, *Etc.* *

My Lord,

It is with a great deal of Pleasure that I lay hold on this first Occasion, which the Accidents of my Life have given me of writing to your Lordship: for since at the same time I write to all the World, it will be a means of publishing (what I would have everybody know) the Respect and Duty which I owe and pay to you. I have so much Inclination to be yours, that I need no other Engagement. But the particular Ties by which I am bound to your Lordship and Family have put it out of my power to make you any Complement, since all Offers of myself, will amount to no more than an honest Acknowledgment, and only shew a willingness in me to be grateful.

I am very near wishing that it were not so much my Interest to be your Lordship's Servant, that it might be more my Merit; not that I would avoid being obliged to you, but I would have my own Choice to run me into the Debt, that I might have it to boast I had distinguished a Man, to whom I would be glad to be obliged, even without the hopes of having it in my Power ever to make him a return.

It is impossible for me to come near your Lordship in any kind, and not to receive some Favour; and while in appearance I am only making an Acknowledgment (with the usual underhand dealing of the World), I am at the same time insinuating my own Interest. I cannot give your Lordship your due, without tacking a Bill of my own Priviledges. 'Tis true, if a Man never committed a Folly, he would never stand in need of a Protection. But then Power would have nothing to do, and good Nature no occasion to shew itself; and where those Vertues are, 'tis pity they should want Objects to shine upon. I must confess this is no reason why a Man should do an idle thing, nor indeed any good Excuse for it, when done; yet it reconciles the uses of such Authority and Goodness to the necessities of our Follies, and is a sort

* Lord Clifford, eldest son of Richard Boyle, Earl of Cork and Burlington, under whom Congreve's father had served as a lieutenant in Ireland. Congreve may have attended a school endowed by the family at Youghal. Here he acknowledges a debt and hopes for further patronage.

of Poetical Logick, which at this time I would make use of, to argue your Lordship into a Protection of this Play. It is the first Offence I have committed in this kind, or indeed in any kind of Poetry, tho' not the first made publick; and, therefore, I hope will the more easily be pardoned. But had it been Acted when it was first written, more might have been said in its behalf; Ignorance of the Town and Stage would then have been Excuses in a young Writer, which now almost four Years experience will scarce allow of. Yet I must declare myself sensible of the good Nature of the Town, in receiving this Play so kindly, with all its Faults, which I must own were for the most part very industriously covered by the care of the Players; for, I think, scarce a Character but receiv'd all the Advantage it would admit of from the justness of Action.

As for the Criticks, my Lord, I have nothing to say to, or against, any of them of any kind; from those who make just Exceptions, to those who find fault in the wrong place. I will only make this general Answer in behalf of my Play (an Answer, which *Epictetus* advises every Man to make for himself to his Censurers) viz. *That if they who find some Faults in it were as intimate with it as I am, they would find a great many more.* This is a Confession which I need not to have made; but, however, I can draw this use from it to my own Advantage, that I think there are no Faults in it but what I do know; which, as I take it, is the first step to an amendment.

Thus I may live in hopes (sometime or other) of making the Town amends; but you, my Lord, I never can, tho' I am ever

Your Lordship's
most obedient and
most humble Servant,
Will. Congreve.

To Mr. *CONGREVE.*

When Virtue in pursuit of Fame appears,
And forward shoots the growth beyond the Years,
We timely court the rising Hero's Cause;
And on his side, the Poet wisely draws;
Bespeaking him hereafter, by Applause.

The days will come when we shall all receive,
Returning Interest from what now we give:
Instructed, and supported by that Praise,
And Reputation, which we strive to raise.
Nature so coy, so hardly to be Woo'd,
Flies, like a Mistress, but to be pursu'd.
O CONGREVE! boldly follow on the Chase;
She looks behind, and wants thy strong Embrace.
She yields, she yields, surrenders all her Charms,
Do you but force her gently to your Arms:
Such Nerves, such Graces, in your Lines appear,
As you were made to be her Ravisher.
DRYDEN has long extended his Command,
By Right-divine, quite through the Muses' Land,
Absolute Lord; and holding now from none,
But great *Apollo,* his undoubted Crown,
(That Empire settled, and grown old in Pow'r)
Can wish for nothing, but a Successor;
Not to enlarge his Limits, but maintain
Those Provinces, which he alone could gain.
His eldest *Wycherley,* in wise Retreat,
Thought it not worth his quiet to be great.
Loose, wand'ring, *Etherege,* in wild Pleasures tost,
And foreign Int'rests, to his hopes long lost;
Poor *Lee* and *Otway* dead! *CONGREVE* appears.
The Darling, and last Comfort of his Years.
May'st thou live long in thy great Master's smiles,
And growing under him, adorn these Isles;
But when—when part of him (be that but late)
His body yielding must submit to Fate.
Leaving his deathless Works, and thee behind,
(The natural Successor of his Mind)
Then may'st thou finish what he has begun:
Heir to his Merit, be in Fame his Son.
What thou hast done, shews all is in thy Power;
And to Write better, only must Write more.
'Tis something to be willing to commend;
But my best Praise is, that I am your Friend.

*THO. SOUTHERNE.**

* (1660-1746): Successful London playwright who admired *The Old Batchelour* in manuscript and carried it to Dryden. Like Congreve, born in Ireland and attended Trinity College.

But he, more Sanguine, trusts in one and twenty,
And impudently hopes he shall content you:
For tho' his Batchelour be worn and cold:
He thinks the Young may club to help the Old:
And what alone can be atchieved by neither,
Is often brought about by both together.
The briskest of you all have felt Allarms
Finding the fair One prostitute her Charms
With broken Sighs, in her old Fumblers Arms.
But for our Spark, he Swears he'll ne're be jealous
Of any Rivals, but young lusty Fellows.
Faith let him try his Chance, and if the Slave,
After his bragging prove a washy Knave;
May he be banish'd to some lonely Den,
And never more have leave to dip his Pen:
But if he be the Champion he pretends,
Both Sexes sure will join to be his Friends;
For all agree, where all can have their ends.
And you must own him for a Man of Might,
If he holds out to please you the third Night.

Prologue

Spoken by Mrs. *Bracegirdle**

How this vile World is chang'd! In former days,
Prologues were serious Speeches before Plays;
Grave solemn Things, as Graces are to Feasts;
Where Poets beg'd a Blessing from their Guests.
But now, no more like Suppliants, we come;
A Play makes War, and Prologue is the Drum:
Arm'd with keen Satyr, and with pointed Wit,
We threaten you who do for Judges sit,
To save our Plays, or else we'll damn your Pit.
But for your Comfort, it falls out today,
We've a young Author and his first-born Play;
So, standing only on his good Behaviour,
He's very civil, and entreats your Favour.
Not but the Man has Malice, would he show it,
But on my Conscience he's a bashful Poet;
You think that strange–
no matter, he'll out-grow it.

* Anne Bracegirdle, famous actress of the day, and intimate friend of Congreve, who wrote leading roles for her in all his plays. Notably discreet in her private life, she and the playwright may have been lovers, but even Colley Cibber, closely associated with her in the theatre, could produce no scandalous information about them.

Well, I'm his Advocate—by me he prays you,
(I don't know whether I shall speak to please you)
He prays—O bless me! what shall I do now!
Hang me if I know what he prays, or how!
And 'twas the prettiest Prologue, as he wrote it!
Well, the Deuce take me, if I han't forgot it.
O Lord, for Heaven's sake excuse the Play,
Because, you know, if it be damn'd today,
I shall be hang'd for wanting what to say.
For my sake then—but I'm in such Confusion,
I cannot stay to hear your Resolution.

Runs off.

Dramatis Personæ

MEN

HEARTWELL, a surly old Batchelour, pretending to slight Women; secretly in Love with SILVIA	Mr. Betterton
BELLMOUR, in Love with BELINDA	Mr. Powel
VAINLOVE, capricious in his Love; in Love with ARAMINTA	Mr. Williams
SHARPER	Mr. Alexander *[later,* Mr. Verbruggen]
SIR JOSEPH WITTOLL	Mr. Bowen
CAPT. BLUFFE	Mr. Hains
FONDLEWIFE, a Banker	Mr. Dogget
SETTER, a *Pimp*	Mr. Underhill
SERVANT to FONDLEWIFE	

WOMEN

ARAMINTA, in Love with VAINLOVE	Mrs. Bracegirdle
BELINDA, her Cousin and affected Lady, in Love with BELLMOUR	Mrs. Mountfort
LÆTITIA, Wife to FONDLEWIFE	Mrs. Barry

SILVIA, VAINLOVE's forsaken Mistress	Mrs. Bowman
LUCY, her Maid	Mrs. Leigh
BETTY	

Boy and Footmen.

The Scene, LONDON.

THE
Old Batchelour.

ACT I. SCENE I. The Street.

Bellmour *and* Vainlove *Meeting.*

BELLMOUR. *Vainlove!* and abroad so early! good Morrow; I thought a Contemplative Lover could no more have parted with his Bed in a Morning, than 'a could have slept in't.

VAINLOVE. *Bellmour,* good Morrow. Why, truth on't is, these early Sallies are not usual to me; but Business as you see Sir—(*Showing Letters.*) And Business must be follow'd, or be lost.

BELLMOUR. Pox o' Business. —And so must Time, my Friend, be close pursued, or lost. Business is the rub of Life, perverts our Aim, casts off the Bias, and leaves us wide and short of the intended Mark.

VAINLOVE. Pleasure, I guess you mean.

BELLMOUR. Ay, what else has meaning?

VAINLOVE. Oh, the Wise will tell you—

BELLMOUR. More than they believe—or understand.

VAINLOVE. How how, *Ned,* a wise Man say more than he understands?

BELLMOUR. Ay, ay, pox Wisdom's nothing but a pretending to know and believe more than really

11 rub of life: Bellmour's philosophy is Epicurean hedonism expressed in the metaphor of a game of English bowls. The rub is any obstacle in the path of a ball slightly misshapen so as to introduce a bias in its motion to be compensated for by the player.

we do. You read of but one wise Man, and all that he knew was that he knew nothing. Come, come, leave Business to Idlers, and Wisdom to Fools; they have need of'em. Wit be my Faculty, and Pleasure my Occupation, and let Father Time shake his Glass. Let low and earthy Souls grovel till they have work'd themselves six foot deep into a Grave. Business is not my Element; I roll in a higher Orb and dwell—

VAINLOVE. In Castles i'th Air of thy own building: That's thy Element, *Ned.* Well, as high a Flyer as you are, I have a Lure may make you stoop.
Flings a Letter.

BELLMOUR. Aye, marry Sir, I have a Hawk's Eye at a Woman's hand. There's more Elegancy in the false Spelling of this Superscription *(Takes up the Letter.)* than in all *Cicero.* Let me see—How now! Dear, perfidious *Vainlove!*

Reads.

VAINLOVE. Hold hold. 'Slife that's the wrong—

BELLMOUR. Nay, let's see the Name—*Silvia!* How can'st thou be ungrateful to that Creature? She's extreamly pretty and loves thee entirely. I have heard her breathe such Raptures about thee—

VAINLOVE. Ay, or anybody that she's about.

BELLMOUR. No, faith, *Frank,* you wrong her. She has been just to you.

VAINLOVE. That's pleasant, by my troth, from thee who hast enjoy'd her.

BELLMOUR. Never her Affections, 'tis true by Heaven; she own'd it to my Face, and blushing like the Virgin Morn when it disclosed the Cheat, which that trusty Bawd of Nature, Night, had hid, confess'd her Soul was true to you, tho' I by treachery had stoll'n the Bliss.

21 *one wise man:* Socrates, whose reputation for disinterested humility is converted here to cynical scepticism.

31 *Lure:* an artificial bird of leather and feathers tossed in the air and baited with meat to lure back a trained hawk.

52 *Bawd of Nature:* night serves as a bawd, or pander, by concealing amorous adventures which morning brings to light. In Dryden's free adaptation of Plautus' *Amphitryon,* 1690, Mercury accuses Night; 'What art thou good for, but to be a bawd?' (I, i, end).

VAINLOVE. So was true as Turtle—in imagination *Ned,* ha? Preach this Doctrin to Husbands, and the married Women will adore thee.

BELLMOUR. Why, faith, I think it will do well enough, if the Husband be out of the way, for the Wife to shew her Fondness and Impatience of his Absence by choosing a Lover as like him as she can, and what is unlike she may help out with her own Fancy.

VAINLOVE. But is it not an Abuse to the Lover to be made a Blind of? For she only stalks under him to take aim at her Husband.

BELLMOUR. As you say, the Abuse is to the Lover, not the Husband; for 'tis an Argument of her great Zeal towards him, that she will enjoy him in Effigie.

VAINLOVE. It must be a very superstitious Country where such Zeal passes for true Devotion. I doubt it will be damn'd by all our Protestant Husbands for flat Idolatry. —But if you can make Alderman *Fondlewife* of your Persuasion, this Letter will be needless.

BELLMOUR. What, the old Banker with the handsome Wife?

VAINLOVE. Ay.

BELLMOUR. Let me see—*Lætitia!* Oh 'tis a delicious Morsel. Dear *Frank,* thou art the truest Friend in the World!

VAINLOVE. Ay, am I not, to be continually starting of Hares for you to course? We were certainly cut out for one another, for my Temper quits an Amour just where thine takes it up. —But read that. It is an Appointment for me this Evening, when *Fondlewife* will be gone out of Town to meet the Master of a Ship about the return of a Venture which he's in

55 *Turtle:* turtledove, proverbially faithful to its mate; a comparison well-worn by Shakespeare's time. Compare Troilus' vows to Cressida, *Troilus and Cressida* (III, ii, 180-189).

65 *Blind:* concealment screening the hunter from his prey.

82 *course:* chase with hounds; another hunting metaphor for the principal activity of these gentlemen.

87 *Venture:* a commercial cargo invested in speculatively.

danger of losing. Read, read.

BELLMOUR *(Reads).* Hum, Hum—*Out of Town this Evening, and talks of sending for* Mr. Spintext *to keep me Company; but I'le take care he shall not be at home.* Good! *Spintext?* Oh, the Fanatick, one-ey'd Parson!

VAINLOVE. Ay.

BELLMOUR. *(Reads).* Hum. Hum—*That your Conversation will be much more agreeable if you can counterfeit his Habit to blind the Servants.* Very good! Then I must be disguised—with all My Heart. It adds a Gusto to an Amour; gives it the greater resemblance of Theft; and among us lewd Mortals, the deeper the Sin the sweeter. *Frank,* I'm amaz'd at thy good Nature.

VAINLOVE. Faith, I hate Love when 'tis forced upon a Man, as I do Wine. And this Business is none of my seeking; I only happened to be once or twice where *Lætitia* was the handsomest Woman in Company, so consequently apply'd myself to her—and it seems she has taken me at my word. Had you been there or anybody, 't had been the same.

VAINLOVE. Never doubt it; for if the Spirit of Cuckoldom be once raised up in a Woman, the Devil can't lay it till she has done't.

BELLMOUR. Prithee, what sort of Fellow is *Fondlewife?*

VAINLOVE. A kind of Mongrel Zealot, sometimes very precise and peevish. But I have seen him pleasant enough in his way; much addicted to Jealousie, but more to Fondness; So that as he is often Jealous without a Cause, he's as often satisfied without Reason.

BELLMOUR. A very even Temper and fit for my purpose. I must get your Man *Setter* to provide my Disguise.

92 *Fanatick:* hostile epithet applied to Puritans and other Protestant nonconformists to the Church of England.

115 *Zealot:* 'One passionately ardent in any cause. Generally used in dispraise.' (Johnson, *Dictionary.*)

118 *Fondness:* doting.

VAINLOVE. Ay, you may take him for good-and-all if you will, for you have made him fit for nobody else. Well–

BELLMOUR. You're going to visit in return of *Silvia's* Letter? Poor Rogue! Any hour of the day or night will serve her. But do you know nothing of a new Rival there?

VAINLOVE. Yes, *Heartwell,* that surly, old, pretended Woman-hater thinks her Virtuous; that's one reason why I fail her. I would have her fret herself out of conceit with me, that she may entertain some Thoughts of him. I know he visits her ev'ry day.

BELLMOUR. Yet rails on still, and thinks his Love unknown to us. A little time will swell him so, he must be forc'd to give it birth, and the discovery must needs be very pleasant from himself, to see what pains he will take, and how he will strain to be deliver'd of a Secret, when he has miscarried on't already.

VAINLOVE. Well good Morrow. Let's dine together; I'll meet at the old place.

BELLMOUR. With all my Heart; it lies convenient for us, to pay our Afternoon Service to our Mistresses. I find I am damnably in Love; I'm so uneasie for not seeing *Belinda* yesterday.

VAINLOVE. But I saw my *Araminta,* yet am as impatient.

Exit.

BELLMOUR. Why, what a Cormorant in Love am I! Who not contented with the slavery of honourable Love in one place, and the pleasure of enjoying some half a score Mistresses of my own acquiring, must yet take *Vainlove's* Business upon my hands, because it lay too heavy upon his. So am not only forc'd to lie with other Men's Wives for 'em, but must also undertake the harder Task, of obliging their Mistresses–

133 *out of conceit with:* no longer satisfied with.

152 *Cormorant:* sea-bird, known for its voracious appetite, used by fishermen to catch fish; hence, Bellmour accuses himself both of greed and of serving another's interest.

I must take up, or I shall never hold out; Flesh and Blood cannot bear it always.

Enter Sharper.

SHARPER. I'm sorry to see this, *Ned.* Once a Man comes to his Soliloques I give him for gone.

BELLMOUR. *Sharper,* I'm glad to see thee.

SHARPER. What, is *Belinda* cruel, that you are so thoughtful?

BELLMOUR. No faith, not for that. —But there's a Business of Consequence fall'n out today that requires some Consideration.

SHARPER. Prithee, what mighty Business of Consequence canst thou have?

BELLMOUR. Why, you must know, 'tis a piece of Work toward the finishing of an Alderman; it seems I must put the last hand to it and dub him Cuckold, that he may be of equal Dignity with the rest of his Brethren. So I must beg *Belinda's* Pardon—

SHARPER. Faith, e'en give her over for good-and-all; you can have no hopes of getting her for a Mistress, and she is too Proud, too Inconstant, too Affected, and too Witty, and too handsome for a Wife.

BELLMOUR. But she can't have too much Mony. —There's twelve thousand Pound, *Tom.* —'Tis true she is excessively foppish and affected, but in my Conscience I believe the Baggage loves me, for she never speaks well of me herself, nor suffers anybody else to rail at me. Then, as I told you, there's twelve thousand Pound—hum—why, faith, upon second Thoughts, she does not appear to be so very affected neither! Give her her due, I think the Woman's a Woman, and that's all. As such I'm sure I shall like her; for the Devil take me if I don't love all the Sex.

SHARPER. And here comes one who Swears as heartily he hates all the Sex.

BELLMOUR. Who, *Heartwell*? Ay, but he knows better things—How now, *George,* where hast thou

160 *take up:* restrain oneself; mend one's ways. 'One that has sown his wild oats . . . begins to take up and be more staied.' (*Dictionary of the Canting Crew,* 1700.)

been snarling odious Truths, and entertaining company like a Physician, with discourse of their diseases and infirmities? What fine Lady hast thou been putting out of conceit with herself, and persuading that the Face she had been making all the morning was none of her own? for I know thou art as unmannerly and as unwelcome to a Woman as a Looking glass after the Small-pox.

HEARTWELL. I confess I have not been sneering fulsome Lies and nauseous Flattery, fawning upon a little tawdry Whore, that will fawn upon me again, and entertain any Puppy that comes, like a Tumbler with the same tricks over and over. For such I guess may have been your late employment.

BELLMOUR. Would thou had'st come a little sooner! *Vainlove* would have wrought thy Conversion and been a Champion for the Cause.

HEARTWELL. What, has he been here? That's one of Love's April-fools, is always upon some errand that's to no purpose, ever embarking in Adventures, yet never comes to harbour.

SHARPER. That's because he always sets out in foul Weather, loves to buffet with the Winds, meet the Tide, and sail in the Teeth of opposition.

HEARTWELL. What, has he not drop't Anchor at *Araminta?*

BELLMOUR. Truth on't is she fits his temper best, is a kind of floating Island; sometimes seems in reach, then vanishes and keeps him busied in the search.

SHARPER. She had need have a good share of sense, to manage so *Capricious* a Lover.

BELLMOUR. Faith, I don't know. He's of a temper the most easy to himself in the World; he takes as much always of an Amour as he cares for, and quits it when it grows stale or unpleasant.

SHARPER. An argument of very little Passion, very good Understanding, and very ill Nature.

HEARTWELL. And proves that *Vainlove* plays the Fool with Discretion.

SHARPER. You, *Bellmour,* are bound in gratitude to stickle for him; you with pleasure reap that fruit which he takes pains to sow. He does the drudgery in the Mine, and you stamp your image on the Gold.

BELLMOUR. He's of another opinion, and says I do the drudgery in the Mine. Well, we have each our share of sport, and each that which he likes best; 'tis his diversion to Set, 'tis mine to Cover the Partridge.

HEARTWELL. And it should be mine to let 'em go again.

SHARPER. Not till you had Mouth'd a little, *George.* I think that's all thou art fit for now.

HEARTWELL. Good Mr. Young-fellow, you're mistaken; as able as yourself and as nimble too, though I mayn't have so much Mercury in my Limbs. 'Tis true indeed, I don't force Appetite, but wait the natural call of my Lust, and think it time enough to be lewd after I have had the temptation.

BELLMOUR. Time enough! Ay, too soon, I should rather have expected, from a person of your gravity.

HEARTWELL. Yet it is oftentimes too late with some of you young, termagant flashy sinners – you have all the guilt of the intention, and none of the pleasure of the practice. 'Tis true you are so eager in pursuit of the temptation that you save the Devil the trouble of leading you into it. Nor is it out of discretion that you don't swallow that very Hook yourselves have baited, but you are cloy'd with the preparative, and what you mean for a Whet turns the edge of your puny Stomacks. Your love is like your courage, which you shew for the first year or two upon all occasions; till in a little time, being disabled or disarm'd, you abate of your vigor; and that daring Blade which was so often drawn is bound to the Peace for ever after.

BELLMOUR. Thou art an old Fornicator of a singular good principle, indeed! And art for encouraging

237 *stickle for:* stand up for.
243 *Set . . . Cover:* Vainlove's role is to locate the game, like a good hunting dog; Bellmour's is to aim at it, but with an obvious *double entendre.*
257 *termagant:* violent and overbearing.

Youth, that they may be as wicked as thou art at thy years.

HEARTWELL. I am for having everybody be what they pretend to be; a Whoremaster be a Whoremaster, and not, like *Vainlove*, kiss a Lap-Dog with passion, when it would disgust him from the Lady's own Lips.

BELLMOUR. That only happens sometimes, where the Dog has the sweeter Breath, for the more cleanly conveyance. But *George*, you must not quarrel with little Gallantries of this nature; Women are often won by 'em. Who would refuse to kiss a Lap-Dog, if it were preliminary to the Lips of his Lady?

SHARPER. Or omit playing with her Fan, and cooling her if she were hot, when it might entitle him to the office of warming her when she should be cold?

BELLMOUR. What is it to read a Play in a rainy day, when it may be the means of getting into a fair Lady's Books? Though you should be now and then interrupted in a witty Scene, and she perhaps preserve her Laughter till the Jest were over, even this may be born with, considering the reward in prospect.

HEARTWELL. I confess you that are Women's Asses, bear greater burdens, are forced to undergo Dressing, Dancing, Singing, Sighing, Whining, Rhyming, Flattering, Lying, Grinning, Cringing, and the drudgery of loving to boot.

BELLMOUR. O Brute, the drudgery of loving!

HEARTWELL. Ay, why to come to Love through all these incumbrances is like coming to an Estate overcharg'd with Debts, which by the time you have pay'd, yields no further profit than what the bare tillage and manuring of the Land will produce at the expense of your own Sweat.

BELLMOUR. Prithee, how dost thou love?

SHARPER. He? he hates the Sex!

HEARTWELL. So I hate Physick too—yet I may love to take it for my health.

309 *Physick:* medicines, at that time often strongly purgative.

BELLMOUR. Well, come off, *George,* if at any time you should be taken straying.

SHARPER. He has need of such an excuse, considering the present state of his Body.

HEARTWELL. How d'ee mean?

SHARPER. Why, if whoring be purging (as you call it), then I may say Marriage is entering into a Course of Physick.

BELLMOUR. How *George,* does the Wind blow there?

HEARTWELL. It will as soon blow North and by South – marry quotha! I hope in Heaven I have a greater portion of Grace, and I think I have baited too many of those Traps, to be caught in one myself.

BELLMOUR. Who the Devil would have thee? Unless 'twere an Oyster-woman, to propagate young Fry for *Bilingsgate* – thy Talent will never recommend thee to anything of better quality.

HEARTWELL. My Talent is chiefly that of speaking truth, which I don't expect should ever recommend me to People of Quality. I thank Heaven I have very honestly purchas'd the hatred of all the great Families in Town.

SHARPER. And you in return of Spleen hate them. But could you hope to be receiv'd into the Alliance of a noble Family–

HEARTWELL. No, I hope I shall never merit that affliction–to be punish'd with a Wife of Birth–be a Stag of the first Head and bear my Horns aloft, like one of the supporters of my Wive's Coat. S'death, I would not be a Cuckold to e'er an illustrious Whore in *England.*

BELLMOUR. What, not to make your family, Man! and provide for your Children!

SHARPER. For her Children, you mean.

327 *Bilingsgate:* London fish market notorious for its abusive language.
339 *Stag of the first Head:* young deer with its first antlers; here, figuratively, a newly made cuckold.
340 *supporters of my Wife's Coat:* Heraldic animals rampant on either side of a coat of arms.

HEARTWELL. Ay, there you've nick't it—there's the Devil upon Devil. Oh, the Pride and Joy of Heart 'twould be to me, to have my Son and heir resemble such a Duke—to have a fleering Coxcomb scoff and cry, Mister, your Son's mighty like his Grace, has just his smile and air of's Face. Then replies another—methink he has more of the Marquess of such a place, about his Nose and Eyes; though 'a has my Lord what d'ee-call's Mouth to a Tittle. Then I to put it off as unconcern'd, come chuck the Infant under the chin, force a smile and cry, ay, the Boy takes after his Mother's relations—when the Devil and she knows 'tis a little Compound of the whole Body of Nobility.

BELLMOUR
SHARPER } Ha, ha, ha!

HEARTWELL. Pox, I have pratled away my time—I hope you are in no haste for an Answer, for I shan't stay now.

Looking on his Watch.

BELLMOUR. Nay, prithee, *George*—

HEARTWELL. No: besides my Business, I see a Fool coming this way. Adieu.

Exit.

BELLMOUR. What does he mean? Oh, here he comes—stand close; let 'em pass.

Sir Joseph Wittoll and *Capt. Bluffe* cross the Stage.

SHARPER. What in the name of wonder is it?

BELLMOUR. Why, a Fool.

SHARPER. 'Tis a tawdry Outside.

BELLMOUR. And a very beggarly Lining—yet he may be worth your acquaintance. A little of thy Chymistry, *Tom*, may extract Gold from that Dirt.

SHARPER. Say you so? faith, I am as poor as a Chymist and would be as industrious. But what was

349 *fleering:* laughing scornfully.

379 *Chymist:* alchemist, who labours hopelessly to create gold from baser materials.

he that follow'd him? is not he a Dragon that watches those Golden Pippins?

BELLMOUR. Hang him, no. He a Dragon! If he be, 'tis a very peaceful one. I can ensure his Anger dormant; or should he seem to rouse, 'tis but well lashing him, and he will sleep like a Top.

SHARPER. Ay, is he of that kidney?

BELLMOUR. Yet is ador'd by that Bigot, Sir *Joseph Wittoll,* as the image of Valour. He calls him his Back, and indeed they are never asunder. Yet last night, I know not by what mischance, the Knight was alone, and had fallen into the hands of some Nightwalkers, who I suppose would have pillag'd him. But I chanc'd to come by and rescued him, though I believe he was heartily frightened; for as soon as ever he was loose, he ran away without staying to see who help'd him.

SHARPER. Is that Bully of his in the Army?

BELLMOUR. No, but is a pretender, and wears the habit of a Soldier, which nowadays as often cloaks Cowardice, as a Black Gown does Atheism. You must know he has been abroad—went purely to run away from a Campagne; enrich'd himself with the plunder of a few Oaths —and here vents 'em against the General, who slighting Men of Merit, and preferring only those of interest, has made him quit the Service.

SHARPER. Wherein, no doubt, he magnifies his own performance.

BELLMOUR. Speaks Miracles, is the Drum to his own praise—the only implement of a Soldier he resembles; like that, being full of blustring noise and emptiness.

SHARPER. And like that, of no use but to be beaten.

BELLMOUR. Right, but then the comparison breaks, for he will take a drubbing with as little noise as a Pulpit Cushion.

381 *Golden Pippins:* golden apples of the Hesperides brought back by Hercules as one of his labours.

404 *those of interest:* those who pay well for their commissions.

414 *Pulpit Cushion:* apt to be thumped by the minister during a vehement sermon.

SHARPER. His name, and I have done.

BELLMOUR. Why that, to pass it current too, he has guilded with a Title; he is call'd *Capt. Bluffe.*

SHARPER. Well, I'll endeavour his acquaintance. You steer another Course; are bound
For Love's Island; I, for the Golden Coast.
May each succeed in what he wishes most.

Exeunt.

ACT II. SCENE I.

Sir Joseph Wittoll, Sharper *following.*

SHARPER. Sure that's he, and alone.

SIR JOSEPH. Um. –Ay, this, this is the very damn'd place; the inhuman Cannibals, the bloody-minded Villains would have Butcher'd me last night. No doubt they would have flayed me alive, have sold my Skin, and devour'd my Members.

SHARPER. How's this!

SIR JOSEPH. An it hadn't been for a civil Gentleman as came by and frightn'd 'em away–but, agad, I durst not stay to give him thanks.

SHARPER. This must be *Bellmour* he means–ha! I have a thought–

SIR JOSEPH. Zooks, would the Captain would come; the very remembrance makes me quake; agad, I shall never be reconciled to this place heartily.

SHARPER. 'Tis but trying, and being where I am at worst. Now, luck! *(Aloud.)* Curs'd fortune! this must be the place, this damn'd unlucky place–

SIR JOSEPH. Agad, and so 'tis–why, here has been more mischief done I perceive.

SHARPER. No, 'tis gone, 'tis lost–ten thousand Devils on that chance which drew me hither; ay here, just here, this spot to me is Hell; nothing to be found but the despair of what I've lost.

Looking about as in search.

13 *Zooks:* 'God's hooks'; Christ's nails on the cross.

SIR JOSEPH. Poor Gentleman—by the Lord *Harry* I'll stay no longer, for I have found too—

SHARPER. Ha! who's that has found? What have you found? Restore it quickly, or by—

SIR JOSEPH. Not I Sir, not I; as I've a Soul to be sav'd, I have found nothing but what has been to my loss, as I may say, and as you were saying, Sir.

SHARPER. Oh, your Servant, Sir; you are safe then it seems. 'Tis an ill Wind that blows nobody good. Well, you may rejoice over my ill fortune, since it pay'd the price of your ransom.

SIR JOSEPH. I rejoice! agad, not I, Sir; I'm sorry for your loss, with all my Heart, Blood and Guts, Sir; and if you did but know me, you'd nere say I were so ill-natur'd.

SHARPER. Know you! Why, can you be so ungrateful, to forget me?

SIR JOSEPH. O Lord, forget him! No no, Sir, I don't forget you—because I never saw your face before, agad. Ha, ha, ha!

Angrily.

SHARPER. How?

SIR JOSEPH. Stay, stay Sir, let me recollect—(*Aside.*) He's a damn'd angry Fellow—I believe I had better remember him till I can get out of his sight, but out o'sight out o'mind, agad.

SHARPER. Methought the service I did you last night Sir, in preserving you from those Ruffians, might have taken better root in your shallow memory.

SIR JOSEPH. Gads-Daggers-Belts-Blades-and Scabbards, this is the very Gentleman! How shall I make him a return suitable to the greatness of his merit? I had a pretty thing to that Purpose, if he han't frighted it out of my memory. Hem, hem! Sir, I must submissively implore your pardon for my transgression of ingratitude and omission; having my intire dependance, Sir, upon the superfluity of your goodness, which, like an innundation will I hope totally immerge the recollection of my errour, and leave me floating in your sight, upon the full-blown Bladders of repentance—by the help of which I shall once more hope to swim into your favour. *Bows.*

SHARPER. So—h, O Sir, I am easily pacify'd. The acknowledgment of a Gentleman—

SIR JOSEPH. Acknowledgment! Sir I am all over acknowledgment, and will not stick to shew it in the greatest extremity, by night, or by day, in sickness, or in health, Winter, or Summer, all Seasons and occasions shall testify the reality and gratitude of your superabundant humble Servant Sir *Joseph Wittoll*, Knight. Hem! Hem!

SHARPER. Sir *Joseph Wittoll!*

SIR JOSEPH. The same, Sir, of *Wittoll-hall* in *Comitatu Bucks.*

SHARPER. Is it possible! Then I am happy to have obliged the Mirrour of Knighthood and Pink of Courtesie in the Age. Let me embrace you.

SIR JOSEPH. O Lord, Sir!

SHARPER. My loss I esteem as a trifle repay'd with interest, since it has purchas'd me the friendship and acquaintance of the person in the World whose Character I admire.

SIR JOSEPH. You are only pleas'd to say so, Sir.—But pray, if I may be so bold, what is that loss you mention?

SHARPER. O term it no longer so, Sir. In the Scuffle last Night I only dropt a Bill of a hundred Pound, which I confess I came half despairing to recover. But thanks to my better Fortune—

SIR JOSEPH. You have found it, Sir, then it seems? I profess I'm heartily glad.

SHARPER. Sir, your humble Servant—I don't question but you are, that you have so cheap an opportunity of expressing your gratitude and generosity; since the refunding so trivial a Sum will wholly acquit you and doubly engage me.

79 *Comitatu Bucks:* Buckinghamshire.

81 *Pink:* the flower, or finest example of excellence.

SIR JOSEPH (*aside*). What a dickens does he means by a trival Sum? But han't you found it, Sir?

SHARPER. No otherwise, I vow to Gad, but in my hopes in you, Sir.

SIR JOSEPH. *Humph!*

SHARPER. But that's sufficient.—'Twere injustice to doubt the honour of Sir *Joseph Wittoll.*

SIR JOSEPH. O Lord, Sir.

SHARPER. You are above (I'm sure) a thought so low, to suffer me to lose what was ventur'd in your service; Nay, 'twas in a manner pay'd down for your deliverance; 'twas so much lent you. And you scorn, I'll say that for you—

SIR JOSEPH. Nay, I'll say that for myself (with your leave, Sir). I do scorn a dirty thing. But agad! I'm a little out of pocket at present.

SHARPER. Pshaw! you can't want a hundred Pound. Your Word is sufficient anywhere. 'Tis but borrowing so much Dirt; you have large Acres and can soon repay it. Mony is but Dirt, Sir *Joseph*—mere Dirt.

SIR JOSEPH. But, I profess, 'tis a Dirt I have wash'd my Hands of at present; I have lay'd it all out upon my Back.

SHARPER. Are you so extravagant in Cloaths, Sir Joseph?

SIR JOSEPH. Ha, ha, ha, a very good Jest, I profess, ha, ha, ha, a very good Jest, and I did not know that I had say'd it and that's a better Jest than tother. 'Tis a sign you and I ha'n't been long acquainted; you have lost a good Jest for want of knowing me.—I only mean a Friend of mine whom I call my Back; he sticks as close to me, and follows me through all dangers. He is indeed Back, Breast and Headpiece as it were to me—agad, he's a brave Fellow. Pauh, I am quite another thing when I am with him; I don't fear the Devil (God bless us) almost if he be by. Ah—had he been with me last night—

SHARPER (*angrily*). If he had Sir, what then? He could have done no more, nor perhaps have suffer'd so much. —Had he a hundred Pound to lose?

SIR JOSEPH. O Lord, Sir, by no means. (But I might have sav'd a hundred Pound.) I meant innocently, as I hope to be sav'd, Sir (a damn'd hot Fellow); only, as I was saying, I let him have all my ready Mony to redeem his great Sword from Limbo.—But Sir, I have a Letter of Credit to Alderman *Fondlewife,* as far as two hundred Pound, and this Afternoon you shall see I am a Person, such a one as you would wish to have met with.

SHARPER (*aside*). That you are I'll be sworn. (*Aloud.*) Why, that's great and like yourself.

Enter Bluffe

SIR JOSEPH. Oh, here 'a comes.—Ah, my Hector of *Troy,* welcome my Bully, my Back; agad, my heart has gone a-pit-pat for thee.

BLUFFE. How how, my young Knight? Not for fear I hope; he that knows me must be a stranger to fear.

SIR JOSEPH. Nay, agad, I hate fear ever since I had like to have dy'd of a fright. But—

BLUFFE. But? Look you here Boy, here's your antidote, here's your Jesuit's Powder for a shaking fit. —But who hast thou got with thee; is he of mettle?
Laying his Hand upon his Sword.

SIR JOSEPH. Ay Bully, a Devilish smart Fellow, 'a will fight like a Cock.

BLUFFE. Say you so? then I honour him. But has he been aboard? for every Cock will fight upon his own Dunghill.

SIR JOSEPH. I don't know, but I'll present you—

BLUFFE. I'll recommend myself.—Sir, I honour you; I understand you love Fighting; I reverence a Man that loves Fighting. Sir, I Kiss your Hilts.

SHARPER. Sir, your Servant. But you are misinform'd, for unless it be to serve my particular Friend, as Sir *Joseph* here, my Country, or my Religion, or in some very Justifiable Cause, I'm not for it.

146 *from Limbo:* out of pawn.
162 *Jesuit's Powder:* quinine, a bark used against malaria by natives of Peru; introduced into Europe by Jesuit missionaries to combat ague.

BLUFFE. O Lord, I beg your pardon, Sir. I find you are not of my Palate; you can't relish a Dish of Fighting without Sweet Sauce. Now I think Fighting for Fighting sake's sufficient Cause; Fighting to me's Religion and the Laws.

SIR JOSEPH. Ah, well said my *Hero;* was not that great, Sir? By the Lord *Harry* he says true; Fighting is Meat, Drink and Cloth to him. But Back, this Gentleman is one of the best Friends I have in the World, and saved my Life last Night.—You know I told you.

BLUFFE. Ay! Then I honour him again.—Sir, may I crave your name?

SHARPER. Ay Sir, my name's *Sharper.*

SIR JOSEPH. Pray, Mr. *Sharper*, embrace my Back. —Very well.—By the Lord *Harry*, Mr. *Sharper*, he's as brave a Fellow as Cannibal, are not you Bully —Back?

SHARPER. *Hannibal,* I believe you mean, Sir *Joseph.*

BLUFFE. Undoubtedly he did, Sir; faith, *Hannibal* was a very pretty Fellow. But, Sir *Joseph,* comparisons are odious—*Hannibal* was a very pretty Fellow in those Days, it must be granted. But Alas, Sir! were he alive now, he would be nothing in the Earth.

SHARPER. How Sir? I make a doubt if there be at this Day a greater General breathing.

BLUFFE. Oh, excuse me, Sir; have you serv'd abroad, Sir?

SHARPER. Not I really, Sir.

BLUFFE. Oh, I thought so. Why then you can know nothing Sir; I'm afraid you scarce know the History of the Late War in *Flanders,* with all its particulars.

SHARPER. Not I, Sir, no more than publick Letters or *Gazettes* tell us.

BLUFFE. *Gazette!* Why, there again now.—Why, Sir, there are not three words of Truth, the Year round, put into the *Gazette.* I'll tell you a strange

211 *Gazettes:* the *London Gazette,* first published in 1666, appearing every Tuesday and Friday with news of the government.

thing now as to that.—You must know, Sir, I was resident in *Flanders* the last Campagn, had a small Post there; but no matter for that. Perhaps, Sir, there was a scarce anything of moment done but an humble Servant of yours, that shall be nameless, was an Eye-witness of. I won't say had the greatest share in't. Tho' I might say that too, since I am nobody you know.—Well, Mr. *Sharper,* would you think it? In all this time—as I hope for a Truncheon—this rascally *Gazette*-writer never so much as once mention'd me—Not once, by the Wars.—Took no more notice than as if *Noll Bluffe* had not been in the Land of the Living.

SHARPER. Strange!

SIR JOSEPH. Yet, by the Lord *Harry* 'tis true, Mr. *Sharper,* for I went every day to Coffee-houses to read the *Gazette* myself.

BLUFFE. Ay, ay, no matter. —You see, Mr. *Sharper,* after all I am content to retire.—Live a private Person. —*Scipio* and others have done it.

SHARPER *(aside).* Impudent Rogue.

SIR JOSEPH. Ay, this damn'd Modesty of yours.—Agad, if he would put in for't he might be made General himself yet.

BLUFFE. Oh, fy, no Sir *Joseph!* You know I hate this.

SIR JOSEPH. Let me but tell Mr. *Sharper* a little; how you eat fire once out of the mouth of a Canon—agad he did; those impenetrable Whiskers of his have confronted Flames.

BLUFFE. Death, what do you mean, Sir *Joseph?*

SIR JOSEPH. Look you now, I tell you he's so modest he'll own nothing.

216 *the last Campagn:* the wars in Flanders between William III and France. Bluffe's cause had recently fared badly; William lost Namur, and was defeated at Steenkirk in the summer of 1692.

223 *Truncheon:* marshal's baton.

234 *Scipio:* Scipio Africanus, Roman general who defeated 'Cannibal', as Sir Joseph would have him, and retired for a time from public life.

BLUFFE. Pish, you have put me out; I have forgot what I was about. Pray hold your Tongue, and give me leave.

Angrily.

SIR JOSEPH. I am dumb.

BLUFFE. This Sword I think I was telling you of, Mr. *Sharper*—this Sword I'll maintain to be the best Divine, Anatomist, Lawyer or Casuist in *Europe;* it shall decide a Controversie or split a Cause—

SIR JOSEPH. Nay, now I must speak; it will split a Hair, by the Lord *Harry;* I have seen it.

BLUFFE. Zoons Sir, it's a Lie; you have not seen it, nor shan't see it; Sir I say you can't see; what d'ye say to that now?

SIR JOSEPH. I am blind.

BLUFFE. Death, had any other Man interrupted me—

SIR JOSEPH. Good Mr. *Sharper,* speak to him; I dare not look that way.

SHARPER. Captain, Sir *Joseph's* penitent.

BLUFFE. O I am calm Sir, calm as a discharg'd Culverin. But 'twas indiscreet, when you know what will provoke me.—Nay, come Sir *Joseph,* you know my Heat's soon over.

SIR JOSEPH. Well, I am a Fool sometimes—but I'm sorry.

BLUFFE. Enough.

SIR JOSEPH. Come, we'll go take a Glass to drown Animosities. Mr. *Sharper,* will you partake?

SHARPER. I wait on you Sir; nay, pray Captain—you are Sir *Joseph's* Back.

Exeunt.

[SCENE II]

SCENE *Changes to Lodging*

Enter Araminta, Belinda.

BELINDA. Ay! nay Dear—prithee good, dear sweet Cousin, no more. Oh Gad, I swear you'd make one sick to hear you.

258 *Zoons:* God's wounds.
266 *Culverin:* large cannon.

ARAMINTA. Bless me! What have I said to move you thus?

BELINDA. Oh, you have raved, talked idly, and all in Commendation of that filthy, awkard, two leg'd Creature, Man.—You don't know what you said; your Fever has transported you.

ARAMINTA. If Love be the Fever which you mean, kind Heav'n avert the cure. Let me have Oil to feed that Flame and never let it be extinct, till I myself am Ashes.

BELINDA. There was a Whine—O Gad, I hate your horrid Fancy. This Love is the Devil, and sure to be in Love is to be possess'd.—Tis in the Head, the Heart, the Blood, the—all over.—O Gad, you are quite spoil'd. I shall loath the sight of Mankind for your sake.

ARAMINTA. Fie, this is gross Affectation.—A little of *Bellmour's* Company would change the Scene.

BELINDA. Filthy Fellow! I wonder Cousin—

ARAMINTA. I wonder, Cousin, you should imagine I don't perceive you love him.

BELINDA. Oh, I love your hideous Fancy! Ha, ha, ha, love a Man!

ARAMINTA. Love a Man! yes—you would not love a Beast.

BELINDA. Of all Beasts not an Ass—which is so like your *Vainlove*.—Lard, I have seen an Ass look so chagrin, Ha, ha, ha, (you must pardon me; I can't help Laughing) that an absolute Lover would have concluded the poor Creature to have had Darts, and Flames, and Altars, and all that in his Breast. *Araminta,* come I'll talk seriously to you now; could you but see with my Eyes the buffoonry of one Scene of Address—a Lover, set out with all his Equipage and Appurtenances; O Gad! sure you would. But you play the Game, and consequently can't see the Miscarriages obvious to every Stander-by.

ARAMINTA. Yes, yes, I can see something near it when you and *Bellmour* meet. You don't know that you dreamt of *Bellmour* last Night, and call'd him aloud in your sleep.

BELINDA. Pish, I can't help dreaming of the Devil sometimes; would you from thence infer I love him?

ARAMINTA. But that's not all; you caught me in your Arms when you named him, and press'd me to your Bosom.—Sure if I had not pinch'd you till you wak'd, you had stifled me with Kisses.

BELINDA. O barbarous Aspersion!

ARAMINTA. No Aspersion, Cousin, we are alone.—Nay, I can tell you more.

BELINDA. I deny it all.

ARAMINTA. What, before you hear it?

BELINDA. My Denial is premeditated like your Malice. Lard, Cousin, you talk odly.—Whatever the Matter is, O my Sol, I'm afraid you'l follow evil Courses.

ARAMINTA. Ha, ha, ha, this is pleasant.

BELINDA. You may laugh, but—

ARAMINTA. Ha, ha, ha!

BELINDA. You think the malicious Grin becomes you. The Devil take *Bellmour!*—Why do you tell me of him?

ARAMINTA. Oh, is it come out? Now you are angry, I am sure you love him. I tell nobody else, Cousin—I have not betray'd you yet.

BELINDA. Prithee, tell it all the World it's false. Betty! *Calls.*

ARAMINTA. Come then, Kiss and Friends.

BELINDA. Pish.

ARAMINTA. Prithee don't be so peevish.

BELINDA. Prithee don't be so impertinent.

ARAMINTA. Ha, ha, ha!

Enter Betty.

BETTY. Did your Ladyship call, Madam?

58 *Sol:* Apollo, the sun. The word occurs in all early editions, but Bateson silently alters it to *soul*, and Summers agrees with him.

BELINDA. Get my Hoods and Tippet, and bid the Footman call a Chair.

Exit Betty.

ARAMINTA. I hope you are not going out in dudgeon, Cousin.

Enter Footman.

FOOTMAN. Madam, there are–

BELINDA. Is there a Chair?

FOOTMAN. No. Madam, there are Mr. *Bellmour* and Mr. *Vainlove* to wait upon your Ladyship.

ARAMINTA. Are they below?

FOOTMAN. No, Madam, they sent before, to know if you were at home.

BELINDA. The Visit's to you, Cousin. I suppose I am at my liberty.

ARAMINTA. Be ready to shew 'em up.

Exit Footman.

I can't tell, Cousin; I believe we are equally concern'd. But if you continue your Humour, it won't be very entertaining–(Aside.) I know she'd fain be persuaded to stay.

BELINDA. I shall oblige you in leaving you to the full and free enjoyment of that Conversation you admire.

Enter Betty, *with Hoods and Looking-glass.*

BELINDA. Let me see; hold the Glass.–Lard I look wretchedly today.

ARAMINTA. *Betty*, why don't you help my Cousin?

Putting on her Hoods

BELINDA. Hold off your Fists, and see that he gets a Chair with a high Roof, or a very low Seat. Stay, Come back here you Mrs. Fidget–you are so ready to go to the Footman.–Here, take 'em all again; my Mind's chang'd; I won't go.

76 *Tippet:* short cloak.
77 *Chair:* sedan-chair, enclosed, carried by two bearers.

Exit Betty *with the Things.*

ARAMINTA. So, this I expected. You won't oblige me then, Cousin, and let me have all the Company to myself?

BELINDA. No; upon deliberation, I have too much Charity to trust you to yourself. The Devil watches all opportunities, and in this favourable disposition of your Mind, Heav'n knows how far you may be tempted. I am tender of your Reputation.

ARAMINTA. I am oblig'd to you—but who's malicious now, *Belinda?*

BELINDA. Not I; witness my Heart I stay out of pure Affection.

ARAMINTA. In my Conscience I believe you.

Enter Bellmour, Vainlove.

BELLMOUR. So Fortune be prais'd! To find you both within, Ladies, is—

ARAMINTA. No Miracle, I hope.

BELLMOUR. Not o' your side, Madam, I confess—but my Tyrant there and I are two Buckets that can never come together.

BELINDA. Nor are ever like—yet we often meet and clash.

BELLMOUR. How never like? marry, *Hymen* forbid. But this it is to run so extravagantly in Debt; I have laid out such a world of Love in your Service that you think you can never be able to pay me all, so shun me for the same reason that you would a Dun.

BELINDA. Ay, on my Conscience, and the most impertinent and troublesome of Duns.—A Dun for Mony will be quiet, when he sees his Debtor has not wherewithal, but a Dun for Love is an eternal Torment that never rests—

BELLMOUR. Till he has created Love where there was none, and then gets it for his pains. For impor-

130 *two Buckets:* hanging in a well on opposite ends of a rope. See Shakespeare, *Richard II* (IV, i, 184-189).

tunity in Love, like importunity at Court, first creates its own Interest, and then pursues it for the Favour.

ARAMINTA. Favours that are got by Impudence and Importunity are like Discoveries from the Rack, when the afflicted Person, for his ease, sometimes confesses Secrets his Heart knows nothing of.

VAINLOVE. I should rather think Favours so gain'd to be due Rewards to indefatigable Devotion. For as Love is a Deity, he must be serv'd by Prayer.

BELINDA. O Gad, would you would all pray to Love then, and let us alone.

VAINLOVE. You are the Temples of Love, and 'tis through you our Devotion must be convey'd.

ARAMINTA. Rather poor silly Idols of your own making, which upon the least displeasure you forsake, and set up new.—Every Man now changes his Mistress and his Religion, as his Humour varies or his Interest.

VAINLOVE. O Madam—

ARAMINTA. Nay come, I find we are growing serious, and then we are in great danger of being dull. If my Musickmaster be not gone, I'll entertain you with a new Song which comes pretty near my own Opinion of Love and your Sex.—Who's there? *Calls.*

Enter Footman.

Is Mr. *Gavot* gone?

FOOTMAN. Only to the next door, Madam; I'll call him.

Exit.

BELLMOUR. Why, you won't hear me with Patience?

ARAMINTA. What's the Matter, Cousin.

BELLMOUR. Nothing, Madam, only—

BELINDA. Prithee hold thy Tongue.—Lard, he has so pester'd me with Flames and Stuff. I think I shan't endure the sight of a Fire this Twelvemonth.

BELLMOUR. Yet all can't melt that cruel, frozen Heart.

BELINDA. O Gad, I hate your hideous Fancy—you said that once before.—If you must talk impertinently, for Heav'ns sake let it be with variety; don't come always, like the Devil, wrapt in Flames. I'll not hear a Sentence more, that begins with an "I burn," or an "I beseech you, Madam."

BELLMOUR. But tell me how you would be Ador'd; I am very tractable.

BELINDA. Then know, I would be Ador'd in Silence.

BELLMOUR. Humph, I thought so, that you might have all the Talk to yourself. You had better let me speak; for if my Thoughts fly to any pitch, I shall make villainous Signs.

BELINDA. What will you get by that? To make such Signs as I won't understand.

BELLMOUR. Ay, but if I'm Tongue-ty'd, I must have all my Actions free to—quicken your Apprehension. And, I-gad, let me tell you, my standing Argument is depress'd in dumb show.

Enter Musick master.

ARAMINTA. Oh, I am glad we shall have a Song to divert the Discourse. Pray oblige us with the last new Song.

SONG.

I.

Thus, to a ripe, consenting Maid,
Poor, old, repenting *Delia* said,
Would you long preserve your Lover?
Would you still his Goddess reign?
Never let him all discover,
Never let him much obtain.

II.

Men will admire, adore and die,
While wishing at your Feet they lie:
But admitting their Embraces,
Wakes 'em from the golden Dream;
Nothing's new besides our Faces,
Every Woman is the same.

ARAMINTA. So, how d'ye like the Song, Gentlemen?

201 *dumb show:* part of a play represented by action without speech. Bellmour finds such gestures insufficient to express his physical passion.
205 *new Song:* set to music by the great Henry Purcell.

BELLMOUR. Oh, very well perform'd—but I don't much admire the Words.

ARAMINTA. I expected it; there's too much Truth in 'em. If Mr. *Gavot* will walk with us in the Garden, we'll have it once again. —You may like it better at second hearing. You'll bring my Cousin?

BELLMOUR. Faith, Madam, I dare not speak to her, but I'll make Signs.

Addresses Belinda *in dumb show.*

BELINDA. O fogh, your dumb Rhetorick is more ridiculous than your talking Impertinence, as an Ape is a much more troublesome Animal than a Parrot.

ARAMINTA. Ay, Cousin, and 'tis a sign the Creatures mimick Nature well, for there are few Men but do more silly things than they say.

BELLMOUR. Well, find my Apishness has paid the Ransom for my Speech, and set it at liberty—tho', I confess, I could be well enough pleas'd to drive on a Love-bargain in that silent manner. —'Twould save a Man a World of Lying and Swearing at the Year's end. Besides, I have had a little Experience, that brings to my mind—

When Wit and Reason both have fail'd to move;
Kind Looks and Action (from Success) do prove,
Ev'n Silence may be Eloquent in Love.

Exeunt Omnes.

ACT III. Scene I. The Street

Silvia *and* Lucy.

SILVIA. Will'a not come then?

LUCY Yes, yes, come, I warrant him, if you will go in and be ready to receive him.

SILVIA. Why did you not tell me? Whom mean you?

LUCY. Whom you should mean; *Heartwell.*

SILVIA. Senseless Creature, I meant my *Vainlove.*

LUCY. You may as soon hope to recover your own Maidenhead as his Love. Therefore e'n set your Heart at rest, and in the name of opportunity mind your own Business. Strike Heartwell home, before the Bait's worn off the Hook; Age will come. He nibbled fairly yesterday, and no doubt will be eager enough to day to swallow the Temptation.

SILVIA. Well, since there's no remedy. Yet tell me—for I would know, though to the anguish of my Soul; how did he refuse? Tell me—how did he receive my letter, in Anger or in Scorn?

LUCY. Neither; but what was ten times worse, with damn'd, senseless indifference. By this Light I could have spit in his Face. Receive it! Why he receiv'd it as I would one of your Lovers that should come empty-handed; as a Court Lord does his Mercer's Bill, or a begging Dedication; —'a receiv'd it, as if 't had been a Letter from his Wife.

SILVIA. What, did he not read it?

LUCY. Hum'd it over, gave you his Respects, and said he would take time to peruse it, but then he was in haste.

SILVIA. Respects, and peruse it! He's gone, and *Araminta* has bewitch'd him from me. —Oh, how the name of Rival fires my Blood! I could curse 'em both; eternal Jealousy attend her Love, and Disappointment meet his Lust. Oh that I could revenge the Torment he has caus'd! —Methinks I feel the Woman strong within me, and Vengeance itches in the room of Love.

LUCY. I have that in my Head may make Mischief.

SILVIA. How, dear *Lucy*?

LUCY. You know *Araminta's* dissembled Coyness has won, and keeps him hers—

SILVIA. Could we persuade him that she Loves another—

LUCY. No, you're out; could we persuade him that she doats on him himself, contrive a kind Letter as from her, 'twould disgust his nicety, and take away his Stomach.

19 *By this Light:* 'by God's light'; a common expression of the day.

22 *Mercer's:* dealer in fabrics.

44 *nicety:* "Fastidious delicacy; punctilious discrimination." (Johnson, *Dictionary.*)

SILVIA. Impossible, 'twill never take.

LUCY. Trouble not your Head. Let me alone; I will inform myself of what past between 'em to day, and about it streight.—Hold, I'm mistaken, or that's *Heartwell* who stands talking at the Corner—'tis he. Go get you in Madam, receive him pleasantly, dress up your Face in Innocence and Smiles, and dissemble the very want of Dissimulation.—You know what will take him.

SILVIA. 'Tis as hard to Counterfeit Love, as it is to conceal it, but I'll do my weak endeavour, though I fear I have not Art.

LUCY. Hang Art, Madam, and trust to Nature for Dissembling.

Man was by Nature Woman's Cully made:
We never are but by ourselves betray'd.

Exeunt.

Enter Heartwell, Vainlove *and* Bellmour *following.*

BELLMOUR. Hist, hist, is not that *Heartwell* going to *Silvia*?

VAINLOVE. He's talking to himself, I think; Prithee let's try if we can hear him.

HEARTWELL. Why, whither in the Devils name am I going now? Hum—Let me think—Is not this *Silvia's* House, the Cave of that Enchantress and which consequently I ought to shun as I would infection? To enter here is to put on the envenom'd Shirt, to run into the Embraces of a Fever, and in some raving fit, be led to plunge myself into that more Consuming Fire, a Woman's Arms. Ha! well recollected. I will recover my reason and be gone.

BELLMOUR. Now *Venus* forbid!

VAINLOVE. Hust—

HEARTWELL. Well, why do you not move? Feet, do your Office.—Not one Inch? No, Foregod, I'm caught! There stands my North, and thither my Needle

60 *Cully:* simpleton easily duped.

72 *envenom'd Shirt:* in Greek mythology, Hercules sought to destroy himself in agony caused by a sacrificial robe rubbed with the blood of the centaur Nessus whom he had killed.

points. –Now could I curse myself, yet cannot repent. O thou Delicious, Damn'd, Dear, Destructive Woman! S'death how the young Fellows will hoot me! I shall be the Jest of the Town. Nay, in two Days, I expect to be chronicled in Ditty, and sung in woful Ballad, to the Tune of the Superanuated Maiden's Comfort, or the Batchelor's Fall; and upon the third, I shall be hang'd in Effigie, pasted up for the exemplary Ornament of necessary Houses and Coblers' Stalls. – Death, I can't think on't–I'll run into the danger to lose the apprehension.

Goes in.

BELLMOUR. A very certain remedy *probatum est*– Ha, ha, ha! Poor *George*, thou art i'th'right, thou hast sold thyself to Laughter; the ill-natur'd Town will find the Jest just where thou hast lost it. Ha, ha, how 'a struggled like an Old Lawyer between two Fees.

VAINLOVE. Or a young Wench, betwixt pleasure and reputation.

BELLMOUR. Or as you did to day, when half afraid you snatch'd a kiss from *Araminta*.

VAINLOVE. She had made a quarrel on't.

BELLMOUR. Pauh, Women are only angry at such offences to have the pleasure of forgiving 'em.

VAINLOVE. And I love to have the pleasure of making my peace. I should not esteem a Pardon if too easy won.

BELLMOUR. Thou dost not know what thou would'st be at; whether thou would'st have her angry or pleas'd. Could'st thou be content to marry *Araminta*?

VAINLOVE. Could you be content to go to Heaven?

BELLMOUR. Hum, not immediately, in my conscience, not heartily. I'd do a little more good in my generation first, in order to deserve it.

VAINLOVE. Nor I to marry *Araminta* till I merit her.

90 *necessary Houses:* privies.

94 *probatum est:* 'it has been tested', referring to a prescription. Bellmour caps Heartwell's medical metaphors.

BELLMOUR. But how the Devil dost thou expect to get her if she never yield?

VAINLOVE. That's true; but I would–

BELLMOUR. Marry her without her Consent; thou'rt a Riddle beyond Woman!

Enter Setter.

Trusty *Setter,* what tidings? How goes the project?

SETTER. As all lewd projects do Sir, where the Devil prevents our endeavours with success.

BELLMOUR. A good hearing, *Setter.*

VAINLOVE. Well, I'll leave you with your Engineer. *Exit.*

BELLMOUR. And hast thou provided necessaries?

SETTER. All, all Sir; the large sanctified Hat, and the little precise Band, with a swinging long Spiritual Cloak to Cover Carnal Knavery–not forgetting the Black Patch, which Tribulation Spintext wears, as I'm inform'd, upon one Eye, as a penal Mourning for the ogling Offences of his Youth; and some say, with that Eye he first discover'd the frailty of his Wife.

BELLMOUR. Well, in this Fanatick Father's habit will I confess *Lætitia.*

SETTER. Rather prepare her for Confession, Sir, by helping her to Sin.

BELLMOUR. Be at your Master's Lodging in the Evening. –I shall use the Robes.

Exit Bellmour.

SETTER. I shall Sir. –I wonder to which of these two Gentlemen I do most properly appertain. The one uses me as his Attendant, the other (being the better acquainted with my parts) employs me as a Pimp; why, that's much the more honourable employment–by all means–I follow one as my Master, but the other follows me as his Conductor.

125 *prevents:* the Devil anticipates us by providing success without our efforts.

Enter Lucy.

LUCY (*aside*). There's the Hang-Dog his Man. I had a power over him in the Reign of my Mistress; but he is too true a *Valet-de-chambre* not to affect his Master's faults, and consequently is revolted from his Allegiance.

SETTER. Undoubtedly 'tis impossible to be a Pimp and not a Man of parts. That is, without being politick, diligent, secret, wary, and soforth—and to all this, valiant as Hercules; that is, passively valiant and actively obedient. Ah, *Setter,* what a treasure is here lost for want of being known!

LUCY. Here's some Villainy afoot, he's so thoughtful. Maybe I may discover something in my Masque. (*Puts on her Masque.*) Worthy Sir, a word with you.

SETTER. Why, if I were known, I might come to be a great Man!

LUCY. Not to interrupt your meditation—

SETTER. And I should not be the first that has procur'd his greatness by Pimping.

LUCY. Now Poverty and the Pox light upon thee, for a Contemplative Pimp.

SETTER. Ha! What art, who thus maliciously hast awakned me from my Dream of Glory? Speak thou vile Disturber!

LUCY. Of thy most vile Cogitations! Thou poor, conceited Wretch, how, wer't thou valuing thyself upon thy Master's employment? For he's the head Pimp to Mr. *Bellmour.*

SETTER. Good Words, Damsel, or I shall—But how dost thou know my master or me?

LUCY. Yes, I know both Master and Man to be—

SETTER. To be Men perhaps? Nay, faith, like enough. I often march in the rear of my Master, and enter the Breaches which he was made.

LUCY. Ay, the Breach of Faith, which he has begun, thou Traitor to thy lawful Princess.

SETTER. Why how now! Prithee who art? Lay that Worldly Face and produce your natural Vizor.

152 *Hang-Dog:* despicable fellow fit only to hang a dog, or be hanged like a dog.

LUCY. No Sirrah, I'll keep it on to abuse thee and leave thee without hopes of revenge.

SETTER. Oh, I begin to smoak ye! Thou art some forsaken *Abigail* we have dallied with heretofore, and art come to tickle thy Imagination with remembrance of iniquity past.

LUCY. No, thou pitiful Flatterer of thy Master's imperfections, thou Maukin made up of the Shreds and Pairings of his superfluous Fopperies!

SETTER. Thou art thy Mistress's foul self, composed of her sully'd iniquities and Cloathing.

LUCY. Hang thee, Beggar's Cur. –Thy Master is but a Mumper in Love; lies Canting at the Gate, but never dare presume to enter the House.

SETTER. Thou art the Wicket to thy Mistress's Gate, to be opened for all Comers. In Fine, thou art the high Road to thy Mistress, as a Clap is to the Pox.

LUCY. Beast, filthy Toad, I can hold no longer. Look and tremble!

Unmasques.

SETTER. How, Mrs. *Lucy!*

LUCY. I wonder thou hast the impudence to look me in the Face.

SETTER. Adsbud who's in fault, Mistress Mine? Who flung the first Stone? Who undervalued my Function? And who the Devil could know you by instinct?

LUCY. You could know my Office by instinct, and be hang'd, which you have slander'd most abominably. It vexes me not what you said of my Person, but that my innocent Calling should be expos'd and scandaliz'd–I cannot bear it.

Cries.

192 *smoak ye:* have an inkling of your plan.

193 *Abigail:* maid or waiting-woman, from the lecherous waiting-woman Abigail in Beaumont and Fletcher's *The Scornful Lady* (1616).

197 *Maukin:* scarecrow.

202 *Mumper:* beggar or sponger.

202 *Canting:* beggarly whining.

SETTER. Nay, faith, *Lucy* I'm sorry; I'll own myself to blame, though we were both in fault as to our Offices. Come, I'll make you any reparation.

LUCY. Swear.

SETTER. I do swear to the utmost of my power.

LUCY. To be brief then; what is the reason your Master did not appear today according to the Summons I brought him?

SETTER. To answer you as briefly—He has a cause to be try'd in another Court.

LUCY. Come, tell me in plain Terms how forward he is with *Araminta.*

SETTER. Too forward to be turn'd back—though he's a little in disgrace at present about a Kiss which he forced. You and I can Kiss *Lucy* without all that.

LUCY. Stand off!—He's a precious Jewel.

SETTER. And therefore you'd have him to set in your Lady's Locket.

LUCY. Where is he now?

SETTER. He'l be in the *Piazza* presently.

LUCY. Remember today's behaviour. Let me see you with a penitent Face.

SETTER. What, no Token of amity, *Lucy?* You and I don't use to part with dry Lips.

LUCY. No, no, avaunt—I'll not be slabber'd and kiss'd now—I'm not i'th' humour.

Exit after her.

Enter Sir Joseph Wittoll, Bluffe.

BLUFFE. And so out of your unwonted Generosity—

SIR JOSEPH. And good Nature, Back; I am good Natur'd and I can't help it.

BLUFFE. You have given him a note upon *Fondlewife* for a hundred Pound.

241 *Piazza:* neo-classical arcade built by Inigo Jones, circa 1633, on two sides of Covent Garden market; a fashionable promenade throughout the century.

SIR JOSEPH. Ay, ay, poor Fellow, he ventur'd fair for't.

BLUFFE. You have disoblig'd me in it, for I have occasion for the Mony, and if you would look me in the Face again and live, go, and force him to redeliver you the Note. Go—and bring it me hither. I'll stay here for you.

SIR JOSEPH. You may stay till the day of Judgement then, by the Lord-*Harry*. I know better things than to be run through the Guts for a hundred Pound. —Why, I gave that hundred Pound for being saved, and d'ye think, an there were no danger, I'll be so ungrateful to take it from the Gentleman again?

BLUFFE. Well, go to him from me.—Tell him, I say he must refund—or Bilbo's the Word, and Slaughter will ensue. If he refuse, tell him—but whisper that—Tell him—I'll pink his Soul—but whisper that softly to him.

SIR JOSEPH. So softly that he shall never hear on't, I warrant you.—Why, what a Devil's the Matter, Bully; are you mad? Or d'ye think I'm mad? Agad, for my part, I don't love to be the Messenger of ill News; 'tis an ungrateful Office—so tell him yourself.

BLUFFE. By these Hilts I believe he frightned you into this Composition; I believe you gave it him out of fear, pure paultry fear—confess.

SIR JOSEPH. No, no, hang't, I was not afraid neither—Tho' I confess he did in a manner snap me up—Yet I can't say that it was altogether out of fear, but partly to prevent mischief, for he was a devilish cholerick Fellow. And if my Choller had been up too, agad there would have been mischief done, that's flat. And yet I believe if you had been by, I would as soon have let him a' had a hundred of my Teeth. Adsheart, if he should come just now when I'm angry, I'd tell him—Mum.

Enter Sharper, Bellmour.

269 *Bilbo:* swashbuckler's term for a sword; from Bilbao, in Spain, where rapiers were made.

289 *Adsheart:* 'God's heart'.

BELLMOUR. Thou'rt a lucky Rogue; there's your Benefactor. You ought to return him Thanks now you have receiv'd the Favour.

SHARPER. Sir *Joseph*,–your Note was accepted, and the Mony paid at sight; I'm come to return my Thanks–

SIR JOSEPH. They won't be accepted so readily as the Bill, Sir.

BELLMOUR. I doubt the Knight repents, *Tom;* he looks like the Knight of the sorrowful Face.

SHARPER. This is a double Generosity.–Do me a Kindness and refuse my Thanks–but I hope you are not offended that I offer'd em.

SIR JOSEPH. Maybe I am, Sir, maybe I am not, Sir, maybe I am both, Sir; what then? I hope I may be offended without any offence to you, Sir.

SHARPER. Hey day! Captain, what's the matter? You can tell.

BLUFFE. Mr. *Sharper,* the matter is plain–Sir *Joseph* has found out your Trick, and does not care to be put upon, being a Man of Honour.

SHARPER. Trick, Sir?

SIR JOSEPH. Ay, Trick, Sir, and won't be put upon, Sir, being a Man of Honour, Sir, and so, Sir–

SHARPER. Hearkee, Sir *Joseph,* a word with ye. In consideration of some favours lately receiv'd, I would not have you draw yourself into a Premunire by trusting to that sign of a Man there–that Pot-gun charg'd with Wind.

SIR JOSEPH. O Lord, O Lord, Captain, come justify yourself–I'll give him the Lie if you'll stand to it.

SHARPER. Nay then I'll be beforehand with you; take that–Oafe!

Cuffs him.

301 *Knight of the sorrowful Face:* Don Quixote's title for himself.

318 *Premunire:* a bad predicament, particularly one requiring an answer to a challenge; in law, the penalty for an act in contempt of the royal prerogative.

319 *Pot-gun:* child's pop-gun.

SIR JOSEPH. Captain, will you see this? Won't you pink his Soul?

BLUFFE. Husht, 'tis not so convenient now.–I shall find a time.

SHARPER. What, do you mutter about a time, Rascal? You were the Incendiary.–There's to put you in mind of your time–a Memorandum.

Kicks him.

BLUFFE. Oh, this is your time, Sir; you had best make use on't.

SHARPER. I Gad and so I will; there's again for you.

Kicks him.

BLUFFE. You are obliging Sir, but this is too publick a Place to thank you in. But in your Ear, you are to be seen again.

SHARPER. Ay, thou inimitable Coward, and to be felt–as for Example.

Kicks him.

BELLMOUR. Ha, ha, ha, prithee come away; 'tis scandalous to kick this Puppy without a Man were cold, and had no other way to get himself a heat.

Exit Bellmour, Sharper.

BLUFFE. Very well–very fine–but 'tis no matter. Is not this fine, Sir *Joseph?*

SIR JOSEPH. Indifferent, agad, in my opinion very indifferent.–I'd rather go plain all my life than wear such Finery.

BLUFFE. Death and Hell to be affronted thus! I'll die before I'll suffer it.

Draws.

SIR JOSEPH. O Lord, his Anger was not raised before.–Nay, dear Captain, don't be in Passion now he's gone. Put up, put up, dear Back, 'tis your Sir *Joseph* begs, come let me kiss thee, so so, put up, put up.

BLUFFE. By Heav'n, 'tis not to be put up!

345 *without:* unless.

SIR JOSEPH. What, Bully?

BLUFFE. Th' Affront.

SIR JOSEPH. No agad, no more 'tis, for that's put up already; thy Sword I mean.

BLUFFE. Well, Sir *Joseph*, at your entreaty—but were not you, my friend, abus'd and cuff'd and kick'd?

Putting up his Sword.

SIR JOSEPH. Ay, ay, so were you too; no matter, 'tis past.

BLUFFE. By the immortal Thunder of great Guns, 'tis false! He sucks not vital Air who dares affirm it to this Face!

Looks big.

SIR JOSEPH. To that Face, I grant you Captain.—No, no, I grant you;—Not to that Face, by the Lord *Harry*. If you had put on your fighting Face before, you had done his Business; he durst as soon have kiss'd you as kick'd you to your Face. But a Man can no more help what's done behind his Back than what's said. Come, we'll think no more of what's past.

BLUFFE. I'll call a Council of War within to consider of my Revenge to come.

Exeunt.

[SCENE II]

SCENE *Changes to* Silvia's *Lodgings.*
Enter Heartwell, Silvia.

SONG.

I.

As *Amoret* and *Thyrsis* lay
Melting the Hours in gentle Play;
Joining Faces, mingling Kisses,
And exchanging harmless Blisses:
He trembling, cry'd with eager haste,
O let me feed as well as taste;
I die, if I'm not wholly blest.

II.

The fearful Nymph reply'd—*Forbear;*
I cannot, dare not, must not hear.

Song: For the same sexual predicament, compare Dryden's 'While Alexis lay prest' in his *Marriage-a-la-Mode* (IV, 2).

Dearest Thyrsis, *do not move me,*
Do not–do not–if you Love me,
O let me–still the Shepherd said;
But while she fond Resistance made,
The hasty Joy, in strugling fled.

III.

Vex'd at the Pleasure she had miss'd,
She frown'd and blush'd, then sigh'd and kiss'd,
And seem'd to moan, in sullen Cooing,
The sad miscarriage of their Wooing:
But vain, alas! were all her Charms;
For *Thyrsis* deaf to Loves allarms,
Baffled and senseless, tir'd her Arms.

After the Song, a Dance of Anticks.

SILVIA. Indeed it is very fine.–I could look upon 'em all day.

HEARTWELL. Well, has this prevail'd for me, and will you look upon me?

SILVIA. If you could Sing and Dance so, I should love to look upon you too.

HEARTWELL. Why, 'twas I Sung and Danc'd; I gave Musick to the Voice, and Life to their Measures. –Look you here *Silvia,* here are Songs and Dances, Poetry and Musick–hark! *(pulling out a Purse and chinking it)* how sweetly one Guinea rhymes to another, and how they dance to the Musick of their own Chink. This buys all the 'tother–and this thou shalt have; and all that I am worth for the purchase of thy Love. Say, is it mine then, ha? Speak, Syren.–Oons, why do I look on her! Yet I must. Speak dear Angel, Devil, Saint, Witch; do not rack me in suspence.

SILVIA. Nay, don't stare at me so–You make me blush –I cannot look.

HEARTWELL. Oh Manhood, where art thou! What am I come to? A Woman's Toy at these years! Death, a bearded Baby for a Girl to dandle. O dotage, dotage! That ever that noble passion, *Lust,* should ebb to this degree. No reflux of vigorous Blood, but milky Love supplies the empty Channels and prompts me

25 *Anticks:* dancers fantastically dressed.
47 *bearded Baby:* a doll.

to the softness of a Child—a meer Infant and would suck. Can you love me *Silvia?* Speak.

SILVIA. I dare not speak till I believe you, and indeed I'm afraid to believe you yet.

HEARTWELL. Pox, how her Innocence torments and pleases me! Lying, Child, is indeed the Art of Love; and Men are generally Masters in it. But I'm so newly entred, you cannot distrust me of any skill in the treacherous Mystery. Now by my soul, I cannot lie, though it were to serve a Friend or gain a Mistress.

SILVIA. Must you lie then, if you say you Love me?

HEARTWELL. No, no, dear ignorance, thou beauteous Changel'ng—I tell thee I do love thee, and tell it for a Truth, a naked Truth, which I'm ashamed to discover.

SILVIA. But Love, they say, is a tender thing that will smooth Frowns, and make calm an angry Face; will soften a rugged Temper, and make ill-humoured People good: You look ready to fright one, and talk as if your Passion were not Love but Anger.

HEARTWELL. 'Tis both; for I am angry with myself, when I am pleased with you—And a Pox upon me for loving thee so well! Yet I must on—'tis a bearded Arrow, and will more easily be thrust forward than drawn back.

SILVIA. Indeed, if I were well assur'd you lov'd; but how can I be well assur'd?

HEARTWELL. Take the Symptoms, and ask all the Tyrants of thy Sex, if their Fools are not known by this Party-coloured Livery: I am Melancholy when thou art absent; look like an Ass when thou art present; Wake for you, when I should Sleep, and even Dream of you, when I am Awake; Sigh much, Drink little, Eat less, court Solitude, am grown very entertaining to myself, and (as I am informed), very troublesome to everybody else. If this be not Love, it is Madness, and then it is pardonable.—Nay yet a more certain Sign than all this; I give thee my Mony.

63 *Changel'ng:* 'The word arises from an odd superstitious opinion, that the fairies steal away children, and put others that are ugly and stupid in their places.' (Johnson, *Dictionary.*)
74 *bearded:* barbed.

SILVIA. Ay, but that is no Sign, for they say Gentlemen will give Mony to any naughty Woman to come to Bed to them—O *Gemini,* I hope you don't mean so—for I won't be a Whore.

HEARTWELL (*aside*). The more is the pity.

SILVIA. Nay, if you would Marry me, you should not come to Bed to me. You have such a Beard and would so prickle one. But do you intend to Marry me?

HEARTWELL (*aside*). That a Fool should ask such a malicious Question! Death, I shall be drawn in before I know where I am. However, I find I am pretty sure of her consent, if I am put to it.
Marry you? no, no, I'll love you.

SILVIA. Nay, but if you love me, you must Marry me; what, don't I know my Father lov'd my Mother, and was married to her?

HEARTWELL. Ay, ay, in old days People married where they lov'd; but that fashion is chang'd, Child.

SILVIA. Never tell me that. I know it is not chang'd by myself; for I love you, and would Marry you.

HEARTWELL. I'll have my Beard shav'd; it shan't hurt thee, and we'l go to Bed—

SILVIA. No, no, I'm not such a Fool neither but I can keep myself—honest. Here, I won't keep anything that's yours. (*Throws the Purse.*) I hate you now, and I'll never see you again, 'cause you'd have me naught.
Going.

HEARTWELL. Damn her, let her go, and a good riddance! Yet so much Tenderness and Beauty and Honesty together is a Jewel.—Stay, *Silvia.*—But then to Marry.—Why, every Man plays the Fool once in his Life, but to Marry is playing the Fool all one's Life long.

SILVIA. What did you call me for?

HEARTWELL. I'll give thee all I have, and thou shalt live with me in every thing so like my Wife the World shall believe it; nay, thou shalt think so thyself—only let me not think so.

SILVIA. No, I'll die before I'll be your Whore—as well as I love you.

HEARTWELL (*aside*). A Woman, and ignorant, may be honest, when 'tis out of Obstinacy and Contradiction—but S'death, it is but a may be, and upon scurvy Terms.—Well, farewell then.—If I can get out of her sight I may get the better of myself.

SILVIA. Well—good by.

Turns and Weeps.

HEARTWELL. Ha! Nay come, we'll kiss at parting (*Kisses her.*) By Heaven, she kisses sweeter than Liberty—I will Marry thee. There, thou hast done't. All my Resolve melted in that Kiss!—One more.

SILVIA. But when?

HEARTWELL. I'm impatient till it be done; I will not give myself liberty to think, lest I should cool—I will about a Licence streight—in the Evening expect me. One Kiss more, to confirm me mad; so.

Exit.

SILVIA. Ha, ha, ha! an old Fox trapt—

Enter Lucy.

Bless me! you frighted me. I thought he had been come again, and had heard me.

LUCY. Lord, Madam, I met your Lover in as much haste as if he had been going for a Midwife.

SILVIA. He's going for a Parson, Girl, the forerunner of a Midwife, some nine Months hence. Well, I find dissembling to our Sex is as natural as swimming to a *Negro;* we may depend upon our skill to save us at a plunge, though till then we never make the experiment. But how hast thou succeeded?

LUCY. As you would wish. Since there is no reclaiming *Vainlove,* I have found out a pique she has taken at him, and have fram'd a Letter that makes her sue for Reconciliation first. I know that will do—walk in and I'll shew it you. Come Madam, you're like to have a happy time on't. Both your Love and Anger satisfied! All that can charm our Sex conspire to please you.

That Woman sure enjoys a blessed Night,
Whom Love and Vengeance do at once delight.

Exeunt.

ACT IV. Scene I. The Street

Enter Bellmour *in Fanatick habit,* Setter.

BELLMOUR. 'Tis pretty near the Hour—

Looking on his Watch.

Well and how, *Setter* hæ, does my Hypocrisy fit me, hæ?
Does it sit easy on me?

SETTER. O most religously well, Sir.

BELLMOUR. I wonder why all our young Fellows should glory in an opinion of Atheism, when they may be so much more conveniently lewd under the Coverlet of Religion.

SETTER. S'bud Sir, away quickly, there's *Fondlewife* just turn'd the Corner, and's coming this way.

BELLMOUR. Gads, so there he is; he must not see me.

Exeunt.

Enter Fondlewife *and* Barnaby.

FONDLEWIFE. I say I will tarry at home.

BARNABY. But Sir.

FONDLEWIFE. Good lack! I profess the Spirit of contradiction hath possess'd the Lad. I say I will tarry at home, *Varlet.*

BARNABY. I have done, Sir; then farewell 500 Pound.

FONDLEWIFE. Ha, how's that? Stay stay, did you leave word, say you, with his Wife? With *Comfort* herself.

BARNABY. I did; and *Comfort* will send *Tribulation* hither as soon as ever he comes home.—I could have brought young Mr. *Prig,* to have kept my Mistress Company in the meantime, but you say—

FONDLEWIFE. How, how; say, *Varlet!* I say let him not come near my Doors. I say he is a wanton young *Levite* and pampereth himself up with Dainties, that he may look lovely in the Eyes of Women. Sincerely I am afraid he hath already defiled the Tabernacle of our Sister *Comfort,* while her good Husband is

31 *Levite:* term, often contemptuous, for a private chaplain; from *Judges,* XVII, 12.

deluded by his Godly appearance. I say that even Lust doth sparkle in his Eyes and glow upon his Cheeks, and that I would as soon trust my Wife with a Lord's high-fed Chaplain.

BARNABY. Sir, the Hour draws nigh—and nothing will be done there till you come.

FONDLEWIFE. And nothing can be done here till I go—so that I'll tarry, d'ye see?

BARNABY. And run the hazard to lose your affair so!

FONDLEWIFE. Good lack, good lack—I profess it is a very sufficient vexation for a Man to have a handsome Wife.

BARNABY. Never Sir, but when the Man is an insufficient Husband. 'Tis then indeed like the vanity of taking a fine House, and yet be forced to let Lodgings to help pay the Rent.

FONDLEWIFE. I profess a very apt Comparison, *Varlet.* Go in and bid my Cocky come out to me. I will give her some instructions; I will reason with her before I go.

Exit Barnaby.

And in the mean time, I will reason with myself—Tell me *Isaac,* why are thee Jealous? Why art thee distrustful of the Wife of thy Bosom?—Because she is young and vigorous, and I am Old and impotent.—Then why didst thee marry *Isaac?*—Because she was beautiful and tempting, and because I was obstinate and doating; so that my inclination was (and is still) greater than my power.— And will not that which tempted thee, also tempt others, who will tempt her, *Isaac?*—I fear it much.—But does not thy Wife love thee, nay doat upon thee?—Yes—why then!—Ay, but to say truth, She's fonder of me than she has reason to be; and in the way of Trade we still suspect the smoothest Dealers of the deepest designs.—And that she has some designs deeper than thou canst reach, th' hast experimented, *Isaac*—but Mum.

Enter Lætitia

LÆTITIA. I hope my dearest Jewel is not going to leave me—are you, *Nykin?*

FONDLEWIFE. Wife—have you throughly consider'd how detestable, how hainous, and how Crying a Sin, the Sin of Adultery is? Have you weigh'd it I say? For it is a very weighty Sin; and although it may lie heavy upon thee, yet thy Husband must also bear his part: for thy iniquity will fall upon his Head.

LÆTITIA. Bless me, what means my Dear?

FONDLEWIFE (*aside*). I profess she has an alluring Eye; I am doubtfull whether I shall trust her even with *Tribulation* himself—

Speak, I say. Have you consider'd what it is to Cuckold your Husband?

LÆTITIA (*aside*). I'm amaz'd; sure he has discover'd nothing.—Who has wrong'd me to my Dearest? I hope my Jewel does not think that ever I had any such thing in my Head, or ever will have.

FONDLEWIFE. No no, I tell you I shall have it in my Head.—You will have it somewhere else.

LÆTITIA (*aside*). I know not what to think. But I'm resolv'd to find the meaning of it—

Unkind Dear! Was it for this you sent to call me? Is it not affliction enough that you are to leave me, but you must study to encrease it by unjust suspicions? (*Crying.*) Well—well—You know my Fondness, and you love to Tyrannize.—Go on cruel Man, do. Triumph over my poor Heart while it holds, which cannot be long with this usage of yours; but that's what you want —Well, you will have your ends soon—you will—you will. Yes, it will break to oblige you.

Sighs.

FONDLEWIFE (*aside*). Verily I fear I have carry'd the Jest too far.—Nay, look you now if she does not weep—'tis the fondest Fool—'

Nay, Cocky, Cocky, nay dear Cocky, don't cry. I was but in Jest, I was not ifeck.

LÆTITIA (*aside*). Oh then all's safe. I was terrible frighted. (*Aloud.*) My affliction is always your Jest, barbarous Man!, Oh that I should love to this degree! yet—

FONDLEWIFE. Nay, Cocky.

109 *ifeck:* 'i 'faith'; in earnest.

LÆTITIA. No no, you are weary of me, that's it—that's all; you would get another Wife—Another fond Fool, to break her Heart. Well, be as cruel as you can to me, I'll pray for you; and when I am dead with grief, may you have one that will love you as well as I have done. I shall be contented to lie at peace in my cold Grave, since it will please you.

Sighs.

FONDLEWIFE. Good lack, good lack, she would melt a Heart of Oak—I profess I can hold no longer. Nay dear Cocky—Ifeck you'l break my Heart—Ifeck you will. See, you have made me weep—made poor *Nykin* weep. Nay, come Kiss, buss poor *Nykin,* and I won't leave thee—I'll lose all first.

LÆTITIA *(aside).* How! Heav'n forbid! that will be carrying the Jest too far indeed.

FONDLEWIFE. Won't you Kiss *Nykin?*

LÆTITIA. Go naughty *Nykin,* you don't love me.

FONDLEWIFE. Kiss, kiss, ifeck I do.

LÆTITIA. No you don't.

She Kisses him.

FONDLEWIFE. What, not love Cocky?

LÆTITIA. No.—o.

FONDLEWIFE. I profess I do love thee better than 500 Pound—and so thou shalt say, for I'll leave it to stay with thee.

LÆTITIA. No, you shan't neglect your business for me—No indeed you san't. *Nykin,* if you don't go, I'll think you been dealous of me still.

FONDLEWIFE. He, he, he, wilt thou, poor Fool? Then I will go, I won't be dealous.—Poor Cocky, Kiss *Nykin,* Kiss *Nykin,* ee, ee, ee. Here will be the good Man anon, to talk to Cocky and teach her how a Wife ought to behave herself.

LÆTITIA *(aside).* I hope to have one that will shew me how a Husband ought to behave himself. (*Aloud.*) I shall be glad to learn, to please my Jewel.

Kiss.

FONDLEWIFE. That's my good Dear. Come, Kiss *Nykin* once more, and then get you in—so. Get you in, get you in. Bye, bye.

LÆTITIA. Bye, *Nykin.*

FONDLEWIFE. Bye, Cocky.

LÆTITIA. Bye, *Nykin.*

She goes in.

FONDLEWIFE. Bye, Cocky, bye, bye.

Exit.

Enter Vainlove, Sharper.

SHARPER. How! *Araminta* lost!

VAINLOVE. To confirm what I have said, read this.

Gives a letter.

SHARPER. (reads). *Hum hum—And what then appear'd a fault, upon reflection, seems only an effect of a too powerful passion. I'm afraid I give too great a Proof of my own at this time—I am in disorder for what I have written. But something, I know not what, forced me. I only beg a favourable Censure of this and your*

Araminta.

SHARPER. Lost! Pray Heaven thou hast not lost thy Wits. Here, here, she's thy own, Man, sign'd and seal'd too.—To her, Man!—A delicious Mellon pure and consenting ripe, and only waits thy Cutting up. She has been breeding Love to thee all this while, and just now she is deliver'd of it.

VAINLOVE. 'Tis an untimely Fruit, and she has miscarried of her Love.

SHARPER. Never leave this damn'd illnatur'd whimsey, *Frank?* Thou hast a sickly peevish Appetite; only chew Love and cannot digest it.

VAINLOVE. Yes, when I feed myself. But I hate to be cram'd.—By Heav'n, there's not a Woman will give a Man the pleasure of a chase: My sport is always balkt or cut short—I stumble o'er the Game I would pursue. 'Tis dull and unnatural to have a Hare run full in the Hounds' Mouth, and would distaste the

171 *Censure*: 'opinion', with no sense of blame.

keenest Hunter. I would have overtaken, not have met my Game.

SHARPER. However, I hope you don't mean to forsake it; that will be but a kind of a Mongrel Cur's trick. Well, are you for the Mall?

VAINLOVE. No, she will be there this evening.—Yes, I will go too, and she shall see her error in—

SHARPER. In her choice,—but thou canst not be so great a Brute as to slight her.

VAINLOVE. I should disappoint her if I did not. By her management, I should think she expects it.

All Naturally fly what does pursue;
'Tis fit Men should be coy, when Women woo.

Exeunt.

[SCENE II]

SCENE *changes to a character in* Fondlewife's *House. A Servant introducing* Bellmour *in Fanatick Habit, with a Patch upon one Eye, and a Book in his Hand.*

SERVANT. Here's a Chair, Sir, if you please to repose yourself. I'll call my Mistress.

Exit Servant.

BELLMOUR. Secure in my Disguise, I have out-fac'd Suspicion, and even dar'd Discovery; this Cloak my Sanctity, and trusty *Scarron's* Novels my Prayer-Book. —Methinks I am the very Picture of *Montufar in the Hypocrites.*—Oh! she comes.

Enter Lætitia.

So breaks Aurora through the Veil of Night;
Thus fly the Clouds, divided by her Light,
And ev'ry Eye receives a new-born Sight.

(Throwing off his Cloak, Patch, &c.)

LÆTITIA. *Thus stew'd with Blushes, like—*

(discovering him, starts)

8 *Hypocrites:* Scarron's novella, translated into English in 1682, dealing with adventures of the Spanish rogue Montufar who disguises himself in clerical costume.

10-14 *So breaks Aurora . . . like:* Herbert Davis connects the figure of the dawn blushing with a similar passage in Dryden's *Amphitryon* (II, ii, 20-22), but such references were a poetic cliché by 1693.

Ah, Heav'n defend me! Who's this?

BELLMOUR. Your Lover.

LÆTITIA *(aside). Vainlove's* Friend! I know his Face, and he has betrayed me to him.

BELLMOUR. You are surpised. Did you not expect a Lover, Madam? Those Eyes shone kindly on my first Appearance, tho' now they are o'er-cast.

LÆTITIA. I may well be surpriz'd at your Person and Impudence; they are both new to me.—You are not what your first Appearance promised: The Piety of your Habit was welcome, but not the Hypocrisie.

BELLMOUR *(aside)*. Rather the Hypocrisie was welcome, but not the Hypocrite.

LÆTITIA. Who are you, Sir? You have mistaken the House, sure.

BELLMOUR. I have Directions in my Pocket, which agree with everything but your Unkindness.

Pulls out the letter.

LÆTITIA *(aside)*. My Letter! Base *Vainlove!* Then 'tis too late to dissemble. 'Tis plain then you have mistaken the Person.

Going.

BELLMOUR *(aside)*. If we part so I'm mistaken. *(Aloud.)* Hold, hold, Madam;—I confess I have run into an Errour:—I beg your Pardon a thousand times.—What an eternal Block-head am I! Can you forgive me the Disorder I have put you into;—But it is a Mistake which anybody might have made.

LÆTITIA *(aside)*. What can this mean! 'Tis impossible he should be mistaken after all this.—A handsome Fellow if he had not surpriz'd me: Methinks, now I look on him again, I would not have him mistaken.

Aloud.

We are all liable to Mistakes, Sir: If you own it to be so, there needs no further Apology.

BELLMOUR. Nay, 'Faith, Madam, 'tis a pleasant one, and worth your hearing. Expecting a Friend last Night at his Lodgings till 'twas late, my Intimacy with him gave me the Freedom of his Bed. He not coming home all Night, a Letter was deliver'd to me by a Servant in the Morning. Upon the Perusal I found the Contents so charming that I cou'd think of nothing all Day but putting 'em in practice—'till just now, (the first time I ever look'd upon the Superscription), I am the most surpriz'd in the World to find it directed to Mr. *Vainlove.* Gad, Madam, I ask you a Million of Pardons, and will make you any Satisfaction.

LÆTITIA *(aside).* I am discover'd:—And either *Vainlove* is not guilty, or he has handsomly excused him.

BELLMOUR. You appear concern'd, Madam.

LÆTITIA. I hope you are a Gentleman, and since you are privy to a weak Woman's Failing, won't turn it to the prejudice of her Reputation. You look as if you had more Honour—

BELLMOUR. And more Love, or my Face is a False-Witness and deserves to be pillory'd.—No, by Heaven, I swear—

LÆTITIA. Nay, don't swear if you'd have me believe you; but promise.

BELLMOUR. Well, I promise.—A promise is so cold.—Give me leave to swear—by those Eyes, those killing Eyes; by those healing Lips.—Oh! press the soft Charm close to mine, and seal 'em up for ever.

He kisses her.

LÆTITIA. Upon that Condition.

BELLMOUR. Eternity was in that Moment.—One more, upon any Condition.

LÆTITIA. Nay, now.—*(Aside.)* I never saw anything so agreeably Impudent. Won't you censure me for this, now;—but 'tis to buy your Silence.

Kiss.

Oh, but what am I doing!

BELLMOUR. Doing! No Tongue can express it,—not thy own; nor anything but thy Lips. I am faint with the Excess of Bliss.—Oh, for Love-sake, lead me any whither, where I may lie down;—quickly, for I'm afraid I shall have a Fit.

LÆTITIA. Bless me! What Fit?

BELLMOUR. Oh, a Convulsion.—I feel the Symptoms.

LÆTITIA. Does it hold you long? I'm afraid to carry you into my Chamber.

BELLMOUR. Oh, No: Let me lie down upon the Bed; the Fit will be soon over.

Exeunt.

[Scene III]

SCENE *changes to* St. James's Park.
Araminta *and* Belinda *meeting.*

BELINDA. Lard, my Dear! I am glad I have met you. I have been at the *Exchange* since, and am so tir'd—

ARAMINTA. Why, What's the matter?

BELINDA. Oh, the most inhuman, barbarous Hackney-Coach! I am jolted to a Jelly.—Am I not horridly touz'd?

Pulls out a Pocket-Glass.

ARAMINTA. Your Head's a little out of Order.

BELINDA. A little! O frightful! What a furious Fiz I have! O most rueful! Ha, ha, ha! O Gad, I hope nobody will come this Way till I put myself a little in Repair.—Ah, my Dear!—I have seen such unhewn Creatures since. Ha, ha, ha! I can't for my Soul help thinking that I look just like one of 'em. Good Dear, pin this, and I'll tell you.—Very well.—So, thank you, my Dear.—But as I was telling you—Pish, this is the untoward'st Lock.—So, as I was telling you—how d'ye like me now? Hideous, ha? Frightful still? O how?

ARAMINTA. No, no; you're very well as can be.

BELINDA. And so—but where did I leave off, my Dear? I was telling you—

ARAMINTA. You were about to tell me something, Child, but you left off before you began.

2 *Exchange:* bazaar featuring milliners' shops on the south side of the Strand. Much of Act III of Wycherley's *The Country Wife* occurs in this lively place of resort.

6 *touz'd:* pulled about, dishevelled.

BELINDA. Oh, a most Comical Sight! A Country-Squire, with the Equipage of a Wife and two Daughters, came to Mrs. *Snipwel's* Shop while I was there.—But, Oh Gad! Two such unlick'd Cubs!

ARAMINTA. I warrant, plump, cherry-cheek'd Country-Girls.

BELINDA. Ay, O my Conscience; fat as Barn-door Fowl, but so bedeck'd you wou'd have taken 'em for *Friezland*-Hens, with their Feathers growing the wrong way.—O such Out-landish Creatures! Such *Tramontanæ,* and Foreigners to the Fashion, or any thing in practice! I had not patience to behold.—I undertook the modelling of one of their Fronts, the more modern Structure.

ARAMINTA. Bless me, Cousin! Why wou'd you affront anybody so? They might be Gentlewomen of a very good Family.

BELINDA. Of a very ancient one, I dare swear, by their Dress.—Affront! Pshaw, how you're mistaken! The poor Creature, I warrant, was as full of Courtesies as if I had been her Godmother. The Truth on't is, I did endeavour to make her look like a Christian——and she was sensible of it, for she thank'd me, and gave me two Apples, piping hot, out of her Under-Petticoat-Pocket, Ha, ha, ha. And t'other did so stare and gape. I fansied her like the Front of her Father's Hall; her Eyes were the two Jut-Windows, and her Mouth the great Door, most hospitably kept open for the Entertainment of travelling Flies.

ARAMINTA. So then; you have been diverted. What did they buy?

BELINDA. Why, the Father bought a Powder-Horn, and an Almanack, and a Comb-Case; the Mother, a great Fruz-Towr, and a Fat-Amber-Necklace; the Daughters only tore two Pair of Kid-Gloves with trying 'em on—Oh Gad, here comes the Fool that din'd at my Lady *Free-love's* t' other Day.

34 *Tramontanae:* those from beyond the mountains; uncouth foreigners.

36 *Fronts:* curls of hair worn over the forehead. Belinda also intends wittily an architectural facade.

50 *Jut-Windows:* bay-windows.

57 *Fruz-Towr:* false hair, piled up and frizzed.

Enter Sir Joseph *and* Bluffe.

ARAMINTA. Maybe he may not know us again.

BELINDA. We'll put on our Masks to secure his Ignorance.

They put on their Masks.

SIR JOSEPH. Nay, gad, I'll pick up; I'm resolv'd to make a Night on't.—I'll go to Alderman *Fondlewife* by-and-by, and get 50 Pieces more from him. Adslidikins, *Bully*, we'll wallow in Wine and Women. Why, this same *Madera*-Wine has made me as light as a Grasshopper.—Hist, hist, *Bully*, dost thou see those Tearers? *(Sings.) Look you what here is,—Look you what here is:—Toll-loll-dera-toll-loll.*—A-Gad, t'other Glass of *Madera*, and I durst have attack'd 'em in my own proper Person, without your help.

BLUFFE. Come on then, Knight.—But d'ye know what to say to 'em?

SIR JOSEPH. Say! Pooh, Pox, I've enough to say, never fear it;—that is, if I can but think on't. Truth is, I have but a treacherous Memory.

BELINDA. O frightful! Cousin, What shall we do? These things come toward us.

ARAMINTA. No matter; I see *Vainlove* coming this way, and, to confess my Failing, I am willing to give him an Opportunity of making his Peace with me; and to rid me of these Coxcombs, when I seem oppress'd with 'em, will be a fair one.

BLUFFE. Ladies, by these Hilts you are well met.

ARAMINTA. We are afraid not.

BLUFFE. What says my pretty little Knapsack-Carrier?

To Belinda.

BELINDA. O monstrous filthy Fellow! Good slovenly Captain *Huffe, Bluffe* (What's your hideous Name?) be gone: You stink of Brandy and Tobacco, most Soldier-like. Foh!

Spits.

72 *Tearers:* Swaggerers; here, whores.
90 *Knapsack-Carrier:* soldier, but also a tramp or camp-follower.

SIR JOSEPH *(aside).* Now am I slap-dash down in the Mouth, and have not one Word to say.

ARAMINTA *(aside).* I hope my Fool has not Confidence enough to be troublesome.

SIR JOSEPH. Hem! Pray Madam, which Way's the Wind?

ARAMINTA. A pithy Question. Have you sent your Wits for a Venture, Sir, that you enquire?

SIR JOSEPH *(aside).* Nay, now I'm in, I can prattle like a Magpye.

Enter Sharper *and* Vainlove, *at a Distance.*

BELINDA. Dear *Araminta,* I'm tir'd.

ARAMINTA. 'Tis but pulling off our Masks and obliging *Vainlove* to know us. I'll be rid of my Fool by fair means,—Well, Sir *Joseph,* you shall see my Face. But, be gone immediately; I see one that will be Jealous to find me in discourse with you.—Be discreet. —No reply, but away.

Unmasks

SIR JOSEPH. *(aside).* The great Fortune, that dined at my Lady *Free-loves!* Sir *Joseph,* thou are a Made-man! Agad, I'm in Love, up to the Ears. But I'll be discreet, and husht.

BLUFFE. Nay, by the World, I'll see your face.

BELINDA. You shall.

Unmasks.

SHARPER. Ladies, your humble Servant.—We were afraid you would not have given us leave to know you.

ARAMINTA. We thought to have been private, but we find fools have the same advantage over a Face in a Mask that a Coward has, while the Sword is in the Scabbard; so were forced to draw in our own defence.

BLUFFE. My Blood rises at that Fellow; I can't stay where he is, and I must not draw in the Park.

To Sir Joseph

131 *draw in the Park:* St. James's Park belonged to the king; to draw a weapon there was a serious offence against the crown.

SIR JOSEPH. I wish I durst stay to let her know my Lodging.—

Exeunt Sir Joseph *and* Bluffe.

SHARPER. There is in true Beauty, as in Courage, somewhat which narrow Souls cannot dare to admire. —And see; the Owls are fled, as at the break of Day.

BELINDA. Very courtly. I believe Mr. *Vainlove* has not rubb'd his Eyes since break of Day neither, he looks as if he durst not approach.—Nay, come Cousin, be friends with him. I swear, he looks so very simply, ha, ha, ha! Well, a Lover in the state of separation from his Mistress is like a Body without a Soul. Mr. *Vainlove,* shall I be bound for your good Behaviour for the future?

VAINLOVE *(aside).* Now must I pretend ignorance equal to hers of what she knows as well as I. *(Aloud.)* Men are apt to offend ('tis true) where they find most Goodness to forgive. But, Madam, I hope I shall prove of a Temper not to abuse Mercy by committing new Offences.

ARAMINTA *(aside).* So cold!

BELINDA. I have broke the ice for you, Mr. *Vainlove,* and so I leave you. Come, Mr. Sharper, you and I will take a turn, and laugh at the Vulgar; both the great Vulgar and the small. —Oh Gad! I have a great Passion for *Cowley.* Don't you admire him?

SHARPER. Oh Madam, he was our English *Horace!*

BELINDA. Ah, so fine! So extreamly fine! So every thing in the World that I like. —Oh Lord, walk this way; I see a couple; I'll give you their History.

Exeunt Belinda *and* Sharper.

VAINLOVE. I find, Madam, the Formality of the Law must be observ'd tho' the Penalty of it be dispens'd with; and an Offender must Plead to his Arraignment, tho' he have his Pardon in his pocket.

ARAMINTA. I'm amaz'd! This Insolence exceeds the t'other. Whoever has encourag'd you to this assurance, presuming upon the easiness of my Temper, has much deceiv'd you, and so you shall find.

156 *both the great Vulgar and the small:* second line of Cowley's imitation of Horace, Book III, Ode 1, in his *Essay on Greatness.*

VAINLOVE (*aside*). Hey-day! Which way now? Here's fine doubling.

ARAMINTA. Base Man! Was it not enough to affront me with your saucy Passion?

VAINLOVE. You have given that Passion a much kinder Epithet than Saucy, in another place.

ARAMINTA. Another place! Some villainous Design to blast my Honour. But tho' thou had'st all the Treachery and Malice of thy Sex, thou canst not lay a Blemish on my Fame. –No, I have not err'd in one favourable Thought of Mankind. How time might have deceiv'd me in you, I know not; my Opinion was but young, and your early baseness has prevented its growing to a wrong Belief. –Unworthy, and ungrateful! Be gone, and never see me more.

VAINLOVE. Did I dream? Or do I dream? Shall I believe my Eyes, or Ears? The Vision is here still. –Your Passion, Madam, will admit of no farther reasoning, but here is a silent Witness of your acquaintance.–

Takes out the Letter, and offers it: She snatches it, and throws it away.

ARAMINTA. There's poison in every thing you touch. Blisters will follow–

VAINLOVE. That Tongue, which denies what the Hands have done.

ARAMINTA. Still mystically senseless and impudent! I find I must leave the place.

VAINLOVE. No, Madam, I'm gone. –She knows her Name's to it, which she will be unwilling to expose to the Censure of the first finder.

ARAMINTA. Woman's Obstinacy made me blind to what Woman's Curiosity now tempts me to see.

Takes up the Letter, and Exit.

Enter Belinda, Sharper.

BELINDA. Nay, we have spared Nobody, I swear. Mr. *Sharper*, you're a pure Man; where did you get this excellent Talent of Railing?

198 *mystically:* mysteriously.
209 *Railing:* 'To treat with satirical merriment.' (Johnson, *Dictionary.*)

SHARPER. Faith, Madam, the Talent was born with men. —I confess, I have taken care to improve it, to qualify me for the society of Ladies.

BELINDA. Nay, sure, Railing is the best qualification in a Woman's Man.

SHARPER. The second-best, indeed I think.

Enter Footman.

BELINDA. How now, *Pace*? Where's my Cousin?

FOOTMAN. She's not very well, Madam, and has sent to know if your Ladyship would have the Coach come again for you?

BELINDA. O Lord, No, I'll go along with her. Come, Mr. *Sharper*.

Exeunt.

[Scene IV]

SCENE *changes to a Chamber in* Fondlewife's *House. Enter* Lætitia *and* Bellmour, *his Cloak, Hat, &c. lying loose about the Chamber.*

BELLMOUR. Here's nobody, nor no noise; 'twas nothing but your fears.

LÆTITIA. I durst have sworn I had heard my Monster's Voice. I swear, I was heartily frightned. —Feel how my heart beats.

BELLMOUR. 'Tis an alarm to love. Come in again, and let us—

FONDLEWIFE *without.* Cocky, Cocky, Where are you, Cocky? I'm come home.

LÆTITIA. Ah! There he is. Make haste, gather up your things.

FONDLEWIFE. Cocky, Cocky, open the door.

BELLMOUR. Pox choak him; would his Horns were in his Throat. My Patch, my Patch.

Looking about, and gathering up his things.

LÆTITIA. My Jewel, Art thou there? No matter for your Patch. —You s'an't tum in, *Nykin*. —Run into my Chamber, quickly, quickly. You s'an't tum in.

Bellmour *goes in.*

FONDLEWIFE. Nay, prithee, Dear, Ifeck I'm in haste.

LÆTITIA. Then I'll let you in.

Opens the Door.

Enter Fondlewife, *and* Sir Joseph.

FONDLEWIFE. Kiss, Dear. –I met the Master of the Ship by the way, and I must have my Papers of Accounts out of your Cabinet.

LÆTITIA (*aside*). Oh, I'm undone!

SIR JOSEPH. Pray, first let me have 50 Pounds, good Alderman, for I'm in haste.

FONDLEWIFE. A Hundred has already been paid by your Order. Fifty? I have the Sum ready in Gold, in my Closet.

Goes into his Closet.

SIR JOSEPH. Agad, it's a curious, fine, pretty Rogue; I'll speak to her. –Pray, Madam, what news d'ye hear?

LÆTITIA. Sir, I seldom stir abroad.

Walks about in disorder.

SIR JOSEPH. I wonder at that, Madam, for 'tis most curious fine Weather.

LÆTITIA. Methinks, 't has been very ill Weather.

SIR JOSEPH. As you say, Madam, 'tis pretty bad Weather, and has been so a great while.

Enter Fondlewife.

FONDLEWIFE. Here are fifty Pieces in this Purse, Sir *Joseph*. If you will tarry a Moment, till I fetch my Papers, I'll wait upon you down-stairs.

LÆTITIA (*aside*). Ruin'd past redemption! What shall I do? –Ha! This fool may be of use. (*As* Fondlewife *is going into the Chamber, she runs to* Sir Joseph, *almost pushes him down, and Cries out.*) Stand off, rude Ruffian! Help me, my Dear –O bless me! Why will you leave me alone with such a Satyr?

FONDLEWIFE. Bless us! What's the matter? What's the matter?

LÆTITIA. Your back was no sooner turn'd, but like a Lion he came open-mouth'd upon me, and would have ravished a kiss from me by main force.

SIR JOSEPH. O Lord! Oh, terrible! Ha, ha, ha! Is your Wife mad, Alderman?

LÆTITIA. Oh! I am sick with the fright; won't you take him out of my sight?

FONDLEWIFE. Oh Traitor! I'm astonished. Oh bloody-minded Traitor!

SIR JOSEPH. Hey day! Traitor yourself. By the Lord-*Harry*, I was in most danger of being ravish'd, if you go to that.

FONDLEWIFE. Oh, how the blasphemous Wretch swears! Out of my house, thou Son of the Whore of *Babylon*; Offspring of *Bell* and the *Dragon*. —Bless us! Ravish my Wife! My *Dinah!* Oh *Schechemite!* Begone, I say.

SIR JOSEPH. Why, the Devil's in the People, I think. *Exit.*

LÆTITIA. Oh! Won't you follow and see him out of Doors, my Dear?

FONDLEWIFE. I'll shut this door, to secure him from coming back.—Give me the Key of your Cabinet, Cocky. —Ravish my Wife before my face! I warrant he's a Papist in his heart, at least, if not a *French*-man.

LÆTITIA. (*aside*). What can I do now! (*Aloud.*) Oh! my Dear, I have been in such a fright that I forgot to tell you; poor Mr. *Spin-text* has a sad Fit of the Cholick and is forced to lie down upon our bed. —You'll disturb him; I can tread softlier.

FONDLEWIFE. Alack poor Man. —No, no, you don't know the Papers. —I won't disturb him; give me the Key.

She gives him the Key, goes to the Chamber-door, and speaks aloud.

71 *Bell and the Dragon:* false gods destroyed by Daniel in the Apocrypha. The name also suggests an ale house, a most suitable origin for Sir Joseph.

72 *Dinah . . . Schechemite:* Dinah, daughter of Jacob and Leah, ravished by Schechem; *Genesis* 34.

LÆTITIA. 'Tis nobody but Mr. *Fondlewife,* Mr. *Spin-text.* Lie still on your Stomach; lying on your Stomach will ease you of the Cholick.

FONDLEWIFE. Ay, ay, lie still, lie still; don't let me disturb you.

Goes in.

LÆTITIA. Sure, when he does not see his face, he won't discover him. Dear Fortune, help me but this once, and I'll never run in thy debt again. But this Opportunity is the Devil.

Fondlewife *returns with Papers.*

FONDLEWIFE. Good Lack! Good Lack! I profess, the poor Man is in great torment, he lies as flat—Dear, you should heat a Trencher, or a Napkin. — Where's *Deborah?* Let her clap a warm thing to his Stomach, or chafe it with a warm-hand, rather than fail. What Book's this?

Sees the Book that Bellmour *forgot.*

LÆTITIA. Mr. *Spintext's* Prayer-Book, Dear. *(Aside.)* Pray Heav'n it be a Prayer-Book.

FONDLEWIFE. Good Man! I warrant he dropp'd it on purpose, that you might take it up and read some of the pious Ejaculations.

Taking up the Book.

O bless me! O monstrous! A Prayer-Book? Ay, this is the Devil's *Pater-noster.* Hold, let me see: *The Innocent Adultery.*

LÆTITIA *(aside).* Misfortune! Now all's ruin'd again.

BELLMOUR *(peeping).* Damn'd Chance! If I had gone a-Whoring with the *Practice of Piety* in my Pocket, I had never been discover'd.

FONDLEWIFE. Adultery, and innocent! O Lord! Here's Doctrine! Ay, here's Discipline!

105 *Trencher:* flat earthenware or metal plate.

117 *The Innocent Adultery:* another of Scarron's translated tales of intrigue and immorality, most unsuitable for Puritan reading.

121 *The Practice of Piety:* often reprinted popular religious manual, first published in 1612.

LÆTITIA. Dear Husband, I'm amaz'd. –Sure it's a good Book, and only tends to the Speculation of Sin.

FONDLEWIFE. Speculation! No, no; something went farther than Speculation when I was not to be let in. –Where is this Apocryphal Elder? I'll ferret him.

LÆTITIA *(aside).* I'm so distracted, I can't think of a Lye.

Fondlewife *haling out* Bellmour.

FONDLEWIFE. Come out here, thou *Ananias* incarnate. –Who, how now! Who have we here?

LÆTITIA. Ha!

Shrieks, as surpriz'd.

FONDLEWIFE. Oh, thou salacious Woman! Am I then brutified? Ay, I feel it here; I sprout, I bud, I blossom, I am ripe-horn-mad. But who, in the Devil's name, are you? Mercy on me for swearing, but–

LÆTITIA. Oh, Goodness keep us! Who's this? Who are you? What are you?

BELLMOUR. Soh.

LÆTITIA. In the Name of the–Oh! Good, my Dear, don't come near it, I'm afraid 'tis the Devil; indeed it has hoofs, Dear.

FONDLEWIFE. Indeed, and I have Horns, Dear. The Devil, no. I'm afraid 'tis the Flesh, thou Harlot, Dear, with the Pox. Come *Syren,* speak, confess, who is this reverend, brawny Pastor?

LÆTITIA. Indeed and indeed. Now my dear *Nykin* –I never saw this wicked Man before.

FONDLEWIFE. Oh, it is a Man then, it seems.

LÆTITIA. Rather, sure it is a Wolf in the cloathing of a Sheep.

FONDLEWIFE. Thou art a Devil in his proper Cloathing, Womans-flesh. What, you know nothing of

126 *Speculation:* 'The contemplation, consideration, or profound study of some subject.' (OED.)

134 *Ananias:* several biblical figures; here, probably the High Priest in Jerusalem who conspired to condemn St. Paul and collaborated with the Romans.

him but his Fleece here!—You don't love Mutton, you *Magdalen* unconverted?

BELLMOUR *(aside)*. Well, now I know my Cue. — That is, very honourably to excuse her, and very impudently accuse myself.

LÆTITIA. Why then, I wish I may never enter into the Heaven of your Embraces again, my Dear, if ever I saw his face before.

FONDLEWIFE. O Lord! O strange! I am in admiration of your impudence. Look at him a little better; he is more modest, I warrant you, than to deny it. Come, were you two never face-to-face before? Speak.

BELLMOUR. Since all Artifice is vain—and I think myself obliged to speak the truth in justice to your Wife—No.

FONDLEWIFE. Humph!

LÆTITIA. No, indeed Dear.

FONDLEWIFE. Nay, I find you are both in a Story; that, I must confess. But, what—not to be cured of the Cholick? Don't you know your Patient, Mrs. *Quack?* Oh, lie upon your Stomach; lying upon your Stomach will cure you of the Cholick. Ah! I wish he has lain upon nobody's stomach but his own. Answer me that, *Jezabel!*

LÆTITIA. Let the wicked Man answer for himself. Does he think that I have nothing to do but excuse him; 'tis enough, if I can clear my own innocence to my own Deare.

BELLMOUR. By my troth, and so 'tis. —*(Aside.)* I have been a little too backward, that's the truth on't.

FONDLEWIFE. Come, Sir, Who are you, in the first place? And what are you?

BELLEMOUR. A Whore-master.

FONDLEWIFE. Very Concise.

LÆTITIA. O beastly, impudent Creature!

FONDLEWIFE. Well, Sir, and what came you hither for?

159 *Mutton:* sexual intercourse.

BELLMOUR. To lie with your Wife.

FONDLEWIFE. Good again. A very civil Person this, and I believe speaks truth.

LÆTITIA. Oh, insupportable Impudence!

FONDLEWIFE. Well, Sir. –Pray be cover'd –and you have –Heh! You have finish'd the matter, heh? And I am, as I should be, a sort of a civil Perquisite to a Whoremaster, called a Cuckold, heh. Is it not so? Come, I'm inclining to believe every word you say.

BELLMOUR. Why, Faith, I must confess, so I design'd you. But you were a little unlucky in coming so soon, and hindred the making of your own Fortune.

FONDLEWIFE. Humph. Nay, if you mince the matter once, and go back of your word, you are not the Person I took you for. Come, come, go on boldly. What, don't be asham'd of your Profession.–Confess, confess, I shall love thee the better for't, I shall, Ifeck. What, dost think I don't know how to behave myself in the Employment of a Cuckold, and have been three Year's Apprentice to Matrimony? Come, come, plain-dealing is a Jewel.

BELLMOUR. Well, since I see thou art a good honest Fellow, I'll confess the whole matter to thee.

FONDLEWIFE. Oh, I am a very honest Fellow. – You never lay with an honester Man's Wife in your life.

LÆTITIA *(aside)*. How my heart aches! All my comfort lies in his impudence, and, Heaven be praised, he has a considerable Portion.

BELLMOUR. In short then, I was informed of the opportunity of your absence by my Spy, (for Faith, honest *Isaac,* I have a long time designed thee this favour.) I knew *Spintext* was to come by your direction, but I laid a trap for him, and procured his Habit, in which I pass'd upon your Servants and was conducted hither. I pretended a Fit of the Cholick to

203 *civil Perquisite:* proper accompaniment.
219 *plain-dealing is a Jewel:* an echo of Wycherley's *The Plain Dealer,* a title which Wycherley proudly applied to himself in his later years.

excuse my lying down upon your Bed, hoping that when she heard of it her good Nature would bring her to administer Remedies for my Distemper. —You know what might have follow'd, but like an uncivil Person, you knock'd at the Door before your Wife was come to me.

FONDLEWIFE. Ha! This is Apocryphal; I may chuse whether I will believe it or no.

BELLMOUR. That you may, Faith, and I hope you won't believe a word on't. —But I can't help telling the truth, for my life.

FONDLEWIFE. How! Would not you have me believe you, say you?

BELLMOUR. No, for then you must of consequence part with your Wife, and there will be some hopes of having her upon the Publick; then the encouragement of a separate maintenance —

FONDLEWIFE. No, no, for that matter, when she and I part, she'll carry her separate maintenance about her.

LÆTITIA. Ah cruel Dear, how can you be so barbarous? You'll break my heart if you talk of parting. *Cries.*

FONDLEWIFE. Ah, dissembling Vermin!

BELLMOUR. How canst thou be so cruel, *Isaac?* Thou hast the Heart of a Mountain-Tyger. By the faith of a sincere Sinner, she's innocent for me. Go to him, Madam; fling your snowy Arms about his stubborn Neck; bathe his relentless face in your salt trickling Tears. —So, a few soft Words, and a Kiss, and the good Man melts. See, how kind Nature works and boils over in him.

She goes and hangs upon his neck, and kisses him. Bellmour *kisses her hand, behind* Fondlewife's *back.*

LÆTITIA. Indeed, my Dear, I was but just coming down-stairs, when you knock'd at the door, and the

241 *Apocryphal:* referring to the Apocrypha, books added to the Bible not required to be believed.

268 *Bellmour kisses her hand:* According to Montague Summers, this action is imitated from Molière's *L'École des Maris* (II, 14), but such bits of comic stage business must have been familiar enough to Congreve.

Maid told me Mr. *Spin-text* was ill of the Cholick, upon our bed. And won't speak to me, cruel *Nykin*? Indeed, I'll die if you don't.

FONDLEWIFE. Ah! No, no, I cannot speak; my heart's so full—I have been a tender Husband, a tender Yoke-fellow; you know I have. But thou hast been a faithless *Dallilah,* and the *Philistines* have been upon thee. Heh! Art thou not vile and unclean, heh? Speak.

Weeping.

LÆTITIA. No-o.

Sighing.

FONDLEWIFE. Oh, that I could believe thee!

LÆTITIIA. Oh, heart will break!

Seeming to faint.

FONDLEWIFE. Heh. How? No, stay, stay, I will believe thee, I will. —Pray, bend her forward, Sir.

LÆTITIIA. Oh! Oh! Where is my Dear.

FONDLEWIFE. Here, here, I do believe thee. —I won't believe my own Eyes.

BELLMOUR. For my part, I am so charm'd with the Love of your Turtle to you that I'll go and sollicit Matrimony with all my might and main.

FONDLEWIFE. Well, well, Sir, as long as I believe it, 'tis well enough. No thanks to you Sir, for her Virtue. —But, I'll show you the way out of my house, if you please. Come, my Dear. Nay, I will believe thee, I do, Ifeck.

BELLMOUR. See the great Blessing of any easy Faith; Opinion cannot err:

No Husband, by his Wife, can be deceiv'd:
She still is Virtuous, if she's so believ'd.

Exeunt.

ACT V. SCENE I. The Street

Enter Bellmour *in Fanatick Habit, and* Setter.

BELLMOUR. *Setter!* Well encounter'd.

SETTER. Joy of your Return, Sir. Have you made a good Voyage. Or have you brought your own Lading back?

BELLMOUR. No, I have brought nothing but Ballast back. Made a delicious Volage, *Setter*, and might have rode at Anchor in the Port till this time, but the Enemy surpriz'd us. I wou'd unrig.

SETTER. I attend you, Sir.

Heartwell *and* Lucy *appear at* Sylvia's *Door.*

BELLMOUR. Ha! Is not that *Heartwell* at *Sylvia's* Door; be gone quickly, I'll follow you;–I wou'd not be known. *(Exit* Setter.) Pox take 'em, they stand just in my Way.

HEARTWELL. I'm impatient till it be done.

LUCY. That may be, without troubling yourself to go again for your Brother's Chaplain. Don't you see that stalking Form of Godliness?

HEARTWELL. O Pox; He's a Fanatick.

LUCY. An Executioner qualified to do your Business. He has been lawfully ordain'd.

HEARTWELL. I'll pay him well if you'll break the Matter to him.

LUCY. *I* warrant you–do you go and prepare your Bride.

Exit Heartwell.

BELLMOUR. Humph, Sits the Wind there? What a lucky Rogue am I! Oh, what Sport will be here, if I can persuade this Wench to Secresie!

LUCY. Sir, Reverend Sir.

BELLMOUR. Madam.

Discovers himself.

LUCY. Now, goodness have Mercy upon me! Mr. *Bellmour!* Is it you?

BELLMOUR. Even I. What dost think?

LUCY. Think? That I shou'd not believe my Eyes, and that you are not what you seem to be.

BELLMOUR. True. But to convince thee who I am, thou know'st my own Token.

Kisses her.

LUCY. Nay, Mr. *Bellmour*. O Lard! I believe you are a Parson in good earnest, you kiss so devoutly.

BELLMOUR. Well, Your Business with me, *Lucy?*

LUCY. I had none, but through Mistake.

BELLMOUR. Which Mistake you must go through with, *Lucy*. Come, I know the Intrigue between *Heartwell* and your Mistress; and you mistook me for *Tribulation Spintext,* to marry 'em – ha? Are not Matters in this posture? Confess. –Come, I'll be faithful; I will, I-faith. –What, Diffide in me *Lucy?*

LUCY. Alas-a-day! You and Mr. *Vainlove* between you have ruin'd my poor Mistress. You have made a Gap in her Reputation, and can you blame her if she stop it up with a Husband?

BELLMOUR. Well, it is as I say?

LUCY. Well, it is then. But you'll be secret?

BELLMOUR. Phuh, Secret, ay. –And to be out of thy Debt, I'll trust thee with another Secret. Your Mistress must not marry *Heartwell, Lucy.*

LUCY. How! O Lord!–

BELLMOUR. Nay, don't be in Passion, Lucy; I'll provide a fitter Husband for her. Come, Here's Earnest of my good Intentions for thee too. Let this mollifie. (*Gives her Money.*) Look you, *Heartwell* is my Friend; and tho' he be blind, I must not see him fall into the Snare and unwittingly marry a Whore.

LUCY. Whore! I'd have you know my Mistress scorns–

BELLMOUR. Nay, nay; Look you, *Lucy;* there are Whores of as good Quality. –But to the purpose, if you will give me Leave to acquaint you with it. Do you carry on the Mistake of me: I'll marry 'em. – Nay, don't pause: If you do, I'll spoil all. I have some private Reasons for what I do, which I'll tell you within. In the mean time, I promise, –and rely upon me to help your Mistress to a Husband. Nay, and thee too, *Lucy*. –Here's my Hand I will, with a fresh Assurance.

Gives her more Money.

50 *Diffide:* have no confidence.

LUCY. Ah, the Devil is not so cunning. You know my easie Nature. –Well, For once I'll venture to serve you; but if you do deceive me, the Curse of all kind, tender-hearted Women light upon you.

BELLMOUR. That's as much as to say, *The Pox take me.*–Well, lead on.

Exeunt.

Enter Vainlove, Sharper *and* Setter.

SHARPER. Just now, say you, gone in with *Lucy*?

SETTER. I saw him, Sir; and stood at the Corner where you found me, and over-heard all they said. Mr. *Bellmour* is to marry 'em.

SHARPER. Ha, ha! 'Twill be a pleasant Cheat. I'll plague *Heartwell* when I see him. Prithee, *Frank,* let's teaze him; make him fret till he foam at the Mouth, and disgorge his Matrimonial Oath with Interest. Come, thou'rt so musty–

SETTER *(to* Sharper). Sir, a Word with you.

Whispers him.

VAINLOVE. *Sharper* swears she has forsworn the Letter. I'm sure he tells me Truth –but I am not sure she told him Truth. Yet she was unaffectedly concern'd, he says, and often blush'd with Anger and Surprize. –And so I remember in the Park. She had reason, if I wrong her. –I begin to doubt.

SHARPER. Say'st thou so!

SETTER. This afternoon, Sir, about an Hour before my Master received the Letter.

SHARPER. In my Conscience, like enough.

SETTER. Ay, I know her, Sir; at least, I'm sure I can fist it out of her. She's the very Sluce to her Lady's Secrets; 'tis but setting her Mill a-going, and I can drain her of 'em all.

SHARPER. Here, *Frank;* your Blood-Hound has made out the Fault. This Letter that so sticks in thy Maw is Counterfeit; only a Trick of *Sylvia* in Revenge, contriv'd by *Lucy.*

103 *She had reason:* 'she was right'; a common Gallicism at that time.

VAINLOVE. Ha! It has a Colour. –But how do you know it, Sirrah?

SETTER. I do suspect as much – because why, Sir? She was pumping me about how your Worship's Affairs stood towards Madam *Araminta*. As, when you had seen her last; when you were to see her next; and, where you were to be found at that time; and such like.

VAINLOVE. And where did you tell her?

SETTER. In the *Piazza*.

VAINLOVE. There I receiv'd the Letter; It must be so. And why did you not find me out to tell me this before, Sot?

SETTER. Sir, I was Pimping for Mr. *Bellmour*.

SHARPER. You were well employ'd. –I think there is no Objection to the Excuse.

VAINLOVE. Pox o' my saucy Credulity! If I have lost her, I deserve it. But if Confession and Repentance be of force, I'll win her, or weary her into a Forgiveness.

Exit.

SHARPER. Methinks I long to see *Bellmour* come forth.

Enter Bellmour.

SETTER. Talk of the Devil! –See where he comes.

SHARPER. Hugging himself in his prosperous Mischief. No real Fanatick can look better pleas'd after a successful Sermon of Sedition.

BELLMOUR. *Sharper*, Fortify thy Spleen! Such a Jest! Speak when thou art ready.

SHARPER. Now, were I ill-natur'd, wou'd I utterly disappoint thy Mirth: Hear thee tell thy mighty Jest with as much Gravity as a Bishop hears Venereal Causes in the Spiritual Court. Not so much as wrinkle my Face with one Smile, but let thee look simply, and laugh by thyself.

149 *Venereal Causes:* matrimonial cases presented in an ecclesiastical court, usually for divorce or annulment.

BELLMOUR. Pshaw, No; I have a better Opinion of thy Wit. –Gad, I defie thee.

SHARPER. Were it not Loss of Time, you should make the Experiment. But honest *Setter* here overheard you with *Lucy,* and has told me all.

BELLMOUR. Nay, then I thank thee for not putting me out of Countenance. But, to tell you something you don't know –I got an Opportunity (after I had marry'd 'em), of discovering the Cheat to *Sylvia.* She took it at first as another Woman would the like Disappointment, but my Promise to make her Amends quickly with another Husband somewhat pacify'd her.

SHARPER. But how the Devil do you think to acquit yourself of your Promise? Will you marry her yourself?

BELLMOUR. I have no such Intentions at present. –Prithee, wilt thou think a little for me? I am sure the ingenious Mr. *Setter* will assist–

SETTER. O Lord, Sir!

BELLMOUR. I'll leave him with you, and go shift my Habit.

Exit.

Enter Sir Joseph *and* Bluffe.

SHARPER. Heh! Sure, Fortune has sent this Fool hither on purpose. *Setter,* stand close. Seem not to observe 'em, and Hark ye.

Whispers.

BLUFFE. Fear him not –I am prepar'd for him now; and he shall find he might have safer rous'd a sleeping Lion.

SIR JOSEPH. Hush, hush! Don't you see him?

BLUFFE. Shew him to me. Where is he?

SIR JOSEPH. Nay, Don't speak so loud. I don't jest, as I did a little while ago. –Look yonder. –A-gad, if he shou'd hear the Lion roar, he'd cudgel him into an Ass, and his primitive Braying. Don't

173 *shift my Habit:* change my clothes.

you remember the Story in *Æsop's Fables,* Bully? A-gad there are good Morals to be pick'd out of *Æsop's Fables,* let me tell you that, and *Reynard the Fox* too.

BLUFFE. Damn your Morals.

SIR JOSEPH. Prithee, don't speak so loud.

BLUFFE *(in a low Voice).* Damn your Morals; I must revenge th'Affront done to my Honour.

SIR JOSEPH *(stealing away upon his Tip-toes).* Ay; Do, do, Captain, if you think fit. –You may dispose of your own Flesh as you think fitting, d'ye see. But, by the Lord *Harry,* I'll leave you.

BLUFFE *(almost whispering, and treading softly after him).* Prodigious! What, will you forsake your Friend in his extremity! You can't, in honour, refuse to carry him a Challenge.

SIR JOSEPH. Prithee, What do you see in my face that looks as if I would carry a Challenge? Honour is your Province, Captain: Take it–All the World know me to be a Knight, and a Man of Worship.

SETTER. I warrant you, Sir, I'm instructed.

SHARPER. Impossible! *Araminta* take a liking to a Fool!

Aloud.

SETTER. Her head runs on nothing else, nor she can talk of nothing else.

SHARPER. I know she commended him all the while we were in the Park; but I thought it had been only to make *Vainlove* jealous.

SIR JOSEPH. How's this! Good Bully, hold your breath, and let's hearken. A-gad, this must be I.

SHARPER. Death, it can't be–an Oaf, an Idiot, a Wittal.

190 *Æsop's Fables:* 'Of the Ass and the Lion's Skin', available to Congreve in several English translations, most recently by Roger L'Estrange (1692).

191 *A-Gad there are good Morals . . . :* in a parody of Dryden partly by Matthew Prior, *The Hind and the Panther Transvers'd* (1687), the caricature of Dryden announces that only Seneca can better the morality of 'the delectable History of Raynard the Fox'.

SIR JOSEPH. Ay, now it's out; 'tis I, my own individual Person.

SHARPER. A Wretch, that has flown for shelter to the lowest shrub of Mankind, and seeks Protection from a blasted Coward.

SIR JOSEPH. That's you, Bully Back.

Bluffe *frowns upon* Sir Joseph.

SHARPER. She has given *Vainlove* her Promise to marry him before tomorrow Morning. –Has she not?

To Setter.

SETTER. She has, Sir; and I have it in Charge to attend her all this Evening, in order to conduct her to the Place appointed.

SHARPER. Well, I'll go and inform your Master; and do you press her to make all the haste imaginable.

Exit.

SETTER. Were I a Rogue now, what a noble *Prize* could I dispose of! A goodly Pinnace, richly laden, and to launch forth under my Auspicious Convoy. Twelve Thousand Pounds, and all her Rigging, besides what lies conceal'd under Hatches. –Ha! All this committed to my Care! Avaunt, Temptation! – *Setter,* shew thyself a Person of Worth; be true to thy Trust, and be reputed honest. Reputed honest? Hum: Is that all? Ay: For to be honest is nothing; the Reputation of it is all, Reputation! What have such poor Rogues as I to do with Reputation? 'Tis above us. –And, for Men of Quality, they are above it. So that Reputation is e'en as foolish as Honesty. –And, for my part, if I meet Sir *Joseph* with a Purse of Gold in his Hand, I'll dispose of mine to the best Advantage.

SIR JOSEPH. Heh, heh, heh. Here, 'tis for you i'Faith, Mr. *Setter.* Nay, I'll take you at your Word.

Chinking a Purse.

SETTER. Sir *Joseph,* and the Captain too! Undone, undone! I'm undone, my Master's undone, my Lady's undone, and all the Business is undone.

SIR JOSEPH. No, no, never fear, Man, the Lady's business shall be done. What–come, Mr. *Setter,* I

240 *Pinnace:* man-of-war's tender boat; figuratively, a mistress.

have over-heard all, and to speak is but loss of time; but if there be occasion, let these worthy Gentlemen intercede for me.

Gives him Gold.

SETTER. O Lord, Sir, What d'ye mean? Corrupt my honesty. –They have indeed, very persuading faces. But–

SIR JOSEPH. 'Tis too little, there's more, Man. There, take all. Now–

SETTER. Well, Sir *Joseph,* you have such a winning way with you.

SIR JOSEPH. And how, and how, good *Setter,* did the little Rogue look when she talk'd of Sir *Joseph?* Did not her Eyes twinkle, and her Mouth water? Did not she pull up her little Bubbies? And–A-gad, I'm so over-joy'd! –And stroke down her Belly, and then step aside to tie her Garter, when she was thinking of her Love. Heh, *Setter?*

SETTER. Oh Yes, Sir.

SIR JOSEPH. How now, Bully? What, melancholy because I'm in the Ladies' favours? –No matter, I'll make your peace. –I know, they were a little smart upon you, but I warrant I'll bring you into the Ladies' good Graces.

BLUFFE. Pshaw, I have Petitions to show from other guess-toys than she. Look here: These were sent me this Morning–There, read. *(Shows Letters.)* That–That's a Scrawl of Quality. Here, here's from a Countess too. Hum–No, hold–That's from a Knight's Wife, she sent it me by her Husband. But here, both these are from Persons of great Quality.

SIR JOSEPH. They are either from Persons of great Quality, or no Quality at all, 'tis such a Damn'd ugly Hand.

While Sir Joseph *reads,* Bluffe *whispers* to Setter.

SETTER. Captain, I wou'd do anything to serve you; but this is so difficult–

288 *other guess-toys:* different sorts of mistresses.

BLUFFE. Not at all. Don't I know him?

SETTER. You'll remember the Conditions?

BLUFFE. I'll give't you under my Hand. In the mean time, here's Earnest. *(Gives him Money).* Come, Knight; I'm capitulating with Mr. *Setter* for you.

SIR JOSEPH. Ah, honest *Setter.* –Sirrah, I'll give thee anything but a Night's Lodging.

Enter Sharper, *tugging in* Heartwell.

SHARPER. Nay, Prithee, leave Railing, and come along with me: Maybe she mayn't be within. 'Tis but to yond' Corner-house.

HEARTWELL. Whither? Whither? Which Corner-House?

SHARPER. Why, there; The Two white Posts.

HEARTWELL. And who wou'd you visit there, say you? (O'ons, How my Heart aches.)

SHARPER. Pshaw, thou'rt so troublesome and inquisitive. Why, I'll tell you; 'Tis a young Creature that *Vainlove* debauch'd, and has forsaken. Did you never hear *Bellmour* chide him about *Sylvia.*

HEARTWELL *(aside).* Death, and Hell, and Marriage! My Wife!

SHARPER. Why, thou art as musty as a new-married Man, that had found his Wife knowing the first Night.

HEARTWELL *(aside).* Hell, and the Devil! Does he know it? But hold – if he shou'd not, I were a Fool to discover it. I'll dissemble, and try him. Ha. ha, ha! Why *Tom,* is that such an Occasion of Melancholy? Is it such an uncommon Mischief?

SHARPER. No, Faith; I believe not. –Few Women but have their Year of Probation, before they are cloister'd in the narrow Joys of Wedlock. But prithee come along with me, or I'll go and have the Lady to myself. B'w'ye, *George.*

Going.

HEARTWELL. O Torture! How he racks and tears me! Death! Shall I own my Shame, or wittingly let him go and whore my Wife? No, That's insupportable.—Oh, *Sharper*.

SHARPER. How now?

HEARTWELL. Oh, I am—married.

SHARPER. (Now hold, Spleen!) Married?

HEARTWELL. Certainly, irrecoverably married.

SHARPER. Heav'n forbid, Man. How long?

HEARTWELL. Oh, an Age, an Age; I have been married these two Hours.

SHARPER. My old Batchelour married! That were a a Jest. Ha, ha, ha!

HEARTWELL. Death! D'ye mock me? Heark-ye. If either you esteem my Friendship, or your own Safety, come not near that House, that Corner-house — that hot Brothel. Ask no Questions.

Exit.

SHARPER. Mad, by this Light!
Thus Grief still treads upon the Heels of Pleasure:
Marry'd in haste, we may repent at leisure.

Setter *Entering*

SETTER. Some by Experience find those Words misplac'd: At leisure marry'd, they repent in haste. As, I suppose, my Master *Heartwell*.

SHARPER. Here again, my *Mercury!*

SETTER. Sublimate, if you please, Sir: I think my Achievements do deserve the Epithet. —*Mercury* was a Pimp too; but, tho' I blush to own it at this time, I must confess I am somewhat fall'n from the Dignity of my Function, and do condescend to be scandalously employ'd in the Promotion of Vulgar Matrimony.

SHARPER. As how, dear dexterous Pimp?

356 *Marry'd in haste, we may repent at leisure:* proverbial expression in many languages; OED gives 1615 as the earliest English appearance in print.

361 *Mercury . . . Epithet:* Mercury serves as a pimp in Dryden's version of Plautus' *Amphitryon*. Setter puns on mercury sublimate and his sublime achievement.

SETTER. Why, to be brief, for I have weighty Affairs depending: Our Stratagem succeeding as you intended, *Bluffe* turns errant Traitor; bribes me to make a private Conveyance of the Lady to him, and put a Sham Settlement upon Sir *Joseph*.

SHARPER. O Rogue! Well, but I hope–

SETTER. No, no; never fear me, Sir. –I privately inform'd the Knight of the Treachery, who has agreed seemingly to be created; that the Captain may be so in reality.

SHARPER. Where's the Bride?

SETTER. Shifting Cloaths for the purpose at a Friend's House of mine. Here's Company coming. If you'll walk this way, Sir, I'll tell you.

Exeunt.

Enter Bellmour, Belinda, Araminta *and* Vainlove.

VAINLOVE (*to* Araminta). Oh, 'twas Frenzy all: Cannot you forgive it? Men in Madness have a Title to your Pity.

ARAMINTA.–Which they forfeit when they are restor'd to their Senses.

VAINLOVE. I am not presuming beyond a Pardon.

ARAMINTA. You who cou'd reproach me with one Counterfeit, how insolent wou'd a real Pardon make you? But there's no need to forgive what is not worth my Anger.

BELINDA (*to* Bellmour). O my Conscience, I cou'd find in my Heart to marry thee, purely to be rid of thee.–At least thou art so troublesome a Lover, there's Hopes thou'lt make a more than ordinary quiet Husband.

BELLMOUR. Say you so?–Is that a Maxim among ye?

BELINDA. Yes! You flattering Men of the Mode have made Marriage a mere *French* Dish.

BELLMORE (*aside*). I hope there's no *French* Sauce.

403 *French Dish:* a showy trifle.

404 *French Sauce:* The French Disease, Syphilis, which appeared in Italy at the time of an invasion by French troops.

BELINDA. You are so curious in the Preparation, that is, your Courtship, one wou'd think you meant a noble Entertainment.—But when we come to feed, 'tis all Froth, and poor, but in show. Nay, often, only Remains which have been, I know not how many times, warm'd for other Company, and at last serv'd up cold to the Wife.

BELLMOUR. That were a miserable Wretch indeed who cou'd not afford one warm Dish for the Wife of his Bosom.—But you timorous Virgins form a dreadful Chimæra of a Husband, as of a Creature contrary to that soft, humble, pliant, easie thing, a Lover; so guess at Plagues in Matrimony in Opposition to the Pleasures of Courtship. Alas! Courtship to Marriage is but as the Musick in the Play-house till the Curtain's drawn; but that once up, then opens the Scene of Pleasure.

BELINDA. Oh, foh, no; rather, Courtship to Marriage as a very witty Prologue to a very dull Play.

Enter Sharper.

SHARPER. Hist, *Bellmour!* If you'll bring the Ladies, make haste to *Silvia's* Lodgings, before *Heartwell* has fretted himself out of breath.—I'm in haste now, but I'll come in at the Catastrophe.

Exit.

BELLMOUR. You have an Opportunity now, Madam, to revenge yourself upon *Heartwell* for affronting your Squirrel.

To Belinda.

BELINDA. Oh, the filthy rude Beast!

ARAMINTA. 'Tis a lasting Quarrel; I think he has never been at our House since.

BELLMOUR. But give yourselves the trouble to walk to that Corner-House, and I'll tell you by the way what may divert and surprize you.

Exeunt.

[Scene II]

SCENE *changes to* Silvia's *Lodgings.*

Enter Heartwell *and* Boy.

HEARTWELL. Gone forth, say you, with her Maid!

BOY. There was a Man too that fetch'd 'em out; *Setter,* I think they call'd him.

HEARTWELL. So-h-that precious Pimp too! Damn'd, damn'd Strumpet! Cou'd she not contain herself on her Wedding-Day! Not hold out till Night! Leave me.

Exit Boy.

O cursed State! How wide we err, when apprehensive of the Lord of Life! We hope to find
That Help which Nature meant in Woman-kind
To Man that Supplemental Self design'd;
But proves a burning Caustick when apply'd.
And *Adam,* sure, cou'd with more Ease abide
The Bone when broken, than when made a Bride.

Enter Bellmour, Belinda, Vainlove, Araminta.

BELLMOUR. Now, *George.* What, Rhyming! I thought the Chimes of Verse were past when once the doleful Marriage-knell was rung.

HEARTWELL. Shame and Confusion! I am exposed.

Vainlove *and* Araminta *talk a-part.*

BELINDA. Joy, Joy Mr. *Bride-groom;* I give you Joy, Sir.

HEARTWELL. 'Tis not in thy Nature to give me Joy. A Woman can as soon give Immortality.

BELINDA. Ha, ha, ha. O Gad, Men grow such Clowns when they are married.

BELLMOUR. That they are fit for no Company but their Wives.

BELINDA. Nor for them neither, in a little time. I swear, at the Month's End, you shall hardly find a Married man that will do a civil thing to his Wife, or say a civil thing to anybody else. *Jesus!* how he looks already. Ha, ha, ha.

BELLMOUR. Ha, ha, ha.

33 *Jesus:* dropped in Congreve's *Works,* 1710; all bawdy or profane references in the original version were softened or omitted in response to attacks. See the Preface.

HEARTWELL. Death, Am I made your Laughing-stock? For you, Sir, I shall find a time; but take off your Wasp here, or the Clown may grow boistrous. I have a Fly-flap.

BELINDA. You have occasion for't; your Wife has been blown upon.

BELLMOUR. That's home.

HEARTWELL. Not Fiends or Furies could have added to my vexation, or anything, but another Woman. You've wrack'd my patience; begone, or by–

BELLMOUR. Hold, hold. What the Devil? Thou wilt not draw upon a Woman?

VAINLOVE. What's the matter?

ARAMINTA. Bless me! What have you done to him?

BELINDA. Only touch'd a gall'd-beast till he winch'd.

VAINLOVE. *Bellmour,* Give it over; you vex him too much; 'tis all serious to him.

BELINDA. Nay, I swear, I begin to pity him myself.

HEARTWELL. Damn your pity! But let me be calm a little.–How have I deserv'd this of you? Any of ye? Sir, have I impair'd the Honour of your House, promis'd your Sister Marriage, and whor'd her? Wherein have I injured you? Did I bring a Physician to your Father when he lay expiring, and endeavour to prolong his life, and you One-and-twenty? Madam, have I had an Opportunity with you and bauk'd it? Did you ever offer me the Favour that I refus'd it? Or–

BELINDA. Oh foh! What does the filthy-fellow mean? Lard, let me be gone.

ARAMINTA. Hang me, if I pity you; you are right enough serv'd.

BELLMOUR. This is a little scurrilous tho'.

VAINLOVE. Nay, 'tis a Sore of your own scratching. Well *George*–

50 *winch'd:* winced.

HEARTWELL. You are the principal Cause of all present Ills. If *Sylvia* had not been your Whore, my Wife might have been honest.

VAINLOVE. And if *Sylvia* had not been your Wife, my Whore might have been just.—There, we are even. —But have a good heart; I heard of your Misfortune, and come to your relief.

HEARTWELL. When Execution's over, you offer a Reprieve.

VAINLOVE. What would you give?

HEARTWELL. Oh! Anything, everything, a Leg or two, or an Arm; nay, I would be divorced from my Virility, to be divorced from my Wife.

Enter Sharper.

VAINLOVE. Faith, that's a sure way.—But here's one can sell you freedom better cheap.

SHARPER. *Vainlove,* I have been a kind of a God-father to you, yonder. I have promised and vow'd some things in your Name, which I think you are bound to perform.

VAINLOVE. No signing to a Blank, friend.

SHARPER. No, I'll deal fairly with you. 'Tis a full and free Discharge to Sir *Joseph Wittoll* and Captain *Bluffe* for all Injuries whatsoever done unto you by them, until the present Date hereof.—How say you?

VAINLOVE. Agreed.

SHARPER. Then, let me beg these Ladies to wear their Masks a Moment.

Exit

HEARTWELL. What the Devil's all this to me.

VAINLOVE. Patience.

Re-enter Sharper, *with* Sir Joseph, Bluffe, Sylvia, Lucy, Setter

BLUFFE. All Injuries whatsoever, Mr. *Sharper.*

SIR JOSEPH. Ay, ay, whatsoever, Captain, stick to that; whatsoever.

SHARPER. 'Tis done; those Gentlemen are witnesses to the general Release.

VAINLOVE. Ay, ay, to this instant Moment.—I have past an Act of Oblivion.

BLUFFE. 'Tis very generous, Sir, since I needs must own—

SIR JOSEPH. No, no, Captain, you need not own, Heh, heh, heh. 'Tis I must own—

BLUFFE.—That you are over-reach'd too, ha, ha, ha; only a little Art military used—only undermined, or so, as shall appear by the fair *Araminta*, my Wife's permission. (Lucy *unmasks.*) Oh the Devil, cheated at last!

SIR JOSEPH. Only a little Art-military Trick, Captain, only countermin'd, or so. Mr. *Vainlove*, I suppose you know whom I have got—now; but all's forgiven.

VAINLOVE. I know whom you have not got; pray Ladies, convince him.

Araminta *and* Belinda *unmask.*

SIR JOSEPH. Ah! O Lord, my heart aches—Ah! *Setter*, a Rogue of all sides.

SHARPER. Sir *Joseph*, you had better have pre-engag'd this Gentleman's Pardon: For though *Vainlove* be so generous to forgive the loss of his Mistress, I know not how *Heartwell* may take the loss of his Wife.

Sylvia *unmasks.*

HEARTWELL. My Wife! By this Light 'tis she, the very Cockatrice—Oh *Sharper!* Let me embrace thee.—But art thou sure she is really married to him?

SETTER. Really and lawfully married; I am witness.

SHARPER. *Bellmour* will unriddle to you.

Heartwell *goes to* Bellmour.

SIR JOSEPH. Pray, Madam, Who are you? For I find you and I are like to be better acquainted.

SYLVIA. The worst of me is, that I am your Wife.

SHARPER. Come, Sir *Joseph*, your Fortune is not so bad as you fear.—A fine Lady, and a Lady of very good Quality.

134 *Cockatrice:* fabulous serpent able to kill with a glance.

SIR JOSEPH. Thanks to my Knight-hood, she's a Lady—

VAINLOVE. That deserves a Fool with a better Title. Pray use her as my Relation, or you shall hear on't.

BLUFFE. What, Are you a Woman of Quality too, Spouse?

SETTER. And my Relation; pray let her be respected accordingly.—Well, honest *Lucy,* Fare-thee-well. I think you and I have been Play-fellows off-and-on any time this Seven Years.

LUCY. Hold your prating; I'm thinking what Vocation I shall follow, while my Spouse is planting Laurels in the Wars.

BLUFFE. No more Wars, Spouse, no more Wars. While I plant Laurels for my Head abroad, I may find the Branches sprout at home.

HEARTWELL. *Bellmour,* I approve thy mirth, and thank thee. And I cannot in gratitude (for I see which way thou art going) see thee fall into the same snare out of which thou hast deliver'd me.

BELLMOUR. I thank thee, *George,* for thy good intention.—But there is a fatality in Marriage, for I find I'm resolute.

HEARTWELL. Then good Counsel will be thrown away upon you. For my part, I have once escap'd. And when I wed again, may she be—ugly as an old Bawd.—

VAINLOVE.—Ill-natur'd as an old Maid—

BELLMOUR. Wanton as a young widow—

SHARPER. And jealous as a barren Wife.

HEARTWELL. Agreed.

BELLMOUR. Well, 'midst of these dreadful Denunciations, and notwithstanding the Warning and Example before me, I commit myself to lasting Durance.

BELINDA. Prisoner, make much of your Fetters.

Giving her Hand.

BELLMOUR. *Frank,* Will you keep us in Countenance.

VAINLOVE. May I presume to hope so great a

Blessing?

To Araminta.

ARAMINTA. We had better take the Advantage of a little of our Friends' Experience first.

BELLMOUR (*aside*). O' my Conscience she dares not consent, for fear he shou'd recant. *(Aloud.)* Well, we shall have your Company to Church in the Morning? Maybe it may get you an Appetite to see us fall to before ye. *Setter,* Did not you tell me—

SETTER. They're at the Door: I'll call 'em in.

A Dance.

BELLMOUR. Now set we forward on a Journey for Life. Come, take your Fellow-Travellers. Old *George,* I'm sorry to see thee still plod on alone.

HEARTWELL.

With gawdy Plumes and jingling Bells made proud,
The youthful Beast sets forth, and neighs aloud.
A Morning-Sun his Tinsell'd Harness gilds,
And the first Stage a Down-hill Green sword yields.
But, Oh,—
What rugged Ways attend the Noon of Life!
(Our Sun declines), and with what anxious Strife,
What Pain we tug that galling Lord, a Wife.
All Courses the first Heat with Vigour run;
But 'tis with Whip and Spur the Race is won.

Exeunt Omnes.

Epilogue,

Spoken by Mrs. *Barry.*[*]

As a rash Girl, who will all Hazards run,
And be enjoy'd, tho' sure to be undone;
Soon as her Curiosity is over,
Would give the World she could her Toy recover:
So fares it with our Poet; and I'm sent
To tell you, he already does repent:
Would you were all as forward, to keep Lent.

[*] Perhaps the greatest of all Restoration actresses, brought on the stage by the Earl of Rochester a generation before *The Old Batchelour.*

7 *to keep Lent:* through fasting and repentance; the play opened during Lent.

To think o'th' Sting, that's in the tail of Pleasure.
Now the Deed's done, the Giddy-thing has leisure
Methinks I hear him in Consideration!
What will the World say? Where's my Reputation?
Now that's at stake—No fool, 'tis out o'fashion,
If loss of that should follow want of Wit,
How many undone Men were in the Pit!
Why that's some Comfort to an Author's fears,
If he's an Ass, he will be try'd by's Peers.
But hold—I am exceeding my Commission;
My Business here, was humbly to petition:
But we're so us'd to Rail on these Occasions,
I could not help one tryal of your Patience:
For 'tis our way (you know) for fear o'th' worst,
To be before-hand still, and cry Fool first.
How say you, Sparks? How do you stand affected?
I swear, young *Bays* within, is so dejected,
'Twould grieve your hearts to see him; shall I call him?
But then you cruel Criticks would so maul him!
Yet, may be, you'll encourage a beginner;
But how?—Just as the Devil does a Sinner.
Women and Wits are used e'en much at one;
You gain your End, and damn 'em when you've done.

FINIS.

23 *Sparks:* rakish young gentlemen.

24 *Bays:* the Duke of Buckingham had satirized Dryden as 'Mr. Bayes' in *The Rehearsal* (1671), and young Congreve was proud to assume the name.

THE DOUBLE DEALER

Introduction

In the dedication to *The Old Batchelour*, Congreve had promised to make amends for the youthful inexperience of his first comedy, and through the summer of 1693 the London audience looked forward eagerly to a second play, on which he was rumoured to be at work. Their curiosity was soon satisfied; after summering outside London in search of quiet and concentration, Congreve reappeared in town, and *The Double Dealer* was announced for November, 1693, roughly eight months after the success of *The Old Batchelour*. The Theatre Royal provided an almost identical cast for the second play, with Betterton ideal in the part of Maskwell, and with the welcome addition of Kynaston as Lord Touchwood. Despite all expectation, however, the play failed to please most of its audience, although Dryden reported to Walsh; "His Double Dealer . . . is defended only by the best Judges, who, you know, are commonly the fewest. Yet it gains ground daily, and has already been acted Eight times."* Both he and the young Jonathan Swift sent commendatory verses to the author; Dryden's fine tribute appeared in the first quarto of the play, published in December. Perhaps less fortunately, Congreve himself added a dedication to Charles Montagu, Earl of Halifax, in which he hectored his critics, and defended in particular his use of soliloquy, the character of his hero, and his satire on women. He was especially proud of the play's tidy construction, claiming for it the neo-Aristotelian unities of time, place, and action. Instead of the loosely connected, almost independent story lines of *The Old Batchelour*, his *Double Dealer* presents the crises of a single evening, springing from the machinations of a villainous character, Maskwell, and of his conscious and unconscious confederates. The elaborate plots and counter-plots necessarily limited the

* See Hodges, *William Congreve: The Man*, p. 46.

amount of witty dialogue included for its own sake, which the audience relished, and which was considered Congreve's greatest gift. In fact, the spectators may have wondered how to classify the play a comedy, although, like its predecessor, it incorporates a number of suggestions from earlier comic writers. It exploits the familiar trio of the deceiving gallant, the frustrated wife, and the doting husband; indeed, Congreve provides two sets of them with the Plyant-Careless, Froth-Brisk intrigues. As Congreve admitted, Maskwell's technique of telling the truth in order to deceive descends from Terence, as a kind of antithesis to the ferocious honesty of Wycherley's plain dealer. The villain's positive delight in his plotting, and his grim silence when finally exposed may even have recalled Iago to the Drury Lane audience, and left them with the uncomfortable impression of a play which cut deeper than expected.

The Double Dealer may at first have been a *succés d'estime,* but Queen Mary was sufficiently impressed by reports of it to order a command performance about a month after its first run. Thereafter, it disappeared for five years, to be revived in 1699 with some expressions softened in response to recent attacks on the alleged immorality of the theatre, and with the innovation of Congreve's name on the playbill. It was the least successful of all Congreve's plays throughout the eighteenth century, appearing with diminishing frequency, was roundly condemned by critics at a revival in 1802, and hardly popular with Victorian audiences. For further information on its history, see Emmett Avery, *Congreve's Plays on the Eighteenth-Century Stage* (MLA Monograph Series, No. 18, 1951).

THE

DOUBLE DEALER,

A

COMEDY.

Acted at the

Theatre Royal,

BY

Their Majesties Servants.

Written by Mr. CONGREVE.

Interdum tamen, vocem Comœdia tollit.[*]

Hor. Ar. Po.

LONDON,

Printed for *Jacob Tonson,* at the *Judges-Head* near the *Inner-Temple-Gate* in *Fleet-street.* 1694.

[*] Yet, sometimes doth the Comedy excite Her Voice. (*Ars Poetica,* **Ben** Jonson's translation, l. 93).

To the Right Honourable Charles Mountague,* *ONE OF THE* Lords *of the TREASURY.*

SIR,

I heartily wish this Play were as perfect as I intended it, that it might be more worthy your acceptance, and that my Dedication of it to you might be more becoming that Honour and Esteem which I, with everybody who are so fortunate as to know you, have for you. It had your Countenance when yet unknown; and now it is made publick, it wants your Protection.

And give me leave, without any Flattery to you or Vanity in myself, to tell my illiterate Criticks, as an answer to their Impotent Objections, that they have found fault with that which has been pleasing to you. This Play, in relation to my concern for its Reputation, succeeded before it was Acted, for thro' your early Patronage it had an audience of several Persons of the first Rank both in Wit and Quality; and their allowance of it was a Consequence of your approbation. Therefore, if I really wish it might have had a more popular reception, it is not at all in consideration of myself, but because I wish well, and would gladly contribute to the benefit of the Stage, and diversion of the Town. They were (not long since) so kind to a very imperfect Comedy of mine, that I thought myself justly indebted to them all my endeavours for an entertainment that might merit some little of that Applause, which they were so lavish of, when I thought I had no Title to it. But I find they are to be treated cheaply, and I have been at an unnecessary expense.

I would not have anybody imagine that I think this Play without its Faults, for I am Conscious of several (and ready to own 'em; but it shall be to those who are able to find 'em out). I confess I design'd (whatever Vanity or Ambition occasion'd that design) to have

* Charles Montagu, later Earl of Halifax, shrewd Whig finance minister and patron of letters. Attacked as a pretender to taste by the Tory satirists Swift and Pope, he nevertheless secured several minor offices for Congreve and assisted numerous writers, Pope, Addison, and Prior among them.

written a true and regular Comedy, but I found it an undertaking which put me in mind of—*Sudet multum, frustraque laboret ausus idem.* And now to make amends for the vanity of such a design, I do confess both the attempt, and the imperfect performance. Yet I must take the boldness to say, I have not miscarried in the whole; for the Mechanical part of it is perfect. That, I may say with as little vanity as a Builder may say he has built a House according to the Model laid down before him, or a Gardener that he has set his Flowers in a knot of such or such a Figure. I design'd the Moral first, and to that Moral I invented the Fable, and do not know that I have borrow'd one hint of it anywhere. I made the Plot as strong as I could, because it was single, and I made it single, because I would avoid confusion, and was resolved to preserve the three Unities of the Drama, which I have visibly done to the utmost severity. This is what I ought not to observe upon myself; but the Ignorance and Malice of the greater part of the Audience is such that they would make a Man turn Herald to his own Play, and Blazon every Character. However, Sir, this Discourse is very impertinent to you, whose Judgment much better can discern the Faults, than I can excuse them; and whose good Nature, like that of a Lover, will find out those hidden Beauties (if there are any such) which it would be great immodesty in me to discover. I think I don't speak improperly when I call you a Lover of Poetry; for it is very well known she has been a kind Mistress to you; she has not deny'd you the last Favour; you have enjoy'd her, and she has been fruitful in a most Beautiful Issue—If I break off abruptly here, I hope everybody will understand that it is to avoid a Commendation, which, as it is your due, would be most easy, for me to pay, and too troublesome for you to receive.

I have, since the Acting of this Play, hearkned after the Objections which have been made to it; for I was Conscious where a true Critick might have put me upon my defence. I was prepared for their Attack; and am pretty confident I could have vindicated some parts, and excused others; and where there were any plain Miscarriages, I would most ingenuously have confess'd 'em. But I have not heard anything said sufficient to provoke an Answer. Some little snarling and barking there has been, but I don't know one well-mouth'd Cur that has opened at all. That, which looks most like an Objection, does not relate in particular to this Play, but to all or most that ever have been written; and that is, Soliloquy. Therefore I will answer it, not only for my own sake, but to save others the trouble, to whom it may hereafter be Objected.

I grant, that for a Man to Talk to himself appears absurd and unnatural; and indeed it is so in most Cases; but the circumstances which may attend the occasion, make great alteration. It oftentimes happens to a Man to have designs which require him to himself, and in their Nature, cannot admit of a Confident. Such, for certain, is all Villainy; and other less mischievous intentions may be very improper to be Communicated to a second Person. In such a case therefore the Audience must observe, whether the Person upon the Stage takes any notice of them at all, or no. For if he supposes anyone to be by when he talks to himself, it is monstrous and ridiculous to the last degree. Nay, not only in this case, but in any part of a Play, if there is expressed any knowledge of an Audience, it is insufferable. But otherwise when a Man in Soliloquy reasons with himself, and *Pro's* and *Con's*, and weighs all his Designs: We ought not to imagine that this Man either talks to us, or to himself; he is only thinking, and thinking such Matter as were inexcusable Folly in him to speak. But because we are conceal'd Spectators of the Plot in agitation, and the Poet finds it necessary to let us know the whole Mystery of his Contrivance, he is willing to inform us of this Person's Thoughts; and to that end is forced to make use of the expedient of Speech, no other better way being yet invented for the Communication of Thought.

Another very wrong Objection has been made by some who have not taken leisure to distinguish the Characters. The Hero of the Play, as they are pleas'd to call him, (meaning *Mellefont*) is a Gull, and made a Fool and cheated. Is every Man a Gull and a Fool that is deceiv'd? At that rate I'm afraid the two Classes of Men will be reduc'd to one, and the Knaves themselves be at a loss to justify their Title: But if an Open-hearted Honest Man, who has an entire Confidence in one whom he takes to be his Friend, and whom he has obliged to be so; and who (to confirm him in his Opinion) in all appearance, and upon several tryals has been so: If this Man be deceived by the Treachery of the other, must he of necessity commence Fool immediately, only because the other has proved a Villain? Ay, but there was Caution given to *Mellefont* in the first Act by his Friend *Careless*. Of what Nature was that Caution? Only to give the Audience some light into the Character of *Maskwell*, before his appearance; and not to convince *Mellefont* of his Treachery; for that was more than *Careless* was then able to do: He never knew *Maskwell* guilty of any Villany; he was only a sort of Man which he did not like. As for his suspecting his Familiarity with my Lady *Touchwood:* Let 'em examine the Answer that *Mellefont* makes him, and compare it with the Conduct of *Maskwell's* Character through the Play.

I would have 'em again look into the Character of *Maskwell*, before they accuse anybody of weakness for being deceiv'd by him. For upon summing up the enquiry into this Objection, [I] find they have only mistaken Cunning in one Character, for Folly in another.

But there is one thing at which I am more concerned than all the false Criticisms that are made upon me; and that is, some of the Ladies are offended. I am heartily sorry for it, for I declare I would rather disoblige all the Criticks in the World, than one of the Fair Sex. They are concerned that I have represented some Women Vicious and Affected: How can I help it? It is the Business of a Comick Poet to paint the Vices and Follies of Humane kind; and there are but two Sexes that I know, *viz. Men and Women,* which have a Title to Humanity: And if I leave one half of them out, the Work will be imperfect. I should be very glad of an opportunity to make my Complement to those Ladies who are offended: But they can no more expect it in a Comedy, than to be Tickled by a Surgeon when he's letting 'em Blood. They who are Virtuous or Discreet, I'm sure cannot be offended, for such Characters as these distinguish them, and make their Beauties more shining and observ'd: And they who are of the other kind, may nevertheless pass for such, by seeming not to be displeased, or touched with the Satire of this *Comedy*. Thus have they also wrongfully accused me of doing them a prejudice, when I have in reality done them a Service.

I have heard some whispering, as if they intended to accuse this Play of Smuttiness and Bawdy: But I declare I took a particular care to avoid it, and if they find any in it, it is of their own making, for I did not design it to be so understood. But to avoid my saying anything upon a Subject which has been so admirably handled before, and for their better instruction, I earnestly recommend to their perusual the Epistle Dedicatory before the *Plain-Dealer*.

You will pardon me, Sir, for the freedom I take of making Answers to other People, in an Epistle which ought wholly to be sacred to you: But since I intend the Play to be so too, I hope I may take the more liberty of Justifying it, where it is in the right. I hear a great many of the Fools are angry at me, and I am glad of it; for I Writ at them, not to 'em. This is a bold confession, and yet I don't think I shall disoblige one Person by it; for nobody can take it to himself, without owning the *Character*.

I must now, Sir, declare to the World, how kind you have been to my Endeavours; for in regard of what was well meant, you have excused what was ill perform'd. I beg you would continue the same Method in your acceptance of this Dedication. I know no other way of making a return to that *Charity* you show'd, in protecting an Infant, but by Enrolling it in your Service, now that it is of Age and come into the World. Therefore be pleased to accept of this as an Acknowledgement of the Favour you have shown me, and an earnest of the real Service and Gratitude of,

SIR,
Your Most Obliged
Humble Servant

William Congreve.

To my Dear Friend Mr. CONGREVE, *On His COMEDY, call'd,* THE DOUBLE DEALER.

Well then; the promis'd hour is come at last;
The present Age of Wit obscures the past:
Strong were our Sires; and as they Fought they Writ,
Conqu'ring with force of Arms, and dint of Wit;
Theirs was the Giant Race before the Flood;
And thus, when *Charles* Return'd, our Empire stood.
Like *Janus,* he the stubborn Soil manur'd,
With Rules of Husbandry the rankness cur'd:
Tam'd us to manners, when the Stage was rude;
And boistrous *English* Wit with Art endu'd.
Our Age was cultivated thus at length;
But what we gain'd in skill we lost in strength.
Our Builders were with want of Genius curst;
The second Temple was not like the first:
'Till You, the best *Vitruvius,* come at length;
Our Beauties equal, but excel our strength.
Firm *Doric* Pillars found Your solid Base:
The Fair *Corinthian* Crowns the higher Space;
Thus all below is Strength, and all above is Grace.
In easy Dialogue is *Fletcher's* Praise:
He mov'd the mind, but had not power to raise.
Great *Johnson* did by strength of Judgment please:
Yet doubling *Fletcher's* Force, he wants his Ease.
In differing Talents both adorn'd their Age;
One for the Study, t'other for the Stage.
But both to *Congreve* justly shall submit,
One match'd in Judgment, both o'er-match'd in Wit.
In Him all Beauties of this Age we see;
Etherege his Courtship, *Southerne's* Purity;
The Satire, Wit, and Strength of Manly *Wycherley.*
All this in blooming Youth you have Achiev'd;
Nor are your foil'd Contemporaries griev'd;
So much the sweetness of your manners move,
We cannot envy you because we Love.

7 *Janus:* Roman god responsible for man's knowledge of agriculture.

15 *Vitruvius:* Ancient Roman architect whose treatise in ten books, *De Architectura,* influenced Renaissance and neo-classical design.

Fabius might joy in *Scipio,* when he saw
A Beardless Consul made against the Law,
And join his Suffrage to the Votes of *Rome;*
Though He with *Hannibal* was overcome.
Thus old *Romano* bow'd to *Raphæl's* Fame;
And Scholar to the Youth he taught, became.

Oh that your Brows my Laurel had sustain'd,
Well had I been Depos'd, if You had reign'd!
The Father had descended for the Son;
For only You are lineal to the Throne.
Thus when the State one *Edward* did depose,
A Greater *Edward* in his room arose.
But now, not I, but Poetry is curs'd;
For *Tom* the Second reigns like *Tom* the first.
But let 'em not mistake my Patron's part,
Nor call his Charity their own desert.
Yet this I Prophecy; Thou shalt be seen,
(Tho' with some short Parenthesis between,)
High on the Throne of Wit; and seated there,
Not mine (that's little) but thy Laurel wear.
Thy first attempt an early promise made;
That early promise this has more than paid.
So bold, yet so judiciously you dare,
That Your least Praise is to be Regular.
Time, Place, and Action, may with pains be wrought,
But Genius must be born, and never can be taught.
This is Your Portion; this Your Native Store;
Heav'n that but once was Prodigal before,
To *Shakespeare* gave as much; she cou'd not give him more.

Maintain Your Post: That's all the Fame You need;
For 'tis impossible you shou'd proceed.
Already I am worn with Cares and Age;
And just abandoning th'Ungrateful Stage:
Unprofitably kept at Heav'ns expence,

35 *Fabius might joy in Scipio:* Fabius, Roman consul and general unable to dislodge Hannibal from Italy in the second Punic War, succeeded by his younger rival Scipio, who finally defeated Hannibal in Africa.

39 *Romano:* Giulio Romano, fellow-artist, friend, and heir of Raphael, actually nine years younger than the Renaissance master.

45 *Edward . . . Edward:* The weak king Edward II, deposed in 1327, succeeded by his son Edward III; see Marlowe's *Edward II.*

48 *Tom the Second:* Thomas Rymer succeeded Thomas Shadwell in 1692 in the post of historiographer royal. Dryden had little love for either of them.

I live a Rent-charge on his Providence:
But You, whom ev'ry Muse and Grace adorn,
Whom I foresee to better Fortune born,
Be kind to my Remains; and, oh defend,
Against Your Judgment, Your departed Friend!
Let not the Insulting Foe my Fame pursue;
But shade those Laurels which descend to You:
And take for Tribute what these Lines express:
You merit more; nor cou'd my Love do less.

John Dryden.

Prologue

Spoken by Mrs. *Bracegirdle**

Moors, have this way (as Story tells) to know
Whether their Brats are truly got, or no;
Into the Sea, the New-born Babe is thrown,
There, as instinct directs, to Swim, or Drown.
A Barbarous Device, to try if Spouse
Have kept Religiously her Nuptial Vows!

Such are the Trials Poets make of Plays:
Only they trust to more inconstant Seas;
So does our Author this his Child commit
To the Tempestuous Mercy of the Pit,
To know if it be truly born of Wit.

Criticks avaunt; for you are Fish of Prey,
And feed, like Sharks, upon an Infant Play.
Be ev'ry Monster of the Deep away;
Let's have a fair Trial, and a clear Sea.

Let Nature work, and do not Damn too soon,
For Life will struggle long, 'ere it sink down:
Let it at least rise thrice, before it Drown.
Let us consider, had it been our Fate,
Thus hardly to be prov'd Legitimate!
I will not say, we'd all in danger been,
Were each to suffer for his Mother's Sin:
But, by my Troth. I cannot avoid thinking
How nearly some Good Men might have scap'd Sinking.
But Heav'n be prais'd, this Custom is confin'd
Alone to the Offspring of the Muses kind:
Our Christian Cuckolds are more bent to pity;

John Dryden: For the relationship of Dryden and Congreve, see the Introduction.

* See note to the Prologue of *The Old Batchelour*.

I know not one *Moor*-Husband in the City.
In th' Good Man's Arms the Chopping Bastard thrives,
For he thinks all his own, that is his Wife's.

Whatever Fate is for this Play design'd,
The Poet's sure he shall some comfort find:
For if his Muse has play'd him false, the worst
That can befal him, is, to be Divorc'd;
You Husbands Judge, if that be to be Curs'd.

Dramatis Personæ

MEN

MASKWELL, A Villain; pretended Friend to MELLEFONT, Gallant to LADY TOUCHWOOD, and in Love with CYNTHIA	Mr. Betterton
LORD TOUCHWOOD, Uncle to MELLEFONT	Mr. Kynaston
MELLEFONT, Promised to, and in Love with CYNTHIA	Mr. Williams
CARELESS, His Friend	Mr. Alexander
LORD FROTH, A Solemn Coxcomb	Mr. Bowman
BRISK, A Pert Coxcomb	Mr. Powell
SIR PAUL PLYANT, An Uxorius, Foolish, old Knight; Brother to LADY TOUCHWOOD, and Father to CYNTHIA	Mr. Dogget

WOMEN

LADY TOUCHWOOD, In Love with MELLEFONT	Mrs. Barry
CYNTHIA, Daughter to SIR PAUL by a former Wife, promised to MELLEFONT	Mrs. Bracegirdle
LADY FROTH, A great Cocquet; pretender to Poetry, Wit, and Learning	Mrs. Mountfort
LADY PLYANT, Insolent to her Husband, and easie to any Pretender	Mrs. Leigh

Chaplain, Boy, Footmen, and *Attendants.*

The SCENE, A Gallery* in the *Lord Touchwood's* House

The Time, from Five o'clock to Eight in the Evening

29 *Chopping:* strapping, vigorous.

* Long upper room popular since the sixteenth century for displaying portraits and entertaining guests.

THE DOUBLE DEALER.

ACT I. SCENE I.

A Gallery in the Lord Touchwood's *House, with Chambers adjoining*

Enter Careless, *Crossing the Stage, with his Hat, Gloves, and Sword in his Hands; as just risen from Table:* Mellefont *following him.*

MELLEFONT. *Ned, Ned,* whither so fast? What, turn'd flincher! Why, you wo' not leave us?

CARELESS. Where are the Women? Pox I'm weary of guzzling, and begin to think them the better Company.

MELLEFONT. Then thy Reason staggers, and thou'rt almost drunk.

CARELESS. No faith, but your Fools grow noisy—and if a man must endure the noise of words without Sense, I think the Women have the more Musical Voices, and become Nonsense better.

MELLEFONT. Why, they are at that end of the Gallery; retired to their Tea, and Scandal, according to their Antient Custom, after Dinner.—But I made a pretence of following you, because I had something to say to you in private, and I am not like to have many opportunities this Evening.

CARELESS. And here's this Cox-Comb most Critically come to interrupt you.

Enter Brisk.

BRISK. Boys, Boys, Lads, where are you? What, do you give ground? Mortgage for a Bottle, ha? *Careless,* this is your trick; you're always spoiling Company by leaving it.

2 *flincher:* one who passes the bottle. 'What! a flincher? Quaff it off, Mulciber.' (Davenant, *Siege of Rhodes,* 1659, IV, 427).

CARELESS. And thou art always spoiling Company by coming into't.

BRISK. Pooh, ha, ha, ha, I know you envy me: spite, proud spite, by the Gods! and burning envy.—I'll be judged by *Mellefont* here, who gives and takes Raillery better, you or I. Pox, Man, when I say you spoil Company by leaving it, I mean you leave Nobody for the Company to Laugh at. I think there I was with you, ha? *Mellefont?*

MELLEFONT. O' my word, *Brisk,* that was a home thrust; you have silenc'd him.

BRISK. Oh, my dear *Mellefont,* let me perish if thou art not the Soul of Conversation, the very Essence of Wit, and Spirit of Wine! The Deuce take me if there were three good things said, or one understood, since thy Amputation from the body of our Society.—He, I think that's pretty and Metaphorical enough: I' gad I could not have said it out of thy Company.—*Careless,* ha?

CARELESS. Hum, ay, what is't?

BRISK. *O, Mon Cœur!* What is't! nay gad, I'll punish you for want of Apprehension: The Deuce take me if I tell you.

MELLEFONT. No, no, hang him, he has no taste.—But, dear *Brisk,* excuse me, I have a little business.

CARELESS. Prithee get thee gone; thou seest we are serious.

MELLFONT. We'll come immediately, if you'll but go in, and keep up good Humour and Sense in the Company: prithee do, they'll fall asleep else.

BRISK. I'gad so they will!—Well I will, I will; gad, you shall Command me from the *Zenith* to the *Nadir.*—But the Deuce take me if I say a good thing till you come.—But prithee, dear Rogue, make haste, prithee make haste, I shall burst else.—And yonder your Uncle, my Lord *Touchwood,* swears he'll Disinherit you, and Sir *Paul Plyant* threatens to disclaim you for a Son-in-Law, and my Lord *Froth* won't Dance at your Wedding tomorrow; nor the Deuce take me, I won't Write your Epithalamium—and see what a condition you're like to be brought to.

63 *Epithalamium:* nuptial song in praise of bride and bridegroom; first recorded in English 1595 as title to Spenser's poem.

MELLEFONT. Well, I'll speak but three words, and follow you.

BRISK. Enough, enough; *Careless,* bring your Apprehension along with you.

Exit.

CARELESS. Pert Cox-Comb!

MELLEFONT. Faith, 'tis a good natur'd Cox-Comb, and has very Entertaining follies—you must be more humane to him; at this Juncture it will do me Service. I'll tell you, I would have mirth continued this day at any rate; tho' Patience purchase folly, and Attention be paid with noise: There are times when Sense may be unseasonable, as well as Truth. Prithee do thou wear none today; but allow *Brisk* to have Wit, that thou may'st seem a Fool.

CARELESS. Why, how now, why this extravagant proposition?

MELLEFONT. O, I would have no room for serious design, for I am Jealous of a Plot. I would have Noise and Impertinence keep my Lady *Touchwood's* Head from Working; for Hell is not more busy than her Brain, nor contains more Devils than that Imaginations.

CARELESS. I thought your fear of her had been over. Is not tomorrow appointed for your Marriage with *Cynthia;* and her Father, Sir *Paul Plyant,* come to settle the Writings this day, on purpose?

MELLEFONT. True; but you shall judge whether I have not reason to be allarm'd. None besides you and *Maskwell* are acquainted with the Secret of my Aunt *Touchwood's* violent Passion for me. Since my first refusal of her Addresses, she has endeavour'd to do me all ill Offices with my Uncle; yet has managed 'em with that subtlety, that to him they have born the face of kindness; while her Malice, like a Dark Lanthorn, only shone upon me where it was directed. Still, it gave me less perplexity to prevent the success of her displeasure than to avoid the importunities of her Love; and of two evils, I thought myself favour'd in her aversion. But whether urged by her despair and

86 *Imaginations:* fancies.

98 *Dark Lanthorn:* lantern fitted with slides to conceal or aim the light.

the short prospect of time she saw to accomplish her designs; whether the hopes of her revenge, or of her Love, terminated in the view of this my Marriage with *Cynthia,* I know not; but this Morning she surpris'd me in my Bed.—

CARELESS. Was there ever such a Fury! 'Tis well Nature has not put it into her Sexes power to Ravish. —Well, bless us! Proceed. What follow'd?

MELLEFONT. What at first amaz'd me; for I look'd to have seen her in all the Transports of a slighted and revengful Woman. But when I expected Thunder from her Voice, and Lightning in her Eyes, I saw her melted into Tears, and hush'd into a Sigh. It was long before either of us spoke; Passion had ty'd her Tongue, and Amazement mine.—In short, the Consequence was thus, she omitted nothing that the most violent Love could urge, or tender words express; which when she saw had no effect, but still I pleaded Honour and nearness of Blood to my Uncle, then came the Storm I fear'd at first. For, starting from my Bed-side like a Fury, she flew to my Sword, and with much ado I prevented her doing me or herself a mischief. Having disarm'd her, in a gust of Passion she left me, and in a resolution confirm'd by a Thousand Curses, not to close her Eyes till she had seen my ruin.

CARELESS. Exquisite Woman! But what the Devil, does she think thou hast no more Sense than to get an Heir upon her Body to Disinherit thyself: for as I take it, this Settlement upon you is with a Proviso that your Uncle have no Children.

MELLEFONT. It is so. Well, the Service that you are to do me will be a Pleasure to yourself; I must get you to engage my Lady *Plyant* all this Evening, that my Pious Aunt may not work her to her Interest. And if you chance to secure her to yourself, you may incline her to mine. She's handsome, and knows it; is very silly, and thinks she has Sense, and has an old fond Husband.

CARELESS. I confess a very fair Foundation for a Lover to build upon.

MELLEFONT. For my Lord *Froth*, he and his Wife will be sufficiently taken up with admiring one another, and *Brisk's* Gallantry, as they call it. I'll observe my Uncle myself; and *Jack Maskwell* has promised me to watch my Aunt narrowly, and give me notice upon any Suspicion. As for Sir *Paul*, my wise Father-in-Law that is to be, my Dear *Cynthia* has such a share in his Fatherly fondness, he would scarce make her a Moment uneasy, to have her happy hereafter.

CARELESS. So, you have Mann'd your Works. But I wish you may not have the weakest Guard where the Enemy is strongest.

MELLEFONT. *Maskwell*, you mean; prithee, why should you suspect him?

CARELESS. Faith, I cannot help it; you know I never lik'd him. I am a little Superstitious in Physiognomy.

MELLEFONT. He has Obligations of Gratitude to bind him to me; his Dependance upon my Uncle is through my means.

CARELESS. Upon your Aunt you mean.

MELLEFONT. My Aunt!

CARELESS. I'm mistaken if there be not a Familiarity between them you do not suspect, for all her Passion for you.

MELLEFONT. Pooh, pooh, nothing in the World but his design to do me Service; and he endeavours to be well in her esteem, that he may be able to effect it.

CARELESS. Well, I shall be glad to be mistaken; but your Aunt's Aversion in her Revenge cannot be any way so effectually shown as in bringing forth a Child to Disinherit you. She is Handsome and cunning, and naturally wanton. *Maskwell* is Flesh and Blood at best, and opportunities between them are frequent. His Affection to you, you have confessed, is grounded upon his Interest; that you have transplanted; and should it take Root in my Lady, I don't see what you can expect from the Fruit.

MELLEFONT. I confess the Consequence is visible, were your suspicions just.—But see, the Company is broke up; let's meet 'em.

Enter Lord Touchwood, Lord Froth, Sir Paul Plyant, *and* Brisk.

LORD TOUCHWOOD. Out upon't, Nephew!—Leave your Father-in-Law and me to maintain our ground against Young People!

MELLEFONT. I beg your Lordship's Pardon—we were just returning.

SIR PAUL. Were you, Son? Gadsbud, much better as it is—good, strange! I swear I'm almost Tipsy—t'other Bottle would have been too powerful for me—as sure as can be it would.—We wanted your Company; but Mr. *Brisk*—where is he? I swear and vow he's a most facetious Person,—and the best Company.—And, my Lord *Froth*, your Lordship is so merry a Man, he, he, he.

LORD FROTH. O foy, Sir *Paul*, what do you mean? Merry! O Barbarous! I'd as lieve you call'd me Fool.

SIR PAUL. Nay, I protest and vow now, 'tis true; when Mr. *Brisk* Jokes, your Lordship's Laugh does so become you, he, he, he.

LORD FROTH. Ridiculous! Sir *Paul*, you're strangely mistaken, I find Champagne is powerful. I assure you, Sir *Paul*, I Laugh at nobody's Jest but my own, or a Lady's; I assure you, Sir *Paul*.

BRISK. How? how my Lord? What, affront my Wit! Let me perish, do I never say anything worthy to be Laugh'd at?

LORD FROTH. O foy, don't misapprehend me. I don't say so, for I often smile at your Conceptions. But there is nothing more unbecoming a Man of Quality than to Laugh; Jesu, 'tis such a Vulgar Expression of the Passion! everybody can Laugh. Then especially to Laugh at the Jest of an Inferiour Person, or when anybody else of the same Quality does not Laugh with him. Ridiculous! To be pleased with what pleases the Crowd! Now, when I Laugh, I always Laugh alone.

BRISK. I suppose that's because you Laugh at your own Jests, I'gad, ha, ha, ha.

LORD FROTH. He, he, I swear, tho', your Raillery provokes me to a smile.

BRISK. Ay, my Lord, it's a sign I hit you in the Teeth, if you show 'em.

LORD FROTH. He, he, he, I swear that's so very pretty, I can't forbear.

CARELESS. I find a Quibble bears more sway in your Lordship's Face than a Jest.

LORD TOUCHWOOD. Sir Paul, if you please, we'll retire to the Ladies, and Drink a Dish of Tea to settle our Heads.

SIR PAUL. With all my heart.—Mr. *Brisk*, you'll come to us, or call me when you're going to Joke; I'll be ready to Laugh incontinently.

Exit Lord Touchwood *and* Sir Paul.

MELLEFONT. But does your Lordship never see Comedies?

LORD FROTH. O yes, sometimes—but I never Laugh.

MELLEFONT. No?

LORD FROTH. Oh, no—never Laugh indeed, Sir.

CARELESS. No? why, what d'ye go there for?

LORD FROTH. To distinguish myself from the Commonalty, and mortify the Poets: the Fellows grow so Conceited when any of their foolish Wits prevails upon the side Boxes, I swear, he, he, he, I have often constrained my Inclinations to Laugh, he, he, he, to avoid giving them encouragement.

MELLEFONT. You are Cruel to yourself, my Lord, as well as Malicious to them.

LORD FROTH. I confess I did myself some violence at first, but now I think I have Conquer'd it.

BRISK. Let me perish, my Lord, but there is something very particular and novel in the Humour; 'tis true, it makes against Wit, and I'm sorry for some Friends of mine that Write, but, I'gad, I love to be malicious.—Nay, Deuce take me, there's Wit in't too —and Wit must be foil'd by Wit; cut a Diamond with a Diamond; no other way, I'gad.

LORD FROTH. Oh, I thought you would not be long before you found out the Wit.

248 *side Boxes:* fashionable seats in the theatre; cf. Pope, *The Rape of the Lock,* V, 14.

CARELESS. Wit! In what? Where the Devil's the Wit in not laughing when a Man has a mind to't.

BRISK. O Lord, why, can't you find it out?—Why, there 'tis, in the not Laughing; don't you Apprehend me?—My Lord, *Careless* is a very honest Fellow, but harkee,—you understand me, somewhat heavy, a little shallow, or so.—Why, I'll tell you now. Suppose now you come up to me—nay, prithee *Careless,* be instructed. Suppose, as I was saying, you come up to me, holding your sides, and Laughing as if you would bepiss yourself. I look grave, and ask the cause of this Immoderate Mirth.—You Laugh on still, and are not able to tell me.—Still I look grave, not so much as smile.—

CARELESS. Smile! no; what the Devil should you smile at, when you suppose I can't tell you?

BRISK. Pshaw, pshaw, prithee don't interrupt me.—But I tell you, you shall tell me—at last—but it shall be a great while first.

CARELESS. Well, but prithee don't let it be a great while, because I long to have it over.

BRISK. Well then, you tell me some good Jest, or very Witty thing, laughing all the while as if you were ready to die—and I hear it, and look thus.—Would not you be disappointed?

CARELESS. No; for if it were a witty thing, I should not expect you to understand it.

LORD FROTH. O foy, Mr. *Careless,* all the World allow Mr. *Brisk* to have Wit; my Wife says he has a great deal. I hope you think her a Judge?

BRISK. Pooh, my Lord, his Voice goes for nothing.—I can't tell how to make him Apprehend.—(*To* Careless.) Take it t'other way. Suppose I say a witty thing to you?

CARELESS. Then I shall be disappointed indeed.

MELLEFONT. Let him alone, *Brisk;* he is obstinately bent not to be instructed.

BRISK. I'm sorry for him, Deuce take me!

MELLEFONT. Shall we go to the Ladies, my Lord?

LORD FROTH.. With all my heart, methinks we are a Solitude without 'em.

MELLEFONT. Or, what say you to another Bottle of Champagne?

LORD FROTH. O, for the Universe, not a drop more I beseech you! O Intemperate! I have a flushing in my Face already.

Takes out a Pocket-Glass, and looks in it.

BRISK. Let me see, let me see, my Lord! I broke my Glass that was in the Lid of my Snuff-Box. Hum! Deuce take me, I have encourag'd a Pimple here too.

Takes the Glass and looks.

LORD FROTH. Then you must mortify him with a Patch; my Wife shall supply you. Come, Gentlemen, *allons.*

Exeunt.

Enter Lady Touchwood, *and* Maskwell.

LADY TOUCHWOOD. I'll hear no more!—Y' are False and Ungrateful; come, I know you false.

MASKWELL. I have been frail, I confess, Madam, for your Ladyship's Service.

LADY TOUCHWOOD. That I should trust a Man whom I had known betray his Friend!

MASKWELL. What Friend have I betray'd? Or to Whom?

LADY TOUCHWOOD. Your fond Friend Mellefont, and to me; can you deny it?

MASKWELL. I do not.

LADY TOUCHWOOD. Have you not wrong'd my Lord, who has been a Father to you in your wants, and given you being? Have you not wrong'd him in the highest manner, in his Bed?

MASKWELL. With your Ladyship's help, and for your Service, as I told you before. I can't deny that neither.—Any thing more, Madam?

LADY TOUCHWOOD. More! Audacious Villain. O, what's more is most my Shame—have you not Dishonoured me?

MASKWELL. No, that I deny; for I never told in all my Life: So that Accusation's Answer'd; on to the next.

LADY TOUCHWOOD. Death, do you dally with my Passion? Insolent Devil! But have a care; provoke me not; For, by the Eternal Fire, you shall not scape my Vengance. —Calm Villain! How unconcern'd he stands, Confessing Treachery and Ingratitude! Is there Vice more black!—O I have Excuses, Thousands, for my Faults! Fire in my Temper, Passions in my Soul, apt to every provocation; oppressed at once with Love and with Despair. But a sedate, a thinking Villain, whose Black Blood runs temperately bad, what excuse can clear? One who is no more moved with the reflection of his Crimes than of his Face, but walks unstartled from the Mirror, and straight forgets the hideous form.

She Walks about Disorder'd.

MASKWELL. Will you be in Temper, Madam? I would not talk, not to be heard. I have been a very great Rogue for your sake, and you reproach me with it; I am ready to be a Rogue still, to do you Service; and you are flinging Conscience and Honour in my Face to rebate my Inclinations. How am I to behave myself? You know I am your Creature, my Life and Fortune in your power; to disoblige you brings me certain Ruin. Allow it, I would betray you, I would not be a Traitor to myself: I don't pretend to Honesty, because you know I am a Rascal, but I would convince you from the necessity of my being firm to you.

LADY TOUCHWOOD. Necessity, Impudence! Can no Gratitude incline you, no Obligations touch you? Have not my Fortune, and my Person, been subjected to your Pleasure? Were you not in the nature of a Servant, and have not I in effect made you Lord of all, of me, and of my Lord? Where is that humble Love, the Languishing, that Adoration, which once was paid me, and everlastingly engaged?

MASKWELL. Fix'd, Rooted in my Heart, whence nothing can remove 'em, yet you—

LADY TOUCHWOOD. Yet! what yet?

359 *in Temper:* mollified, composed.

MASKWELL. Nay, Misconceive me not, Madam, when I say I have had a Generous and a Faithful Passion, which you had never favour'd but through Revenge and Policy.

LADY TOUCHWOOD. Ha!

MASKWELL. Look you, Madam, we are alone—pray contain yourself, and hear me. You know you Lov'd your Nephew when I first Sigh'd for you; I quickly found it an Argument that I Lov'd, for with that Art you veil'd your Passion; 'twas imperceptible to all but Jealous Eyes. This discovery made me bold: I confess it; for by it I thought you in my Power. Your Nephew's Scorn of you added to my hopes; I watch'd the Occasion, and took you, just Repulsed by him, warm at once with Love and Indignation; your Disposition, my Arguments, and happy Opportunity, accomplish'd my Design; I prest the yielding Minute and was blest. How I have Lov'd you since, Words have not shown, then how should Words express?

LADY TOUCHWOOD. Well, mollifying Devil!—And have I not met your Love with forward Fire?

MASKWELL. Your Zeal I grant was Ardent, but misplac'd; there was Revenge in view; that Woman's Idol had defil'd the Temple of the God, and Love was made a Mock-Worship. A Son and Heir would have edg'd Young *Mellefont* upon the brink of Ruin, and left him nought but you to catch at for Prevention.

LADY TOUCHWOOD. Again, provoke me! Do you wind me like a Larum, only to rouse my own still'd Soul for your Diversion? Confusion!

MASKWELL. Na, Madam, I'm gone, if you Relapse. —What needs this? I say nothing but what yourself, in open hours of Love, have told me. Why should you deny it? Nay, how can you? Is not all this present Heat owing to the same Fire? Do you not Love him still? How have I this day Offended you, but in not breaking off his Match with *Cynthia*? Which ere to Morrow shall be done—had you but Patience.

LADY TOUCHWOOD. How, what said you *Maskwell*? another Caprice to unwind my temper?

MASKWELL. By heaven, no; I am your Slave, the Slave of all your Pleasures, and will not rest till I have given you peace, would you suffer me.

LADY TOUCHWOOD. O, *Maskwell,* in Vain I do disguise me from thee; thou know'st me, know'st the very inmost Windings and Recesses of my Soul.—Oh *Mellefont!* I burn; Married tomorrow! Despair strikes me. Yet my Soul knows I hate him too! Let him but once be mine, and next immediate Ruin seize him.

MASKWELL. Compose yourself; You shall Enjoy and and Ruin him too.—Will that please you?

LADY TOUCHWOOD. How, how? Thou Dear, thou precious Villain, how?

MASKWELL. You have already been tampering with my Lady *Plyant?*

LADY TOUCHWOOD. I have: She is ready for any Impression I think fit.

MASKWELL. She must be throughly persuaded that *Mellefont* Loves her.

LADY TOUCHWOOD. She is so Credulous that way naturally, and likes him so well, that she will believe it faster than I can persuade her. But I don't see what you can propose from such a trifling design, for her first Conversing with *Mellefont* will convince her of the contrary.

MASKWELL. I know it.—I don't depend upon it.—But it will prepare something else, and gain us leisure to lay a stronger Plot. If I gain a little time, I shall not want Contrivance.

One Minute gives Invention to Destroy,
What, to Rebuild, will a whole Age Employ.

Exeunt.

ACT II. SCENE I.

Enter Lady Froth *and* Cynthia.

CYNTHIA. Indeed, Madam! Is it Possible your Ladyship could have been so much in Love?

LADY FROTH. I could not sleep; I did not sleep one wink for Three Weeks together.

CYNTHIA. Prodigious! I wonder want of sleep, and so much Love and so much Wit as your Ladyship has, did not turn your Brain.

LADY FROTH. O my Dear *Cynthia,* you must not rally your Friend.—But really, as you say, I wonder too; but then I had a way.—For between you and I, I had Whymsies and Vapours, but I gave them vent.

CYNTHIA. How pray, Madam?

LADY FROTH. O I Writ, Writ abundantly!—Do you never Write?

CYNTHIA. Write what?

LADY FROTH. Songs, Elegies, Satires, Encomiums, Panegyricks, Lampoons, Plays, or Heroick Poems.

CYNTHIA. O Lord, not I, Madam; I'm content to be a Courteous Reader.

LADY FROTH. O Inconsistent! In Love, and not Write! if my Lord and I had been both of your Temper, we had never come together.—O bless me! What a sad thing would that have been, if my Lord and I should never have met!

CYNTHIA. Then neither my Lord nor you would ever have met with your Match, on my Conscience.

LADY FROTH. O' my Conscience, no more we should; thou say'st right—for sure my Lord *Froth* is as fine a Gentleman, and as much a Man of Quality! Ah! Nothing at all of the Common Air.—I think I may say he wants nothing but a Blue Ribbon and a Star to make him Shine the very Phosphorus of our Hemisphere. Do you understand those Two hard Words? If you don't, I'll explain 'em to you.

CYNTHIA. Yes, yes, Madam, I'm not so Ignorant.—(*Aside.*) At least I won't own it, to be troubled with your Instructions.

LADY FROTH. Nay, I beg your Pardon; but being Derived from the *Greek,* I thought you might have

16-17 Songs . . . Poems: Lady Froth's catalogue includes many of the major genres of poetry of the time, capped by epic, the loftiest genre of all.

31 Blue Ribbon and a Star: worn by members of the order of the Garter.

escap'd the Etymology.—But I'm the more amazed to find you a Woman of Letters, and not Write! Bless me! how can *Mellefont* believe you Love him?

CYNTHIA. Why Faith, Madam, he that won't take my Word shall never have it under my Hand.

LADY FROTH. I Vow *Mellefont's* a pretty Gentleman, but Methinks he wants a Manner.

CYNTHIA. A Manner! what's that, Madam?

LADY FROTH. Some distinguishing Quality, as for example, the *Belle-air* or *Brillant* of Mr. *Brisk;* the Solemnity, yet Complaisance of my Lord, or something of his own that should look a little *Je-ne-scay quoysh;* he is too much a Mediocrity, in my mind.

CYNTHIA. He does not indeed affect either pertness or formality; for which I like him. Here he comes.

LADY FROTH. And my Lord with him; pray observe the difference.

Enter Lord Froth, Mellefont, Brisk.

CYNTHIA *(aside).* Impertinent Creature! I could almost be angry with her now.

LADY FROTH. My Lord, I have been telling my dear *Cynthia* how much I have been in Love with you; I swear I have; I'm not asham'd to own it now; ah! it makes my heart leap, I vow I sigh when I think on't. My dear Lord, ha, ha, ha! do you remember, my Lord?

Squeezes him by the hand, looks kindly on him, sighs, and then laughs out.

LORD FROTH. Pleasant Creature! perfectly well, ah! that look, ay, there it is; who could resist? 'Twas so my heart was made a Captive first, and ever since 't has been in Love with happy Slavery.

LADY FROTH. O that Tongue, that dear deceitful Tongue! that Charming Softness in your Mien and your Expression, and then your Bow! Good my Lord, bow as you did when I gave you my Picture; here, suppose this is my Picture—

Gives him a Pocket-glass.

Pray mind, my Lord; ah! he bows Charmingly; nay my Lord, you sha'n't kiss it so much; I shall grow jealous, I vow now.

He bows profoundly low, then kisses the Glass.

LORD FROTH. I saw myself there, and kissed it for your sake.

LADY FROTH. Ah! Gallantry to the last degree.—Mr. *Brisk,* you're a Judge; was ever anything so well-bred as my Lord?

BRISK. Never anything but your Ladyship, let me perish.

LADY FROTH. O prettily turn'd again; let me die but you have a great deal of Wit. Mr. *Mellefont,* don't you think Mr. *Brisk* has a World of Wit?

MELLEFONT. O yes, Madam.

BRISK. O Lord, Madam—

LADY FROTH. An infinite deal!

BRISK. O Jesu, Madam—

LADY FROTH. More Wit than anybody.

BRISK. I'm everlastingly our humble Servant, Deuce take me, Madam.

LORD FROTH. Don't you think us a happy Couple?

CYNTHIA. I vow, my Lord, I think you the happiest Couple in the World; for you are not only happy in one another, and when you are together, but happy in yourselves and by yourselves.

LORD FROTH. I hope *Mellefont* will make a good Husband too.

CYNTHIA. 'Tis my Interest to believe he will, my Lord.

LORD FROTH. D'e think he'll Love you as well as I do my Wife? I'm afraid not.

CYNTHIA. I believe he'll Love me better.

LORD FROTH. Heavens! that can never be; but why do you think so?

CYNTHIA. Because he has not so much reason to be fond of himself.

LORD FROTH. Oh, your humble Servant for that, dear Madam; well, *Mellefont*, you'll be a happy Creature.

MELLEFONT. Ay, my Lord, I shall have the same reason for my happiness that our Lordship has; I shall think myself happy.

LORD FROTH. Ah, that's all.

BRISK (*to Lady* Froth). Your Ladyship is in the right; but, I'gad, I'm wholly turn'd into Satire. I confess I Write but seldom, but when I do—keen *Iambicks,* I'gad. But my Lord was telling me your Ladyship has made an Essay toward an Heroick Poem.

LADY FROTH. Did my Lord tell you? Yes I vow, and the Subject is my Lord's Love to me. And what do you think I call it? I dare Swear you won't guess—*The Sillibub,* ha, ha, ha!

BRISK. Because my Lord's Title's *Froth,* I'gad, ha, ha, ha. Deuce take me very a *Propos* and Surprizing, ha, ha, ha!

LADY FROTH. He, Ay, is not it?—And then I call my Lord *Spumoso;* and myself, what d'e think I call myself?

BRISK. *Lactilla* maybe—'gad, I cannot tell.

LADY FROTH. *Biddy,* that's all; just my own Name.

BRISK. *Biddy!* I'gad, very pretty! Deuce take me if your Ladyship has not the Art of Surprizing the most Naturally in the World.—I hope you'll make me happy in Communicating the Poem.

LADY FROTH. O, you must be my Confident; I must ask your Advice.

BRISK. I'm your Humble Servant, let me perish. I presume your Ladyship has Read *Bossu?*

124 keen Iambicks: Horace, *Odes,* I, xvi, 24, 'in celeres iambos'; iambic trimeter traditionally first used by ancient Greek satirists.

130 Sillibub: frothy drink of milk beaten with wine and flavourings.

146-147 Bossu, Rapine, Dacier: influential neo-classical French critics. Bossu's *Traité du Poème epique,* 1675, was soon to appear in English; Rymer's translation of Rapin, *Reflections on Aristotle's Art of Poetry,* had come out in 1674; Dacier's ten-volume translation with commentary of Horace, 1681-9, was famous, and his French translation of Aristotle had recently been published.

LADY FROTH. O yes, and *Rapine,* and *Dacier* upon *Aristotle* and *Horace.*—My Lord, you must not be Jealous, I'm Communicating all to Mr. *Brisk.*

LORD FROTH. No, no, I'll allow Mr. *Brisk;* have you nothing about you to shew him, my Dear?

LADY FROTH. Yes, I believe I have.—Mr. *Brisk,* come, will you go into the next Room? and there I'll shew you all I have.

Exit Lady Froth *and* Brisk.

LORD FROTH. I'll walk a turn in the Garden, and come to you.

Exit.

MELLEFONT. You're thoughful, *Cynthia?*

CYNTHIA. I'm thinking, that tho' Marriage makes Man and Wife One Flesh, it leaves 'em still Two Fools; and they become more Conspicuous by setting off one another.

MELLEFONT. That's only when Two Fools meet, and their follies are oppos'd.

CYNTHIA. Nay, I have known Two Wits meet, and by the opposition of their Wits, render themselves as ridiculous as Fools. 'Tis an odd Game we're going to Play at; what think you of drawing Stakes, and giving over in time?

MELLEFONT. No, hang't, that's not endeavouring to Win, because it's possible we may lose; since we have Shuffled and Cut, let's e'en turn up Trump now.

CYNTHIA. Then I find it's like Cards: if either of us have a good Hand, it is an Accident of Fortune.

MELLEFONT. No, Marriage is rather like a Game at Bowls; Fortune indeed makes the match, and the Two nearest, and sometimes the Two farthest are together, but the Game depends entirely upon Judgment.

CYNTHIA. Still it is a Game, and Consequently one of us must be a Loser.

MELLEFONT. Not at all; only a Friendly Trial of Skill, and the Winnings to be Shared between us.—

169 *drawing Stakes:* withdrawing bets.

What's here, the Musick?—Oh, my Lord has promised the Company a New Song; we'll get 'em to give it us by the way.

Musicians crossing the Stage.

Pray let us have the Favour of you to practice the Song before the Company hear it.

SONG.

I.

Cynthia frowns whene'r I Woo her,
Yet she's vext if I give over;
Much she fears I should undo her,
But much more, to lose her Lover:
Thus, in doubting, she refuses;
And not Winning, thus she loses.

II.

Prithee, *Cynthia,* look behind you,
Age and Wrinkles will o'ertake you;
Then, too late, desire will find you,
When the power does forsake you:
Think, O think, o'th' sad Condition,
To be past, yet wish Fruition!

MELLEFONT. You shall have my thanks below.

To the Musick, they go out.

Enter Sir Paul Plyant *and* Lady Plyant.

SIR PAUL. Gadsbud! I am provoked into a Fermentation, as my Lady *Froth* says; was ever the like read of in Story?

LADY PLYANT. Sir *Paul* have patience; let me alone to rattle him up.

SIR PAUL. Pray, your Ladyship, give me leave to be Angry—I'll rattle him up, I Warrant you; I'll firk him with a *Certiorari.*

LADY PLYANT. You firk him, I'll firk him myself; pray, Sir *Paul,* hold you Contented.

191 *Song:* set by Purcell and sung by Mrs. Ayliff; she was given a larger role in Congreve's next play, *Love for Love.*

215 *firk:* drive by whipping.

216 *Certiorari:* Latin, to be certified, informed; legal writ from a superior court requesting records of a case from a lower court for review.

CYNTHIA. Bless me, what makes my Father in such a Passion! I never saw him thus before.

SIR PAUL. Hold yourself Contented, my Lady *Plyant.* I find Passion coming upon me by inspiration, and I cannot submit as formerly, therefore give way.

LADY PLYANT. How now! will you be pleased to retire and–

SIR PAUL. No, marry will I not be pleased; I am pleased to be angry, that's my pleasure at this time.

MELLEFONT. What can this mean?

LADY PLYANT. Gad's my life, the man's Distracted; why how now, who are you? What am I? 'Slidikins, can't I govern you? What did I Marry you for? Am I not to be absolute and uncontrollable? Is it fit a Woman of my Spirit and Conduct should be contradicted in a matter of this Concern?

SIR PAUL. It concerns me, and only me; besides, I'm not to be govern'd at all times. When I am in Tranquility, my Lady *Plyant* shall Command Sir *Paul;* but when I am provoked to fury, I cannot incorporate with Patience and Reason. As soon may Tygers Match with Tygers, Lambs with Lambs, and every Creature couple with its Foe, as the Poet says.

LADY PLYANT. He's hot-headed still! 'Tis in vain to talk to you; but remember I have a Curtain-Lecture for you, you disobedient, headstrong Brute.

SIR PAUL. No, 'tis because I won't be headstrong, because I won't be a Brute, and have my Head fortifi'd, that I am thus exasperated. But I will protect my Honour, and yonder is the Violater of my Fame.

LADY PLYANT. 'Tis my Honour that is concern'd, and the violation was intended to me. Your Honour! You have none but what is in my keeping, and I can dispose of it when I please–therefore don't provoke me.

SIR PAUL. Hum, gadsbud, she says true!–Well, my my Lady, March on; I will fight under you, then; I am convinced, as far as Passion will permit.

Lady Plyant *and* Sir Paul *come up to* Mellefont.

243 Curtain-Lecture: 'A reproof given by a wife to her husband in bed.' (Johnson, *Dictionary.*)

LADY PLYANT. Inhuman and Treacherous!

SIR PAUL. Thou Serpent and first Tempter of Womankind.—

CYNTHIA. Bless me! Sir; Madam; what mean you?

SIR PAUL. *Thy, Thy,* come away *Thy,* touch him not, come hither Girl, go not near him, there's nothing but deceit about him; Snakes are in his Peruke, and the Crocodile of *Nilus* in his Belly; he will eat thee up alive.

LADY PLYANT. Dishonourable, impudent Creature!

MELLEFONT. For Heaven's sake, Madam, to whom do you direct this Language?

LADY PLYANT. Have I behaved myself with all the decorum and nicety befitting the Person of Sir *Paul's* Wife? Have I preserved my Honour as it were in a Snow-House for this three year past? Have I been white and unsulli'd even by Sir *Paul* himself?

SIR PAUL. Nay, she has been an impenetrable Wife, even to me; that's the truth on't.

LADY PLYANT. Have I, I say, preserv'd myself, like a fair Sheet of Paper, for you to make a Blot upon—

SIR PAUL. And she shall make a Simile with any Woman in *England.*

MELLEFONT. I am so amazed, I know not what to speak.

SIR PAUL. Do you think my Daughter, this pretty Creature— gadsbud, she's a Wife for a Cherubin! Do you think her fit for nothing but to be a Stalking-Horse, to stand before you while you take aim at my Wife? Gadsbud, I was never angry before in my Life, and I'll never be appeased again.

MELLEFONT *(aside).* Hell and Damnation! this is my Aunt; such malice can be engendred nowhere else.

LADY PLYANT. Sir *Paul,* take *Cynthia* from his sight; leave me to strike him with the remorse of his intended Crime.

CYNTHIA. Pray, Sir, stay, hear him, I dare affirm he's innocent.

SIR PAUL. Innocent! why heark'ee, come hither, *Thy*, heark'ee, I had it from his Aunt, my Sister *Touchwood*.—Gadsbud, he does not care a Farthing for anything of thee but thy Portion. Why, he's in Love with my Wife; he would have tantalized thee, and made a Cuckold of thy poor Father—and that would certainly have broke my Heart.—I'm sure, if ever I should have Horns, they would kill me; they would never come kindly, I should dye of 'em, like any Child that were cutting his Teeth—I should, indeed, *Thy*.—Therefore come away; but providence has prevented all, therefore come away when I bid you.

CYNTHIA. I must obey.

Exit Sir Paul *and* Cynthia.

LADY PLYANT. O, such a thing! the Impiety of it startles me—to wrong so good, so fair a Creature, and one that lov'd you tenderly—'tis a barbarity of barbarities, and nothing could be guilty of it—

MELLEFONT. But the greatest Villain imagination can form, I grant it; and next to the Villainy of such a fact is the Villainy of aspersing me with the guilt. How? Which way was I to wrong her? for yet I understand you not.

LADY PLYANT. Why, gads my life, Cousin *Mellefont*, you cannot be so peremptory as to deny it, when I tax you with it to your face! for, now Sir *Paul's* gone, you are *Corum Nobus*.

MELLEFONT. By Heaven, I love her more than life, or—

LADY PLYANT. Fiddle, faddle, don't tell me of this and that, and every thing in the World, but give me Mathemacular Demonstration; answer me directly.—But I have not patience.—Oh, the Impiety of it, as I was saying, and the unparallel'd wickedness! O merciful Father! how could you think to reverse Nature so, to make the Daughter the means of procuring the Mother?

MELLEFONT. The Daughter procure the Mother!

LADY PLYANT. Ay, for tho' I am not *Cynthia's* own Mother, I am her Father's Wife, and that's near enough to make it Incest.

323 *Corum Nobus: Coram nobis;* in our presence, in our court.

MELLEFONT *(aside)*. Incest! Oh, my precious Aunt and the Devil in Conjunction.

LADY PLYANT. Oh, reflect upon the horror of that and then the guilt of deceiving everybody! Marrying the Daughter, only to make a Cuckold of the Father; and then seducing me, debauching my purity, and perverting me from the road of Virtue in which I have trod thus long, and never made one Trip, not one *faux pas*. Oh, consider it, what would you have to answer for, if you should provoke me to frailty? Alas! Humanity is feeble, Heaven knows! very feeble, and unable to support itself.

MELLEFONT. Where am I? sure, is it day? and am I awake? Madam—

LADY PLYANT. And nobody knows how Circumstances may happen together.—To my thinking, now, I could resist the strongest Temptation.—But yet I know, 'tis impossible for me to know whether I could or not; there is no certainty in the things of this life.

MELLEFONT. Madam, pray give me leave to ask you one question—

LADY PLYANT. O Lord, ask me the question; I'll swear I'll refuse it, I swear I'll deny it—therefore don't ask me. Nay you shan't ask me; I swear I'll deny it. O Gemini, you have brought all the Blood into my face. I warrant I am as red as a Turky-Cock; O fie, Cousin *Mellefont!*

MELLEFONT. Nay, Madam, hear me; I mean—

LADY PLYANT. Hear you, no, no; I'll deny you first, and hear you afterwards. For one does not know how one's mind may change upon hearing—hearing is one of the Senses, and all the Senses are fallible; I won't trust my Honour, I assure you; my Honour is infallible and uncomatible.

MELLEFONT. For Heaven's sake, Madam—

LADY PLYANT. O name it no more—bless me, how can you talk of Heaven, and have so much wickedness in your Heart? Maybe you don't think it a sin—they say some of you Gentlemen don't think it a sin.—Maybe it is no sin to them that don't think it so;—indeed, if I did not think it a sin—but still my honour, if it were no sin.—But then, to Marry my Daughter, for the Conveniency of frequent Opportunities—I'll never consent to that; as sure as can be I'll break the Match.

MELLEFONT. Death and amazement! Madam, upon my knees—

LADY PLYANT. Nay, nay, rise up; come, you shall see my good Nature. I know Love is powerful, and nobody can help his passion: 'Tis not your fault; nor, I swear, it is not mine. How can I help it, if I have Charms? And how can you help it, if you are made a Captive? I swear it's pity it should be a fault,—but my honour—well, but your honour, too—but the sin!—well, but the necessity—O Lord, here's somebody coming, I dare not stay. Well, you must consider of your Crime, and strive as much as can be against it. Strive, be sure—but don't be melancholly, don't despair,—but never think that I'll grant you anything; O Lord, no,—but be sure you lay aside all thought of the Marriage, for tho' I know you don't Love *Cynthia*, only as a blind for your Passion to me, yet it will make me jealous.—O Lord, what did I say? Jealous! no, no, I can't be jealous, for I must not Love you; therefore don't hope—but don't despair neither.—Oh, they're coming, I must fly.

Exit.

MELLEFONT *(after a pause)*. So then, spite of my care and foresight, I am caught, in my security.—Yet this was but a shallow artifice, unworthy of my Matchiavilian Aunt. There must be more behind; this is but the first flash, the priming of her Engine; destruction follows hard, if not most presently prevented.

Enter Maskwell.

Maskwell, welcome. Thy presence is a view of Land, appearing to my Shipwrack'd hopes: The Witch has rais'd the Storm, and her Ministers have done their Work; you see the Vessels are parted.

MASKWELL. I know it; I met Sir *Paul* towing away *Cynthia*. Come, trouble not your head, I'll join you together ere tomorrow Morning, or drown between you in the attempt.

MELLFONT. There's comfort in a hand stretch'd out to one that's sinking, tho' ne'er so far off.

MASKWELL. No sinking, nor no danger.—Come, cheer up; why, you don't know that while I plead for you, your Aunt has given me a retaining Fee; nay, I am your greatest Enemy, and she does but Journey-Work under me.

MELLEFONT. Ha! how's this?

MASKWELL. What d'e think of my being employ'd in the execution of all her Plots? Ha, ha, ha, by Heaven it's true: I have undertaken to break the Match; I have undertaken to make your Uncle Disinherit you; to get you turn'd out of Door; and to—ha, ha, ha, I can't tell you for Laughing. Oh, she has open'd her heart to me! I am to turn you a Grazing, and to—ha, ha, ha, Marry *Cynthia* myself. There's a Plot for you!

MELLEFONT. Ha! O I see, my Rising Sun! Light breaks thro' Clouds upon me, and I shall live in Day. O my *Maskwell!* how shall I thank or praise thee? Thou hast outwitted Woman.—But tell me, how could'st thou thus get into her Confidence, ha? How? But was it her Contrivance to persuade my Lady *Plyant* to this extravagant belief?

MASKWELL. It was, and to tell you the truth, I encouraged it for your diversion. Tho' it made you a little uneasy for the present, yet the reflection of it must needs be entertaining.—I warrant she was very Violent at first.

MELLEFONT. Ha, ha, ha, a very Fury; but I was most afraid of her violence at last. If you had not come as you did, I don't know what she might have attempted.

MASKWELL. Ha, ha, ha, I know her temper.—Well, you must know then that all my Contrivances were but Bubbles, till at last I pretended to have been long Secretly in Love with *Cynthia;* that did my business; that convinced your Aunt I might be trusted, since it was as much my interest as hers to break the Match: Then she thought my Jealousy might qualify

427 *Journey-Work:* work done for hire by the day.
456 *Bubbles:* deceptions.

me to assist her in her Revenge. And, in short, in that belief, told me the Secrets of her heart. At length we made this agreement, if I accomplish her designs (as I told you before) she has ingaged to put *Cynthia* with all her Fortune into my Power.

MELLEFONT. She is most gracious in her Favour.—Well, and dear *Jack*, how hast thou Contrived?

MASKWELL. I would not have you stay to hear it now, for I don't know but she may come this way. I am to meet her anon; after that I'll tell you the whole matter. Be here in this Gallery an hour hence; by that time I imagine our Consultation may be over.

MELLEFONT. I will; till then, success attend thee.

Exit.

MASKWELL. Till then, Success will attend me; for when I meet you, I meet the only Obstacle to my Fortune. *Cynthia*, let thy Beauty gild my Crimes; and whatsoever I commit of Treachery or Deceit shall be imputed to me as a Merit.—Treachery? What Treachery? Love cancels all the Bonds of Friendship, and sets Men right upon their first Foundations.

Duty to Kings, Piety to Parents, Gratitude to Benefactors, and Fidelity to Friends, are different and particular Ties: but the Name of Rival cuts 'em all asunder, and is a general acquittance. Rival is equal, and Love like Death an universal Leveller of Mankind. Ha! But is there not such a thing as Honesty? Yes, and whosoever has it about him, bears an Enemy in his Breast. For your honest man, as I take it, is that nice, scrupulous, conscientious Person, who will cheat no body but himself; such another Coxcomb as your wise man, who is too hard for all the World, and will be made a Fool of by nobody but himself; Ha, ha, ha. Well, for Wisdom and Honesty, give me Cunning and Hypocristy; oh, 'tis such a pleasure to angle for fair-faced Fools! Then that hungry Gudgeon Credulity will bite at anything.—Why, let me see, I have the same Face, the same Words and Accents when I speak what I do think, and when I speak what I do not think—the very same—and dear dissimulation is the only Art not to be known from Nature.

496 *hungry Gudgeon Credulity:* the gudgeon, a common fish easily caught; hence, as Summers points out, a gull who will take any bait.

Why will Mankind be Fools, and be deceiv'd?
And why are Friends and Lovers' Oaths believ'd,
When each, who searches strictly his own mind,
May so much Fraud and Power of Baseness find?

ACT III. SCENE I.

Enter Lord Touchwood, *and* Lady Touchwood.

LADY TOUCHWOOD. My Lord, can you blame my Brother *Plyant* if he refuse his Daughter upon this Provocation? The Contract's void by this unheard-of Impiety.

LORD TOUCHWOOD. I don't believe it true; he has better Principles—Pho, 'tis nonsense. Come, come; I know my Lady *Plyant* has a large Eye, and wou'd centre everything in her own Circle; 'tis not the first time she has mistaken Respect for Love, and made Sir *Paul* jealous of the Civility of an undesigning person, the better to bespeak his security in her unfeigned Pleasures.

LADY TOUCHWOOD. You censure hardly, my Lord; my Sister's Honour is very well known.

LORD TOUCHWOOD. Yes, I believe I know some that have been familiarly acquainted with it. This is a little Trick wrought by some pitiful Contriver, envious of my Nephew's Merit.

LADY TOUCHWOOD. Nay, my Lord, it may be so, and I hope it will be found so: but that will require some time for in such a Case as this, demonstration is necessary.

LORD TOUCHWOOD. There should have been demonstration of the contrary too, before it had been believ'd—

LADY TOUCHWOOD. So I suppose there was.

LORD TOUCHWOOD. How! Where? When?

LADY TOUCHWOOD. That I can't tell: nay, I don't say there was.—I am willing to believe as favorably of my Nephew as I can.

11 *bespeak his security:* engage his trust.

LORD TOUCHWOOD *(half aside)*. I don't know that.

LADY TOUCHWOOD. How? Don't you believe that, say you, my Lord?

LORD TOUCHWOOD. No, I don't say so. I confess I am troubled to find you so cold in his Defence.

LADY TOUCHWOOD. His Defence! Bless me, wou'd you have me defend an ill thing?

LORD TOUCHWOOD. You believe it then?

LADY TOUCHWOOD. I don't know; I am very unwilling to speak my Thoughts in anything that may be to my Cousin's disadvantage; besides, I find, my Lord, you are prepared to receive an ill impression from any opinion of mine which is not consenting with your own. But, since I am like to be suspected in the end, and 'tis a pain any longer to dissemble, I own it to you; in short, I do believe it, nay, and can believe anything worse if it were laid to his charge.—Don't ask me my Reasons, my Lord, for they are not fit to be told.

LORD TOUCHWOOD *(aside)*. I'm amaz'd; here must be something more than ordinary in this.—*(Aloud.)* Not fit to be told me, Madam? You can have no Interests wherein I am not concern'd, and consequently the same Reasons ought to be convincing to me, which create your satisfaction or disquiet.

LADY TOUCHWOOD. But those which cause my disquiet I am willing to have remote from your hearing. Good my Lord, don't press me.

LORD TOUCHWOOD. Don't oblige me to press you.

LADY TOUCHWOOD. Whatever it was, 'tis past. And that is better to be unknown which cannot be prevented; therefore let me beg you rest satisfied—

LORD TOUCHWOOD. When you have told me, I will.

LADY TOUCHWOOD. You won't.

LORD TOUCHWOOD. By my Life, my Dear, I will.

LADY TOUCHWOOD. What if you can't?

LORD TOUCHWOOD. How? Then I must know; nay I will! No more trifling—I charge you tell me—by all our mutual Peace to come; upon your Duty—

LADY TOUCHWOOD. Nay, my Lord, you need say no more to make me lay my heart before you, but don't be thus transported; compose yourself; It is not of Concern to make you lose one minute's temper. 'Tis not indeed, my Dear. Nay, by this kiss you shan't be angry. O Lord, I wish I had not told you anything. —Indeed, my Lord, you have frighted me. Nay, look pleas'd; I'll tell you.

LORD TOUCHWOOD. Well, well.

LADY TOUCHWOOD. Nay, but will you be calm?—Indeed, it's nothing but—

LORD TOUCHWOOD. But what?

LADY TOUCHWOOD. But will you promise me not to be angry—nay, you must—not to be angry with *Mellefont*? I dare swear he's sorry—and were it to do again, would not—

LORD TOUCHWOOD. Sorry for what? 'Death, you rack me with delay.

LADY TOUCHWOOD. Nay, no great matter, only—well, I have your promise—Pho, why nothing, only your Nephew had a mind to amuse himself sometimes with a little Gallantry towards me. Nay, I can't think he meant anything seriously, but methought it look'd oddly.

LORD TOUCHWOOD. Confusion and Hell, what do I hear!

LADY TOUCHWOOD. Or, maybe, he thought he was not enough a-kin to me, upon your account, and had a mind to create a nearer relation on his own; a Lover you know, my Lord—Ha, ha, ha. Well, but that's all—now you have it. Well, remember your promise, my Lord, and don't take any notice of it to him.

LORD TOUCHWOOD. No, no, no—Damnation!

LADY TOUCHWOOD. Nay, I swear you must not.—A little harmless mirth—only misplac'd, that's all—but if it were more, 'tis over now, and all well. For my part I have forgot it, and so has he, I hope—for I have not heard anything from him these two days.

LORD TOUCHWOOD. These two days! Is it so fresh? Unnatural Villain! 'Death, I'll have him stripp'd and turn'd naked out of my doors this moment, and let him rot and perish, incestuous Brute!

LADY TOUCHWOOD. O for Heaven's sake, my Lord, you'll ruin me if you take such publick notice of it; it will be a Town-talk. Consider your own and my Honour—nay, I told you you would not be satisfied when you knew it.

LORD TOUCHWOOD. Before I've done, I will be satisfied. Ungrateful Monster, how long?—

LADY TOUCHWOOD. Lord, I don't know; I wish my Lips had grown together when I told you.—Almost a Twelve-month—nay, I won't tell you any more till you are yourself. Pray, my Lord, don't let the Company see you in this disorder. Yet, I confess, I can't blame you; for I think I was never so surpris'd in my Life. Who would have thought my Nephew could have so misconstrued my Kindness? But will you go into your Closet, and recover your Temper; I'll make an excuse of sudden Business to the Company, and come to you. Pray, good dear my Lord, let me beg you do now. I'll come immediately and tell you all; will you, my Lord?

LORD TOUCHWOOD. I will.—I am mute with wonder.

LADY TOUCHWOOD. Well but go now, here's somebody coming.

LORD TOUCHWOOD. Well I go.—You won't stay? For I would hear more of this.

Exit Lord Touchwood.

LADY TOUCHWOOD. I follow instantly.—So.

Enter Maskwell.

MASKWELL. This was a Master-piece, and did not need my help; tho' I stood ready for a Cue to come in and confirm all, had there been occasion.

LADY TOUCHWOOOD. Have you seen *Mellefont?*

MASKWELL. I have, and am to meet him here about this time.

LADY TOUCHWOOD. How does he bear his Disappointment?

MASKWELL. Secure in my Assistance, he seem'd not much afflicted, but rather laugh'd at the shallow Artifice, which so little time must of necessity discover. Yet he is apprehensive of some farther design of yours, and has engaged me to watch you. I believe he will hardly be able to prevent your Plot, yet I would have you use Caution and Expedition.

LADY TOUCHWOOD. Expedition indeed; for all we do must be perform'd in the remaining part of this Evening and before the Company break up, lest my Lord should cool and have an opportunity to talk with him privately.—My Lord must not see him again.

MASKWELL. By no means; therefore you must aggravate my Lord's Displeasure to a degree that will admit of no Conference with him.—What think you of mentioning me?

LADY TOUCHWOOD. How?

MASKWELL. To my Lord, as having been privy to *Mellefont's* design upon you, but still using my utmost Endeavours to dissuade him. Tho' my Friendship and Love to him has made me conceal it; yet you may say I threatened the next time he attempted anything of that kind to discover it to my Lord.

LADY TOUCHWOOD. To what end is this?

MASKWELL. It will confirm my Lord's opinion of my Honour and Honesty, and create in him a new Confidence in me, which (should this design miscarry) will be necessary to the forming of another Plot that I have in my head— *(Aside.)* to cheat you, as well as the rest.

LADY TOUCHWOOD. I'll do it.—I'll tell him you hindered him once from forcing me.

MASKWELL. Excellent! your Ladyship has a most improving Fancy. You had best go to my Lord, keep him as long as you can in his Closet, and I doubt not but you will mould him to what you please; your Guests are so engaged in their own Follies and Intrigues, they'll miss neither of you.

LADY TOUCHWOOD. When shall we meet?—At eight this Evening in my Chamber; there rejoice at our success, and toy away an hour in mirth.

MASKWELL. I will not fail.

Exit Lady Touchwood.

I know what she means by toying away an hour well enough. Pox, I have lost all Appetite to her; yet she's a fine Woman, and I lov'd her once. But I don't know: since I have been in a great measure kept by her, the case is alter'd; what was my Pleasure is become my Duty, and I have as little stomach to her now as if I were her Husband. Should she smoke my design upon *Cynthia,* I were in a fine pickle. She has a damn'd penetrating head, and knows how to interpret a Coldness the right way; therefore I must dissemble Ardour and Ecstasie; that's resolv'd. How easily and pleasantly is that dissembled before Fruition! Pox on't that a Man can't drink without quenching his Thirst. Ha! Yonder comes *Mellefont* thoughtful. Let me think: Meet her at eight–hum–ha! By Heaven I have it, if I can speak to my Lord before.–Was it my Brain or Providence? No Matter which–I will deceive 'em all, and yet secure myself. 'Twas a lucky thought! Well, this Double-Dealing is a Jewel.

Maskwell, *pretending not to see him, walks by him, and speaks as it were to himself.*

Here he comes, now for me–

Enter Mellefont *musing.*

Mercy on us, What will the Wickedness of this World come to?

MELLEFONT. How now, *Jack?* What, so full of Contemplation that you run over!

MASKWELL. I'm glad you're come, for I could not contain myself any longer, and was just going to give vent to a Secret, which nobody but you ought to drink down. Your Aunt's just gone from hence.

MELLEFONT. And having trusted thee with the Secrets of her Soul, thou art villainously bent to discover all to me, ha?

MASKWELL. I'm afraid my frailty leans that way–but I don't know whether I can in honour discover all.

198 *smoke my design:* detect my plot.

210 *Double-Dealing is a Jewel:* cynical alteration of a proverbial form. Davis cites Nashe, 'Learning is a Jewel.' *Works,* III, 388, 11.

MELLEFONT. All, all, man; what! You may in honour betray her as far as she betrays herself. No tragical design upon my Person, I hope?

MASKWELL. No, but it's a Comical design upon mine.

MELLEFONT. What dost thou mean?

MASKWELL. Listen and be dumb; we have been bargaining about the rate of your ruin—

MELLEFONT. Like any two Guardians to an Orphan Heiress—Well?

MASKWELL. And whereas pleasure is generally paid with mischief, what mischief I shall do is to be paid with Pleasure.

MELLEFONTE. So when you've swallow'd the Potion, you sweeten your mouth with a plumb.

MASKWELL. You are merry, Sir, but I shall probe your Constitution. In short, the price of your Banishment is to be paid with the Person of—

MELLEFONTE. Of *Cynthia,* and her Fortune. Why, you forget you told me this before.

MASKWELL. No, no. – So far you are right; and I am, as an earnest of that Bargain, to have full and free possession of the person of—your Aunt.

MELLEFONTE. Ha! – Pho, you trifle.

MASKWELL. By this Light, I'm serious; all raillery apart. – I knew 'twould stun you: this Evening at eight she will receive me in her Bed-Chamber.

MELLEFONTE. Hell and the Devil, is she abandon'd of all Grace? Why, the Woman is possess'd!

MASKWELL. Well, will you go in my stead?

MELLEFONTE. By Heav'n, into a hot Furnace sooner!

MASKWELL. No, you would not; it would not be so convenient, as I can order Matters.

MELLEFONTE. What d'ye mean?

MASKWELL. Mean? Not to disappoint the Lady, I assure you. Ha, ha, ha, how gravely he looks.—Come,

come, I won't perplex you. 'Tis the only thing that Providence could have contriv'd to make me capable of serving you, either to my Inclination or your own necessity.

MELLEFONTE. How, how, for Heaven's sake, dear *Maskwell?*

MASKWELL. Why thus—I'll go according to Appointment; you shall have notice at the critical minute to come and surprise your Aunt and me together: counterfeit a rage against me, and I'll make my escape through the private passage from her Chamber, which I'll take care to leave open: 'twill be hard if then you can't bring her to any Conditions. For this Discovery will disarm her of all Defence, and leave her entirely at your Mercy: nay, she must ever after be in awe of you.

MELLEFONTE. Let me adore thee, my better *Genius!* By Heav'n I think it is not in the power of Fate to disappoint my hopes—my hopes? my certainty!

MASKWELL. Well, I'll meet you here, within a quarter of eight, and give you notice.

MELLEFONTE. Good Fortune ever go along with thee.

Enter to him Careless.

CARELESS. Mellefont, get out o'th' way, my Lady *Plyant's* coming, and I shall never succeed while thou art in sight—tho' she begins to tack about; but I made Love a great while to no purpose.

MELLEFONTE. Why, what's the Matter? She's convinc'd that I don't care for her.

CARELESS. 'Pox, I can't get an Answer from her that does not begin with her Honour, or her Virtue, her Religion, or some such Cant. Then, she has told me the whole History of Sir *Paul's* nine years' Courtship; how he has lain for whole nights together upon the Stairs before her Chamber door; and that the first Favour he receiv'd from her was a piece of an old Scarlet Petticoat for a Stomacher, which, since the day of his Marriage, he has, out of a piece of Gallantry, converted into a Night-Cap, and wears it still with such Solemnity on his anniversary Wedding-night.

301 *Stomacher:* waistcoat.

MELLEFONT. That I have seen, with the Ceremony thereunto belonging—for on that night he creeps in at the Bed's Feet like a gull'd Bassa that has married a Relation of the *Grand Signior's*, and that night he has his arms at liberty. Did not she tell you at what a distance she keeps him? He has confess'd to me that but at some certain times, that is I suppose when she apprehends being with Child, he never has the privilege of using the familiarity of a Husband with his Wife. He was once given to scrambling with his hands and sprawling in his Sleep, and ever since she has him swaddled up in Blankets, and his hands and feet swath'd down, and so put to bed; and there he lies with a great Beard, like a *Russian* Bear upon a drift of Snow. You are very great with him; I wonder he never told you his Grievances. He will, I warrant you.

CARELESS. Excessively foolish! --But that which gives me most hopes of her is her telling me of the many Temptations she has resisted.

MELLEFONT. Nay, then you have her; for a woman's bragging to a man that she has overcome Temptations is an argument that they were weakly offered, and a challenge to him to engage her more irresistably. 'Tis only an enhancing the price of the Commodity by telling you how many Customers have underbid her.

CARELESS. Nay, I don't despair. —But still she has a grudging to you. I talk'd to her t'other night at my Lord *Froth's* Masquerade, when I'm satisfied she knew me, and I had no reason to complain of my Reception; but I find women are not the same bare-faced and in Masks, and a Vizor disguises their Inclinations as much as their Faces.

MELLEFONT. 'Tis a mistake, for women may most properly be said to be unmask'd when they wear Vizors; for that secures them from blushing and being out of Countenance, and next to being in the dark, or alone, they are most truly themselves in a Vizor Mask. Here they come, I'll leave you. Ply her close, and by and by clap a *Billet doux* into her hand. For a

306 *he creeps in . . . :* Rycaut's *History of the Present State of the Ottoman Empire,* 5th ed. (1682) pp. 132-134, describes how the Grand Signior checks the power of an ambitious Pashaw by forcing him to marry one of the Signior's relatives and to humble himself on their wedding night.

woman never thinks a man truly in love with her, till he has been fool enough to think of her out of her sight, and to lose so much time as to write to her.

Exit.

Enter Sir Paul *and* Lady Plyant.

SIR PAUL. Shan't we disturb your Meditation, Mr. *Careless*? You wou'd be private?

CARELESS. You bring that along with you, Sir *Paul*, that shall be always welcome to my privacy.

SIR PAUL. O, sweet Sir, you load your humble Servants, both me and my Wife, with continual Favours.

LADY PLYANT. Jesu, Sir *Paul*, what a Phrase was there? You will be making Answers, and taking that upon you which ought to lie upon me! That you should have so little breeding to think Mr. *Careless* did not apply himself to me. Pray, what have you about you to entertain anybody's privacy? I swear and declare in the face of the World, I'm ready to blush for your Ignorance.

SIR PAUL. *(aside to her).* I acquiesce, my Lady; but don't snub so loud.

LADY PLYANT. Mr. *Careless*, If a person that is wholly illiterate might be supposed to be capable of being qualified to make a suitable return to those Obligations which you are pleased to confer upon one that is wholly incapable of being qualified in all those Circumstances, I'm sure I should rather attempt it than anything in the World; *(Curtesies.)* for I'm sure there's nothing in the World that I would rather. *(Curtesies.)* But I know Mr. *Careless* is so great a Critick and so fine a Gentleman that it is impossible for me–

CARELESS. O Heavens! Madam, you confound me.

SIR PAUL. Gadsbud, she's a fine person–

LADY PLYANT. O Lord! Sir, pardon me, we women have not those Advantages; I know my own Imperfections–but at the same time you must give me leave to declare in the face of the World that nobody is more sensible of Favours and Things; for with the Reserve of my Honour, I assure you, Mr. *Careless*, I don't know anything in the World I would refuse to a person so meritorious.—You'll pardon my want of Expression.

CARELESS. O, your Ladyship is abounding in all Excellence, particularly that of Phrase.

LADY PLYANT. You are so obliging, Sir.

CARELESS. Your Ladyship is so charming.

SIR PAUL. So, now, now; now, my Lady.

LADY PLYANT. So well bred.

CARELESS. So surprizing.

LADY PLYANT. So well drest, so boon mein, so eloquent, so unaffected, so easy, so free, so particular, so agreeable—

SIR PAUL. Ay, so, so, there.

CARELESS. O Lord, I beseech you, Madam, don't—

LADY PLYANT. So gay, so graceful, so good teeth, so fine shape, so fine limbs, so fine linen, and I don't doubt but you have a very good skin, Sir.

CARELESS. For Heaven's sake, Madam—I'm quite out of Countenance.

SIR PAUL. And my Lady's quite out of Breath; or else you should hear—Gadsbud, you may talk of my Lady *Froth*.

CARELESS. O fie, fie, not to be named of a day. My Lady *Froth* is very well in her Accomplishments; but it is when my Lady *Plyant* is not thought of, if that can ever be.

LADY PLYANT. O, you overcome me!—That is so excessive—

SIR PAUL. Nay, I swear and vow, that was pretty.

CARELESS. O, Sir *Paul*, you are the happiest man alive. Such a Lady! that is the envy of her Sex, and the admiration of ours.

SIR PAUL. Your humble Servant, I am I thank Heaven in a fine way of living, as I may say, peacefully and happily, and I think need not envy any of my Neighbours, blessed be Providence. Ay, truly, Mr. *Careless,* my Lady is a great Blessing, a fine, discreet, well-spoken woman as you shall see—if it becomes me to say so; and we live very comfortably together; she's a little hasty sometimes, and so am I; but mine's soon over, and then I'm so sorry.—O, Mr. *Careless,* if it were not for one thing—

Enter Boy *with a Letter, carries it to* Sir Paul.

LADY PLYANT. How often have you been told of that, you Jack-a-napes?

SIR PAUL. Gad so, gadsbud—*Tim,* carry it to my Lady; you should have carry'd it to my Lady first.

BOY. 'Tis directed to your Worship.

SIR PAUL. Well, well, my Lady reads all Letters first.—Child, do so no more; d'ye hear, *Tim?*

BOY. No, an please you.

Carries the Letter to my Lady, and Exit.

SIR PAUL. A humour of my wife's; you know women have little fancies. But as I was telling you, Mr. *Careless,* if it were not for one thing, I should think myself the happiest man in the World; indeed, that touches me near, very near.

CARELESS. What can that be, Sir *Paul?*

SIR PAUL. Why, I have, I thank Heaven, a very plentiful Fortune, a good Estate in the Country, some houses in Town, and some money, a pretty tolerable personal Estate; and it is a great grief to me, indeed it is Mr. *Careless,* that I have not a Son to inherit this.—'Tis true I have a Daughter, and a fine dutiful Child she is, though I say it, blessed be Providence I may say; for indeed, Mr. *Careless,* I am mightily beholding to Providence, a poor unworthy Sinner.—But if I had a Son, ah, that's my affliction, and my only affliction; indeed I cannot refrain Tears when it comes in my mind.

Cries.

CARELESS. Why, methinks that might be easily remedied. My Lady's a fine likely Woman—

SIR PAUL. Oh, a fine likely Woman as you shall see in a Summer's-day.—Indeed she is, Mr. *Careless,* in all respects.

CARELESS. And I should not have taken you to have been so old—

SIR PAUL. Alas, that's not it, Mr. *Careless;* ah! that's not it; no, no, you shoot wide of the mark a mile; indeed you do; that's not it, Mr. *Careless;* no, no, that's not it.

CARELESS. No? What can be the matter then?

SIR PAUL. You'll scarcely believe me, when I shall tell you—my Lady is so nice—it's very strange, but it's true; too true—she's so very nice, that I don't believe she would touch a Man for the World—at least not above once a year; I'm sure I have found it so; and, alas, what's once a year to an Old Man, who would do good in his Generation? indeed it's true, Mr. *Careless,* it breaks my heart.—I am her Husband, as I may say, though far unworthy of that honour, yet I am her Husband; but alas-a-day, I have no more familiarity with her Person—as to that matter —than with my own Mother—no indeed.

CARELESS. Alas-a-day, this is a lamentable story; my Lady must be told on't; she must i'faith, Sir *Paul;* 'tis an injury to the World.

SIR PAUL. Ah! would to Heav'n you would, Mr. *Careless;* you are mightily in her favour.

CARELESS. I warrant you. What, we must have a Son some way or other!

SIR PAUL. Indeed, I should be mighty bound to you if you could bring it about, Mr. *Careless* . . .

LADY PLYANT. Here, Sir *Paul,* it's from your Steward. Here's a return of 600 Pounds; you may take fifty of it for your next half year.

Gives him the Letter.

Enter Lord Froth, Cynthia.

SIR PAUL. How does my Girl? come hither to thy Father, poor Lamb, thou'rt melancholy.

LORD FROTH. Heav'n Sir *Paul*, you amaze me, of all things in the World. You are never pleased but when we are all upon the broad grin; all laugh and no Company; ah, then 'tis such a sight to see some teeth. Sure you're a great admirer of my Lady *Whifler*, Mr. *Sneer*, and Sir *Laurence Loud*, and that gang.

SIR PAUL. I vow and swear she's a very merry Woman, but I think she laughs a little too much.

LORD FROTH. Merry! O Lord, what a character that is of a Woman of Quality. You have been at my Lady *Whifler's* upon her day, Madam?

CYNTHIA. Yes, my Lord—*(Aside.)* I must humour this Fool.

LORD FROTH. Well and how? hee! What is your sense of the Conversation there?

CYNTHIA. O, most ridiculous—a perpetual consort of laughing without any harmony; for sure, my Lord, to laugh out of time is as disagreeable as to sing out of time or out of tune.

LORD FROTH. Hee, hee, hee, right; and then my Lady *Whifler* is so ready—she always comes in three bars too soon—and then, what do they laugh at? For you know laughing without a jest is as impertinent, hee! as, as—

CYNTHIA. As dancing without a Fiddle.

LORD FROTH. Just, i'faith. That was at my tongue's end.

CYNTHIA. But that cannot be properly said of them, for I think they are all in good nature with the World, and only laugh at one another; and you must allow they have all jests in their Persons, though they have none in their Conversation.

LORD FROTH. True, as I'm a Person of Honour. For Heaven's sake let us sacrifice 'em to mirth a little.

Enter Boy *and whispers* Sir Paul.

SIR PAUL. 'Gads so—Wife, Wife, my Lady *Plyant!* I have a word.

511 *consort:* a group of singers or instruments making chamber music.

LADY PLYANT. I'm busy, Sir *Paul;* I wonder at your impertinence.

CARELESS. Sir *Paul,* harkee, I'm reasoning the matter you know; Madam,—if your Ladyship please, we'll discourse of this in the next Room.

Exit Careless *and* Lady Plyant.

SIR PAUL. O ho, I wish you good success, I wish you good success. Boy, tell my Lady, when she has done I would speak with her below.

Exit Sir Paul.

Enter Lady Froth *and* Brisk.

LADY FROTH. Then you think that Episode between *Susan,* the Dairymaid, and our Coach-man is not amiss; you know, I may suppose the Dairy in Town, as well as in the Country.

BRISK. Incomparable, let me perish!—But then being an Heroick Poem, had not you better call him a *Charioteer? Charioteer* sounds great; besides your Ladyship's Coach-man having a red face, and you comparing him to the Sun—and you know the Sun is call'd Heav'n's *Charioteer.*

LADY FROTH. Oh, infinitely better; I'm extremely beholding to you for the hint. Stay, we'll read over those half a score lines again. (*Pulls out a Paper.*) Let me see here, you know what goes before, the comparison, you know.

Reads.

For as the Sun shines every day,
So, of our Coach-man I may say—

BRISK. I'm afraid that simile won't do in wet Weather, because you say the Sun shines every day.

LADY FROTH. No, for the Sun it won't, but it will do for the Coachman, for you know there's most occasion for a Coach in wet Weather.

BRISK. Right, right, that saves all.

LADY FROTH. Then I don't say the Sun shines all the day, but that he peeps now and then, yet he does shine all the day too, you know, tho' we don't see him.

BRISK. Right, but the vulgar will never comprehend that.

LADY FROTH. Well, you shall hear.—Let me see.
Reads.

For as the Sun shines every day,
So, of our Coach-man I may say,
He shows his drunken fiery Face.
Just as the Sun does, more or less.

BRISK. That's right, all's well, all's well.

LADY FROTH *(reads).*

And when at night his labour's done,
Then too like Heav'n's Charioteer, the Sun:

Ay, *Charioteer* does better.

Into the Dairy he descends,
And there his whipping and his driving ends;
There he's secure from danger of a bilk,
His fare is paid him, and he sets in Milk.

For *Susan*, you know, is *Thetis,* and so—

BRISK. Incomparable well and proper, Igad!—But I have one exception to make.—Don't you think *bilk* (I know it's good Rhyme), but don't you think *bilk* and *fare* are too like a Hackney Coach-man?

LADY FROTH. I swear and vow I'm afraid so.—And yet our *Jehu* was a Hackney Coach-man when my Lord took him.

BRISK. Was he? Then I'm answered, if *Jehu* was a Hackney Coach-man. You may put that into the marginal Notes, tho', to prevent Criticisms—only mark it with a small asterism, and say, *Jehu* was formerly a Hackney Coachman.

LADY FROTH. I will; you'd oblige me extremely to write Notes to the whole Poem.

BRISK. With all my Heart and Soul, and proud of the vast honour, let me perish.

LORD FROTH. Hee, hee, hee, my Dear, have you done? Won't you join with us; we were laughing at my Lady *Whifler,* and Mr. *Sneer.*

589 *Thetis:* sea goddess who bore Achilles and whose marriage feast with Peleus started the chain of events leading to the Trojan war.

LADY FROTH. —Ay, my Dear—were you? Oh filthy Mr. *Sneer;* he's a nauseous figure, a most fulsamick Fop, Foh! He spent two days together in going about *Covent-Garden* to suit the lining of his Coach with his complexion.

LORD FROTH. O silly! yet his Aunt is as fond of him as if she had brought the Ape into the World herself.

BRISK. Who, my Lady *Toothless!* O, she's a mortifying Spectacle; she's always chewing the Cud like an old *Yew.*

CYNTHIA. Fie, Mr. *Brisk;* 'tis *Eringo's* for her Cough.

LADY FROTH. I have seen her take 'em half chew'd out of her Mouth, to Laugh, and then put 'em in again—Foh.

LORD FROTH. Foh!

LADY FROTH. Then she's always ready to Laugh when *Sneer* offers to speak, and sits in expectation of his no Jest, with her Gums bare, and her Mouth open—

BRISK. Like an Oyster at low Ebb, I'gad—ha, ha, ha!

CYNTHIA *(aside)*. Well, I find there are no Fools so inconsiderable in themselves but they can render other People contemptible in exposing their Infirmities.

LADY FROTH. Then that t'other great strapping Lady—I can't hit of her Name; the old fat Fool that Paints so exorbitantly.

BRISK. I know whom you mean—but Deuce take me, I can't hit of her Name neither. Paints, d'ye say? Why she lays it on with a Trowel. Then she has a great Beard that bristles though it, and makes her look as if she were plastered with Lime and Hair, let me perish.

LADY FROTH. Oh, you made a Song upon her, Mr. *Brisk.*

BRISK. He? e'gad, so I did.—My Lord can sing it.

610 *fulsamick:* overbearing and wearisome.
619 *Eringos:* an herb candied and eaten at that time as an aphrodisiac.

CYNTHIA. O good my Lord, let's hear it.

BRISK. 'Tis not a Song neither—it's a sort of an Epigram, or rather an Epigrammatick Sonnet; I don't know what to call it, but it's Satire. Sing it, my Lord.

SONG.

LORD FROTH *(sings).*

Ancient *Phillis* has young Graces,
'Tis a strange thing, but a true one;
Shall I tell you how?
She herself makes her own Faces,
And each Morning wears a new one;
Where's the Wonder now?

BRISK. Short, but there's Salt in't, my way of writing, I'gad.

Enter Footman.

LADY FROTH. How now?

FOOTMAN. Your Ladyship's Chair is come.

LADY FROTH. Is Nurse and the Child in it?

FOOTMAN. Yes, Madam.

LADY FROTH. O the dear Creature! Let's go see it.

LORD FROTH. I swear, my Dear, you'll spoil that Child, with sending it to and again so often; this is the seventh time the Chair has gone for her today.

LADY FROTH. O law, I swear it's but the sixth,—and I han't seen her these two hours.—The poor dear Creature—I swear, my Lord, you don't Love poor litle *Sapho*.—Come my dear *Cynthia*. Mr. *Brisk*, we'll go see *Sapho*, tho' my Lord won't.

CYNTHIA. I'll wait upon your Ladiship.

BRISK. Pray, Madam, how old is Lady *Sapho*?

LADY FROTH. Three Quarters, but I swear she has a World of Wit, and can sing a Tune already. My Lord, won't you go? Won't you? What! not to see *Saph*? Pray, My Lord, come see little *Saph*. I knew you cou'd not stay.

Exeunt.

649 *Song:* composed and sung by John Bowman, an actor famous for his singing.

CYNTHIA. 'Tis not so hard to counterfeit Joy in the depth of Affliction, as to dissemble Mirth in Company of Fools.—Why should I call 'em Fools? The World thinks better of 'em; for these have Quality and Education, Wit and fine Conversation, are receiv'd by the World.—If not, they like and admire themselves.—And why is not that true Wisdom, for 'tis Happiness? And for aught I know, we have misapply'd the Name all this while, and mistaken the thing; since

If Happiness in Self-content is plac'd,
The Wise are Wretched, and Fools only Bless'd

Exit.

ACT IV. SCENE I.

Enter Mellefont *and* Cynthia.

CYNTHIA. I heard him loud as I came by the Closet-Door, and my Lady with him, but she seem'd to moderate his Passion.

MELLEFONT. Ay, Hell thank her, as gentle breezes moderate a fire; but I shall counter-work her Spells, and ride the Witch in her own Bridle.

CYNTHIA. It's impossible; she'll cast beyond you still. I'll lay my Life it will never be a Match.

MELLEFONT. What?

CYNTHIA. Between you and me.

MELLEFONT. Why so?

CYNTHIA. My Mind gives me it won't—because we are both willing; we each of us strive to reach the Goal, and hinder one another in the Race; I swear it never does well when the Parties are so agreed. For when People walk hand in hand, there's neither overtaking nor meeting: we Hunt in Couples where we both pursue the same Game, but forget one another; and 'tis because we are so near that we don't think of coming together.

6 *ride the Witch:* by throwing a bridle over a man's head, a witch could compel him to serve her as a horse. Shadwell's *Lancashire Witches,* 1682, revived 1691, provided such a spectacle.

MELLEFONT. Hum, 'gad I believe there's something in't;—Marriage is the Game that we Hunt, and while we think that we only have it in view, I don't see but we have it in our power.

CYNTHIA. Within reach; for example, give me your hand; why have you look'd through the wrong end of the Perspective all this while, for nothing has been between us but our fears.

MELLEFONT. I don't know why we should not steal out of the House this moment and Marry one another, without Consideration or the fear of Repentance. Pox o'Fortune, Portion, Settlements and Jointures.

CYNTHIA. Ay, ay, what have we to do with 'em? You know we Marry for Love.

MELLEFONT. Love, Love, downright, very Villainous Love.

CYNTHIA. And he that can't live upon Love deserves to die in a Ditch.—Here then, I give you my promise, in spite of Duty, any temptation of Wealth, your inconstancy, or my own inclination to change—

MELLEFONT. To run most wilfully and unreasonably away with me this moment and be Married.

CYNTHIA. Hold!—Never to Marry anybody else.

MELLEFONT. That's but a kind of Negative Consent.—Why, you won't balk the Frollick?

CYNTHIA. If you had not been so assured of your own Conduct I would not; but 'tis but reasonable that since I consent to like a Man without the vile Consideration of Money, He should give me a very evident demonstration of his Wit: therefore let me see you undermine my Lady *Touchwood* as you boasted, and force her to give her Consent, and then—

MELLEFONT. I'll do't!

CYNTHIA. And I'll do't.

MELLEFONT. This very next ensuing hour of Eight o'Clock is the last Minute of her Reign, unless the Devil assist her in *propria persona.*

27 *Perspective:* telescope.

CYNTHIA. Well, if the Devil should assist her, and your Plot miscarry–

MELLEFONT. Ay, what am I to trust to then?

CYNTHIA. Why, if you give me very clear demonstration that it was the Devil, I'll allow for irresistable odds. But if I find it to be only chance, or destiny, or unlucky Stars, or any thing but the very Devil, I'm inexorable; only still I'll keep my word and live a Maid, for your sake.

MELLEFONT. And you won't die one, for your own, so still there's hope.

CYNTHIA. Here's my Mother-in-Law and your Friend *Careless*. I would not have 'em see us together yet.

Exeunt.

Enter Careless *and* Lady Plyant.

LADY PLYANT. I swear, Mr. *Careless,* you are very alluring, and say so many fine things, and nothing is so moving to me as a fine thing. Well, I must do you this justice, and declare in the face of the World never anybody gain'd so far upon me as yourself; with Blushes I must own it, you have shaken, as I may say, the very foundation of my Honour.–Well, sure if I escape your Importunities, I shall value myself as long as I live, I swear.

CARELESS *(sighing).* And Despise me.

LADY PLYANT. The last of any Man in the World, by my purity; now you make me swear.–O Gratitude forbid that I should ever be wanting in a respectful acknowledgment of an entire resignation of all my best Wishes, for the Person and Parts of so accomplish'd a Person, whose Merit challenges much more, I'm sure, than my illiterate Praises can description.

CARELESS *(in a Whining Tone).* Ah Heavens, Madam, you ruin me with Kindness, your charming Tongue pursues the Victory of your Eyes, while at your Feet your poor Adorer dies.

LADY PLYANT. Ah! Very fine.

70 *Mother-in-Law:* step-mother.

90 *description:* used here oddly as a verb, illustrating Lady Plyant's laboured attempts at fine language.

CARELESS *(still Whining).* Ah, why are you so Fair, so bewitching Fair? O let me grow to the ground here, and feast upon that hand; O let me press it to my heart, my aching trembling heart! The nimble movement shall instruct your Pulse, and teach it to alarm Desire. *(Aside.)* Zoons! I'm almost at the end of my Cant if she does not yield quickly.

LADY PLYANT. Oh, that's so passionate and fine I cannot hear it.—I am not safe if I stay, and must leave you.

CARELESS. And must you leave me! Rather let me Languish out a Wretched Life, and breath my Soul beneath your Feet. *(Aside.)* I must say the same thing over again, and can't help it.

LADY PLYANT. I swear I am ready to Languish too.—O my Honour! Whither is it going? I protest you have given me the Palpitation of the Heart.

CARELESS. Can you be so cruel—

LADY PLYANT. O rise, I beseech you, say no more till you rise.—Why did you kneel so long? I swear I was so transported I did not see it.—Well, to show you how far you have gain'd upon me, I assure you if Sir *Paul* should die, of all Mankind there's none I'd sooner make my second choice.

CARELESS. O Heaven! I can't out-live this Night without your favour!—I feel my Spirits faint, a general dampness overspreads my face, a cold deadly dew already vents through all my Pores, and will tomorrow wash me forever from your sight, and drown me in my Tomb.

LADY PLYANT. Oh, you have Conquered, sweet, melting, moving Sir, you have Conquered. What heart of Marble can refrain to weep and yield to such sad Sayings?

Cries.

CARELESS. I thank Heav'n, they are the saddest that I ever said—Oh! *(Aside.)* I shall never contain Laughter.

LADY PLYANT. Oh, I yield myself all up to your uncontrollable Embraces. Say, thou dear, dying Man, when, where, and how—Ah, there's Sir *Paul!*

Enter Sir Paul *and* Cynthia.

CARELESS. 'Slife, yonder's Sir *Paul,* but if he were not come, I'm so transported I cannot speak.—This Note will inform you. *(Gives her a Note.)*

Exit.

SIR PAUL. Tho art my tender Lambkin, and shalt do what thou wilt—but endeavour to forget this *Mellefont.*

CYNTHIA. I would obey you to my power, Sir; but if I have not him, I have sworn never to Marry.

SIR PAUL. Never to Marry! Heaven forbid; must I neither have Sons nor Grandsons? Must the Family of the *Plyants* be utterly extinct for want of Issue Male. Oh Impiety! But did you swear, did that sweet Creature swear? ha! How durst you swear without my Consent, ha? Gadsbud, who am I?

CYNTHIA. Pray don't be angry, Sir; when I swore, I had your Consent, and therefore I swore.

SIR PAUL. Why then the revoking my Consent does annul, or make of none effect your Oath; So you may unswear it again;—The Law will allow it.

CYNTHIA. Ay, but my Conscience never will.

SIR PAUL. Gadsbud, no matter for that; Conscience and Law never go together; you must not expect that.

LADY PLYANT. Ay, but Sir *Paul,* I conceive if she has sworn, d'ye mark me, if she has once sworn, It is most unchristian, inhumane, and obscene that she should break it. (*Aside.*) I'll make up this Match again, because Mr. *Careless* said it would oblige him.

SIR PAUL. Does your Ladyship conceive so? Why, I was of that Opinion once too. Nay, if your Ladyship conceives so, I'm of that Opinion again; but I can neither find my Lord nor my Lady to know what they intend.

LADY PLYANT. I'm satisfied that my Cousin *Mellefont* has been much wrong'd.

CYNTHIA *(aside)*. I'm amazed to find her of our side, for I'm sure she lov'd him.

LADY PLYANT. I know my Lady *Touchwood* has no kindness for him; and besides, I have been inform'd by Mr. *Careless* that *Mellefont* had never anything more than a profound respect.—That he has own'd himself to be my Admirer 'tis true, but he never was so presumptuous to entertain any dishonourable Notions of things; so that if this be made plain; I don't see how my Daughter can in Conscience, or Honour, or anything in the World—

SIR PAUL. Indeed, if this be made plain, as my Lady your Mother says, Child —

LADY PLYANT. Plain! I was inform'd of it by Mr. *Careless.*— And I assure you Mr. *Careless* is a Person —that has a most extraordinary respect and honour for you, Sir *Paul.*

CYNTHIA *(aside).* And for your Ladyship too, I believe, or else you had not chang'd sides so soon; now I begin to find it.

SIR PAUL. I am much obliged to Mr. *Careless* really; he is a Person that I have a great value for, not only for that, but because he has a great veneration for your Ladyship.

LADY PLYANT. O las, indeed, Sir *Paul;* 'tis upon your account.

SIR PAUL. No, I protest and vow, I have no title to his esteem, but in having the honour to appertain in some measure to your Ladyship, that's all.

LADY PLYANT. O la now, I swear and declare it shan't be so; you're too modest, Sir *Paul.*

SIR PAUL. It becomes me, when there is any comparison made between—

LADY PLYANT. O fy, fy, Sir *Paul!* you'll put me out of Countenance. Your very obedient and affectionate Wife, that's all, and highly honoured in that Title.

SIR PAUL. Gadsbud, I am transported! Give me leave to kiss your Ladyship's Hand.

CYNTHIA *(aside).* That my poor Father should be so very silly.

LADY PLYANT. My Lip indeed, Sir *Paul*, I swear you shall.

He kisses her, and bows very low.

SIR PAUL. I humbly thank your Ladyship.—I don't know whether I fly on Ground, or walk in Air. Gadsbud, she was never thus before.—Well, I must own myself the most beholden to Mr. *Careless*.—As sure as can be this is all his doings; something that he has said. Well, 'tis a rare thing to have an ingenious Friend. Well, your Ladyship is of opinion that the Match may go forward.

LADY PLYANT. By all means; Mr. *Careless* has satisfied me of the matter.

SIR PAUL. Well, why then, Lamb, you may keep your Oath, but have a care of making rash Vows. Come hither to me, and kiss *Papa*.

LADY PLYANT. I swear and declare, I am in such a twitter to read Mr. *Careless* his Letter that I can't forbear any longer.—But though I may read all Letters first by Prerogative, yet I'll be sure to be unsuspected this time.—Sir *Paul!*

SIR PAUL. Did your Ladyship call?

LADY PLYANT. Nay, not to interrupt you, my Dear —only lend me your Letter, which you had from your Steward today; I would look upon the Account again, and maybe increase your Allowance.

SIR PAUL. There it is, Madam. Do you want a Pen and Ink?

Bows and gives the Letter.

LADY PLYANT. No, no, nothing else, I thank you, Sir Paul. (*Aside.*) So now I can read my own Letter under the cover of his.

SIR PAUL. He? And wilt thou bring a Grandson at 9 Months' end—He? A brave Chopping Boy.—I'll settle a Thousand pounds a Year upon the Rogue as soon as ever he looks me in the Face, I will Gadsbud. I'm overjoy'd to think I have any of my Family that will bring Children into the World. For I would fain have some resemblance of myself in my Posterity, he, *Thy?* Can't you contrive that affair, Girl? Do gadsbud, think on thy old Father, Heh? Make the young Rogue as like as you can.

CYNTHIA. I'm glad to see you so merry, Sir.

SIR PAUL. Merry! Gadsbud, I'm serious; I'll give thee *500 l.* for every inch of him that resembles me; ah this Eye, this Left Eye! A *1000 l.* for this Left Eye. This has done Execution in its time, Girl; why thou hast my Leer Hussey, just thy Father's Leer.—Let it be transmitted to the young Rogue by the help of imagination; why, 'tis the mark of our Family, *Thy;* our House is distinguished by a Languishing Eye, as the House of *Austria* is by a thick Lip.—Ah! when I was of your Age, Hussy, I would have held fifty to one I could have drawn my own Picture—Gadsbud I could have done—not so much as you, neither, but —nay, don't Blush—

CYNTHIA. I don't Blush, Sir, for I vow I don't understand—

SIR PAUL. Pshaw, Pshaw, you fib, you Baggage; you do understand, and you shall understand; come, don't be so nice, Gadsbud, don't learn after your Mother-in-Law my Lady here. Marry, Heaven forbid that you should follow her Example; that would spoil all indeed. Bless us, if you should take a Vagary and make a rash Resolution on your Wedding Night to die a Maid, as she did, all were ruin'd, all my hopes lost!—My Heart would break, and my Estate would be left to the wide World, he? I hope you are a better Christian than to think of being a Nun, he? Answer me.

CYNTHIA. I'm all Obedience, Sir, to your Commands.

LADY PLYANT *(having read the Letter).* O dear Mr. *Careless,* I swear he writes charmingly, and he talks charmingly, and he looks charmingly, and he has charm'd me, as much as I have charm'd him; and so I'll tell him in the Wardrobe when 'tis Dark. O Crimine! I hope, Sir *Paul* has not seen both Letters. —*(Puts the wrong Letter hastily up, and gives him*

265 *House of Austria . . . by a thick Lip:* Hapsburg family trait, easily recognized in their portraits, of a protruding lower lip and jaw. Jonson jokes at it in the *Alchemist,* IV, i, 56.

290 *Wardrobe:* dressing-room adjoining a bedroom.

291 *Crimine:* affected version of *Gemini,* an oath often indicating pseudo-gentility in a character in plays of the period.

her own.) Sir *Paul,* here's your Letter; tomorrow Morning I'll settle the Accounts to your Advantage.

Enter Brisk.

BRISK. Sir *Paul,* Gadsbud you're an uncivil Person, let me tell you, and all that; and I did not think it had been in you.

SIR PAUL. O La! what's the matter now? I hope you are not angry, Mr. *Brisk.*

BRISK. Deuce take me, I believe you intend to Marry your Daughter yourself; you're always brooding over her like an Old Hen, as if she were not well hatch'd, I'gad, he?

SIR PAUL. Good, strange! Mr. *Brisk* is such a Merry, Facetious Person, he, he, he! No, No, I have done with her, I have done with her now.

BRISK. The Fiddles have stay'd this hour in the Hall, and my Lord *Froth* wants a Partner; we can never begin without her.

SIR PAUL. Go, go Child, go, go get you gone and Dance and be Merry; I'll come and look at you by and by. Where's my Son *Mellefont?*

Exit Cynthia.

LADY PLYANT. I'll send him to them. I know where he is.

Exit.

BRISK. Sir *Paul,* will you send *Careless* into the Hall if you meet him.

SIR PAUL. I will, I will; I'll go and look for him on purpose.

Exit.

BRISK. So now they are all gone, and I have an opportunity to practice.—Ah! My dear Lady *Froth!* She's a most engaging Creature, if she were not so fond of that damn'd coxcombly Lord of hers; and yet I am forced to allow him Wit too, to keep in with him.—No matter, she's a Woman of parts, and, I'gad, parts will carry her. She said she would follow me into the Gallery.—Now to make my Approaches.—Hem, Hem! *(Bows.)* Ah Madam!—Pox on't, why should I disparage my parts by thinking what to say? None but dull

Rogues *think;* witty Men, like rich Fellows, are always ready for all Expenses; while your Blockheads, like poor needy Scoundrels, are forced to examine their Stock, and forecast the Charges of the Day. Here she comes; I'll seem not to see her, and try to win her with a new airy invention of my own, hem!

Enter Lady Froth.

BRISK *(sings). I'm sick with Love,* ha ha ha, *prithee come walking about. Cure me.*

I'm sick with, &c.

O ye Powers! O my Lady *Froth,* my Lady *Froth!* My Lady *Froth!* Heigho! Break Heart; Gods, I thank you.

Stands musing with his Arms across.

LADY FROTH. O Heavens, Mr. *Brisk!* What's the matter?

BRISK. My Lady *Froth!* Your Ladyship's most humble Servant.—The matter, Madam? Nothing, Madam, nothing at all, I'gad. I was fallen into the most agreeable amusement in the whole Province of Contemplation, That's all.—*(Aside.)* I'll seem to conceal my Passion, and that will look like Respect.

LADY FROTH. Bless me, why did you call out upon me so loud?

BRISK. O Lord, I, Madam? I beseech your Ladyship. when?

LADY FROTH. Just now as I came in, bless me. Why, don't you know it?

BRISK. Not I, let me perish.—But did I? Strange! I confess your Ladyship was in my Thoughts; and I was in a sort of Dream that did in a manner represent a very pleasing Object to my imagination, but—but did I indeed?—To see how Love and Murder will out! But did I really name my Lady *Froth?*

LADY FROTH. Three times aloud, as I love Letters.—But did you talk of Love? O *Parnassus!* Who would have thought Mr. *Brisk* could have been in Love, ha ha ha! O Heaven's, I thought you cou'd have no Mistress but the Nine Muses.

BRISK. No more I have, I'gad, for I adore 'em all in your Ladyship.—Let me perish, I don't know whether to be splenatick, or airy upon't; the Deuce take me if I can tell whether I am glad or sorry that your Ladyship has made the Discovery.

LADY FROTH. O be merry by all means.—Prince *Volscius* in Love! Ha ha ha!

BRISK. O barbarous, to turn me into ridicule! Yet, ha ha ha, The Deuce take me, I can't help laughing myself neither, ha ha ha; yet by Heavens, I have a violent passion for your Ladyship, seriously.

LADY FROTH. *Seriously?* Ha ha ha.

BRISK. *Seriously,* ha ha ha. Gad, I have, for all I Laugh.

LADY FROTH. Ha ha ha! What d'e think I Laugh at? Ha ha ha.

BRISK. Me I' gad, ha, ha.

LADY FROTH. No, the Deuce take me if I don't Laugh at myself; for hang me if I have not a violent Passion for Mr. *Brisk,* ha ha ha.

BRISK. Seriously?

LADY FROTH. Seriously, ha ha ha.

BRISK. That's well enough; let me perish, ha ha ha. O Miraculous; what a happy Discovery! Ah, my dear charming Lady *Froth!*

LADY FROTH. Oh my adored Mr. *Brisk!*

Embrace.

Enter Lord Froth.

LORD FROTH. The Company are all ready.—How now!

BRISK *(softly to her).* Zoons, Madam, there's my Lord.

LADY FROTH *(aside to Brisk).* Take no notice—but observe me.—*(Aloud.)* Now cast off, and meet me at the lower end of the Room, and then join hands again; I could teach my Lord this Dance purely, but I vow, Mr. *Brisk,* I can't tell how to come so near any other Man. Oh, here's my Lord; now you shall see me do it with him.

They pretend to practice part of a Country-Dance.

376-7 *Prince Volscius in Love:* parody of the lover in heroic drama, given to absurd extremes of passion, in Buckingham's *The Rehearsal,* 1671.

LORD FROTH *(aside).*—Oh, I see there's no harm yet. But I don't like this familiarity.

LADY FROTH. Shall you and I do our close Dance to show Mr. *Brisk?*

LORD FROTH. No, my Dear, do it with him.

LADY FROTH. I'll do it with him, my Lord, when you are out of the way.

BRISK *(aside).* That's good I'gad, that's good. Deuce take me, I can hardly hold Laughing in his Face.

LORD FROTH. Any other time, my Dear, or we'll Dance it below.

LADY FROTH. With all my heart.

BRISK. Come my Lord, I'll wait on you.—*(To her.)* My charming witty Angel!

LADY FROTH. We shall have whispering time enough, you know, since we are Partners.

Exeunt.

Enter Lady Plyant, *and* Careless.

LADY PLYANT. O Mr. *Careless,* Mr. *Careless,* I'm ruin'd, I'm undone.

CARELESS. What's the matter, Madam?

LADY PLYANT. O the unlucki'st Accident, I'm afraid I shan't live to tell it you.

CARELESS. Heav'n forbid! What is it?

LADY PLYANT. I'm in such a fright; the strangest Quandary and Premunire! I'm all over in a Universal Agitation, I dare swear every Circumstance of me trembles.—O your Letter, your Letter! By an Unfortunate Mistake, I have given Sir *Paul* your Letter instead of his own.

CARELESS. That was unlucky.

LADY PLYANT. Oh, yonder he comes reading of it; for Heaven's sake step in here and advise me quickly before he sees.

Exeunt.

435 *Premunire:* cf. n. to *The Old Batchelour,* III, i, 318.

Enter Sir Paul *with the Letter.*

SIR PAUL. O Providence, what a Conspiracy have I discover'd! But let me see to make an end on't.—(*Reads.*) Hum—*After Supper in the Wardrobe by the Gallery. If Sir* Paul *should surprize us, I have a Commission for him to treat with you about the very matter of Fact.*—Matter of Fact! Very pretty; it seems than I am conducting to my own Cuckoldom, Why, this is the very traiterous Position of taking up Arms by my Authority, against my Person! Well, let me see—*Till then I Languish in expectation of my Adored Charmer.*

Dying Ned Careless.

Gadsbud, would that were Matter of Fact too! Die and be Damn'd for a *Judas Maccabeus,* and *Iscariot* both! O friendship! What art thou but a Name! Henceforward, let no Man make a Friend that would not be a Cuckold. For whomsoever he receives into his bosom will find the way to his Bed, and there return his Caresses with interest to his Wife. Have I for this been pinion'd Night after Night for three Years past? Have I been swath'd in Blankets till I have even been depriv'd of motion, and render'd uncapable of suing the common benefits of Nature? Have I approach'd the Marriage Bed with reverence as to a sacred shrine, and deny'd myself the enjoyment of lawful Domestick Pleasures to preserve its Purity, and must I now find it polluted by Foreign Iniquity? O my Lady *Plyant,* you were Chaste as Ice, but you are melted now, and false as Water!—But Providence has been constant to me in discovering this Conspiracy; still I am beholden to Providence. If it were not for Providence, sure, poor Sir *Paul,* thy Heart would break.

Enter Lady Plyant.

LADY PLYANT. So, Sir, I see you have read the Letter.—Well now, Sir *Paul,* what do you think of your Friend *Careless?* Has he been Treacherous, or did you give his insolence a License to make trial of your Wife's suspected Virtue? De'e see here? Look, read it? (*Snatches the Letter as in anger.*) Gad's my

459 *Judas Maccabeus and Iscariot both:* Sir Paul lumps together the Hebrew hero, who fought to liberate Israel from the Greeks, with the greatest villain of religious history.

Life if I thought it were so, I would this moment renounce all Communication with you. Ungrateful Monster! He? Is it so? Ay, I see it, a Plot upon my Honour; your guilty Cheeks confess it. Oh, where shall wrong'd Virtue fly for Reparation! I'll be Divorced this instant.

SIR PAUL. Gadsbud, what shall I say? This is the strangest Surprise! Why, I don't know anything at all, nor I don't know whether there be anything at all in the World, or no.

LADY PLYANT. I thought I should try you, false Man! I that never dissembled in my Life. Yet to make trial of you, pretended to like that Monster of Inquity, *Careless,* and found out that contrivance to let you see this Letter; which now I find was of your own inditing.—I do, Heathen, I do. See my Face no more; there has hardly been Consummation between us, and I'll be Divorced presently.

SIR PAUL. O strange, what will become of me? I'm so amazed, and so overjoy'd, so afraid, and so sorry.—But did you give me this Letter on purpose, he? Did you?

LADY PLYANT. Did I? Do you doubt me, Turk, Sarazen? I have a Cousin that's a Proctor in the Commons, I'll go to him instantly—

SIR PAUL. Hold, stay, I beseech your Ladyship.—I'm so overjoy'd, stay; I'll confess all.

LADY PLYANT. What will you confess, Jew?

SIR PAUL. Why, now, as I hope to be saved, I had no hand in this Letter—Nay, hear me, I beseech your Ladyship. The Devil take me now if he did not go beyond my Commission.—If I desired him to do any more than speak a good word only just for me. Gadsbud, only for poor Sir *Paul,* I'm an Anabaptist, or a Jew, or what you please to call me.

LADY PLYANT. Why, is not here Matter of Fact?

SIR PAUL. Ay, but by your own Virtue and Continency, that matter of Fact is all his own doing.—I confess I had a great desire to have some Honours Conferr'd upon me, which lie all in your Ladyship's

509 *Proctor in the Commons:* lawyer in charge of matrimonial cases.

Breast, and he being a well spoken Man, I desired him to intercede for me.

LADY PLYANT. Did you so, Presumption! Well, remember for this, your Right Hand shall be swathed down again tonight—and I thought to have always allow'd you that Liberty—

SIR PAUL. Nay but Madam, I shall offend again if you don't allow me that to reach—

LADY PLYANT. Drink the less you Sot, and do't before you come to Bed.

Exit.

Enter Careless.

CARELESS. Sir *Paul,* I'm glad I've met with you: gad, I have said all I could, but can't prevail.—Then my Friendship to you has carried me a little farther in this matter—

SIR PLYANT. Indeed—Well, Sir—*(Aside.)* I'll dissemble with him a little.

CARELESS. Why, faith, I have in my time known Honest Gentlemen abused by a pretended Coyness in their Wives, and I had a mind to try my Lady's Virtue. And when I could not prevail for you, 'gad, I pretended to be in Love myself;—but all in vain, she would not hear a word upon that Subject. Then I writ a Letter to her; I don't know what effects that will have, but I'll be sure to tell you when I do, tho' by this Light I believe her Virtue is impregnable.

SIR PAUL. O Providence! Providence! What Discoveries are here made? Why, this is better and more Miraculous than the rest.

CARELESS. What do you mean?

SIR PAUL. I can't tell you, I'm so overjoy'd; come along with me to my Lady. I can't contain myself; come my dear Friend.

Exeunt.

CARELESS *(aside).* So, so, so, this difficulty's over.

Enter Mellefont *and* Maskwell *severally.*

MELLEFONT. *Maskwell!* I have been looking for you—'tis within a Quarter of Eight.

MASKWELL. My Lady is just gone down from my Lord's Closet; you had best steal into her Chamber before she comes, and lie conceal'd there; otherwise she may Lock the Door when we are together, and you not easily get in to surprise us.

MELLEFONT. Ha! you say true.

MASKWELL. You had best make haste, for she's but gone to make some Apology to the Company for her own and my Lord's absence all this while, and will to her Chamber instantly.

MELLEFONT. I go this moment: Now, Fortune, I defy thee!

Exit.

MASKWELL. I confess you may be allow'd to be secure in your own Opinion; the appearance is very fair, but I have an After-Game to play that shall turn the Tables, and here comes the Man that I must Manage.

Enter Lord Touchwood.

LORD TOUCHWOOD. *Maskwell,* you are the Man I wish'd to meet.

MASKWELL. I am happy to be in the way of your Lordship's Commands.

LORD TOUCHWOOD. I have always found you prudent and careful in anything that has concern'd me or my Family.

MASKWELL. I were a Villain else.—I am bound by duty and Gratitude, and my own Inclination, to be ever your Lordship's Servant.

LORD TOUCHWOOD. Enough—You are my Friend; I know it. Yet there has been a thing in your Knowledge which has concern'd me nearly, that you have conceal'd from me.

MASKWELL. My Lord!

LORD TOUCHWOOD. Nay, I excuse your Friendship to my unnatural Nephew thus far.—But I know you have been Privy to his impious Designs upon my Wife. This Evening she has told me all. Her good Nature conceal'd it as long as was possible, but he perseveres so in Villainy, that she has told me even you were weary of dissuading him, though you have once actually hindered him from forcing her.

MASKWELL. I am sorry, my Lord, I can make you no Answer; this is an Occasion in which I would not willingly be so silent

LORD TOUCHWOOD. I know you would excuse him —and I know as well that you can't.

MASKWELL. Indeed I was in hopes 't had been a youthful Heat that might have soon boil'd over, but—

LORD TOUCHWOOD. Say on.

MASKWELL. I have nothing more to say, my Lord— but to express my Concern, for I think his Frenzy increases daily.

LORD TOUCHWOOD. How! Give me but Proof of it, Ocular Proof, that I may justify my Dealing with him to the World, and share my Fortunes.

MASKWELL. O my Lord! consider that is hard: besides, time may work upon him—then, for me to do it! I have profess'd an everlasting Friendship to him.

LORD TOUCHWOOD. He is your Friend, and what am I?

MASKWELL. I am answered.

LORD TOUCHWOOD. Fear not his Displeasure; I will put you out of his, and Fortune's Power, and for that thou art scrupulously honest, I will secure thy Fidelity to him, and give my Honour never to own any Discovery that you shall make me. Can you give me a demonstrative Proof? Speak.

MASKWELL. I wish I could not!—To be plain, my Lord, I intended this Evening to have try'd all Arguments to dissuade him from a Design which I suspect; and if I had not succeeded, to have informed your Lordship of what I knew.

LORD TOUCHWOOD. I thank you. What is the Villain's Purpose?

MASKWELL. He has own'd nothing to me of late, and what I mean now is only a bare Suspicion of my own. If your Lordship will meet me a quarter of an Hour hence there, in that Lobby by my Lady's Bed-Chamber, I shall be able to tell you more.

LORD TOUCHWOOD. I will.

MASKWELL. My Duty to your Lordship makes me do a severe Piece of Justice—

LORD TOUCHWOOD. I will be secret, and reward your Honesty beyond your Hopes.

Exeunt, severally.

[SCENE II]

SCENE *opening, shows* Lady Touchwood's *Chamber.*

Mellefont, *Solus.*

MELLEFONT. Pray Heaven my Aunt keep with her Assignation! Oh that her Lord were but sweating behind this Hanging, with the Expectation of what I shall see.—Hist, she comes. Little does she think what a Mine is just ready to spring under her Feet. But to my Post.

Goes behind the Hanging.

Enter Lady Touchwood

LADY TOUCHWOOD. 'Tis Eight O'Clock: Methinks I should have found him here. Who does not prevent the Hour of Love outstays the Time; for to be dully punctual is too slow.—I was accusing you of Neglect.

Enter Maskwell

MASKWELL. I confess you do Reproach me when I see you here before me; but 'tis fit I should be still behind hand, still to be more and more indebted to your goodness.

LADY TOUCHWOOD. You can excuse a fault too well, not to have been to blame. A ready Answer shows you were prepar'd.

MASKWELL. Guilt is ever at a loss and confusion waits upon it; when Innocence and bold Truth are always ready for expression—

10 *prevent:* anticipate.

LADY TOUCHWOOD. Not in Love; Words are the weak support of Cold indifference; Love has no Language to be heard.

MASKWELL. Excess of Joy had made me stupid! Thus may my Lips be ever clos'd. (*Kisses her.*) And thus —Oh, who would not lose his Speech, upon condition to have Joys above it?

LADY TOUCHWOOD. Hold, let me Lock the Door first.

Goes to the door.

MASKWELL *(aside).* That I believ'd; 'twas well I left the private passage open.

LADY TOUCHWOOD. So, that safe.

MASKWELL. And so may all your Pleasures be, and secret as this kiss—

MELLEFONT. And may all Treachery be thus discovered.

Leaps out.

LADY TOUCHWOOD. Ah! *(Shrieks.)*

MELLEFONT. Villain! (*Offers to Draw.*)

MASKWELL. Nay! then, there's but one way.

Runs out.

MELLEFONT. Say you so, were you provided for an Escape? Hold, Madam, you have no more holes to your Burrow. I'll stand between you and this Sally-Port.

LADY TOUCHWOOD. Thunder strike thee Dead for this Deceit, immediate Lightning blast thee, me, and the whole World! Oh! I could rack myself, play the Vulture to my own Heart, and gnaw it piece-meal, for not boding to me this misfortune.

MELLEFONT. Be Patient—

LADY TOUCHWOOD. Be Damn'd!

MELLEFONT. Consider, I have you on the hook; you will but flounder yourself a-weary, and be nevertheless my Prisoner.

LADY TOUCHWOOD. I'll hold my breath and die, but I'll be free!

MELLEFONT. O Madam, have a care of dying unprepared! I doubt you have some unrepented Sins that may hang heavy and retard your flight.

LADY TOUCHWOOD. O! What shall I do? Say? Whither shall I turn? Has Hell no remedy?

MELLEFONT. None; Hell has served you even as Heaven has done, left you to yourself.—You're in a kind of *Erasmus* Paradise; yet if you please you may make it a Purgatory, and with a little Penance and my Absolution, all this may turn to good account.

LADY TOUCHWOOD (*aside*). Hold in my passion, and fall, fall, a little, thou swelling Heart! Let me have some intermission of this rage, and one minute's coolness to dissemble.

She Weeps.

MELLEFONT. You have been to blame. I like those Tears, and hope they are of the purest kind—Penitential Tears.

LADY TOUCHWOOD. O the Scene was shifted quick before me! I had not time to think—I was surprised to see a Monster in the Glass, and now I find it is myself. Can you have mercy to forgive the faults I have imagined, but never put in practice?—O Consider, Consider, how fatal you have been to me! You have already killed the quiet of this Life; the love of you was the first wandring fire that e'er misled my steps, and while I had only that in view, I was betray'd into unthought-of ways of ruin.

MELLEFONT. May I believe this true?

LADY TOUCHWOOD. O be not cruelly incredulous! —How can you doubt these streaming Eyes? Keep the severest Eye o'er all my future Conduct, and if I once relapse, let me not hope forgiveness; 'twill ever be in your power to ruin me. —My Lord shall sign to your desires; I will myself create your Happiness, and *Cynthia* shall be this night your Bride. —Do but conceal my failings, and forgive.

69 *Erasmus Paradise:* attempts at moderation in the Reformation controversies made the humanist philospher Erasmus suspect by members of each side, and barred from both the Catholic and the Protestant Heaven.

70 *Purgatory:* unlike Erasmus, the orthodox Catholic may proceed through Purgatory to Heaven.

MELLEFONT. Upon such terms I will ever yours in every honest way.

Enter Lord Touchwood, Maskwell *softly behind him.*

MASKWELL. I have kept my word, he's here, but I must not be seen.

Exit

LORD TOUCHWOOD. Hell and Amazement, she's in Tears.

LADY TOUCHWOOD *(kneeling).* Eternal Blessings thank you.—*(Aside.)* Ha! my Lord listning! O Fortune has o'er paid me all! all's my own!

MELLEFONT. Nay, I beseech you rise.

LADY TOUCHWOOD *(aloud).* Never, never! I'll grow to the Ground, be buried quick beneath it, e'er I be consenting to so damn'd a Sin as Incest, unnatural Incest!

MELLEFONT. Ha!

LADY TOUCHWOOD. O cruel Man, will you not let me go?—I'll forgive all that's past.—O Heaven, you will not ravish me!

MELLEFONT. Damnation!

LORD TOUCHWOOD. Monster! Dog! Your life shall answer this—

Draws, and runs at Mellefont, *is held by* Lady Touchwood.

LADY TOUCHWOOD. O Heavens, my Lord! hold, hold, for Heaven's sake.

MELLEFONT. Confusion—my Uncle! O the damn'd Sorceress.

LADY TOUCHWOOD. Moderate your rage, good my Lord! He's mad, alas, he's mad!—Indeed he is, my Lord, and knows not what he does—see how wild he looks.

MELLEFONT. By Heaven, 'twere senseless not to be mad, and see such Witchcraft.

LADY TOUCHWOOD. My Lord, you hear him—he talks Idly.

LORD TOUCHWOOD. Hence from my sight, thou living infamy to my Name; when next I see that Face, I'll write Villain in't with my Swords point.

MELLEFONT. Now, by my Soul, I will not go till I have made known my wrongs!—Nay, till I have made known yours, which (if possible) are greater—though she has all the Host of Hell her Servants! Though she can wear more shapes in shining day than fear shows Cowards in the dark—

LADY TOUCHWOOD. Alas, he raves! talks very Poetry! for Heaven's sake away, my Lord; he'll either tempt you to extravagance, or commit some himself.

MELLEFONT. Death and Furies, will you not hear me?—Why, by Heaven she laughs, grins, points to your Back; she forks out Cuckoldom with her Fingers, and you're running Horn-mad after your Fortune.

As she is going she turns back and smiles at him.

LORD TOUCHWOOD. I fear he's mad indeed.—Let's send *Maskwell* to him.

MELLEFONT. Send him to her.

LADY TOUCHWOOD. Come, come, good my Lord, my Heart aches so, I shall faint if I stay.

Exeunt

MELLEFONT. Oh, I could curse my Stars, Fate, and Chance; all Causes and Accidents of Fortune in this Life! But to what purpose? Yet, 'sdeath, for a Man to have the fruit of all his Industry grown full and ripe, ready to drop into his mouth, and just when he holds out his hand to gather it, to have a sudden Whirlwind come, tear up Tree and all, and bear away the very root and foundation of his hopes, what temper can contain? They talk of sending *Maskwell* to me; I never had more need of him.—But what can he do? Imagination cannot form a fairer and more plausible design than this of his which has miscarried.—O my Precious Aunt! I shall never thrive without I deal with the Devil, or another Woman.

Women like flames have a destroying pow'r,
Ne'er to be quench'd, till they themselves devour.

Exit.

SCENE shuts.

ACT V. Scene I.

Enter Lady Touchwood *and* Maskwell.

LADY TOUCHWOOD. Was't not Lucky?

MASKWELL. Lucky! Fortune is your own, and 'tis her interest so to be. By Heaven I believe you can control her power, and she fears it: though chance brought my Lord, 'twas your own art that turned it to advantage.

LADY TOUCHWOOD. 'Tis true it might have been my ruin—but yonder's my Lord. I believe he's coming to find you; I'll not be seen.

Exit.

MASKWELL. So; I durst not own my introducing my Lord, though it succeeded well for her, for she would have suspected a design which I could have been puzzled to excuse. My Lord is thoughtful—I'll be so too; yet he shall know my thoughts, or think he does—

Enter Lord Touchwood.

MASKWELL. What have I done?

LORD TOUCHWOD. Talking to himself!

MASKWELL. 'Twas honest—and shall I be rewarded for it? No, 'twas honest, therefore I shan't.—Nay, rather therefore I ought not, for it rewards itself.

LORD TOUCHWOOD *(aside)*. Unequall'd Virtue!

MASKWELL. But should it be known! Then I have lost a Friend! He was an ill Man, and I have gain'd; for half my self I lent him, and that I have recall'd: so I have served myself, and what is yet better, I have served a worthy Lord to whom I owe myself.

LORD TOUCHWOOD *(aside)*. Excellent Man!

MASKWELL. Yet I am wretched.—Oh, there is a secret burns within this Breast, which, should it once blaze forth, would ruin all, consume my honest Character, and brand me with the name of Villain.

LORD TOUCHWOOD. Ha!

MASKWELL. Why do I love! yet Heaven and my waking Conscience are my Witnesses, I never gave one working thought a vent which might discover that I lov'd, nor ever must; no, let it prey upon my Heart; for I would rather die, than seem once, barely seem, dishonest.—Oh, should it once be known I love fair *Cynthia,* all this that I have done would look like Rival's Malice, false Friendship to my Lord, and base Self-interest. Let me perish first, and from this hour avoid all sight and speech, and, if I can, all thought of that pernicious Beauty. Ha! but what is my distraction doing? I am wildly talking to myself, and some ill Chance might have directed malicious Ears this way.

Seems to start, seeing my Lord.

LORD TOUCHWOOD. Start not—let guilty and dishonest Souls start at the revelation of their thoughts, but be thou fix'd, as is thy Virtue.

MASKWELL. I am confounded, and beg your Lordship's pardon for those free discourses which I have had with myself.

LORD TOUCHWOOD. Come, I beg your pardon that I over-heard you, and yet it shall not need.—Honest *Maskwell!* thy and my good Genius led me hither: mine, in that I have discovered so much Manly Virtue; thine, in that thou shalt have due reward of all thy worth. Give me thy hand—my Nephew is the alone remaining Branch of all our ancient Family; him I thus blow away, and constitute thee in his room to be my Heir.

MASKWELL. Now Heaven forbid—

LORD TOUCHWOOD. No more—I have resolv'd.—The Writings are ready drawn, and wanted nothing but to be sign'd, and have his name inserted—yours will fill the Blank as well—I will have no reply.—Let me command this time; for 'tis the last in which I will assume Authority. Hereafter, you shall rule where I have Power.

MASKWELL. I humbly would petition—

Maskwell *pauses.*

LORD TOUCHWOOD. Is't for yourself?—I'll hear of nought for anybody else.

MASKWELL. Then witness Heaven for me, this Wealth and Honour was not of my seeking, nor would I build my Fortune on another's ruin. I had but one desire—

LORD TOUCHWOOD. Thou shalt enjoy it.—If all I'm worth in Wealth or Interest can purchase *Cynthia*, she is thine. I'm sure Sir *Paul's* Consent will follow Fortune; I'll quickly show him which way that is going.

MASKWELL. You oppress me with Bounty; my Gratitude is weak, and shrinks beneath the weight, and cannot rise to thank you.—What, enjoy my Love! Forgive the Transports of a Blessing so unexpected, so unhop'd for, so unthought of!

LORD TOUCHWOOD. I will confirm it, and rejoice with thee.

Exit.

MASKWELL. This is prosperous indeed!—Why, let him find me out a Villain. Settled in possession of a fair Estate and full fruition of my Love, I'll bear the railings of a losing Gamester. But should he find me out before! 'Tis dangerous to delay.—Let me think.—Should my Lord proceed to treat openly of my Marriage with *Cynthia*, all must be discover'd, and *Mellefont* can be no longer blinded.—It must not be; nay, should my Lady know it—ay, then were fine work indeed! Her fury would spare nothing, tho' she involv'd herself in ruin. No, it must be by Stratagem.—I must deceive *Mellefont* once more, and get my Lord to consent to my private management. He comes opportunely. Now will I, in my old way, discover the whole and real truth of the matter to him, that he may not suspect one word on't.

No Mask like open Truth to cover Lies,
As to go naked is the best disguise.

Enter Mellefont.

MELLEFONT. O *Maskwell*, what hopes? I am confounded in a maze of thoughts, each leading into one another, and all ending in perplexity. My uncle will not see nor hear me.

106 in my old way: the title page of the 1706 edition of the play bore lines from Terence's play *Heautontimoroumenos*, in which the villain Syrus boasts of cheating by telling the truth.

MASKWELL. No matter, Sir, don't trouble your head; all's in my power.

MELLEFONT. How, for Heaven's sake?

MASKWELL. Little do you think that your Aunt has kept her word. How the Devil she wrought my Lord into this dotage, I know not, but he's gone to Sir *Paul* about my Marriage with *Cynthia*, and has appointed me his Heir.

MELLEFONT. The Devil he has! What's to be done?

MASKWELL. I have it! It must be by Stratagem, for it's in vain to make Application to him. I think I have that in my head that cannot fail. Where's *Cynthia?*

MELLEFONT. In the Garden.

MASKWELL. Let us go and consult her. My life for yours, I cheat my Lord.

Exeunt.

Enter Lord Touchwood, Lady Touchwood.

LADY TOUCHWOOD. *Maskwell* your Heir, and Marry *Cynthia!*

LORD TOUCHWOOD. I cannot do too much for so much merit.

LADY TOUCHWOOD. But this is a thing of too great moment to be so suddenly resolv'd. Why *Cynthia?* Why must he be Married? Is there not reward enough in raising his low Fortune, but he must mix his Blood with mine, and Wed my Niece? How know you that my Brother will consent, or she? May, he himself perhaps may have Affections otherwise.

LORD TOUCHWOOD. No, I am convinced he loves her.

LADY TOUCHWOOD. *Maskwell* love *Cynthia?* Impossible!

LORD TOUCHWOOD. I told you, he confess'd it to me.

LADY TOUCHWOOD *(aside)*. Confusion! How's this?

LORD TOUCHWOOD. His humility long stifled his Passion, and his Love of *Mellefont* would have made him still conceal it. But by Encouragement I wrung the secret from him, and know he's no way to be rewarded but in her. I'll defer my farther proceedings in it till you have consider'd it, but remember how we are both indebted to him.

Exit.

LADY TOUCHWOOD. Both indebted to him! Yes, we are both indebted to him, if you knew all, damn'd Villain! oh, I am wild with this surprize of Treachery: Hell and Fire, it is impossible, it cannot be!—He Love *Cynthia!* What, have I been Bawd to his designs, his Property only, a baiting place to stay his stomach in the road to her? Now I see what made him false to *Mellefont.*—Shame and Destruction! I cannot bear it, oh! What Woman can bear to be a Property? To be kindled to a flame, only to light him to another's Arms! Oh, that I were Fire indeed, that I might burn the vile Traitor to a Hell of Torments.—But he's Damnation proof, a Devil already, and Fire is his Element. What shall I do? How shall I think? I cannot think.—All my designs are lost, my Love unsated, my Revenge unfinished, and fresh cause of fury from unthought-of Plagues.

Enter Sir Paul.

SIR PAUL. Madam, Sister, my Lady Sister, did you see my Lady my Wife?

LADY TOUCHWOOD. Oh! Torture!

SIR PAUL. Gadsbud, I can't find her high nor low; where can she be, think you?

LADY TOUCHWOOD. Where she's serving you as all your Sex ought to be served; making you a Beast. Don't you know that you're a Fool, Brother?

SIR PAUL. A Fool; he, he, he, you're merry.—No, no, not I, I know no such matter.

LADY TOUCHWOOD. Why then you don't know half your happiness.

SIR PAUL. That's a jest with all my heart, faith and troth.—But hearkee, my Lord told me something of a Revolution of things; I don't know what to make on't.

164 *Property:* Compare Lady Wishfort's rage at becoming another's property in *The Way of the World,* V, i, 50.

—Gadsbud, I must consult my Wife.—He talks of disinheriting his Nephew, and I don't know what.—Look you, Sister, I must know what my Girl has to trust to, or not a syllable of a Wedding, gadsbud, to show you that I am not a Fool.

LADY TOUCHWOOD. Hear me; consent to the breaking off this Marriage, and the promoting any other without consulting me, and I'll renounce all Blood, all relation and concern with you for ever;—nay, I'll be your Enemy, and pursue you to Destruction; I'll tear your Eyes out, and tread you under my feet!

SIR PAUL. Why, what's the matter now? Good Lord, what's all this for? Pooh, here's a joke, indeed!—Why, where's my Wife?

LADY TOUCHWOOD. With *Charles,* in the close Arbour; he may want you by this time, as much as you want her.

SIR PAUL. O, if she be with Mr. *Careless,* 'tis well enough.

LADY TOUCHWOOD. Fool, Sot, insensible Ox! But remember what I said to you, or you had better eat your own Horns, and Pimp for your living, by this light you had.

Exit.

SIR PAUL. She's a passionate Woman, gadsbud!—But to say truth, all our Family are Cholerick; I am the only peaceable Person amongst 'em.

Exit.

Enter Mellefont, Maskwell, *and* Cynthia.

MELLEFONT. I know no other way but this he has proposed, If you have Love enough to run the venture.

CYNTHIA. I don't know whether I have Love enough, but I find I have obstinacy enough to pursue whatever I have once resolved, and a true Female courage to oppose anything that resists my will, tho' 'twere reason itself.

MASKWELL. That's right.—Well, I'll secure the Writings and run the hazard along with you.

CYNTHIA. But how can the Coach and six Horses be got ready without suspicion?

MASKWELL. Leave it to my care; that shall be so far from being suspected, that it shall be got ready by my Lord's own order.

MELLEFONT. How?

MASKWELL. Why, I intend to tell my Lord the whole matter of our Contrivance; that's my way.

MELLEFONT. I don't understand you.

MASKWELL. Why, I'll tell my Lord I laid this Plot with you on purpose to betray you; and that which put me upon it was the finding it impossible to gain the Lady any other way, but in the hopes of her Marrying you.—

MELLEFONT. So—

MASKWELL. So, why so, while you are busied in making yourself ready, I'll wheedle her into the Coach; and instead of you, borrow my Lord's Chaplain, and so run away with her myself.

MELLEFONT. O I conceive you; you'll tell him so?

MASKWELL. Tell him so! Ay; why, you don't think I mean to do so?

MELLEFONT. No, no; ha, ha, I dare swear thou wilt not.

MASKWELL *(aside)*. You may be deceiv'd.—Therefore, for our farther Security, I would have you Disguis'd like a Parson, that if my Lord should have Curiosity to peep, he may not discover you in the Coach, but think the Cheat is carried on as he would have it.

MELLEFONT. Excellent *Maskwell*, thou wer't certainly meant for a Statesman or a Jesuit; but that thou'rt too honest for one, and too pious for the other.

MASKWELL. Well, get yourselves ready, and meet me in half an hour yonder in my Lady's Dressing-Room; go by the back Stairs, and so we may slip down without being observ'd.—I'll send the Chaplain to you with his Robes; I have made him my own, and ordered him to meet us tomorrow Morning at St. *Albans;* there we will Sum up this Account to all our satisfactions.

MELLEFONT. Should I begin to thank or praise thee, I should waste the little time we have.

Exit.

MASKWELL. Madam, you will be ready?

CYNTHIA. I will be punctual to the Minute.

Going.

MASKWELL. Stay, I have a doubt.—Upon second thoughts, we had better meet in the Chaplain's Chamber here, the corner Chamber at this end of the Gallery; there is a back way into it, so that you need not come thro' this Door, and a Pair of private Stairs leads down to the Stables. —It will be more convenient.

CYNTHIA. I am guided by you,—but *Mellefont* will mistake.

MASKWELL. No, no, I'll after him immediately, and tell him.

CYNTHIA. I will not fail.

Exit.

MASKWELL. Why, *qui vult decipi decipiatur.*—'Tis no fault of mine; I have told 'em in plain terms how easy 'tis for me to cheat 'em, and if they will not hear the Serpent's hiss, they must be stung into experience, and future caution.—Now to prepare my Lord to consent to this.— But first I must instruct my little Levite; there is no Plot, publick or private, that can expect to prosper without one of 'em have a finger in't. He promised me to be within at this hour.—Mr. *Saygrace,* Mr. *Saygrace.*

Goes to the Chamber Door and knocks.

SAYGRACE *(looking out).* Sweet Sir, I will but pen the last Line of an Acrostick, and be with you in the twinkling of an Ejaculation, in the pronouncing of an *Amen,* or before you can—

291 *qui vult,* etc.: Latin proverb. 'If the world will be gulled, let it be gulled.' Burton, *Anatomy of Melancholy* (1621).

297 *Levite:* cf. n. to *The Old Batchelour,* IV, i, 31.

MASKWELL. Nay, good Mr. *Saygrace,* do not prolong the time by describing to me the shortness of your stay; rather, if you please, defer the finishing of your Wit, and let us talk about our business. It shall be Tithes in your way.

SAYGRACE *(enters)*. You shall prevail; I would break off in the middle of a Sermon to do you pleasure.

MASKWELL. You could not do me a greater,—except the business in hand. Have you provided a Habit for *Mellefont?*

SAYGRACE. I have; they are ready in my Chamber, together with a clean starch'd Band and Cuffs.

MASKWELL. Good, let them be carried to him.—Have you stitch'd the Gown Sleeve, that he may be puzzled, and waste time in putting it on?

SAYGRACE. I have; the Gown will not be indued without perplexity.

MASKWELL. Meet me in half an Hour here in your own Chamber. When *Cynthia* comes, let there be no Light, and do not speak, that she may not distinguish you from *Mellefont.* I'll urge haste, to excuse your silence.

SAYGRACE. You have no more Commands?

MASKWELL. None; your Text is short.

SAYGRACE. But pithy, and I will handle it with discretion.

Exit.

MASKWELL. It will be the first you have so serv'd.

Enter Lord Touchwood.

LORD TOUCHWOOD. Sure I was born to be controlled by those I should Command. My very Slaves will shortly give me Rules how I shall govern them.

MASKWELL. I am concern'd to see your Lordship discomposed—

LORD TOUCHWOOD. Have you seen my Wife lately, or disobliged her?

MASKWELL. No, my Lord. *(Aside.)* What can this mean?

LORD TOUCHWOOD. Then *Mellefont* has urg'd somebody to incense her.—Something she has heard of you which carries her beyond the bounds of Patience.

MASKWELL *(aside)*. This I fear'd. Did not your Lordship tell her of the Honours you designed me?

LORD TOUCHWOOD. Yes.

MASKWELL. 'Tis that; you know my Lady has a high Spirit; she thinks I am unworthy.

LORD TOUCHWOOD. Unworthy! 'tis an ignorant Pride in her to think so. Honesty to me is true Nobility. However, 'tis my Will it should be so, and that shou'd be convincing to her as much as reason.—By Heav'n, I'll not be Wife-ridden; were it possible it should be done this night.

MASKWELL *(aside)*. By Heav'n, he meets my wishes. Few things are impossible to willing minds.

LORD TOUCHWOOD. Instruct me how this may be done; you shall see I want no inclination.

MASKWELL. I had laid a small design for tomorrow (as Love will be inventing) which I thought to communicate to your Lordship—but it may be as well done tonight.

LORD TOUCHWOOD. Here's Company. Come this way and tell me.

Exeunt.

Enter Careless *and* Cynthia.

CARELESS. Is not that he, now gone out with my Lord?

CYNTHIA. Yes.

CARELESS. By Heaven, there's Treachery! The Confusion that I saw your Father in, my Lady *Touchwood's* Passion, with what imperfectly I overheard between my Lord and her, confirm me in my fears. Where's *Mellefont*?

CYNTHIA. Here he comes.

Enter Mellefont.

Did *Maskwell* tell you anything of the Chaplain's Chamber?

MELLEFONT. No; my Dear, will you get ready?——The things are all in my Chamber; I want nothing but the Habit.

CARELESS. You are betray'd, and *Maskwell* is the Villain that I always thought him.

CYNTHIA. When you were gone, he said his mind was chang'd, and bid me meet him in the Chaplain's Room, pretending immediately to follow you and give you notice.

MELLEFONT. How.!

CARELESS. There's *Saygrace* tripping by with a bundle under his Arm. He cannot be ignorant that *Maskwell* means to use his Chamber; let's follow and examine him.

MELLEFONT. 'Tis loss of time—I cannot think him false.

Exeunt Mellefont *and* Careless.

Enter Lord Touchwood.

CYNTHIA *(aside)*. My Lord musing!

LORD TOUCHWOOD. He has a quick invention, if this were suddenly design'd; yet he says he had prepar'd my Chaplain already.

CYNTHIA. How's this? Now I fear indeed.

LORD TOUCHWOOD. *Cynthia* here! Alone, fair Cousin, and melancholly?

CYNTHIA. Your Lordship was thoughtful.

LORD TOUCHWOOD. My thoughts were on serious business, not worth your hearing.

CYNTHIA. Mine were on Treachery concerning you, and may be worth your hearing.

LORD TOUCHWOOD. Treachery concerning me? Pray be plain.—Hark! what noise!

MASKWELL *(within)*. Will you not hear me?

LADY TOUCHWOOD *(within)*. No, Monster! Hellish Traitor, no!

CYNTHIA. My Lady and *Maskwell!* This may be lucky.—My Lord, let me entreat you to stand behind this Screen and listen; perhaps this chance may give you proof of what you ne'er could have believ'd from my suspicions.

They abscond.

Enter Lady Touchwood *with a Dagger,* Maskwell.

LADY TOUCHWOOD. You want but leasure to invent fresh falsehood, and soothe me to a fond belief of all your fictions; but I will stab the Lie that's forming in your heart, and save a Sin in pity to your Soul.

MASKWELL. Strike then!—Since you will have it so.

LADY TOUCHWOOD. Ha! a steady Villain to the last!

MASKWELL. Come, why do you dally with me thus?

LADY TOUCHWOOD. Thy stubborn temper shocks me, and you knew it would.—By Heav'n, this is Cunning all, and not Courage; no, I know thee well: but thou shalt miss thy aim.

MASKWELL. Ha, ha, ha.

LADY TOUCHWOOD. Ha! do you mock my Rage? Then this shall punish your fond, rash Contempt! Again smile!

Goes to strike.

And such a smile as speaks in Ambiguity! Ten thousand meanings lurk in each corner of that various face. Oh that they were written in thy heart! That I, with this, might lay thee open to my sight! But then 'twill be too late to know.—Thou hast, thou hast found the only way to turn my Rage. Too well thou know'st my jealous Soul could ever bear Uncertainty. Speak, then, and tell me.—Yet are you silent? Oh, I am wilder'd in all Passions! But thus my Anger melts. (*Weeps.*) Here, take this Poniard, for my very Spirits faint, and I want strength to hold it; thou hast disarm'd my Soul.

Gives the Dagger.

452 *wilder'd:* confused.

LORD TOUCHWOOD. Amazement shakes me—where will this end?

MASKWELL. So, 'tis well.—Let your wild fury have a vent; and when you have temper, tell me.

LADY TOUCHWOOD. Now, now, now I am calm, and can hear you.

MASKWELL *(aside)*. Thanks, my invention; and now I have it for you.—First tell me what urg'd you to this violence? For your Passion broke in such imperfect terms that yet I am to learn the cause.

LADY TOUCHWOOD. My Lord himself surpris'd me with the News You were to marry *Cynthia*—that you had own'd your Love to him, and his indulgence would assist you to attain your ends.

CYNTHIA *(aside to Lord Touchwood)*. How, my Lord!

LORD TOUCHWOOD *(aside to Cynthia)*. Pray forbear all Resentments for a while, and let us hear the rest.

MASKWELL. I grant you in appearance all is true; I seem'd consenting to my Lord; nay, transported with the Blessing—but could you think that I who had been happy in your lov'd Embraces, could e'er be fond of an inferiour Slavery?

LORD TOUCHWOOD *(aside)*. Ha! O poison to my Ears! What do I hear!

CYNTHIA *(aside)*. Nay, good my Lord, forbear Resentment; let us hear it out.

LORD TOUCHWOOD *(aside)*. Yes, I will contain, tho' I could burst.

MASKWELL. I that had wanton'd in the wide Circle of your World of Love, could be confin'd within the puny Province of a Girl? No. —Yet tho' I doat on each last Favour more than all the rest; though I would give a Limb for every look you cheaply throw away on any other Object of your Love; yet so far I prize your Pleasures o'er my own, that all this seeming Plot that I have laid has been to gratify your taste and cheat the World, to prove a faithful Rogue to you.

LADY TOUCHWOOD. If this were true!—But how can it be?

MASKWELL. I have so contriv'd that *Mellefont* will presently, in the Chaplain's habit, wait for *Cynthia* in your Dressing-Room: but I have put the change upon her that she may be otherwhere employ'd.—Do you procure her Night-Gown, and with your Hoods tied over your face, meet him in her stead. You may go privately by the back Stairs, and unperceiv'd, there you may propose to reinstate him in his Uncle's favour, if he'll comply with your desires; his Case is desperate, and I believe he'll yield to any Conditions. —If not, here, take this; you may employ it better than in the Death of one who is nothing when not yours.

Gives the Dagger.

LADY TOUCHWOOD. Thou can'st deceive everybody.—Nay, thou hast deceiv'd me; but 'tis as I would wish—trusty Villain! I could worship thee.

MASKWELL. No more; there want but a few Minutes of the time, and *Mellefont's* Love will carry him there before his hour.

LADY TOUCHWOOD. I go, I fly, incomparable *Maskwell*.

Exit.

MASKWELL. So, this was a pinch indeed; my invention was upon the Rack, and made discov'ry of her last Plot. I hope *Cynthia* and my Chaplain will be ready; I'll prepare for the Expedition.

Exit.

Cynthia *and* Lord Touchwood *come forward.*

CYNTHIA. Now, my Lord?

LORD TOUCHWOOD. Astonishment binds up my rage! Villainy upon Villainy! Heavens, what a long track of dark deceit has this discover'd! I am confounded when I look back, and want a Clue to guide me through the various mazes of unheard-of Treachery. My Wife! Damnation—my Hell!

CYNTHIA. My Lord, have patience, and be sensible how great our happiness is that this discovery was not made too late.

LORD TOUCHWOOD. I thank you, yet it may be still too late, if we don't presently prevent the Execution of their plots.—Ha, I'll do't. Where's *Mellefont,* my poor injured Nephew? How shall I make him ample satisfaction?

CYNTHIA. I dare answer for him.

LORD TOUCHWOOD. I do him fresh wrong to question his forgivness, for I know him to be all goodness. —Yet my Wife! Damn her: she'll think to meet him in that Dressing-Room—was't not so? And *Maskwell* will expect you in the Chaplain's Chamber.—For once, I'll add to my Plot too. Let us haste to find out, and inform my Nephew, and do you quickly as you can bring all the Company into this Gallery.—I'll expose the Strumpet, and the Villain.

Exeunt.

Enter Lord Froth, *and* Sir Paul.

LORD FROTH. By Heavens, I have slept an Age.— Sir *Paul,* what o'Clock is't? Past Eight, on my Conscience; my Lady's is the most inviting Couch, and a slumber there is the prettiest amusement! But where's all the Company?

SIR PAUL. The Company, gadsbud, I don't know, my Lord, but here's the strangest Revolution; all turn'd topsy-turvy, as I hope for Providence.

LORD FROTH. O Heavens, what's the matter? Where's my Wife?

SIR PAUL. All turn'd topsy-turvy, as sure as a Gun.

LORD FROTH. How do you mean? My Wife?

SIR PAUL. The strangest posture of Affairs!

LORD FROTH. What, my Wife?

SIR PAUL. No, no, I mean the Family.—Your Lady's Affairs may be in a very good posture; I saw her go into the Garden with Mr. *Brisk.*

LORD FROTH. How? where? when? what to do?

SIR PAUL. I suppose they have been laying their heads together.

LORD FROTH. How?

SIR PAUL. Nay, only about Poetry, I suppose, my Lord; making Couplets.

LORD FROTH. Couplets!

SIR PAUL. O, here they come.

Enter Lady Froth, Brisk.

BRISK. My Lord, your humble Servant; Sir *Paul* yours.—The finest night!

LADY FROTH. My dear, Mr. *Brisk* and I have been Star-gazing, I don't know how long.

SIR PAUL. Does it not tire your Ladyship? Are not you weary with looking up?

LADY FROTH. Oh, no, I love it violently.—My dear, you're melancholly.

LORD FROTH. No, my dear; I'm but just awake.

LADY FROTH. Snuff some of my Spirit of Hartshorn.

LORD FROTH. I've some of my own, thank you my dear.

LADY FROTH. Well, I swear, Mr. *Brisk*, you understood Astronomy like an old *Egyptian.*

BRISK. Not comparable to your Ladyship; you are the very *Cynthia* of the Skies, and Queen of Stars.

LADY FROTH. That's because I've no light but what's by Reflection from you, who are the Sun.

BRISK. O Jesu! Madam, you have Eclips'd me quite, let me perish.—I can't answer that.

LADY FROTH. No matter.—Heark'ee, shall you and I make an Almanack together?

BRISK. With all my Soul.—Your Ladyship has made me the Man in't already, I'm so full of the Wounds which you have given.

589 *Spirit of Hartshorn:* ammonia derived from stag's horn, ironically suitable for Lord Froth.

595 *Cynthia:* epithet of Artemis, born near Mt Cynthus, identified with hunting and the moon.

601-3 *Almanack . . . Man in't:* old almanacks often show a man surrounded by the twelve signs of the celestial Zodiac, each sign next to the part of the body it is said to influence.

LADY FROTH. O finely taken! I swear now you are even with me. O *Parnassus*, you have an infinite deal of Wit.

SIR PAUL. So he has, gadsbud, and so has your Ladyship.

Enter Lady Plyant, Careless, Cynthia.

LADY PLYANT. You tell me most surprising things; bless me, who would ever trust a man? O my heart aches for fear they should be all deceitful alike.

CARELESS. You need not fear, Madam; you have Charms to fix Inconstancy itself.

LADY PLYANT. O dear, you make me blush.

LORD FROTH. Come my dear, shall we take leave of my Lord and Lady?

CYNTHIA. They'll wait upon your Lordship presently.

LORD FROTH. Mr. *Brisk*, my Coach shall set you down.

A great shriek from the corner of the Stage. Lady Touchwood *runs out affrighted, my Lord after her, like a Parson.*

ALL. What's the matter?

LADY TOUCHWOOOD. O, I'm betray'd!—Save me, help me!

LORD TOUCHWOOD. Now what Evasion, Strumpet?

LADY TOUCHWOOD. Stand off, let me go, and Plagues and Curses seize you all.

Runs out.

LORD TOUCHWOOD. Go, and thy own Infamy pursue thee.—You stare as you were all amazed,—I don't wonder at it, but too soon you'll know mine, and that Woman's shame.

Enter Mellefont *lugging in* Maskwell *from the other side of the Stage,* Mellefont *like a Parson.*

MELLEFONT. Nay, by Heaven you shall be seen.—*Careless*, your hand;—do you hold down your head? Yes, I am your Chaplain; look in the Face of your injur'd Friend, thou wonder of all Falsehood.

LORD TOUCHWOOD. Are you silent, Monster?

MELLEFONT. Good Heavens! How I believ'd and Lov'd this Man!—Take him hence, for he's a Disease to my Sight.

LORD TOUCHWOOD. Secure that manifold Villain.

CARELESS. Miracle of Ingratitude!

They carry out Maskwell, *who hangs down his head.*

BRISK. This is all very surprising, let me perish.

LADY FROTH. You know I told you *Saturn* look'd a little more angry than usual.

LORD TOUCHWOOD. We'll think of punishment at leasure, but let me hasten to do Justice in rewarding Virtue and wrong'd Innocence.—Nephew, I hope I have your pardon, and *Cynthia's.*

MELLEFONT. We are your Lordship's Creatures.

LORD TOUCHWOOD. And be each other's comfort.—Let me join your hands.—Unwearied Nights, and wishing Days attend you both; mutual Love, lasting Health, and Circling Joys, tread round each happy Year of your long Lives.

Let secret Villainy from hence be warn'd;
Howe'er in private, Mischiefs are conceiv'd,
Torture and shame attend their open Birth;
Like Vipers in the Womb, base Treach'ry lies,
Still gnawing that, whence first it did arise;
No sooner born, but the Vile Parent dies.

Exeunt Omnes.

FINIS.

Epilogue

Spoken by Mrs. *Mountford.**

Could Poets but forsee how Plays would take,
Then they could tell what Epilogues to make;
Whether to thank, or blame their Audience most:
But that late knowledge, does much hazard cost:
Till Dice are thrown, there's nothing won, nor lost.

* Lady Froth in the play; widow of a famous actor murdered the year before.

So till the Thief has stoll'n, he cannot know
Whether he shall escape the Law, or no.
But Poets run much greater hazards far,
Than they who stand their Trials at the Bar;
The Law provides a curb for its own Fury,
And suffers Judges to direct the Jury.
But in this Court, what difference does appear!
For every one's both Judge and Jury here;
Nay, and what's worse, an Executioner.
All have a Right and Title to some part,
Each chusing that in which he has most Art.
The dreadful men of Learning all Confound,
Unless the Fable's good, and Moral sound.
The Vizor-Masks, that are in Pit and Gallery,
Approve, or Damn the Repartee and Rallery.
The Lady Criticks, who are better Read,
Enquire if Characters are nicely bred;
If the soft things are Penn'd and spoke with grace;
They Judge of Action too, and Time, and Place;
In which, we do not doubt but they're discerning,
For that's a kind of *Assignation Learning.*
Beaus Judge of Dress; the Witlings Judge of Songs;
The Cuckoldom, of Ancient Right, to Cits belongs.
Poor Poets thus the Favour are deny'd
Even to make exceptions, when they're Try'd.
'Tis hard that they must every one admit;
Methinks I see some Faces in the Pit
Which must of Consequence be Foes to Wit.
You who can Judge, to Sentence may proceed;
But tho' he cannot Write, let him be freed
At least from their Contempt, who cannot Read.

19 *Vizor-Masks:* worn by available ladies who plied the theatre.

26 *Assignation Learning:* 'Learning picked up from others indirectly, not gained by one's own efforts.' (Quoted by Davis from Blount, *Law Dictionary*).

28 *Cits:* 'Inhabitant of a city, in an ill sense; a pert low townsman; a pragmatical trader.' (Johnson, *Dictionary.*)

LOVE FOR LOVE

Introduction

Approximately a year after the indifferent reception of *The Double Dealer,* Congreve was ready with a third comedy, *Love For Love.* The death of Queen Mary in December 1694, closed the theatre, however, and at the same time a quarrel between actors and management split the Theatre Royal. Virtually all the players who had performed in Congreve's early comedies left Drury Lane, and, in March 1695, secured a royal license to set up a rival theatre in a tennis court behind Lincoln's Inn Fields. Congreve and his latest comedy went with them, and the new house opened with *Love for Love* on 30 April, including with it two prologues and an epilogue commenting on the circumstances of its performance. The sympathetic audience was disposed to like whatever the new company put on, and found itself presented with a masterpiece. It ran for thirteen days, rivalling the success of *The Old Batchelour.* Congreve had continued to draw on traditional comic characters and situations in this, his third offering on the stage, but both the skill of the language, and the brilliance of the performance enchanted the onlookers. In fact, Congreve took particular care in tailoring his parts to fit his performers; the acting of Doggett in the role of Ben the sailor was especially admired. His plot is nicely calculated to furnish opportunites for glittering dialogue, without the atmosphere of devious villainy in *The Double Dealer.* Foresight's astrological lore may seem hopelessly recondite to the modern reader, but Congreve had a number of well-known volumes on the subject in his library, and many of the technical terms would have been familiar from monthly almanacs to a public for whom astrology was even more popular than it is today.

Congreve's reputation was firmly established by *Love for Love,* and it became his most popular play throughout the next century, although often presented in shortened and 'purified' versions. By the early nineteenth century, however, as Charles Lamb noted: 'Con-

* Avery, *Congreve's Plays on the Eighteenth-Century Stage,* p. 16.

greve and Farquhar show their heads once in seven years only, to be exploded and put down instantly,'* but it did continue to be performed at irregular intervals. Since its revival at the Aldwych in 1917 as part of a cycle of Congreve's plays over a nine-year period, it has approached the reputation of *The Way of the World,* with several fine productions, and a complete long-playing recording by the National Theatre of Great Britain. Single volumes of the play are available in editions by Emmett Avery for the Regents Restoration Drama Series, 1966, and by M. M. Kelsall in a New Mermaids Dramabook, 1969.

Love for Love:

A

COMEDY.

Acted at the

THEATRE in Little Lincolns-Inn Fields,

BY

His Majesty's Servants.

Written by Mr. *CONGREVE.*

Nudus agris, nudus nummis paternis,
Insanire parat certa ratione modoque.
Hor.

LONDON:

Printed for *Jacob Tonson* at the *Judge's-Head,* near the *Inner-Temple-Gate* in *Fleetstreet,* 1695.

Nudus agris, etc.: 'Stripped of his lands, stripped of his patrimony, he prepares to go mad by fixed rule and regulation.' (Horace, *Satires,* II, iii, 184 and 271.) Congreve, or his typesetter, has altered *paret* to *parat.*

To the Right Honourable Charles

Earl of *Dorset* and *Middlesex*,*

Lord Chamberlain of His Majesty's Household, and Knight of the Most Noble Order of the Garter, &c.

MY LORD,

A young Poet is liable to the same Vanity and Indiscretion with a Young Lover; and the Great Man that smiles upon one, and the Fine Woman that looks kindly upon t'other, are each of 'em in Danger of having the Favour publish'd with the first Opportunity.

But there may be a different Motive, which will a little distinguish the Offenders. For tho' one should have a Vanity in ruining another's Reputation, yet the other may only have an Ambition to advance his own. And I beg leave, my Lord, that I may plead the latter, both as the Cause and Excuse of this Dedication.

Whoever is King, is also the Father of his Country; and as nobody can dispute Your Lordship's *Monarchy* in *Poetry*, so all that are concern'd ought to acknowledge Your Universal Patronage: And it is only presuming on the Priviledge of a Loyal Subject that I have ventur'd to make this my Address of Thanks to Your Lordship; which at the same time, includes a Prayer for Your Protection.

I am not Ignorant of the Common Form of Poetical Dedications, which are generally made up of Panegyricks, where the Authors endeavour to distinguish their Patrons, by the shining Characters they give them, above other Men. But that, my Lord, is not my business at this time, nor is Your Lordship *now* to be distinguish'd. I am contented with the Honour I do myself in this Epistle, without the Vanity of attempting to add to, or explain, Your Lordship's Character.

I confess it is not without some struggling that I behave myself in this Case as I ought: For it is very hard to be pleased with a Subject, and yet forbear it. But I chuse rather to follow *Pliny's* Precept than his Example, when in his Panegyrick to the Emperour *Trajan*, he says,

* Charles Earl of Dorset, aristocratic poet, wit, and patron of letters; as Lord Chamberlain he licensed the new Lincoln's Inn Theatre, which opened with *Love for Love*.

Nec minus considerabo quid aures ejus pati possint, Quam quid virtutibus debeatur.•

I hope I may be excus'd the Pedantry of a Quotation when it is so justly apply'd. Here are some Lines in the Print (and which your Lordship read before this Play was Acted) that were omitted on the Stage; and particularly one whole Scene in the Third Act,★ which not only helps the Design forward with less Precipitation, but also heightens the ridiculous Character of *Foresight,* which indeed seems to be maim'd without it. But I found myself in great danger of a long Play, and was glad to help it where I could. Tho' notwithstanding my Care, and the kind Reception it had from the Town, I could heartily wish it yet shorter: But the Number of Different Characters represented in it would have been too much crowded in less room.

This Reflection on Prolixity (a Fault, for which scarce any one Beauty will attone) warns me not to be tedious now, and detain Your Lordship any longer with the Trifles of,

MY LORD,
Your Lordship's
Most Obedient
and Most Humble
Servant,
WILL. CONGREVE.

A Prologue For

The opening of the new Play-House,* propos'd to be spoken by Mrs. *Bracegirdle*† in Man's Cloaths.

Sent from an unknown Hand.

Custom, which everywhere bears mighty Sway,
Brings me to act the Orator today:
But Women, you will say, are ill at Speeches—

• 'I shall consider what his ears can endure hearing no less than what may be owed to his virtues.'

★ probably the scene in which Scandal introduces doubts into Foresight's mind; perhaps omitted to give more time for the interludes of music and dancing in which the play is unusually rich.

* see Introductory Note.

† see note to the Prologue of *The Old Batchelour.*

'Tis true, and therefore I appear in Breeches:
Not for Example to you City-Wives,
That by Prescription's settled for your Lives.
Was it for gain the Husband first consented?
O yes, their Gains are mightily augmented:

Making Horns with her Hands over her Head.

And yet, methinks, it must have cost some Strife:
A Passive Husband, and an Active Wife!
'Tis awkward, very awkward, by my Life.
But to my Speech-Assemblies of all Nations
Still are suppos'd to open with Orations:
Mine shall begin, to shew our Obligations.
To you, our Benefactors, lowly Bowing,
Whose Favours have prevented our undoing;
A long *Egyptian* Bondage we endur'd,
Till Freedom, by our Justice we procur'd:
Our Taskmasters were grown such very *Jews*,
We must at length have Play'd in Wooden Shoes,
Had not your Bounty taught us to refuse.
Freedom's of *English* growth, I think, alone;
What for lost *English* Freedom can attone?
A Free-born Player loathes to be compell'd;
Our Rulers Tyrannized, and We Rebell'd.
Freedom! the Wise Man's Wish, the Poor Man's Wealth;
Which you, and I, and most of us enjoy by Stealth;
The Soul of Pleasure, and the Sweet of Life.
The Woman's Charter, Widow, Maid or Wife,
This they'd have cancell'd, and thence grew the Strife.
But you perhaps wou'd have me here confess
How we obtain'd the Favour–Can't you guess?
Why then I'll tell you (for I hate a Lie)
By Brib'ry, errant Brib'ry, let me dye:
I was their Agent, but by Jove I swear
No honourable Member had a share,
Tho' young and able Members bid me Fair:
I chose a wiser way to make you willing,
Which has not cost the House a single Shilling;
Now you suspect at least I went a-Billing.
You see I'm Young, and to that Air of Youth,
Some will add Beauty, and a little Truth;
These Pow'rful Charms, improv'd by Pow'rful Arts,
Prevail'd to captivate your op'ning Hearts.

21 *Taskmasters:* patentees of Drury Lane, whose monopoly of the stage was broken by the new Lincoln's Inn Theatre.

Thus furnish'd, I prefer'd my poor Petition,
And brib'd ye to commiserate our Condition:
I Laugh'd, and Sigh'd, and Sung, and Leer'd upon ye;
With Roguish Loving Looks, and that way won ye:
The Young Men kiss'd me, and the Old I kiss'd,
And luringly I led them as I list.
The Ladies in mere Pity took our Parts,
Pity's the darling Passion of their Hearts.
Thus Bribing, or thus Brib'd, fear no Disgraces;
For thus you may take Bribes, and keep your Places.

Prologue.

Spoken at the opening of the New House,

By Mr. *Betterton.*[*]

The Husbandman in vain renews his Toil,
To cultivate each Year a hungry Soil;
And fondly hopes for rich and generous Fruit,
When what should feed the Tree, devours the Root:
Th' unladen Boughs, he sees, bode certain Dearth,
Unless transplanted to more kindly Earth.
So, the poor Husbands of the Stage, who found
Their Labours lost upon the ungrateful Ground,
This last and only Remedy have prov'd;
And hope new Fruit from ancient Stocks remov'd.
Well may they hope, when you so kindly aid,
And plant a Soil which you so rich have made.
As Nature gave the World to Man's first Age,
So from your Bounty, we receive this Stage;
The Freedom Man was born to, you've restor'd,
And to our World, such Plenty you afford,
It seems like *Eden,* fruitful of its own accord.
But since in *Paradise* frail Flesh give way,
And when but two were made, both went astray;
Forbear your Wonder, and the Fault forgive,
If in our larger Family we grieve
One falling *Adam,* and one tempted *Eve.*

* leader of the revolt from Drury Lane; although sixty years old, he filled the role of Valentine with great success.

22 *Adam . . . Eve:* Joseph Williams and Susanna Mountfort, actors who deserted the new company to return to Drury Lane.

We who remain, would gratefully repay
What our Endeavours can, and bring this day,
The First-fruit Offering of a Virgin Play.
We hope there's something that may please each Taste,
And tho' of Homely Fare we make the Feast,
Yet you will find variety at least.
There's Humour, which for chearful Friends we got,
And for the thinking Party there's a Plot.
We've something too, to gratify ill Nature
(If there be any here) and that is Satire.
Though Satire scarce dares grin, 'tis grown so mild;
Or only shews its Teeth, as if it smil'd.
As Asses Thistles, Poets mumble Wit,
And dare not bite, for fear of being bit.
They hold their Pens, as Swords are held by Fools,
And are afraid to use their own Edge-Tools.
Since the *Plain-Dealer's* Scenes of Manly Rage,
Not one has dar'd to lash this Crying Age.
This time the Poet owns the bold Essay,
Yet hopes there's no ill-manners in his Play:
And he declares by me, he has design'd
Affront to none, but frankly speaks his mind.
And shou'd th' ensuing Scenes not chance to hit,
He offers but this one Excuse: 'twas writ
Before your late Encouragement of Wit.

Dramatis Personæ

MEN

SIR SAMPSON LEGEND, Father to VALENTINE and BEN.	Mr. Underhill
VALENTINE, Fallen under his Father's Displeasure by his expensive way of living, in love with ANGELICA.	Mr. Betterton
SCANDAL, His Friend, a Free Speaker.	Mr. Smith
TATTLE, A half-witted Beau, vain of his Amours, yet valuing himself for Secrecy.	Mr. Bowman

40 *Plain-Dealer's . . .Manly Rage:* Manly, a principal character in Wycherley's biting comedy of 1676.

BEN, SIR SAMPSON's Younger Son, half home-bred, and half Sea-bred, design'd to marry MISS PRUE.	Mr. Dogget
FORESIGHT, An illiterate Old Fellow, peevish and positive, superstitious, and pretending to understand Astrology, Palmistry, Physiognomy, Omens, Dreams, *Etc.* Uncle to ANGELICA.	Mr. Sanford
JEREMY, Servant to VALENTINE.	Mr. Bowen
TRAPLAND, A Scrivener.	Mr. Triffusis
BUCKRAM, A Lawyer.	Mr. Freeman

WOMEN

ANGELICA, Niece to FORESIGHT, of a considerable Fortune in her own Hands.	Mrs. Bracegirdle
MRS. FORESIGHT, Second Wife to FORESIGHT.	Mrs. Bowman
MRS. FRAIL, Sister to MRS. FORESIGHT, a Woman of the Town.	Mrs. Barry
MISS PRUE, Daughter to FORESIGHT by a former Wife, a silly, awkward, Country Girl.	Mrs. Ayliff
NURSE, to MISS PRUE.	Mrs. Leigh
JENNY, Maid to ANGELICA.	Mrs. Lawson

A Steward, Officers, Sailers, and several Servants.

The SCENE in LONDON

LOVE FOR LOVE.

ACT I. SCENE I.

Valentine *in his Chamber, Reading.* Jeremy *waiting.*

Several Books upon the Table.

VALENTINE. *Jeremy.*

JEREMY. Sir.

VALENTINE. Here, take away. I'll walk a turn and digest what I have read–

JEREMY (*aside and taking away the Books*). You'll grow Devilish fat upon this Paper Diet.

VALENTINE. And d'ye hear, go you to Breakfast.– There's a Page doubled down in *Epictetus* that is a Feast for an Emperor.

JEREMY. Was *Epictetus* a real Cook, or did he only write Receipts?

VALENTINE. Read, read, Sirrah, and refine your Appetite; learn to live upon Instruction; feast your Mind, and mortify your Flesh; Read, and take your Nourishment in at your Eyes; shut up your Mouth, and chew the Cud of Understanding. So *Epictetus* advises.

JEREMY. O Lord! I have heard much of him when I waited upon a Gentleman at *Cambridge*: Pray, what was that *Epictetus?*

VALENTINE. A very rich Man.–Not worth a Groat.

JEREMY. Humph, and so he has made a very fine Feast, where there is nothing to be eaten.

VALENTINE. Yes.

JEREMY. Sir, you're a Gentleman, and probably understand this fine Feeding; but if you please, I had rather be at Board-Wages. Does your *Epictetus,* or your *Seneca* here, or any of these poor rich Rogues, teach you how to pay your Debts without Money? Will they shut up the Mouths of your Creditors? Will *Plato* be Bail for you? Or *Diogenes,* because he understands Confinement and liv'd in a Tub, go to Prison for you? 'Slife, Sir, what do you mean, to mew yourself up here with Three or Four musty Books in commendation of Starving and Poverty?

VALENTINE. Why, Sirrah, I have no Money, you know it; and therefore resolve to rail at all that have: and in that I but follow the Examples of the wisest and wittiest Men in all Ages; these Poets and Philosophers whom you naturally hate, for just such another Reason: because they abound in Sense, and you are a Fool.

8 *Epictetus:* Greek Stoic philospher who preached indifference to life's evils.

JEREMY. Aye, Sir, I am a Fool, I know it; And yet, Heav'n help me, I'm poor enough to be a Wit. But I was always a Fool when I told you what your Expences would bring you to; your Coaches and your Liveries; your Treats and your Balls; your being in Love with a Lady that did not care a Farthing for you in your Prosperity; and keeping Company with Wits that car'd for nothing but your Prosperity; and now when you are poor, hate you as much as they do one another.

VALENTINE. Well, and now I am poor, I have an opportunity to be reveng'd on 'em all; I'll pursue *Angelica* with more Love than ever, and appear more notoriously her Admirer in this Restraint, than when I openly rival'd the rich Fops that made Court to her; so shall my Poverty be a Mortification to her Pride, and perhaps, make her compassionate that Love which has principally reduc'd me to this Lowness of Fortune. And for the Wits, I'm sure I'm in a Condition to be even with them—

JEREMY. Nay, your Condition is pretty even with theirs, that's the truth on't.

VALENTINE. I'll take some of their Trade out of their Hands.

JEREMY. Now Heav'n of Mercy continue the Tax upon Paper; you don't mean to write!

VALENTINE. Yes, I do; I'll write a Play.

JEREMY. Hem!—Sir, if you please to give me a small Certificate of Three Lines—only to certify those whom it may concern: that the Bearer hereof, *Jeremy Fetch* by Name, has for the space of Sev'n Years truly and faithfully serv'd *Valentine Legend* Esq; and that he is not now turn'd away for any Misdemeanour; but does voluntarily dismiss his Master from any future Authority over him—

VALENTINE. No, Sirrah, you shall live with me still.

JEREMY. Sir, it's impossible—I may die with you, starve with you, or be damn'd with your Works; But to live even Three days, the Life of a Play, I no more

58 *compassionate:* take pity on.
80 *three days:* house receipts on the third night went to the author.

expect it than to be Canoniz'd for a Muse after my Decease.

VALENTINE. You are witty, you Rogue! I shall want your Help; I'll have you learn to make Couplets, to tag the ends of Acts, d'ye hear, get the Maids to Crambo in an Evening, and learn the knack of Rhyming: you may arrive at the height of a Song, sent by an unknown Hand, or a Chocolate-House Lampoon.

JEREMY. But Sir, is this the way to recover your Father's Favour? Why, Sir *Sampson* will be irreconcilable. If your Younger Brother shou'd come from Sea, he'd never look upon you again. You're undone, Sir; you're ruin'd; you won't have a Friend left in the World if you turn Poet.—Ah, Pox confound that *Will's* Coffee-House; it has ruin'd more Young Men than the *Royal Oak* Lottery. Nothing thrives that belongs to't. The Man of the House would have been an Alderman by this time with half the Trade if he had set up in the City. For my part, I never sit at the Door that I don't get double the Stomach that I do at a Horse-Race. The Air upon *Banstead Downs* is nothing to it for a Whetter; yet I never see it, but the Spirit of Famine appears to me; sometimes like a decay'd Porter, worn out with pimping and carrying *Billet-doux* and Songs; not like other Porters for Hire, but for the Jest's sake; now like a thin Chairman, melted down to half his Proportion with carrying a Poet upon Tick to visit some great Fortune; and his Fare to be paid him like the Wages of Sin, either at the Day of Marriage, or the Day of Death.

VALENTINE. Very well, Sir; can you proceed?

JEREMY. Sometimes like a bilk'd Bookseller, with a meagre terrify'd Countenance, that looks as if he had written for himself, or were resolv'd to turn Author and bring the rest of his Brethren into the same Condition. And Lastly, In the Form of a worn-out Punk, with Verses in her Hand, which her Vanity had pre-

85 *Crambo:* 'A play at which one gives a word, to which another finds a rhyme.' (Johnson, *Dictionary.*)
94 *Will's:* resort of Congreve and the literati, presided over by Dryden.
96 *Royal Oak Lottery:* yearly lottery suppressed in 1699.
101 *Banstead Downs:* racecourse near Epsom in Surrey known for its bracing air.
116 *Punk:* prostitiute.

ferr'd to Settlements, without a whole Tatter to her Tail, but as ragged as one of the Muses; or as if she were carrying her Linen to the Paper Mill, to be converted into Folio Books, of Warning to all Young Maids not to prefer Poetry to good Sense; or lying in the Arms of a needy Wit, before the Embraces of a wealthy Fool.

Enter Scandal.

SCANDAL. What, *Jeremy* holding forth?

VALENTINE. The Rogue has (with all the Wit he could muster up) been declaiming against Wit.

SCANDAL. Aye? Why then I'm afraid *Jeremy* has Wit; for wherever it is, it's always contriving its own Ruin.

JEREMY. Why, so I have been telling my Master, Sir. Mr. *Scandal,* for Heaven's sake, Sir, try if you can dissuade him from turning Poet.

SCANDAL. Poet! He shall turn Soldier first, and rather depend upon the outside of his Head than the Lining. Why, what the Devil, has not your Poverty made you Enemies enough? Must you needs show your Wit to get more?

JEREMY. Ay, more indeed; for who cares for anybody that has more Wit than himself?

SCANDAL. *Jeremy* speaks like an Oracle. Don't you see how worthless great Men, and dull rich Rogues, avoid a witty Man of small Fortune? Why, he looks like a Writ of Enquiry into their Titles and Estates; and seems Commission'd by Heav'n to seize the better half.

VALENTINE. Therefore, I would rail in my Writings, and be reveng'd.

SCANDAL. Rail? At whom? the whole World? Impotent and vain! Who would die a Martyr to Sense in a Country where the Religion is Folly? You may stand at Bay for a while; but when the full Cry is against you, you won't have fair Play for your Life. If you can't be fairly run down by the Hounds, you will be treacherously shot by the Huntsmen.—No, turn Pimp, Flatterer, Quack, Lawyer, Parson, be Chaplain to an Atheist, or Stallion to an Old Woman, anything but

Poet; a Modern Poet is worse, more servile, timorous, and fawning, than any I have nam'd; without you could retrieve the Ancient Honours of the Name, recall the Stage of *Athens*, and be allow'd the force of open honest Satire.

VALENTINE. You are as inveterate against our Poets as if your Character had been lately expos'd upon the Stage.—Nay, I am not violently bent upon the Trade.

One Knocks.

Jeremy, see who's there.

Exit Jeremy.

But tell me what you would have me do?—What do the World say of me, and of my forc'd Confinement?

SCANDAL. The World behaves itself as it used to do on such Occasions; some pity you, and condemn your Father; Others excuse him, and blame you; only the Ladies are merciful and wish you well, since Love and Pleasurable Expence have been your greatest faults.

Enter Jeremy.

VALENTINE. How now?

JEREMY. Nothing new, Sir; I have dispatch'd some half a Dozen Duns with as much Dexterity as a hungry Judge does Causes at Dinner time.

VALENTINE. What answer have you given 'em?

SCANDAL. Patience, I suppose, the old Receipt.

JEREMY. No, faith, Sir; I have put 'em off so long with patience and forbearance and other fair words, that I was forc'd now to tell 'em in plain downright *English*—

VALENTINE. What?

JEREMY. That they should be paid.

VALENTINE. When?

JEREMY. Tomorrow.

159 *without:* unless.

179 *Duns:* debt collectors.

180 *hungry Judges:* a common jibe of the time. 'The hungry Judges soon the Sentence sign,/And Wretches hang that Jury-men may Dine.' (Pope, *Rape of the Lock*, iii, 21-22.)

VALENTINE. And how the Devil do you mean to keep your word?

JEREMY. Keep it? Not at all; it has been so very much stretch'd, that I reckon it will break of course by tomorrow, and nobody be surpris'd at the Matter. *(Knocking.)* Again! Sir, if you don't like my Negotiation, will you be pleas'd to answer these yourself.

VALENTINE. See who they are.

Exit Jeremy.

By this, *Scandal*, you may see what it is to be great; Secretaries of State, Presidents of the Council, and Generals of an Army lead just such a life as I do, have just such Crowds of Visitants in a morning, all soliciting of past promises; which are but a civiller sort of Duns, that lay claim to voluntary Debts.

SCANDAL. And you, like a true great Man, having engaged their Attendance, and promis'd more than ever you intend to perform, are more perplex'd to find Evasions than you would be to invent the honest means of keeping your word, and gratifying your Creditors.

VALENTINE. *Scandal*, learn to spare your Friends, and do not provoke your Enemies; this liberty of your Tongue will one day bring a Confinement on your Body, my Friend.

Re-enter Jeremy.

JEREMY. O Sir, there's *Trapland* the Scrivener, with two suspicious Fellows like lawful Pads, that wou'd knock a Man down with Pocket-Tipstaves—and there's your Father's Steward, and the Nurse with one of your Children from *Twitnam*.

VALENTINE. Pox on her, cou'd she find no other time to fling my Sins in my Face? Here, give her this, *(Gives Money.)* and bid her trouble me no more. A thoughtless two-handed Whore, she knows my Condition well enough and might have overlaid the Child a Fortnight ago if she had had any forecast in her.

217 *Scrivener:* here, a money lender.
218 *lawful Pads:* robbers, but with the law on their side.
219 *Pocket-Tipstaves:* bailiff's staffs with a metal head.
221 *Twitnam:* Twickenham.
226 *overlaid:* smothered.
227 *forecast:* foresight.

SCANDAL. What, is it Bouncing *Margery* and my Godson?

JEREMY. Yes, Sir.

SCANDAL. My Blessing to the Boy, with this Token *(Gives Money.)* of my Love. And d'ye hear, bid *Margery* put more Flocks in her Bed, shift twice a Week, and not work so hard, that she may not smell so vigorously.—I shall take the Air shortly.

VALENTINE. *Scandal,* don't spoil my Boy's Milk.—Bid *Trapland* come in.

Exit Jeremy.

If I can give that *Cerberus* a Sop, I shall be at rest for one day.

Enter Trapland *and* Jeremy

O Mr. *Trapland!* my old Friend! Welcome. *Jeremy,* a Chair quickly; a Bottle of Sack and a Toast—fly—a Chair first.

TRAPLAND. A good Morning to you, Mr. *Valentine,* and to you, Mr. *Scandal.*

SCANDAL. The Morning's a very good Morning, if you don't spoil it.

VALENTINE. Come sit you down, you know his way.

TRAPLAND *(sits).* There is a Debt, Mr. *Valentine,* of 1500 *l.* of pretty long standing—

VALENTINE. I cannot talk about Business with a Thirsty Palate.—Sirrah, the Sack.—

TRAPLAND. And I desire to know what Course you have taken for the Payment?

VALENTINE. Faith and Troth, I am heartily glad to see you—my Service to you—fill, fill, to honest Mr. *Trapland,* fuller.

TRAPLAND. Hold, Sweet-heart. This is not to our Business—my Service to you, Mr. *Scandal.* *(Drinks.)* I have forborn as long—

VALENTINE. T'other Glass, and then we'll talk. Fill, *Jeremy.*

243 *Sack:* sherry.

TRAPLAND. No more, in truth.—I have forborn, I say—

VALENTINE. Sirrah, fill when I bid you.—And how do's your handsome Daughter? Come, a good Husband to her.

Drinks.

TRAPLAND. Thank you.—I have been out of this Money—

VALENTINE. Drink first. *Scandal,* why do you not Drink?

They Drink.

TRAPLAND. And in short, I can be put off no longer.

VALENTINE. I was much oblig'd to you for your Supply: It did me Signal Service in my necessity. But you delight in doing good.—*Scandal,* Drink to me my Friend *Trapland's* Health. An honester Man lives not, nor one more ready to serve his Friend in Distress, tho' I say it to his face. Come, fill each Man his Glass.

SCANDAL. What, I know *Trapland* has been a Whoremaster, and loves a Wench still. You never knew a Whoremaster that was not an honest Fellow.

TRAPLAND. Fie, Mr. *Scandal,* you never knew—

SCANDAL. What don't I know?—I know the Buxom black Widow in the *Poultry—800 l.* a Year Jointure, and *20000 l.* in Money. Ahah, Old *Trap!*

VALENTINE. Say you so, I'faith! Come, we'll remember the Widow; I know whereabouts you are. Come, to the Widow!

TRAPLAND. No more indeed.

VALENTINE. What, the Widow's Health; give it him —off with it!

They Drink.

A Lovely Girl, I'faith, black sparkling Eyes, soft pouting Ruby-Lips! Better sealing there than a Bond for a Million, hah!

TRAPLAND. No, no, there's no such thing; we'd better mind our business.—You're a Wag.

288 *Poultry:* street east of Cheapside containing poulterers' shops.

VALENTINE. No, faith, we'll mind the Widow's business. Fill again. Pretty round heaving Breasts, a *Barbary* shape, and a Jut with her Bum would stir an *Anchoret;* And the prettiest Foot! Oh, if a Man could but fasten his Eyes to her Feet, as they steal in and out, and play at Bo-peep under her Petticoats, ah, Mr. *Trapland?*

TRAPLAND. Verily, give me a Glass—you're a Wag—and here's to the Widow.

Drinks.

SCANDAL. He begins to Chuckle; ply him close, or he'll relapse into a Dun.

Enter Officer.

OFFICER. By your leave, Gentlemen.—Mr. *Trapland* if we must do our Office, tell us. We have half a dozen Gentlemen to Arrest in *Pall-Mall* and *Covent-Garden;* and if we don't make haste the Chairmen will be abroad and block up the Chocolate-Houses, and then our labour's lost.

TRAPLAND. Udso, that's true. Mr. *Valentine,* I love Mirth, but business must be done. Are you ready to—

JEREMY. Sir, your Father's Steward says he comes to make Proposals concerning your Debts.

VALENTINE. Bid him come in. Mr. *Trapland,* send away your Officer. You shall have an answer presently.

TRAPLAND. Mr. *Snap,* stay within Call.

Exit Officer.

Enter Steward and Whispers Valentine.

SCANDAL. Here's a Dog now, a Traitor in his Wine. *(To Trapland.)* Sirrah, refund the Sack: *Jeremy,* fetch him some warm water, or I'll rip up his Stomach and go the shortest way to his Conscience.

TRAPLAND. Mr. *Scandal,* you are Uncivil; I did not value your Sack; but you cannot expect it again when I have drank it.

303 *Barbary shape:* as well-shaped as an Arabian horse from North Africa.
305 *Anchoret:* anchorite, a desert hermit.

SCANDAL. And how do you expect to have your Money again when a Gentleman has spent it?

VALENTINE. You need say no more; I understand the Conditions; they are very hard, but my Necessity is very pressing: I agree to 'em; take Mr. *Trapland* with you, and let him draw the Writing.—Mr. *Trapland,* you know this Man; he shall satisfy you.

TRAPLAND. Sincerely, I am loth to be thus pressing, but my necessity—

VALENTINE. No Apology, good Mr. Scrivener; you shall be paid.

TRAPLAND. I hope you forgive me; my business requires—

Exeunt Steward, Trapland *and* Jeremy.

SCANDAL. He begs Pardon like a Hangman at an Execution.

VALENTINE. But I have got a Reprieve.

SCANDAL. I am surpris'd; what, does your Father relent?

VALENTINE. No; He has sent me the hardest Conditions in the World. You have heard of a Booby Brother of mine that was sent to Sea three Years ago? This Brother, my Father hears, is Landed; whereupon he very affectionately sends me word, if I will make a Deed of Conveyance of my Right to his Estate after his Death to my younger Brother, he will immediately furnish me with Four thousand Pound to pay my Debts, and make my Fortune. This present impatience of my Creditors for their Money, and my own impatience of Confinement and absence from *Angelica,* force me to consent.

SCANDAL. A very desperate demonstration of your love to *Angelica;* and I think she has never given you any assurance of hers.

VALENTINE. You know her temper; she never gave me any great reason either for hope or despair.

SCANDAL. Women of her airy temper, as they seldom think before they act, so they rarely give us any light to guess at what they mean: but you have little reason to believe that a Woman of this Age, who has had an indifference for you in your Prosperity, will fall in love with your ill Fortune; besides, *Angelica* has a great Fortune of her own; and great Fortunes either expect another great Fortune, or a Fool.

Enter Jeremy.

JEREMY. More Misfortunes, Sir.

VALENTINE. What, another Dun?

JEREMY. No Sir, but Mr. *Tattle* is come to wait upon you.

VALENTINE. Well, I can't help it,—you must bring him up; He knows I don't go abroad.

Exit Jeremy.

SCANDAL. Pox on him, I'll be gone.

VALENTINE. No, prithee stay: *Tattle* and you should never be asunder; you are light and shadow, and show one another; he is perfectly thy reverse both in humour and understanding; and as you set up for Defamation, he is a mender of Reputations.

SCANDAL. A mender of Reputations! Aye, just as he is a keeper of secrets, another Virtue that he sets up for in the same manner. For the Rogue will speak aloud in the posture of a Whisper, and deny a Woman's name while he gives you the marks of her Person. He will forswear receiving a Letter from her, and at the same time show you her Hand upon the Superscription; and yet perhaps he has Counterfeited the Hand too; and sworn to a truth; but he hopes not to be believ'd; and refuses the reputation of a Lady's favour, as a Doctor says No to a Bishopric, only that it may be granted him. In short, he is a publick Professor of Secrecy, and makes Proclamation that he holds private Intelligence.—He's here.

Enter Tattle.

TATTLE. *Valentine,* good Morrow; *Scandal* I am Yours—That is, when you speak well of me.

SCANDAL. That is, when I am yours; for while I am

TATTLE. How Inhuman!

my own, or anybody's else, that will never happen.

VALENTINE. Why *Tattle,* you need not be much concern'd at anything that he says: for to converse with *Scandal* is to play at *Losing Loadum;* you must lose a good Name to him before you can win it for yourself.

TATTLE. But how Barbarous that is, and how unfortunate for him, that the World shall think the better of any Person for his Calumniation! I thank Heav'n it has always been a part of my Character to handle the Reputation of others very tenderly.

SCANDAL. Ay, such rotten Reputations as you have to deal with are to be handl'd tenderly indeed.

TATTLE. Nay, but why rotten? Why should you say rotten, when you know not the persons of whom you speak? How cruel that is.

SCANDAL. Not know 'em? Why, thou never hadst to do with anybody that did not stink to all the Town.

TATTLE. Ha, ha, ha! Nay, now you make a Jest of it indeed. For there is nothing more known, than that nobody knows anything of that nature of me. As I hope to be sav'd, *Valentine,* I never expos'd a Woman since I knew what Woman was.

VALENTINE. And yet you have convers'd with several.

TATTLE. To be free with you, I have—I don't care if I own that. Nay more (I'm going to say a bold Word now), I never could meddle with a Woman that had to do with anybody else.

SCANDAL. How!

VALENTINE. Nay faith, I'm apt to believe him.—Except her Husband, *Tattle.*

TATTLE. O that—

SCANDAL. What think you of that Noble Commoner, Mrs. *Drab* ?

TATTLE. Pooh, I know Madam *Drab* has made her Brags in three or four places that I said this and that, and writ to her, and did I know not what—but, upon

418 *Losing Loadum:* card game in which the winner takes the fewest tricks.

my Reputation, she did me wrong.—Well, well, that was Malice—but I know the bottom of it. She was brib'd to that by one that we all know—A Man too—only to bring me into Disgrace with a certain Woman of Quality—

SCANDAL. Whom we all know.

TATTLE. No matter for that.—Yes, yes, everybody knows—No doubt on't, everybody knows my Secrets. But I soon satisfied the Lady of my Innocence; for I told her—Madam, says I, there are some Persons who make it their Business to tell Stories, and say this and that of one and t'other, and everything in the World; and, says I, if your Grace—

SCANDAL. Grace!

TATTLE. O Lord, what have I said? My Unlucky Tongue!

VALENTINE. Ha, ha, ha!

SCANDAL. Why, Tattle, thou has more Impudence than one can in reason expect: I shall have an esteem for thee. Well, and ha, ha, ha! well, go on, and what did you say to her Grace?

VALENTINE. I confess this is something extraordinary.

TATTLE. Not a word, as I hope to be sav'd; an errant *Lapsus Linguæ.* Come, let's talk of something else.

VALENTINE. Well, but how did you acquit yourself?

TATTLE. Pooh, pooh, nothing at all, I only rallied with you.—A Woman of ord'nary Rank was a little jealous of me, and I told her something or other, faith —I know not what.—Come, let's talk of something else. *Hums a Song.*

SCANDEL. Hang him, let him alone; he has a mind we should enquire.

TATTLE. *Valentine,* I Supp'd last Night with your Mistress, and her Uncle, Old *Foresight.* I think your Father lies at *Foresight's?*

VALENTINE. Yes.

TATTLE. Upon my Soul, *Angelica's* a fine Woman—and so is Mrs. *Foresight,* and her Sister Mrs. *Frail.*

SCANDEL. Yes, Mrs. *Frail* is a very fine Woman; we all know her.

TATTLE. Oh, that is not fair.

SCANDAL. What?

TATTLE. To tell.

SCANDAL. To tell what? Why, what do you know of Mrs. *Frail*?

TATTLE. Who, I? Upon Honour I don't know whether she be Man or Woman but by the smoothness of her Chin and roundness of her Lips.

SCANDAL. No!

TATTLE. No.

SCANDAL. She says otherwise.

TATTLE. Impossible!

SCANDAL. Yes, Faith. Ask *Valentine* else.

TATTLE. Why then, as I hope to be sav'd, I believe a Woman only obliges a Man to Secrecy that she may have the pleasure of telling herself.

SCANDAL. No doubt on't. Well, but has she done you wrong, or no? You have had her? Ha?

TATTLE. Tho' I have more Honour than to tell first, I have more Manners than to contradict what a Lady has declar'd.

SCANDAL. Well, you own it?

TATTLE. I am strangely surpris'd! Yes, yes, I can't deny't, if she taxes me with it.

SCANDAL. She'll be here by and by; she sees *Valentine* every Morning.

TATTLE. How!

VALENTINE. She does me the favour—I mean of a Visit sometimes. I did not think she had granted more to anybody.

SCANDAL. Nor I, faith—but *Tattle* does not use to bely a Lady; it is contrary to his Character.—How one may be deceiv'd in a Woman, *Valentine!*

TATTLE. Nay, what do you mean, Gentlemen?

SCANDAL. I'm resolv'd I'll ask her.

TATTLE. O Barbarous! Why did you not tell me—

SCANDAL. No, you told us.

TATTLE. And bid me ask *Valentine.*

VALENTINE. What did I say? I hope you won't bring me to confess an Answer, when you never ask'd me the Question.

TATTLE. But, Gentlemen, this is the most inhuman Proceeding—

VALENTINE. Nay, if you have known *Scandal* thus long, and cannot avoid such a palpable Decoy as this was, the Ladies have a fine time whose Reputations are in your keeping.

Enter Jeremy.

JEREMY. Sir, Mrs. *Frail* has sent to know if you are stirring.

VALENTINE. Show her up when she comes.

Exit Jeremy.

TATTLE. I'll be gone.

VALENTINE. You'll meet her.

TATTLE. Have you not a back way?

VALENTINE. If there were, you have more Discretion than to give *Scandal* such an Advantage; why, your running away will prove all that he can tell her.

TATTLE. *Scandal,* you will not be so ungenerous.—O, I shall lose my Reputation of Secrecy forever.—I shall never be receiv'd but upon Publick Days, and my Visits will never be admitted beyond a Drawing Room: I shall never see a Bed Chamber again, never be lock't in a Closet, nor run behind a Screen, or under a Table; never be distinguish'd among the Waiting-Women by the Name of Trusty Mr. *Tattle* more.—You will not be so cruel!

VALENTINE. *Scandal,* have pity on him; he'll yield to any Conditions.

TATTLE. Any, any Terms.

SCANDAL. Come then, sacrifice half a Dozen Women of good Reputation to me presently. Come, where are you familiar?—And see that they are Women of Quality too, the first Quality.

TATTLE. 'Tis very hard. Won't a Baronet's Lady pass?

SCANDAL. No, nothing under a Right Honourable.

TATTLE. O inhuman! You don't expect their Names.

SCANDAL. No, their Titles shall serve.

TATTLE. Alas, that's the same thing. Pray spare me their Titles; I'll describe their Persons.

SCANDAL. Well, begin then; but take notice, if you are so ill a Painter that I cannot know the Person by your Picture of her, you must be condemned, like other bad Painters, to write the Name at the bottom.

TATTLE. Well, first then—

Enter Mrs. Frail.

O unfortunate! She's come already; will you have Patience till another time—I'll double the number.

SCANDAL. Well, on that Condition. Take heed you don't fail me.

MRS. FRAIL. Hey day! I shall get a fine Reputation by coming to see Fellows in a Morning. *Scandal,* you Devil, are you here too? Oh Mr. *Tattle,* everything is safe with you, we know.

SCANDAL. *Tattle!*

TATTLE. Mum.—O, Madam, you do me too much Honour.

VALENTINE. Well Lady Galloper, how does *Angelica?*

MRS. FRAIL. *Angelica?* Manners!

VALENTINE. What, you will allow an absent Lover—

MRS. FRAIL. No, I'll allow a Lover present with his Mistress to be particular, but otherwise I think his Passion ought to give place to his Manners.

VALENTINE. But what if he have more Passion than Manners?

MRS. FRAIL. Then let him Marry and reform.

VALENTINE. Marriage indeed may qualify the Fury of his Passion, but it very rarely mends a Man's Manners.

MRS. FRAIL. You are the most mistaken in the World; there is no Creature perfectly Civil but a Husband. For in a little time he grows only rude to his Wife, and that is the highest good Breeding, for it begets his Civility to other People. Well, I'll tell you News; but I suppose you hear your Brother *Benjamin* is landed. And my Brother *Foresight's* Daughter is come out of the Country.—I assure you, there's a Match talk'd of by the Old People.—Well, if he be but as great a Sea-Beast as she is a Land-Monster, we shall have a most Amphibious Breed. The Progeny will be all Otters; he has been bred at Sea, and she has never been out of the Country.

VALENTINE. Pox take 'em, their Conjunction bodes no good, I'm sure.

MRS. FRAIL. Now you talk of Conjunction, my Brother *Foresight* has cast both their Nativities, and prognosticates an Admiral and an eminent Justice of the Peace to be the Issue-Male of their two Bodies. Tis the most superstitious Old Fool! He would have persuaded me that this was an Unlucky Day and wou'd not let me come abroad. But I invented a Dream, and sent him to *Artimedorus* for Interpretation, and so stole out to see you. Well, and what will you give me now? Come, I must have something.

VALENTINE. Step into the next Room—and I'll give you something.

SCANDAL. Ay, we'll all give you something.

MRS. FRAIL. Well, what will you all give me?

VALENTINE. Mine's a Secret.

MRS. FRAIL. I thought you would give me something that would be a trouble to you to keep.

627 *Artemidorus:* Greek soothsayer, second century A.D. His *Oneirocritica* was the authoritative work on the interpretation of dreams.

VALENTINE. And *Scandal* shall give you a good Name.

MRS. FRAIL. That's more than he has for himself. And what will you give me, Mr. *Tattle?*

TATTLE. I? My Soul, Madam.

MRS. FRAIL. Pooh, No, I thank you; I have enough to do to take care of my own. Well; but I'll come and see you one of these Mornings: I hear you have a great many Pictures.

TATTLE. I have a pretty good Collection at your Service, some Originals.

SCANDAL. Hang him, he has nothing but the *Seasons* and the *Twelve Cæsars,* paltry Copies; and the *Five Senses,* as ill represented as they are in himself. And he himself is the only Original you will see there.

MRS. FRAIL. Ay, but I hear he has a Closet of Beauties.

SCANDAL. Yes, all that have done him Favours, if you will believe him.

MRS. FRAIL. Ay, let me see those, Mr. *Tattle.*

TATTLE. Oh Madam, those are Sacred to Love and Contemplation. No Man but the Painter and myself was ever blest with the Sight.

MRS. FRAIL. Well, but a Woman–

TATTLE. Nor Woman, till she consented to have her Picture there too–for then she is obliged to keep the Secret.

SCANDAL. No, no; come to me if you wou'd see Pictures.

MRS. FRAIL. You?

SCANDAL. Yes, Faith, I can show you your own Picture, and most of your Acquaintance to the Life, and as like as at *Kneller's.*

648-50 *Seasons . . . Five Senses:* cheap popular prints of the day. Several modern editions of *Love for Love* note that the Twelve Caesars, ascribed to Titian, are present on the wall of the brothel in Hogarth's *Rakes Progress,* III.

669 *Kneller's:* Sir Godfrey Kneller (1646-1726), fashionable portrait painter.

MRS. FRAIL. O lying Creature—*Valentine*, does not he lie?—I can't believe a word he says.

VALENTINE. No indeed, he speaks truth now: for as *Tattle* has Pictures of all that have granted him favours, he has the Pictures of all that have refus'd him; if Satires, Descriptions, Characters, and Lampoons are Pictures.

SCANDAL. Yes, mine are most in black and white.—And yet there are some set out in their true Colours, both Men and Women. I can show you Pride, Folly, Affectation, Wantonness, Inconstancy, Covetousness, Dissimulation, Malice, and Ignorance, all in one Piece. Then I can show you Lying, Foppery, Vanity, Cowardice, Bragging, Lechery, Impotence, and Ugliness in another Piece; and yet one of these is a celebrated Beauty, and t'other a profest Beau. I have Paintings too, some pleasant enough.

MRS. FRAIL. Come, let's hear 'em.

SCANDAL. Why, I have a Beau in a Bagnio, Cupping for a Complexion, and Sweating for a Shape.

MRS. FRAIL. So.

SCANDAL. Then I have a Lady burning of Brandy in a Cellar with a Hackney-Coachman.

MRS. FRAIL. O Devil! Well, but that Story is not true.

SCANDAL. I have some Hieroglyphicks too; I have a Lawyer with a hundred Hands, two Heads, and but one Face; a Divine with two Faces, and one Head; and I have a Solider with his Brains in his Belly, and his Heart where his Head shou'd be.

MRS. FRAIL. And no Head?

SCANDAL. No Head.

MRS. FRAIL. Pooh, this is all Invention. Have you ne'er a Poet?

SCANDAL. Yes, I have a Poet weighing Words, and selling Praise for Praise, and a Critick picking his Pocket. I have another large Piece too, representing a

688 *Bagnio:* turkish bath, often disreputable.
688 *Cupping for a Complexion:* bleeding to ensure a fashionable paleness.

School, where there are huge Proportion'd Criticks, with long Wigs, Lac'd Coats, *Steinkirk* Cravats, and terrible Faces; with Catcalls in their Hands, and Horn-Books about their Necks. I have many more of this kind, very well Painted, as you shall see.

MRS. FRAIL. Well, I'll come, if it be only to disprove you.

Enter Jeremy.

JEREMY. Sir, here's the Steward again from your Father.

VALENTINE. I'll come to him.—Will you give me leave, I'll wait on you again presently.

MRS. FRAIL. No, I'll be gone. Come, who Squires me to the *Exchange?* I must call my Sister *Foresight* there.

SCANDAL. I will; I have a mind to your Sister.

MRS. FRAIL. Civil!

TATTLE. I will; because I have a tender for your Ladyship.

MRS. FRAIL. That's somewhat the better reason, to my Opinion.

SCANDAL. Well, if *Tattle* entertains you, I have the better opportunity to engage your Sister.

VALENTINE. Tell *Angelica* I am about making hard Conditions to come abroad and be at Liberty to see her.

SCANDAL. I'll give an account of you, and your Proceedings. If Indiscretion be a sign of Love, you are the most a Lover of anybody that I know: you fancy that parting with your Estate will help you to your Mistress.—In my mind he is a thoughtless Adventurer.

708 *Steinkirk Cravats:* casually tied flowing neckcloths, named after the battle of Steenkirk, 1692, at which the French officers lacked time to tie them properly before the battle.
709 *Catcalls:* shrill pocket whistles used to express disapproval at the theatre.
709 *Hornbooks:* child's cards for learning the alphabet, originally protected by horn covers.
720 *Exchange:* fashionable shops with covered walkways in the Strand.

Who hopes to purchase Wealth, by selling Land;
Or win a Mistress, with a losing hand.

Exeunt.

ACT II. Scene I.

A Room in Foresight's *House.*

Foresight and Servant.

FORESIGHT. Hey day! What, are all the Women of my Family abroad? Is not my Wife come home? Nor my Sister, nor my Daughter?

SERVANT. No, Sir.

FORESIGHT. Mercy on us, what can be the meaning of it? Sure the Moon is in all her Fortitudes. Is my Niece *Angelica* at home?

SERVANT. Yes, Sir.

FORESIGHT. I believe you lie, Sir.

SERVANT. Sir?

FORESIGHT. I say you lie, Sir. It is impossible that anything should be as I would have it; for I was born, Sir, when the Crab was ascending, and all my Affairs go backward.

SERVANT. I can't tell indeed, Sir.

FORESIGHT. No, I know you can't, Sir: but I can tell, Sir, and foretell, Sir.

Enter Nurse.

Nurse, Where's your young Mistress?

NURSE. Wee'st heart, I know not; they're none of 'em come home yet: Poor Child, I warrant she's fond o'seeing the Town—marry, pray Heav'n they ha' given her any Dinner.—Good lack-a-day, ha, ha, ha, O strange; I'll vow and swear now, ha, ha, ha, marry, and did you ever see the like!

6 *Moon in all her Fortitudes:* the inconstant moon exerting her full influence, causing changes and uncertainty on earth.
13 *Crab ascending:* Cancer, the fourth sign of the Zodiac. Davis cites W. Ramesey, *Astrologie Restored* (1660), as Congreve's source for much of the astrological lore in the play.
20 *Wee'st heart:* woe's my heart.

FORESIGHT. Why, how now, what's the matter?

NURSE. Pray Heav'n send your Worship good Luck, marry and Amen with all my heart, for you have put on one Stocking with the wrong side outward.

FORESIGHT. Ha, how? Faith and troth I'm glad of it, and so I have! That may be good Luck in troth, in troth it may, very good Luck. Nay, I have had some Omens: I got out of Bed backwards too this morning, without Premeditation; pretty good that too. But then I stumbl'd coming downstairs, and met a Weasel; bad Omens those. Some bad, some good, our lives are checquer'd. Mirth and Sorrow, Want and Plenty, Night and Day, make up our time.—But in troth I am pleas'd at my Stocking, very well pleas'd at my Stocking.—Oh, here's my Niece!

Enter Angelica.

Sirrah, go tell Sir *Sampson Legend* I'll wait on him, if he's at leisure.—'Tis now Three o'clock, a very good hour for Business; *Mercury* governs this hour.

Exit Servant.

ANGELICA. Is not it a good hour for Pleasure too? Uncle, pray lend me your Coach; mine's out of Order.

FORESIGHT. What' wou'd you be gadding too? Sure all Females are mad today. It is of evil portent, and bodes Mischief to the Master of a Family.—I remember an old Prophecy written by Messehalah the *Arabian*, and thus translated by a Reverend *Buckinghamshire* Bard.

When Housewifes all the House forsake,
And leave good Man to Brew and Bake,
Withouten Guile, then be it said,
That House doth stond upon its Head;
And when the Head is set in Grond,
Ne marl, if it be fruitful fond.

Fruitful, the Head fruitful, that bodes Horns; the Fruit of the Head is Horns.—Dear Niece, stay at home

35 *Weasel:* favorite shape for a witch's familiar.
51 *Messahalah:* 9th century Jewish astrologer. Congreve drew several of these esoteric scholars from Ramesey, *op. cit.*, and from his own copy of William Lilly, *England's Phrophetícall Merline* (1644).
52 *Buckinghamshire Bard:* John Mason, contemporary hymn writer who attracted a following with his fanatical belief in the coming millennium.

—For by the Head of the House is meant the Husband; the Prophecy needs no Explanation.

ANGELICA. Well, but I can neither make you a Cuckold, Uncle, by going abroad, nor secure you from being one by staying at home.

FORESIGHT. Yes, yes; while there's one Woman left, the Prophecy is not in full Force.

ANGELICA. But my Inclinations are in force; I have a mind to go abroad, and if you won't lend me your Coach, I'll take a Hackney or a Chair and leave you to erect a Scheme and find who's in Conjunction with your Wife. Why don't you keep her at Home, if you're Jealous when she's abroad? You know my Aunt is a little Retrograde (as you call it) in her Nature. Uncle, I'm afraid you are not Lord of the Ascendant, ha, ha, ha.

FORESIGHT. Well, Jill-flirt, you are very pert—and always ridiculing that Celestrial Science.

ANGELICA. Nay Uncle, don't be angry.—If you are, I'll reap up all your false Prophecies, ridiculous Dreams, and idle Divinations. I'll swear you are a Nuisance to the Neighbourhood. What a Bustle did you keep against the last Invisible Eclipse, laying in Provision as 'twere for a Siege? What a World of Fire and Candle, Matches and Tinderboxes did you purchase! One would have thought we were ever after to live under Ground, or at least making a Voyage to *Greenland*, to inhabit there all the dark Season.

FORESIGHT. Why, you malapert Slut—

ANGELICA. Will you lend me your Coach, or I'll go on.—Nay, I'll declare how you prophesied Popery was coming, only because the Butler had mislaid some of the Apostle's Spoons, and thought they were lost. Away went Religion and Spoon-meat together. Indeed, Uncle, I'll indite you for a Wizard.

72-76 *erect a Scheme . . . Ascendant:* astrologer's terms from Ramesey, here with obvious double meanings.
84 *Last Invisible Eclipse:* Davis notes two eclipses of the sun during 1695 listed in almanacs as "not visible in London."
95 *Spoon-meat:* stew eaten with spoons like soup.

FORESIGHT. How, Hussie! Was there ever such a provoking Minx?

NURSE. O merciful Father, how she talks!

ANGELICA. Yes, I can make Oath of your unlawful Midnight Practices; you and the old Nurse there—

NURSE. Marry, Heav'n defend! I at Midnight Practices! —O Lord, what's here to do?—I in unlawful Doings with my Master's Worship?—Why, did you ever hear the like now?—Sir, did ever I do anything of your Midnight Concerns but warm your Bed, and tuck you up, and set the Candle, and your Tobacco-Box, and your Urinal by you, and now and then rub the Soles of your Feet?—O Lord, I!

ANGELICA. Yes, I saw you together, through the Key-hole of the Closet one Night, like *Saul* and the Witch of *Endor*, turning the Sieve and Sheers, and pricking Thumbs, to write poor innocent Servants' Names in Blood, about a little Nutmeg-Grater which she had forgot in the Caudle-Cup.—Nay, I know something worse, if I would speak of it—

FORESIGHT. I defie you, Hussy! But I'll remember this, I'll be reveng'd on you, Cockatrice; I'll hamper you.—You have your Fortune in your own Hands, but I'll find a way to make your Lover, your Prodigal Spendthrift Gallant, *Valentine*, pay for all, I will.

ANGELICA. Will you? I care not, but all shall out then.—Look to it, Nurse; I can bring Witness that you have a great unnatural Teat under your Left Arm, and he another, and that you Suckle a Young Devil in the Shape of a Tabby-Cat by turns, I can.

NURSE. A Teat, a Teat, I an unnatural Teat! O the false slanderous thing; feel, feel here, if I have any thing but like another Christian, *(Crying.)* or any Teats, but two that han't given Suck this Thirty Years.

FORESIGHT. I will have Patience, since it is the Will of the Stars I should be thus tormented. This

111 *Saul and the Witch of Endor:* see I. Samuel xxviii: 3-25.
112 *Sieve and shears:* divination by holding a sieve between the open points of a shears.
115 *Caudle:* spiced gruel mixed with wine.
118 *Cockatrice:* a fabulous monster, a prostitute.

is the effect of the malicious Conjunctions and Oppositions in the Third House of my Nativity; there the Curse of Kindred was foretold.—But I will have my Doors lock'd up—I'll punish you; not a Man shall enter my House.

ANGELICA. Do, Uncle, lock 'em up quickly before my Aunt come home. You'll have a Letter for Alimony tomorrow morning.—But let me be gone first, and then let no Mankind come near the House, but Converse with Spirits and the Celestial Signs, the Bull, and the Ram, and the Goat. Bless me! There are a great many Horn'd Beasts among the Twelve Signs, Uncle. But Cuckolds go to Heav'n.

FORESIGHT. But there's but one Virgin among the Twelve Signs, Spitfire, but one Virgin.

ANGELICA. Nor there had not been that one, if she had had to do with anything but Astrologers, Uncle. That makes my Aunt go abroad.

FORESIGHT. How? How? Is that the reason? Come, you know something; tell me, and I'll forgive you; do, good Niece.—Come, you shall have my Coach and Horses—Faith and Troth you shall—Does my Wife complain? Come, I know Women tell one another. She is young and sanguine, has a wanton Eye, and was born under *Gemini,* which may incline her to Society; she has a Mole upon her Lip, with a moist Palm, and an open Liberality on the Mount of *Venus.*

ANGELICA. Ha, ha, ha!

FORESIGHT. Do you laugh? Well, Gentlewoman, I'll —But come, be a good Girl, don't perplex your poor Uncle; tell me—won't you speak? Odd, I'll—

Enter Servant.

SERVANT. Sir *Sampson* is coming down to wait upon you—

ANGELICA. Goodbye, Uncle. *(To servant.)* Call me a Chair. I'll find out my Aunt, and tell her she must not come home.

Exit Angelica *and Servant.*

133 *Oppositions in the Third House:* the heavenly bodies influencing family relationships are 180° apart, indicating a falling-out.
157-9 *Gemini . . . Venus:* all signs of sensuality.

FORESIGHT. I'm so perplex'd and vex'd, I am not fit to receive him; I shall scarce recover myself before the Hour be past. Go, Nurse, tell Sir *Sampson* I'm ready to wait on him.

NURSE. Yes, Sir.

Exit.

FORESIGHT. Well—Why, if I was born to be a Cuckold, there's no more to be said—

Enter Sir Sampson Legend *with a Paper.*

SIR SAMPSON. Nor no more to be done, Old Boy, that's plain. Here 'tis, I have it in my Hand, Old *Ptolomee;* I'll make the ungracious Prodigal know who begat him, I will, old *Nostrodamus.* What, I warrant my Son thought nothing belong'd to a Father but Forgiveness and Affection; no Authority, no Correction, no Arbitrary Power; nothing to be done but for him to offend and me to pardon. I warrant you, if he danc'd till Doomsday, he thought I was to pay the Piper. Well, but here it is under Black and White, *Signatum, Sigillatum,* and *Deliberatum;* that as soon as my Son *Benjamin* is arriv'd he is to make over to him his Right of Inheritance. Where's my Daughter that is to be?—Hah! old *Merlin,* body o' me, I'm so glad I'm reveng'd on this undutiful Rogue.

FORESIGHT. Odso, let me see. Let me see the Paper. —Ay, faith and troth, here 'tis, if it will but hold. I wish things were done, and the Conveyance made.— When was this Sign'd, what Hour? Odso, you should have consulted me for the time. Well, but we'll make haste—

SIR SAMPSON. Haste, ay, ay, haste enough. My Son *Ben* will be in Town tonight. I have order'd my Lawyer to draw up Writings of Settlement and Jointure. All shall be done tonight. No matter for the time. Prithee, Brother *Foresight,* leave Superstition. —Pox o'th 'time! There's no time but the time present; there's no more to be said of what's past, and all that

181 *Old Ptolomee:* Ptolemaeus Alexandrinus, 2nd century A.D., in his *Almagest* the medieval authority on astronomy and astrology.

183 *Nostrodamus:* 16th-century French physician and astrologer; his *Centuries,* much translated, offer obscure predictions.

193 *Merlin:* the Arthurian magician reappeared in almanacs and as a character in Restoration plays.

is to come will happen. If the Sun shine by Day, and the Stars by Night, why, we shall know one another's Faces without the help of a Candle, and that's all the Stars are good for.

FORESIGHT. How, how? Sir *Sampson*, that all? Give me leave to contradict you, and tell you you are ignorant .

SIR SAMPSON. I tell you I am wise, and *sapiens dominabitur astris;* there's Latin for you to prove it, and an Argument to confound your *Ephemeris.*—Ignorant!—I tell you, I have travell'd, old *Fircu,* and know the Globe. I have seen the *Antipodes,* where the Sun rises at Midnight and sets at Noon-day.

FORESIGHT. But I tell you, I have travell'd, and travell'd in the Cœlestial *Spheres,* know the *Signs* and the *Planets,* and their Houses: Can judge of Motions Direct and Retrograde, of *Sextiles, Quadrates, Trines* and *Oppositions,* Fiery *Trigons* and Aquatical *Trigons;* know whether Life shall be long or short, Happy or Unhappy; whether Diseases are Cureable or Incurable; if Journeys shall be prosperous, Undertakings successful, or Goods stoll'n recover'd. I know—

SIR SAMPSON. I know the length of the Emperour of *China's* Foot, have kiss'd the Great *Mogul's* Slipper, and rid a Hunting upon an Elephant with the Cham of *Tartary.*—Body o' me, I have made a Cuckold of a King, and the present Majesty of *Bantam* is the Issue of these Loins.

FORESIGHT. I know when Travellers lie or speak Truth, when they don't know it themselves.

SIR SAMPSON. I have known an Astrologer made a Cuckold in the twinkling of a Star, and seen a Con-

215 *sapiens dominabitur astris:* "The wise man will be governed by the stars." Familiar tag ascribed, probably inaccurately, to Ptolemy.
217 *Ephemeris:* table showing predicted positions of heavenly bodies; the name of a monthly almanac.
218 *Fircu:* corrupt name for witch's familiar.
224 *Sextiles . . . Oppositions:* aspect of two heavenly bodies seen from earth separated from each other by a sixth, a quarter, a third, or half the circle of the Zodiac.
225 *Trigons:* conjunction of three signs of the Zodiac.
234 *Bantam:* port in western Java from which the English had recently been forced by the Dutch.

jurer that cou'd not keep the Devil out of his Wife's Circle.

FORESIGHT *(aside).* What, does he twit me with my Wife too? I must be better inform'd of this.—Do you mean my Wife, Sir *Sampson?* Tho' you made a Cuckold of the King of *Bantam*, yet by the Body of the Sun—

SIR SAMPSON. By the Horns of the Moon, you wou'd say, Brother *Capricorn.*

FORESIGHT. *Capricorn* in your Teeth, thou Modern *Mandevil; Ferdinand Mandez Pinto* was but a Type of thee, thou Liar of the first Magnitude. Take back your Paper of Inheritance; send your Son to Sea again. I'll wed my Daughter to an *Egyptian* Mummy, ere she shall Incorporate with a Contemner of Sciences, and a defamer of Virtue.

SIR SAMPSON. Body o' me, I have gone too far; I must not provoke honest *Albumazar.*—An *Egyptian* Mummy is an Illustrious Creature, my trusty Hieroglyphick, and may have significations of futurity about him; odsbud, I wou'd my Son were an *Egyptian* Mummy for thy sake. What, thou art not angry for a Jest, my good *Haly?* I Reverence the Sun, Moon and Stars with all my heart.—What, I'll make thee a Present of a Mummy. Now I think on't, Body o' me, I have a Shoulder of an *Egyptian* King that I purloin'd from one of the Pyramids, powder'd with Hieroglyphicks; thou shalt have it sent home to thy House, and make an Entertainment for all the *Philomaths* and Students in Physick and Astrology in and about *London.*

FORESIGHT. But what do you know of my Wife, Sir *Sampson?*

SIR SAMPSON. Thy Wife is a Constellation of Virtues; she's the Moon, and thou art the Man in the

248 *Capricorn:* the goat; a horned cuckold.

250 *Mandeville . . . Pinto:* Pinto's *Peregrinations* (1614) rivalled the supposed Sir John Mandeville's incredible tales of fourteenth-century travel in the East.

257: *Albumazar:* ninth-century Arabian astrologer, subject of an Italian play adapted for the Jacobean stage, revived 1668 and during Congreve's lifetime.

262: *Haly:* another esoteric ninth-century Arabian astrologer, familiar to Congreve from Ramesey and Lilly.

268 *Philomaths:* pedantic scholars.

Moon. Nay, she is more Illustrious than the Moon, for she has her Chastity without her Inconstancy. 'Sbud, I was but in Jest.

Enter Jeremy.

How now, who sent for you? Ha! what wou'd you have?

FORESIGHT. Nay, if you were but in Jest.—Who's that Fellow? I don't like his Physiognomy.

SIR SAMPSON. My Son, Sir? What Son, Sir? My Son *Benjamin*, hoh?

JEREMY. No, Sir, Mr. *Valentine*, my master; 'tis the first time he has been abroad since his Confinement, and he comes to pay his Duty to you.

SIR SAMPSON. Well, Sir.

Enter Valentine.

JEREMY. He is here, Sir.

VALENTINE. Your Blessing, Sir.

SIR SAMPSON. You've had it already, Sir: I think I sent it you today in a Bill of Four thousand Pound. A great deal of Money, Brother *Foresight*.

FORESIGHT. Aye, indeed, Sir *Sampson*, a great deal of Money for a young Man; I wonder what he can do with it!

SIR SAMPSON. Body o' me, so do I.—Hark ye, *Valentine*, if there is too much, refund the Superfluity; Do'st hear, Boy?

VALENTINE. Superfluity, Sir; it will scarce pay my Debts. I hope you will have more Indulgence than to oblige me to those hard Conditions which my necessity Sign'd to.

SIR SAMPSON. Sir, how; I beseech you, what were you pleas'd to intimate concerning Indulgence?

VALENTINE. Why, Sir, that you wou'd not go to the extremity of the Conditions, but release me at least from some part.

SIR SAMPSON. Oh Sir, I understand you,—that's all, ha?

VALENTINE. Yes, Sir, all that I presume to ask.— But what you, out of Fatherly fondness, will be pleas'd to add, shall be doubly welcome.

SIR SAMPSON. No doubt of it, sweet Sir, but your filial Piety and my Fatherly fondness wou'd fit like two Tallies.— Here's a Rogue, Brother *Foresight*, makes a Bargain under Hand and Seal in the Morning, and would be releas'd from it in the Afternoon.— Here's a Rogue, Dog, here's Conscience and Honesty; this is your Wit now, this is the Morality of your Wits! You are a Wit, and have been a Beau, and may be a —why, Sirrah, is it not here under Hand and Seal? Can you deny it?

VALENTINE. Sir, I don't deny it.

SIR SAMPSON. Sirrah, you'll be hang'd; I shall live to see you go up *Holborn-hill*.—Has he not a Rogue's face?—Speak, Brother, you understand Physiognomy; a hanging look to me; of all my Boys the most unlike me; 'a has a damn'd *Tyburn* face, without the benefit o' the Clergy.

FORESIGHT. Hum—truly I don't care to discourage a young Man; he has a violent death in his face, but I hope no danger of Hanging.

VALENTINE. Sir, is this Usage for your Son? For that old, Weatherheaded fool, I know how to laugh at him; but you, Sir—

SIR SAMPSON. You, Sir; and you, Sir!—Why, who are you, Sir?

VALENTINE. Your Son, Sir.

SIR SAMPSON. That's more than I know, Sir, and I believe not.

VALENTINE. Faith, I hope not.

SIR SAMPSON. What, wou'd you have your Mother a Whore! Did you ever hear the like! Did you ever hear the like! Body o' me—

VALENTINE. I would have an excuse for your Barbarity and Unnatural Usage.

326 *Holborn Hill:* part way from Newgate Prison to the gallows at Tyburn.

SIR SAMPSON. Excuse! Impudence! Why, Sirrah, mayn't I do what I please? Are not you my Slave? Did not I beget you? And might not I have chosen whether I would have begot you or no? Ouns, who are you? Whence came you? What brought you into the World? How came you here, Sir? Here, to stand here, upon those two Legs, and look erect with that audacious face, hah? Answer me that! Did you come a Volunteer into the World? Or did I beat up for you with the lawful Authority of a Parent, and press you to service?

VALENTINE. I know no more why I came, than you do why you call'd me. But here I am, and if you don't mean to provide for me, I desire you wou'd leave me as you found me.

SIR SAMPSON. With all my heart. Come, uncase, strip, and go naked out of the World as you came into't.

VALENTINE. My clothes are soon put off; but you must also deprive me of Reason, Thought, Passions, Inclinations, Affections, Appetites, Senses, and the huge Train of Attendants that you begot along with me.

SIR SAMPSON. Body o' me, what a many-headed Monster have I propagated!

VALENTINE. I am of myself a plain easy simple Creature, and to be kept at small expence; but the Retinue that you gave me are craving and invincible; they are so many Devils that you have rais'd, and will have employment.

SIR SAMPSON. 'Oons, what had I to do to get Children? Can't a private man be born without all these followers? Why, nothing under an Emperour should be born with Appetites. Why, at this rate a fellow that has but a Groat in his Pocket may have a Stomach capable of a Ten Shilling Ordinary.

JEREMY. Nay, that's as clear as the Sun; I'll make Oath of it before any Justice in *Middlesex*.

SIR SAMPSON. Here's a Cormorant too.—'Sheart, this Fellow was not born with you?—I did not beget him, did I?

383 *Ordinary:* eating house.
386 *Cormorant:* sea bird known for its appetite; a glutton.

JEREMY. By the Provision that's made for me, you might have begot me too: nay, and to tell your Worship another truth, I believe you did, for I find I was born with those same Whoreson Appetites too, that my Master speaks of.

SIR SAMPSON. Why look you there now. I'll maintain it, that by the rule of right Reason, this fellow ought to have been born without a Palate.—'S'heart, what shou'd he do with a distinguishing taste?—I warrant now he'd rather eat a Pheasant than a piece of poor *John;* and smell, now, why I warrant he can smell, and loves Perfumes above a stink.—Why there's it; and Musick—don't you love Musick, Scoundrel?

JEREMY. Yes, I have a reasonable good Ear, Sir, as to Jigs and Country Dances and the like; I don't much matter your *Sola's* or *Sonata's;* they give me the Spleen.

SIR SAMPSON. The Spleen, ha, ha, ha! A Pox confound you—*Sola's* and *Sonata's?* 'Oons, whose Son are you? How were you engendred, Muckworm?

JEREMY. I am, by my Father, the Son of a Chairman; my Mother sold Oysters in Winter and Cucumbers in Summer; and I came up Stairs into the World, for I was born in a Cellar.

FORESIGHT. By your Looks, you shou'd go up Stairs out of the World too, Friend.

SIR SAMPSON. And if this Rogue were Anatomiz'd now, and dissected, he has his Vessels of Digestion and Concoction, and so forth, large enough for the inside of a Cardinal, this Son of a Cucumber. These things are unaccountable and unreasonable. Body o' me, why was not I a Bear, that my Cubs might have liv'd upon sucking their Paws? Nature has been provident only to Bears and Spiders; the one has its Nutriment in his own hands, and t'other spins his Habitation out of his Entrails.

VALENTINE. Fortune was provident enough to supply all the Necessities of my Nature, if I had my right of Inheritance.

399 *poor* John: cheap dried salt fish.
404 *matter:* care for.
413 *up Stairs out of the World:* i.e., up the steps of the gallows.

SIR SAMPSON. Again! 'Ouns, han't you four thousand Pound? If I had it again, I wou'd not give thee a Groat.–What, would'st thou have me turn Pelican, and feed thee out of my own Vitals? 'S'heart, live by your Wits.–You were always fond of the Wits, now let's see if you have Wit enough to keep yourself. Your Brother will be in Town tonight, or tomorrow morning, and then look you perform Covenants, and so your Friend and Servant.–Come, Brother *Foresight.*

Exeunt Sir Sampson *and* Foresight.

JEREMY. I told you what your Visit wou'd come to.

VALENTINE. 'Tis as much as I expected–I did not come to see him: I came to *Angelica;* but since she was gone abroad, it was easily turn'd another way, and at least look'd well on my side.–What's here? Mrs. *Foresight* and Mrs. *Frail;* they are earnest.–I'll avoid 'em. Come this way, and go and inquire when *Angelica* will return.

Exeunt.

Enter Mrs. Foresight *and* Mrs. Frail.

MRS. FRAIL. What have you to do to watch me? 'Slife, I'll do what I please.

MRS. FORESIGHT. You will?

MRS. FRAIL. Yes, marry will I. A great piece of busines to go to *Covent-Garden Square* in a Hackney-Coach and take a turn with one's Friend.

MRS. FORESIGHT. Nay, two or three Turns, I'll take my Oath.

MRS. FRAIL. Well, what if I took twenty? I warrant if you had been there, it had been only innocent Recreation.–Lord, where's the comfort of this Life, if we can't have the happiness of conversing where we like.

MRS. FORESIGHT. But can't you converse at home? I own it, I think there's no happiness like conversing with an agreeable man; I don't quarrel at that, nor I don't think but your Conversation was very innocent; but the place is publick, and to be seen with a man

430 *Pelican:* often pictured tearing its own breast to feed its young.

in a Hackney-Coach is scandalous. What if anybody else shou'd have seen you alight as I did?—How can anybody be happy, while they're in perpetual fear of being seen and censur'd? Besides, it wou'd not only reflect upon you, Sister, but me.

MRS. FRAIL. Pooh, here's a Clutter. Why should it reflect upon you? I don't doubt but you have thought yourself happy in a Hackney-Coach before now.—If I had gone to *Knights-bridge*, or to *Chelsey*, or to *Spring-Garden*, or *Barn-Elms* with a man alone, something might have been said.

MRS. FORESIGHT. Why, was I ever in any of these places? What do you mean Sister?

MRS. FRAIL. Was I? What do you mean?

MRS. FORESIGHT. You have been at a worst place.

MRS. FRAIL. I at a worse place, and with a man!

MRS. FORESIGHT. I suppose you would not go alone to the *World's-End*.

MRS. FRAIL. The World's end! What, do you mean to banter me?

MRS. FORESIGHT. Poor innocent! You don't know that there's a place call'd the *World's-End*? I'll swear you can keep your Countenance purely; you'd make an Admirable Player.

MRS. FRAIL. I'll swear you have a great deal of Impudence, and in my mind too much for the Stage.

MRS. FORESIGHT. Very well, that will appear who has most. You never were at the *World's End*?

MRS. FRAIL. No.

MRS. FORESIGHT. You deny it positively to my Face.

MRS. FRAIL. Your Face, what's Your Face?

MRS. FORESIGHT. No matter for that; it's as good a Face as yours.

484: World's-End: two contemporary inns, in Knightsbridge and Chelsea. The other places named provided inns, or outdoor privacy, for clandestine meetings on the edge of town.

MRS. FRAIL. Not by a Dozen Year's wearing.—But I do deny it positively to your Face then.

MRS. FORESIGHT. I'll allow you now to find fault with my Face; for I'll swear your impudence has put me out of Countenance. But look you here now—where did you lose this Gold Bodkin?—Oh, Sister, Sister!

MRS. FRAIL. My Bodkin!

MRS. FORESIGHT. Nay, 'tis Yours, look at it.

MRS. FRAIL. Well, if you go to that, where did you find this Bodkin?—Oh, Sister, Sister!—Sister every way.

MRS. FORESIGHT *(aside)*. O Devil on't, that I cou'd not discover her without betraying myself!

MRS. FRAIL. I have heard Gentlemen say, Sister, that one should take great care when one makes a thrust in Fencing, not to lie open one's self.

MRS. FORESIGHT. It's very true, Sister. Well, since all's out, and as you say, since we are both Wounded, let us do that is often done in Duels, take care of one another, and grow better Friends than before.

MRS. FRAIL. With all my heart; ours are but slight Fleshwounds, and if we keep 'em from Air, not at all dangerous. Well, give me your Hand in token of sisterly secrecy and affection.

MRS. FORESIGHT. Here 'tis with all my heart.

MRS. FRAIL. Well, as an earnest of Friendship and Confidence, I'll acquaint you with a design that I have. To tell Truth, and speak openly one to another, I'm afraid the World have observ'd us more than we have observ'd one another. You have a Rich Husband and are provided for; I am at a loss and have no great Stock either of Fortune or Reputation, and therefore must look sharply about me. Sir *Sampson* has a Son that is expected tonight, and by the Account I have heard of his Education can be no Conjurer; the Estate, You know, is to be made over to him.—Now if I cou'd wheedle him, Sister, ha? You understand me?

506 *Gold Bodkin:* ornamental hairpin.

MRS. FORESIGHT. I do; and will help you to the utmost of my power.—And I can tell you one thing that falls out luckily enough: my awkard Daughter-in-Law, who you know is design'd for his Wife, is grown fond of Mr. *Tattle;* now if we can improve that, and make her have an Aversion for the Booby, it may go a great way towards his liking of you. Here they come together; and let us contrive some way or other to leave 'em together.

Enter Tattle, *and* Miss Prue.

MISS PRUE. Mother, Mother, Mother, look you here.

MRS. FORESIGHT. Fie, fie, Miss, how you bawl. Besides, I have told you, you must not call me Mother.

MISS PRUE. What must I call you then? Are not you my Father's Wife?

MRS. FORESIGHT. Madam; you must say Madam. By my Soul, I shall fancy myself Old indeed, to have this great Girl call me Mother.—Well, but, Miss, what are you so overjoy'd at?

MISS PRUE. Look you here, Madam, then, what Mr. *Tattle* has giv'n me—Look you here, Cousin, here's a Snuff-box; nay, there's Snuff in't;—here, will you have any?—Oh good! How sweet it is.—Mr. *Tattle* is all over sweet, his Peruke is sweet and his Gloves are sweet, and his Handerchief is sweet, pure sweet, sweeter than Roses.—Smell him Mother—Madam, I mean. He gave me this Ring for a kiss.

TATTLE. O fie, Miss, you must not kiss and tell.

MISS PRUE. Yes; I may tell my Mother.—And he says he'll give me something to make me smell so. Oh, pray lend me your Handkerchief.—Smell, Cousin; he says he'll give me something that will make my Smocks smell this way. Is not it pure?—It's better than Lavender, mun. I'm resolv'd I won't let Nurse put any more Lavender among my Smocks—ha, Cousin?

MRS. FRAIL. Fie, Miss; amongst your Linen, you must say. You must never say Smock.

541 *Daughter-in-law:* step-daughter.

MISS PRUE. Why, It is not bawdy, is it, Cousin?

TATTLE. Oh, Madam, you are too severe upon Miss; you must not find fault with her pretty simplicity, it becomes her strangely.—Pretty Miss, don't let 'em persuade you out of your Innocency.

MRS. FORESIGHT. Oh, Demm you, Toad!—I wish you don't persuade her out of her Innocency.

TATTLE. Who I, Madam? Oh Lord, how can your Ladyship have such a thought? Sure, you don't know me.

MRS. FRAIL. Ah Devil, sly Devil.—He's as close, Sister, as a Confessor. He thinks we don't observe him.

MRS. FORESIGHT. A cunning Cur; how soon he cou'd find out a fresh harmless Creature, and left us, Sister, presently.

TATTLE. Upon Reputation—

MRS. FORESIGHT. They're all so, Sister, these Men. They love to have the spoiling of a Young Thing; they are as fond of it, as of being first in the Fashion, or of seeing a new Play the first day.—I warrant it wou'd break Mr. *Tattle's* Heart to think that anybody else shou'd be before-hand with him.

TATTLE. Oh Lord, I swear I wou'd not for the World—

MRS. FRAIL. O hang you; who'll believe you? You'd be hang'd before you'd confess.—We know you.—She's very pretty! Lord, what pure red and white!—She looks so wholsome; ne'er stir, I don't know, but I fancy, if I were a Man—

MISS PRUE. How you love to jeer one, Cousin.

MRS. FORESIGHT. Heark'ee, Sister, by my Soul, the Girl is spoil'd already. D'ye think she'll ever endure a great lubberly Tarpawlin? Gad, I warrant you, she won't let him come near her, after Mr. *Tattle*.

MRS. FRAIL. O' my Soul, I'm afraid not. Eh! filthy Creature, that smells all of Pitch and Tar!—Devil take you, you confounded Toad; why did you see her before she was Married?

MRS. FORESIGHT. Nay, why did we let him? My Husband will hang us. He'll think we brought 'em acquainted.

MRS. FRAIL. Come, Faith let us be gone. If my Brother *Foresight* shou'd find us with them, he'd think so, sure enough.

MRS. FORESIGHT. So he wou'd—but then, leaving 'em together is as bad. And he's such a sly Devil, he'll never miss an opportunity.

MRS. FRAIL. I don't care; I won't be seen in't.

MRS. FORESIGHT. Well, if you should, Mr. *Tattle,* you'll have a world to answer for. Remember I wash my Hands of it; I'm thoroughly Innocent.

Exeunt Mrs. Foresight *and* Mrs. Frail.

MISS PRUE. What makes 'em go away, Mr. *Tattle?* What do they mean, do you know?

TATTLE. Yes, my Dear—I think I can guess. But hang me if I know the reason of it.

MISS PRUE. Come, must not we go too?

TATTLE. No, no, they don't mean that.

MISS PRUE. No! What then? What shall you and I do together?

TATTLE. I must make Love to you, pretty Miss; will you let me make Love to you?

MISS PRUE. Yes, if you please.

TATTLE *(aside)*. Frank, egad at least. What a Pox does Mrs. *Foresight* mean by this Civility? Is it to make a Fool of me? Or does she leave us together out of good Morality, and do as she would be done by? Gad, I'll understand it so.

MISS PRUE. Well, and how will you make Love to me? Come, I long to have you begin. Must I make Love too? You must tell me how.

TATTLE. You must let me speak Miss; you must not speak first. I must ask you Questions, and you must answer.

MISS PRUE. What, is it like the Catechism?—Come then, ask me.

TATTLE. D'ye you think you can Love me?

MISS PRUE. Yes.

TATTLE. Pooh, Pox, you must not say yes already; I shan't care a Farthing for you then in a twinkling.

MISS PRUE. What must I say then?

TATTLE. Why you must say no, or you believe not, or you can't tell—

MISS PRUE. Why, must I tell a Lie then?

TATTLE. Yes, if you would be well-bred. All well-bred Persons Lie. —Besides, you are a Woman; you must never speak what you think; Your words must contradict your thoughts; but your Actions may contradict your words. So, when I ask you if you can Love me, you must say no, but you must Love me too. If I tell you you are Handsome, you must deny it, and say I flatter you. But you must think yourself more Charming than I speak you, and like me for the Beauty which I say you have as much as if I had it myself. If I ask you to Kiss me, you must be angry, but you must not refuse me. If I ask you for more, you must be more angry—but more complying; and as soon as ever I make you say you'll cry out, you must be sure to hold your Tongue.

MISS PRUE. O Lord, I swear this is pure. I like it better than our old-fashion'd Country way of speaking one's mind;— and must not you lie too?

TATTLE. Hum—yes—but you must believe I speak Truth.

MISS PRUE. O *Gemini!* well, I always had a great mind to tell Lies—but they frighted me, and said it was a sin.

TATTLE. Well, my pretty Creature; will you make me happy by giving me a Kiss?

MISS PRUE. No, indeed; I'm angry at you.

Runs and Kisses him.

TATTLE. Hold, hold, that's pretty well, but you should not have given it me, but have suffer'd me to take it.

MISS PRUE. Well, we'll do it again.

TATTLE. With all my heart. Now then, my little Angel.

Kisses her.

MISS PRUE. Pish.

TATTLE. That's right.—Again, my Charmer.

Kisses again.

MISS PRUE. O fie, now I can't abide you.

TATTLE. Admirable! That was as well as if you had been born and bred in *Covent-Garden* all the days of your Life. And won't you show me, pretty *Miss*, where your Bed-Chamber is?

MISS PRUE. No, indeed won't I: but I'll run there, and hide myself from you behind the Curtains.

TATTLE. I'll follow you.

MISS PRUE. Ah, but I'll hold the Door with both Hands, and be angry—and you shall push me down before you come in.

TATTLE. No, I'll come in first, and push you down afterwards.

MISS PRUE. Will you? Then I'll be more angry, and more complying.

TATTLE. Then I'll make you cry out.

MISS PRUE. Oh, but you shan't, for I'll hold my Tongue.—

TATTLE. O my dear, apt Scholar.

MISS PRUE. Well, now I'll run and make more haste than you.

Exit Miss Prue.

TATTLE. You shall not fly so fast, as I'll pursue.

Exit after her.

ACT III. Scene I.

Enter Nurse.

NURSE. Miss, Miss, Miss *Prue*—Mercy on me, marry and Amen. Why, what's become of the Child?—Why

Miss, Miss *Foresight!* Sure she has not lock'd herself up in her Chamber and gone to sleep, or to Prayers. Miss, Miss! I hear her.—Come to your Father, Child; Open the Door. Open the Door, Miss. I hear you cry husht. O Lord, who's there? (*Peeps.*) What's here to do?—O the Father! a Man with her! Why, Miss I say, God's my Life, here's fine doings towards.—O Lord, We're all undone. O you young Harlotry. (*Knocks.*) Od's my Life, won't you open the Door? I'll come in the back way.

Exit.

Tattle *and* Miss Prue *at the Door.*

MISS PRUE. O Lord, she's coming—and she'll tell my Father. What shall I do now?

TATTLE. Pox take her; if she had stayed two Minutes longer, I shou'd have wish'd for her coming.

MISS PRUE. O Dear, what shall I say? Tell me, Mr. *Tattle,* tell me a Lie.

TATTLE. There's no occasion for a Lie; I cou'd never tell a Lie to no purpose. But since we have done nothing, we must say nothing, I think. I hear her. I'll leave you together, and come off as you can.

Thrusts her in, and shuts the Door.

Enter Valentine, Scandal, *and* Angelica.

ANGELICA. You can't accuse me of Inconstancy; I never told you that I lov'd you.

VALENTINE. But I can accuse you of Uncertainty, for not telling me whether you did or no.

ANGELICA. You mistake Indifference for Uncertainty; I never had Concern enough to ask myself the Question.

SCANDAL. Nor good Nature enough to answer him that did ask you; I'll say that for you, Madam.

ANGELICA. What, are you setting up for good Nature?

SCANDAL. Only for the affectation of it, as the Women do for ill Nature.

ANGELICA. Persuade your Friend that it is all Affectation.

VALENTINE. I shall receive no Benefit from the Opinion: for I know no effectual Difference between continued Affectation and Reality.

TATTLE (*coming up. Aside to* Scandal.) *Scandal,* are you in private Discourse, anything of Secrecy?

SCANDAL. Yes, but I dare trust you; we were talking of *Angelica's* Love for *Valentine.* You won't speak of it?

TATTLE. No, no, not a Syllable. I know that's a Secret, for it's whisper'd everywhere.

SCANDAL. Ha, ha, ha.

ANGELICA. What is, Mr. *Tattle?* I heard you say something was whisper'd everywhere.

SCANDAL. Your Love of *Valentine.*

ANGELICA. How!

TATTLE. No, Madam, his Love for your Ladyship. —Gad take me, I beg your Pardon—for I never heard a Word of your Ladyship's Passion till this instant.

ANGELICA. My Passion! And who told you of my Passion, pray, Sir?

SCANDAL. Why, is the Devil in you? Did not I tell it you for a Secret?

TATTLE. Gadso; but I thought she might have been trusted with her own Affairs.

SCANDAL. Is that your Discretion? Trust a Woman with herself?

TATTLE. You say true, I beg your Pardon; I'll bring all off.—It was impossible, Madam, for me to imagine that a Person of your Ladyship's Wit and Gallantry could have so long receiv'd the passionate Addresses of the accomplisht *Valentine,* and yet remain insensible; therefore, you will pardon me if from a just weight of his Merit, with your Ladyship's good Judgment, I form'd the Balance of a reciprocal Affection.

VALENTINE. O the Devil, what damn'd Costive Poet has given thee this Lesson of Fustian to get by Rote?

76 *Costive:* constipated.

ANGELICA. I dare swear you wrong him; it is his own. And Mr. *Tattle* only judges of the Success of others from the Effects of his own Merit. For certainly Mr. *Tattle* was never deny'd anything in his Life.

TATTLE. O Lord! Yes indeed, Madam, several times.

ANGELICA. I swear I don't think 'tis possible.

TATTLE. Yes, I vow and swear I have: Lord, Madam, I'm the most unfortunate Man in the World, and the most cruelly us'd by the Ladies.

ANGELICA. Nay, now you're ungrateful.

TATTLE. No, I hope not. 'Tis as much Ingratitude to own some Favours, as to conceal others.

VALENTINE. There, now it's out.

ANGELICA. I don't understand you now. I thought you had never ask'd anything, but what a Lady might modestly grant, and you confess.

SCANDAL. So faith, your Business is done here; now you may go brag somewhere else.

TATTLE. Brag! O Heav'ns! Why, did I name anybody?

ANGELICA. No; I suppose that is not in your Power; but you wou'd if you cou'd, no doubt on't.

TATTLE. Not in my Power, Madam! What does your Ladyship mean, that I have no Woman's Reputation in my Power?

SCANDAL *(aside)*. Ouns, why you won't own it, will you?

TATTLE. Faith, Madam, you're in the right; no more I have, as I hope to be sav'd; I never had it in my Power to say anything to a Lady's Prejudice in my Life. For as I was telling you Madam, I have been the most unsuccessful Creature living in things of that nature, and never had the good Fortune to be trusted with a Lady's Secret, not once.

ANGELICA. No?

VALENTINE. Not once, I dare answer for him.

SCANDAL. And I'll answer for him; for I'm sure if he had, he wou'd have told me. I find, Madam, you don't know Mr. *Tattle.*

TATTLE. No indeed, Madam, you don't know me at all I find: for sure my intimate Friends wou'd have known—

ANGELICA. Then it seems you would have told, if you had been trusted.

TATTLE. O pox, *Scandal,* that was too far put.—Never have told Particulars, Madam. Perhaps I might have talk'd as of a Third Person, or have introduc'd an Amour of my own in Conversation by way of Novel; but never have explain'd Particulars.

ANGELICA. But whence comes the Reputation of Mr. *Tattle's* Secrecy, if he was never trusted?

SCANDAL. Why thence it arises—the thing is proverbially spoken, but may be apply'd to him—as if we shou'd say in general Terms, He only is Secret who never was trusted: a Satirical Proverb upon our Sex. There's another upon yours—as she is chaste, who was never ask'd the Question. That's all.

VALENTINE. A couple of very civil Proverbs, truly: 'tis hard to tell whether the Lady or Mr. *Tattle* be the more obliged to you. For you found her Virtue upon the Backwardness of the Men; and his Secrecy, upon the mistrust of the Women.

TATTLE. Gad, it's very true, Madam; I think we are oblig'd to acquit ourselves. And for my part—but your Ladyship is to speak first—

ANGELICA. Am I? Well, I freely confess I have resisted a great deal of Temptation.

TATTLE. And I, Gad, I have given some Temptation that has not been resisted.

VALENTINE. Good.

ANGELICA. I cite *Valentine* here, to declare to the Court how fruitless he has found his Endeavours, and to confess all his Solicitations and my Denials.

135 *As . . . Question: casta est, quam nemo rogavit.* (Ovid, *Amores,* I, viii, 43.)

VALENTINE. I am ready to plead, Not guilty for you; and Guilty for myself.

SCANDAL. So, why this is fair, here's Demonstration with a Witness.

TATTLE. Well, my Witnesses are not present. But I confess I have had Favours from Persons—but as the Favours are numberless, so the Persons are nameless.

SCANDAL. Pooh, pox, this proves nothing.

TATTLE. No? I can show Letters, Locketts, Pictures, and Rings, and if there be occasion for Witnesses, I can summon the Maids at the Chocolate-Houses, all the Porters of *Pall-Mall* and *Covent-Garden,* the Door-keepers at the Play-House, the Drawers at *Locket's, Pontack's,* the *Rummer, Spring Garden;* my own Land-lady and *Valet de Chambre;* all who shall make Oath that I receive more Letters than the Secretary's Office, and that I have more Vizor-Masks to enquire for me than ever went to see the Hermaphrodite, or the Naked Prince. And it is notorious that in a Country Church, once, an Enquiry being made who I was, it was answer'd, I was the famous *Tattle,* who had ruin'd so many Women.

VALENTINE. It was there, I suppose, you got the Nickname of the *Great Turk.*

TATTLE. True; I was call'd *Turk-Tattle* all over the Parish. The next *Sunday* all the old Women kept their Daughters at home, and the Parson had not half his Congregation. He wou'd have brought me into the Spiritual Court, but I was reveng'd upon him, for he had a handsome Daughter whom I initiated into the Science. But I repented it afterwards, for it was talk'd of in Town—and a Lady of Quality that shall be nameless, in a raging Fit of Jealousy, came down in her Coach and Six Horses, and expos'd herself upon my Account; Gad, I was sorry for it with all my Heart.—You know whom I mean—You know where we raffled—

SCANDAL. Mum, *Tattle.*

165 *Locket's etc.:* well-known eating houses, often mentioned in plays.
170 *Hermaphrodite:* such bi-sexual freaks of nature were a popular attraction in London.
171 *Naked Prince:* tattoed south-sea islander exhibited at that time.

VALENTINE. 'Sdeath, are not you asham'd?

ANGELICA. O barbarous! I never heard so insolent a piece of Vanity. Fie, Mr. *Tattle,* I'll swear I could not have believ'd it.—Is this your Secrecy?

TATTLE. Gad so, the Heat of my Story carry'd me beyond my Discretion, as the Heat of the Lady's Passion hurry'd her beyond her Reputation. But I hope you don't know whom I mean, for there were a great many Ladies raffled.—Pox on't, now could I bite off my Tongue.

SCANDAL. No don't; for then you'll tell us no more. *(Goes to the Door.)* Come, I'll recommend a Song to you upon the Hint of my two Proverbs, and I see one in the next Room that will sing it.

TATTLE. For Heaven's sake, if you do guess, say nothing. Gad, I'm very unfortunate.

Re-enter Scandal, *with one to Sing.*

SCANDAL. Pray sing the first Song in the last new Play.

SONG.

Set by Mr. *John Eccles.*

A Nymph and a Swain to *Apollo* once pray'd,
The Swain had been Jilted, the Nymph been Betray'd;
Their Intent was to try if his Oracle knew
E'er a Nymph that was Chaste, or a Swain that was True.

2.

Apollo was mute, and had like t' have been pos'd,
But sagely at length he this Secret disclos'd:
He alone won't Betray in whom none will Confide,
And the Nymph may be Chaste that has never been Try'd.

Enter Sir Sampson, Mrs. Frail, Miss Prue, *and Servant.*

SIR SAMPSON. Is *Ben* come? Odso, my Son *Ben* come? Odd, I'm glad on't. Where is he? I long to see

208 *Song in the last new Play:* in fact written by Congreve for *Love for Love.* According to Summers, John Eccles composed the music for songs in more than fifty plays in the period 1681-1707.
218 *pos'd:* baffled.

him. Now, Mrs. *Frail,* you shall see my Son *Ben.* Body o'me, he's the Hopes of my Family. I han't seen him these Three Years—I warrant he's grown. Call him in, bid him make haste. I'm ready to cry for Joy.

Exit Servant.

MRS. FRAIL. Now Miss, you shall see your Husband.

MISS PRUE *(aside to* Mrs. Frail). Pish, he shall be none of my Husband.

MRS. FRAIL. Hush. Well he shan't, leave that to me.—I'll beckon Mr. *Tattle* to us.

ANGELICA. Won't you stay and see your Brother?

VALENTINE. We are the Twin Stars and cannot shine in one Sphere: when he Rises I must set. Besides, if I shou'd stay, I don't know but my Father in good Nature may press me to the immediate Signing the Deed of Conveyance of my Estate, and I'll defer it as long as I can. Well, you'll come to a Resolution.

ANGELICA. I can't. Resolution must come to me, or I shall never have one.

SCANDAL. Come, *Valentine,* I'll go with you; I've something in my Head to communicate to you.

Exit Valentine *and* Scandal.

SIR SAMPSON. What, is my Son *Valentine* gone? What, is he sneak'd off, and would not see his Brother? There's an Unnatural Whelp! There's an ill-natur'd Dog! What, were you here too, Madam, and could not keep him! Cou'd neither Love, nor Duty, nor Natural Affection oblige him? Odsbud, Madam, have no more to say to him; he is not worth your Consideration. The Rogue has not a Dram of Generous Love about him: all Interest, all Interest; he's an undone Scoundrel, and courts your Estate. Body o' me, he does not care a Doit for your Person.

ANGELICA. I'm pretty even with him, Sir *Sampson;* for if ever I cou'd have lik'd anything in him, it shou'd have been his Estate too. But since that's gone, the Bait's off, and the naked Hook appears.

238 *Twin Stars:* Castor and Pollux, the Gemini allowed by Zeus to visit heaven on alternate days.
259 *Doit:* Dutch coin of little value.

SIR SAMPSON. Odsbud, well spoken, and you are a Wiser Woman than I thought you were; for most young Women now-a-days are to be tempted with a naked hook.

ANGELICA. If I marry, Sir *Sampson,* I'm for a good Estate with any Man, and for any Man with a good Estate. Therefore, if I were obliged to make a Choice, I declare I'd rather have you than your Son.

SIR SAMPSON. Faith and Troth, you're a wise Woman, and I'm glad to hear you say so; I was afraid you were in Love with the Reprobate. Odd, I was sorry for you with all my Heart. Hang him, Mongrel! cast him off; you shall see the Rogue show himself and make Love to some desponding *Cadua* of Fourscore for Sustenance. Odd, I love to see a young Spendthrift forc'd to cling to an Old Woman for Support, like Ivy round a dead Oak. Faith, I do; I love to see 'em hug and cotten together, like Down upon a Thistle.

Enter Ben, Legend *and Servant.*

BEN. Where's Father?

SERVANT. There, Sir, his back's toward you.

SIR SAMPSON. My Son *Ben!* Bless thee, my dear Boy; body o' me, thou are heartily welcome.

BEN. Thank you Father, and I'm glad to see you.

SIR SAMPSON. Odsbud, and I'm glad to see thee; kiss me Boy, kiss me again and again, dear *Ben.*

Kisses him.

BEN. So, so, enough Father.—Mess, I'd rather kiss these Gentlewomen.

SIR SAMPSON. And so thou shalt.—Mrs. *Angelica,* my Son *Ben.*

BEN. Forsooth an you please—*(Salutes her.)* Nay Mistress, I'm not for dropping Anchor here; About Ship, i' faith—

Kisses Mrs. Frail.

Nay, and you too, my little Cock-boat—so—

Kisses Miss Prue.

277 *Cadua:* amorous rich old woman.

TATTLE. Sir, you're welcome ashore.

BEN. Thank you, thank you, Friend.

SIR SAMPSON. Thou hast been many a weary League, *Ben,* since I saw thee.

BEN. Ay, ay, been! Been far enough, an that be all.—Well Father, and how do all at home? How do's Brother *Dick*, and Brother *Val?*

SIR SAMPSON. *Dick,* body o' me, *Dick* has been dead these two Years; I writ you word when you were at *Legorne.*

BEN. Mess, and that's true; marry I had forgot. *Dick's* dead as you say—well, and how? I have a many Questions to ask you. Well, you ben't Marry'd again, Father, be you?

SIR SAMPSON. No, I intend you shall Marry, *Ben;* I would not Marry for thy sake.

BEN. Nay, what do's that signify? An you Marry again—why then, I'll go to Sea again, so there's one for t'other, an that be all. Pray don't let me be your hindrance; e'en Marry a God's Name, an the wind sit that way. As for my part, mayhap I have no mind to Marry.

MRS. FRAIL. That wou'd be pity, such a Handsome Young Gentleman.

BEN. Handsome! he, he he, nay forsooth, an you be for Joking, I'll Joke with you, for I love my jest, an the Ship were sinking, as we say'n at Sea. But I'll tell you why I don't much stand towards Matrimony. I love to roam about from Port to Port, and from Land to Land: I could never abide to be Port-bound as we call it. Now a man that is married has, as it were, d'ye see, his feet in the Bilboes, and mayhap mayn't get 'em out again when he wou'd.

SIR SAMPSON. *Ben's* a Wag.

BEN. A man that is married, d'ye see, is no more like another man than a Galley slave is like one of us free

311 *Legorne:* Livorno, in English Leghorn, on the north-west coast of Italy.
333 *Bilboes:* ship's irons.

Sailors; he is chain'd to an Oar all his life, and mayhap forc'd to tug a leaky Vessel into the Bargain.

SIR SAMPSON. A very Wag, *Ben's* a very Wag; only a little rough, he wants a little Polishing.

MRS. FRAIL. Not at all; I like his humour mightily, it's plain and honest. I shou'd like such a humour in a Husband extremely.

BEN. Say'n you so, forsooth? Marry and I shou'd like such a handsome Gentlewoman for a Bed-fellow hugely. How say you Mistress, wou'd you like going to Sea? Mess, you're a tight Vessel and well rigg'd, an you were but as well Mann'd.

MRS. FRAIL. I shou'd not doubt that, if you were Master of me.

BEN. But I'll tell you one thing, an you come to Sea in a high Wind, or that Lady, You mayn't carry so much Sail o' your Head—Top and Top-gallant, by the Mess.

MRS. FRAIL. No, why so?

BEN. Why, an you do, You may run the risk to be overset, and then you'll carry your Keels above Water, he, he, he.

ANGELICA. I swear, Mr. *Benjamin* is the veriest Wag in nature; an absolute Sea-wit.

SIR SAMPSON. Nay, *Ben* has Parts, but as I told you before, they want a little Polishing: you must not take anything ill, Madam.

BEN. No, I hope the Gentlewoman is not angry; I mean all in good part: for if I give a Jest, I'll take a Jest. And so forsooth you may be as free with me.

ANGELICA. I thank you, Sir, I am not at all offended; but methinks, Sir *Sampson*, You shou'd leave him alone with his Mistress. Mr. *Tattle*, we must not hinder Lovers.

TATTLE. Well *Miss*, I have your promise.

Aside to Miss Prue.

SIR SAMPSON. Body o' me, Madam, you say true. Look you *Ben;* this is your Mistress.—Come *Miss*, you must not be shame-fac'd; we'll leave you together.

354 Top and Top-gallant: upper sails on a square-rigged ship. Ben is amused by the fashionable towering hairdos.

MISS PRUE. I can't abide to be left alone. Mayn't my Cousin stay with me?

SIR SAMPSON. No, no. Come, let's away.

BEN. Look you Father, mayhap the young Woman mayn't take a liking to me.

SIR SAMPSON. I warrant thee, Boy. Come, come, we'll be gone; I'll venture that.

Exeunt all but Ben *and* Miss Prue.

BEN. Come Mistress, will you please to sit down, for an you stand a stern a that'n, we shall never grapple together.—Come, I'll haul a Chair; there, an you please to sit, I'll sit by you.

MISS PRUE. You need not sit so near one; if you have anything to say, I can hear you farther off, I an't deaf.

BEN. Why, that's true, as you say, nor I an't dumb, I can be heard as far as another.—I'll heave off to please you.

Sits further off.

An we were a League asunder, I'd undertake to hold Discourse with you, an 'twere not a main high Wind indeed, and full in my Teeth. Look you forsooth, I am as it were, bound for the Land of Martimony; 'tis a Voyage d'ye see that was none of my seeking. I was commanded by Father, and if you like of it, mayhap I may steer into your Harbour. How say you, Mistress? The short of the thing is this, that if you like me, and I like you, we may chance to swing in a Hammock together.

MISS PRUE. I don't know what to say to you, nor I don't care to speak with you at all.

BEN. No? I'm sorry for that. But pray, why are you so scornful?

MISS PRUE. As long as one must not speak one's mind, one had better not speak at all, I think, and truly I won't tell a lie for the matter.

BEN. Nay, You say true in that; it's but a folly to lie. For to speak one thing, and to think just the contrary way is, as it were, to look one way, and to row another. Now, for my part, d'ye see, I'm for carrying things

386 *a stern a that'n:* with her back turned.

above Board, I'm not for keeping anything under Hatches;—so that if you ben't as willing as I, say so, a God's name, there's no harm done; mayhap you may be shame-fac'd; some Maidens tho'f they love a man well enough, yet they don't care to tell'n so to's face. If that's the Case, why, silence gives consent.

MISS PRUE. But I'm sure it is not so, for I'll speak sooner than you should believe that; and I'll speak truth, tho' one should always tell a lie to a man; and I don't care, let my Father do what he will; I'm too big to be whipt, so I'll tell you plainly, I don't like you, nor love you at all, nor never will, that's more. So, there's your answer for you, and don't trouble me no more, you ugly thing.

BEN. Look you, Young Woman. You may learn to give good words, however. I spoke you fair, d'ye see, and civil.—As for your Love or your liking, I don't value it of a Rope's end; and mayhap I like you as little as you do me. What I said was in Obedience to Father; Gad, I fear a Whipping no more than you do. But I tell you one thing, if you shou'd give such Language at Sea, you'd have a Cat o' Nine-tails laid cross your Shoulders. Flesh! who are you? You heard t'other handsome Young Woman speak civilly to me, of her own accord. Whatever you think of yourself, Gad, I don't think you are any more to compare to her than a Can of Small-beer to a Bowl of Punch.

MISS PRUE. Well, and there's a handsome Gentleman, and a fine Gentleman, and a sweet Gentleman, that was here that loves me, and I love him; and if he sees you speak to me any more, he'll thrash your Jacket for you, he will, you great Sea-calf.

BEN. What, do you mean that fair-Weather Spark that was here just now? Will he thrash my Jacket?—Let'n, let'n.— But an he comes near me, mayhap I may giv'n a Salt Eel for's Supper, for all that. What do's Father mean to leave me alone as soon as I come home with such a dirty dowdy.—Sea-calf? I an't Calf enough to lick your Chalk'd face, You Cheese-curd you.—Marry thee! Oons, I'll Marry a *Lapland* Witch as soon, and live upon selling of contrary Winds and Wrack'd Vessels.

455 *Lapland Witch:* witches had power to raise storms.

MISS PRUE. I won't be call'd Names, nor I won't abus'd thus, so I won't–If I were a man, (*Cries.*) you durst not talk at this rate–no you durst not, you stinking Tar-barrel.

Enter Mrs. Foresight, *and* Mrs. Frail.

MRS. FORESIGHT. They have quarrel'd just as we cou'd wish.

BEN. Tar-barrel? Let your Sweet-heart there call me so, if he'll take your part, Your *Tom Essence*, and I'll say something to him; Gad, I'll lace his Musk-Doublet for him, I'll make him stink; he shall smell more like a Weasel than a Civet-Cat afore I ha' done with 'en.

MRS. FORESIGHT. Bless me, what's the matter? *Miss*–what, does she cry?–Mr. *Benjamin,* what have you done to her?

BEN. Let her cry: The more she cries, the less she'll–she has been gathering foul weather in her Mouth, and now it rains out at her Eyes.

MRS. FORESIGHT. Come, *Miss*, come along with me, and tell me, poor Child.

MRS. FRAIL. Lord, what shall we do? There's my Brother *Foresight* and Sir *Sampson* coming. Sister, do you take *Miss* down into the Parlour, and I'll carry Mr. *Benjamin* into my Chamber, for they must not know that they are fall'n out. Come, Sir, will you venture yourself with me?

Looks kindly on him.

BEN. Venture, *Mess,* and that I will, tho' 'twere to Sea in a Storm.

Exeunt.

Enter Sir Sampson *and* Foresight.

SIR SAMPSON. I left 'em together here. What, are they gone? *Ben's* a brisk Boy: he has got her into a Corner, Father's own Son! faith, he'll touzle her and mouzle her: The Rogue's sharp set, coming from Sea. If he should not stay for saying Grace, old *Foresight,* but fall too without the help of a Parson, ha? Odd, if he should, I cou'd not be angry with him; twould

466 *Tom Essence:* comedy by Thomas Rawlins (1676), after Molière.
469 *Civet Cat:* animal yielding civet, an ingredient in perfumes.

be but like me, *A Chip of the Old Block*. Ha! thou'rt melancholly, old Prognostication; As melancholly as if thou hadst spilt the Salt, or par'd thy Nails of a Sunday.—Come, Cheer up, look about thee. Look up, old Star-Gazer. Now is he poring upon the Ground for a crooked Pin, or an old Horse-nail with the head towards him.

FORESIGHT. Sir *Sampson*, we'll have the Wedding tomorrow morning.

SIR SAMPSON. With all my Heart.

FORESIGHT. At Ten o'clock, punctually at Ten.

SIR SAMPSON. To a Minute, to a Second; thou shall set thy Watch, and the Bridegroom shall observe it's Motions; they shall be married to a Minute, go to Bed to a Minute; and when the Alarm strikes, they shall keep time like the Figures of St. *Dunstan's* Clock, and *Consummatum est* shall ring all over the Parish.

Enter Scandal.

SCANDAL. Sir *Sampson*, sad News.

FORESIGHT. Bless us!

SIR SAMPSON. Why, what's the matter?

SCANDAL. Can't you guess at what ought to afflict you and him, and all of us, more than anything else?

SIR SAMPSON. Body o' me, I don't know any universal Grievance, but a new Tax and the loss of the Canary Fleet. Without Popery shou'd be landed in the *West*, or the *French* Fleet were at Anchor at *Blackwall*.

SCANDAL. No. Undoubtedly Mr. *Foresight* knew all this, and might have prevented it.

FORESIGHT. 'Tis no Earthquake!

SCANDAL. No, not yet; nor Whirlwind. But we don't know what it may come to. But it has had a Consequence already that touches us all.

511 *Figures of St. Dunstan's Clock:* painted mechanical figures appearing on the quarter hour.

522 *Canary Fleet:* in 1694, British ships were attempting to seek out and engage a French fleet along the coast of Spain and Africa.

524 *Blackwall:* site of dockyards on the Thames below Greenwich.

SIR SAMPSON. Why, body o'me, out with't.

SCANDAL. Something has appear'd to your Son *Valentine.* He's gone to Bed upon't, and very ill. He speaks little, yet says he has a World to say; asks for his Father and the Wise *Foresight;* talks of *Raymond Lully*, and the Ghost of *Lilly*. He has Secrets to impart, I suppose, to you two. I can get nothing out of him but Sighs. He desires he may see you in the Morning, but would not be disturb'd tonight, because he has some Business to do in a Dream.

SIR SAMPSON. Hoity toity! What have I to do with his Dreams or his Divination? Body o' me, this is a Trick to defer Signing the Conveyance. I warrant the Devil will tell him in a Dream that he must not part with his Estate: but I'll bring him a Parson to tell him that the Devil's a Liar.—Or if that won't do, I'll bring a Lawyer that shall out-lie the Devil. And so I'll try whether my Black-Guard or his shall get the better of the Day.

Exit.

SCANDAL. Alas, Mr. *Foresight,* I'm afraid all is not right.—You are a Wise Man, and a Conscientious Man; a Searcher into Obscurity and Futurity; and if you commit an Error, it is with a great deal of Consideration, and Discretion, and Caution.

FORESIGHT. Ah, good Mr. *Scandal*—

SCANDAL. Nay, nay, 'tis manifest; I do not flatter you. But Sir *Sampson* is hasty, very hasty;—I'm afraid he is not scrupulous enough, Mr. *Foresight.* He has been wicked, and Heav'n grant he may mean well in his Affair with you—but my Mind gives me, these things cannot be wholly insignificant. You are wise, and shou'd not be over-reach'd, methinks you shou'd not—

FORESIGHT. Alas Mr. *Scandal—Humanum est errare.*

SCANDAL. You say true, Man will err; mere Man will err—but you are something more. There have been wise Men; but they were such as you: Men who

536 *Raymond Lully:* thirteenth-century philospher and missionary to the Moslems.

536 *Ghost of Lilly:* William Lilly (1602-1681), famous English astrologer who predicted the Plague and Great Fire of London.

consulted the Stars, and were Observers of Omens. *Solomon* was wise, but how?—By his Judgment in Astrology. So says *Pineda* in his Third Book and Eighth Chapter—

FORESIGHT. You are learn'd, Mr. *Scandal.*

SCANDAL. A Trifler—but a Lover of Art—and the Wise Men of the *East* ow'd their Instruction to a Star, which is rightly observ'd by *Gregory* the Great in favour of Astrology! And *Albertus Magnus* makes it the most valuable Science, Because, says he, it teaches us to consider the Causation of Causes, in the Causes of things.

FORESIGHT. I protest I honour you, Mr. *Scandal*—I did not think you had read in these matters. Few Young Men are inclin'd—

SCANDAL. I thank my Stars that have inclin'd me. But I fear this Marriage and making over this Estate, this transferring of a rightful Inheritance, will bring Judgments upon us. I prophesy it, and I wou'd not have the Fate of *Cassandra* not to be believ'd. *Valentine* is disturb'd; what can be the Cause of that? And Sir *Sampson* is hurried on by an unusual Violence.—I fear he does not act wholly from himself; methinks he does not look as he used to do.

FORESIGHT. He was always of an impetuous Nature. But as to this marriage, I have consulted the Stars, and all Appearances are prosperous—

SCANDAL. Come, come, Mr. *Foresight,* let not the Prospect of Worldly Lucre carry you beyond your Judgment, nor against your Conscience. You are not satisfied that you act justly.

FORESIGHT. How!

SCANDAL. You are not satisfied, I say.—I am loath to discourage you, but it is palpable that you are not satisfied.

571 *Pineda:* Spanish Jesuit scholar best known for a commentary on Solomon, published Lyons, 1609.

576 *Gregory the Great:* distinguished sixth-century pope, honored as one of the four greater Doctors of the Roman Catholic Church.

577 *Albertus Magnus:* Dominican scholastic, teacher of Thomas Aquinas, and a believer in alchemy and astrology.

FORESIGHT. How does it appear, Mr. *Scandal?* I think I am very well satisfied.

SCANDAL. Either you suffer yourself to deceive yourself, or you do not know yourself.

FORESIGHT. Pray explain yourself.

SCANDAL. Do you sleep well o'nights?

FORESIGHT. Very well.

SCANDAL. Are you certain? You do not look so.

FORESIGHT. I am in Health, I think.

SCANDAL. So was *Valentine* this Morning, and look'd just so.

FORESIGHT. How! Am I alter'd any way? I don't perceive it.

SCANDAL. That may be, but your Beard is longer than it was two Hours ago.

FORESIGHT. Indeed? bless me!

Enter Mrs. Foresight.

MRS. FORESIGHT. Husband, will you go to Bed? It's Ten o'Clock. Mr. *Scandal,* your Servant—

SCANDAL. Pox on her, she has interrupted my Design. But I must work her into the Project.—You keep early Hours, Madam.

MRS. FORESIGHT. Mr. *Foresight* is punctual; we sit up after him.

FORESIGHT. My Dear, pray lend me your Glass, your little Looking-glass.

SCANDAL. Pray lend it him, Madam—I'll tell you the reason. (*She gives him the Glass:* Scandal *and she whisper.*) My Passion for you is grown so violent—that I am no longer Master of myself. I was interrupted in the morning, when you had Charity enough to give me your Attention, and I had Hopes of finding another opportunity of explaining myself to you, but was disappointed all this day; and the Uneasiness that has attended me ever since brings me now hither at this unseasonable hour.

MRS. FORESIGHT. Was there ever such Impudence, to make Love to me before my Husband's Face? I'll Swear I'll tell him.

SCANDAL. Do; I'll die a Martyr, rather than disclaim my Passion. But come a little farther this way, and I'll tell you what Project I had to get him out of the way, that I might have an opportunity of waiting upon you.

Whisper.

FORESIGHT *(looking in the Glass)*. I do not see any Revolution here. Methinks I look with a serene and benign aspect—pale, a little pale—but the Roses of these Cheeks have been gather'd many Years. Ha! I do not like that sudden flushing—gone already!—Hem, hem, hem! faintish. My Heart is pretty good; yet it beats; and my Pulses, ha!—I have none—Mercy on me!—Hum—Yes, here they are. Gallop, gallop, gallop, gallop, gallop, gallop, hey! Whither will they hurry me?—Now they're gone again. And now I'm faint again; and pale again, and hem! and my hem!—breath, hem!—grows short; hem! hem! he, he, hem!

SCANDAL. It takes; pursue it in the name of Love and Pleasure.

MRS. FORESIGHT. How do you do, Mr. *Foresight*?

FORESIGHT. Hum, not so well as I thought I was. Lend me your Hand.

SCANDAL. Look you there now. Your Lady says your Sleep has been unquiet of late.

FORESIGHT. Very likely.

MRS. FORESIGHT. O, mighty restless, but I was afraid to tell him so. He has been subject to Talking and Starting.

SCANDAL. And he did not use to be so.

MRS. FORESIGHT. Never, never; till within these three Nights; I cannot say that he has once broken my Rest since we have been Married.

FORESIGHT. I will go to Bed.

SCANDAL. Do so, Mr. *Foresight*, and say your Pray'rs. He looks better than he did.

MRS. FORESIGHT *(calls).* Nurse, Nurse!

FORESIGHT. Do you think so, Mr. *Scandal?*

SCANDAL. Yes, yes, I hope this will be gone by Morning, taking it in time.

FORESIGHT. I hope so.

Enter Nurse.

MRS. FORESIGHT. Nurse, your Master is not well; put him to Bed.

SCANDAL. I hope you will be able to see *Valentine* in the Morning. You had best take a little Diacodion and Cowslip water, and lie upon your back; maybe you may dream.

FORESIGHT. I thank you, Mr. *Scandal,* I will.—Nurse, let me have a Watch-light, and lay the Crums of Comfort by me.

NURSE. Yes, Sir.

FORESIGHT. And—hem, hem! I am very faint.

SCANDAL. No, no, you look much better.

FORESIGHT. Do I? And d'ye hear—bring me, let me see—within a quarter of Twelve—hem—he, hem!—just upon the turning of the Tide, bring me the Urinal;—and I hope neither the Lord of my Ascendant nor the Moon will be combust, and then I may do well.

SCANDAL. I hope so. Leave that to me; I will erect a Scheme; and I hope I shall find both *Sol* and *Venus* in the sixth House.

FORESIGHT. I thank you, Mr. *Scandal.* Indeed, that wou'd be a great Comfort to me. Hem, hem! Good Night.

Exit.

SCANDAL. Good Night, good Mr. *Foresight;* and I hope *Mars* and *Venus* will be in Conjunction—while your Wife and I are together.

688 *Diacodion:* narcotic similar to morphine.
692 *Crumbs of Comfort:* popular devotional manual (1628), by Michael Sparkes.
701 *Combust:* without influence.
703 *Sol and Venus in the sixth House:* in Virgo, a desirable sign for which Foresight is grateful, but also implying his impotence and still-virgin wife.

MRS. FORESIGHT. Well; and what use do you hope to make of this Project? You don't think that you are ever like to succeed in your design upon me?

SCANDAL. Yes, Faith I do; I have a better Opinion both of you and myself than to despair.

MRS. FORESIGHT. Did you ever hear such a Toad? Heark'ee Devil; do you think any Woman Honest?

SCANDAL. Yes, several, very honest; they'll cheat a little at Cards, sometimes, but that's nothing.

MRS. FORESIGHT. Pshaw! but Virtuous, I mean.

SCANDAL. Yes, Faith, I believe some Women are Virtuous too; but 'tis as I believe some Men are Valiant, thro' fear. For why shou'd a Man court Danger, or a Woman shun Pleasure?

MRS. FORESIGHT. O Monstrous! What are Conscience and Honour?

SCANDAL. Why, Honour is a publick Enemy, and Conscience a Domestick Thief; and he that wou'd secure his Pleasure, must pay a Tribute to one, and go halves with the t'other. As for Honour, that you have secur'd, for you have purchas'd a perpetual opportunity for Pleasure.

MRS. FORESIGHT. An Opportunity for Pleasure!

SCANDAL. Aye, your Husband. A Husband is an opportunity for Pleasure, so you have taken care of Honour, and 'tis the least I can do to take care of Conscience.

MRS. FORESIGHT. And so you think we are free for one another?

SCANDAL. Yes Faith, I think so; I love to speak my mind.

MRS. FORESIGHT. Why then, I'll speak my mind. Now as to this Affair between you and me. Here you make love to me; why, I'll confess it does not displease me. Your Person is well enough, and your Understanding is not amiss.

SCANDAL. I have no great Opinion of myself; yet I think I'm neither Deform'd, nor a Fool.

MRS. FORESIGHT. But you have a Villainous Character; you are a Libertine in Speech as well as Practice.

SCANDAL. Come, I know what you wou'd say. You think it more dangerous to be seen in Conversation with me, than to allow some other Men the last Favour. You mistake; the liberty I take in Talking is purely affected for the Service of your Sex. He that first cries out stop Thief, is often he that has stolen the Treasure. I am a Juggler that acts by Confederacy; and if you please, we'll put a Trick upon the world.

MRS. FORESIGHT. Aye; but you are such an universal Juggler—that I'm afraid you have a great many Confederates.

SCANDAL. Faith, I'm sound.

MRS. FORESIGHT. O, fie—I'll Swear you're Impudent.

SCANDAL. I'll Swear you're Handsome.

MRS. FORESIGHT. Pish, you'd tell me so, tho' you did not think so.

SCANDAL. And you'd think so, tho' I should not tell you so: and now I think we know one another pretty well.

MRS. FORESIGHT. O Lord, who's here?

Enter Mrs. Frail, *and* Ben.

BEN. Mess, I love to speak my mind. Father has nothing to do with me.—Nay, I can't say that neither; he has something to do with me. But what do's that signify? If so be that I ben't minded to be steer'd by him, 'tis as tho'f should strive against Wind and Tide.

MRS. FRAIL. Aye, but, my Dear, we must keep it secret, till the Estate be settled; for you know, Marrying without an Estate is like Sailing in a Ship without Ballast.

BEN. He, he, he; why, that's true; just so for all the World it is indeed, as like as two Cable Ropes.

MRS. FRAIL. And tho' I have a good Portion, you know one wou'd not venture all in one Bottom.

BEN. Why that's true again; for mayhap one Bottom may spring a Leak. You have hit it indeed; Mess, you've nick'd the Channel.

MRS. FRAIL. Well, but if you shou'd forsake me after all, you'd break my Heart.

BEN. Break your Heart? I'd rather the Marigold shou'd break her Cable in a storm, as well as I love her. Flesh, you don't think I'm false-hearted, like a Landman? A Sailer will be honest, tho'f mayhap he has never a Penny of Mony in his Pocket. Mayhap I may not have so fair a Face as a Citizen or a Courtier, but for all that, I've as good Blood in my Veins, and a Heart as sound as a Bisket.

MRS. FRAIL. And will you love me always?

BEN. Nay, an I love once, I'll stick like pitch; I'll tell you that. Come, I'll sing you a Song of a Sailor.

MRS. FRAIL. Hold, there's my Sister; I'll call her to hear it.

MRS. FORESIGHT. Well; I won't go to Bed to my Husband tonight, because I'll retire to my own Chamber and think of what you have said.

SCANDAL. Well, You'll give me leave to wait upon you to your Chamber-door, and leave you my last Instructions?

MRS. FORESIGHT. Hold, here's my Sister coming toward us.

MRS. FRAIL. If it won't interrupt you, I'll entertain you with a Song.

BEN. The Song was made upon one of our Ship's Crew's Wife; our Boatswain made the Song; mayhap you may know her, Sir. Before she was Married, she was call'd buxom *Joan* of *Deptford*.

SCANDAL. I have heard of her.

Ben *Sings.*

BALLAD.

Set by Mr. *John Eccles.*

A Soldier and a Sailor,
A Tinker, and a Tailor,
Had once a doubtful strife, Sir,
To make a Maid a Wife, Sir,
Whose Name was *Buxom Joan.*
For now the time was ended,
When she no more intended,
To lick her Lips at Men, Sir,
And gnaw the Sheets in vain, Sir,
And lie o'Nights alone.

2.

The Soldier Swore like Thunder,
He lov'd her more than Plunder;
And show'd her many a Scar, Sir,
That he had brought from far, Sir,
With Fighting for her sake.
The Tailor thought to please her,
With off'ring her his Measure.
The Tinker too with Mettle,
Said he could mend her Kettle,
And stop up ev'ry leak.

3.

But while these three were prating,
The Sailor slyly waiting,
Thought if it came about, Sir,
That they should all fall out, Sir;
He then might play his part.
And just e'en as he meant, Sir,
To Loggerheads they went, Sir,
And then he let fly at her,
A shot 'twixt wind and water,
That won this Fair Maid's Heart.

BEN. If some of our Crew that came to see me are not gone, you shall see that we Sailors can Dance sometimes as well as other Folks.

Whistles.

I warrant that brings 'em, an' they be within hearing.

Enter Seamen.

823 *Ballad:* Davis notes the great success of this song, reprinted with additional stanzas not by Congreve.

Oh, here they be—and Fiddles along with 'em. Come my Lads, let's have a round, and I'll make one.

Dance.

We're merry Folk, we Sailors; we han't much to care for. Thus we live at Sea; eat Bisket, and drink Flip, put on a clean Shirt once a Quarter, come home and lie with our Landladies once a Year, get rid of a little Mony; and then put off with the next fair wind. How d'ye like us?

MRS. FRAIL. O' you are the happiest, merriest Men alive.

MRS. FORESIGHT. We're beholding to Mr. *Benjamin* for this Entertainment. I believe it's late.

BEN. Why, forsooth, an you think so, you had best go to Bed. For my part, I mean to toss a Can and remember my Sweet-Heart a-fore I turn in; mayhap I may dream of her.

MRS. FORESIGHT. Mr. *Scandal,* you had best go to Bed and Dream too.

SCANDAL. Why Faith, I have a good lively Imagination, and can Dream as much to the purpose as another, if I set about it. But Dreaming is the poor retreat of a lazy, hopeless, and imperfect Lover; 'tis the last glimpse of Love to worn out Sinners, and the faint dawning of a Bliss to wishing Girls and growing Boys.

There's nought but willing, waking Love, that can
Make Blest the Ripen'd Maid, and Finish'd Man.

Exeunt.

ACT IV. Scene I.

Valentine's *Lodging.*

Enter Scandal, *and* Jeremy.

SCANDAL. Well, Is your Master ready? Does he look madly, and talk madly?

JEREMY. Yes, Sir; you need make no great doubt of that; he that was so near turning Poet yesterday morning can't be much to seek in playing the Madman today.

867 *Flip:* concoction of sweetened brandy and beer, drunk hot like most fortified drinks of the day.

SCANDAL. Would he have *Angelica* acquainted with the Reason of his design?

JEREMY. No, Sir, not yet. He has a mind to try whether his playing the Madman won't make her play the Fool, and fall in Love with him; or at least own that she has lov'd him all this while and conceal'd it.

SCANDAL. I saw her take Coach just now with her Maid, and think I heard her bid the Coach-man drive hither.

JEREMY. Like enough, Sir, for I told her Maid this morning my Master was run stark mad only for Love of her Mistress. I hear a Coach stop; if it should be she, Sir, I believe he would not see her till he hears how she takes it.

SCANDAL. Well, I'll try her.—'Tis she, here she comes.

Enter Angelica *with* Jenny.

ANGELICA. Mr. *Scandal,* I suppose you don't think it a Novelty to see a Woman visit a Man at his own Lodgings in a morning.

SCANDAL. Not upon a kind occasion, Madam. But when a Lady comes Tyrannically to insult a ruin'd Lover, and make manifest the cruel Triumphs of her Beauty, the barbarity of it something surprizes me.

ANGELICA. I don't like Raillery from a serious Face. Pray tell me what is the matter.

JEREMY. No strange matter, Madam; my Master's mad, that's all. I suppose your Ladyship has thought him so a great while.

ANGELICA. How d'ye mean, mad?

JEREMY. Why faith, Madam, he's mad for want of his Wits, just as he was poor for want of Money; his Head is e'en as light as his Pockets, and anybody that has a mind to a bad Bargain can't do better than to beg him for his Estate.

ANGELICA. If you speak Truth, your endeavouring at Wit is very unseasonable—

SCANDAL *(aside).* She's concern'd, and loves him.

ANGELICA. Mr. *Scandal,* you can't think me guilty of so much Inhumanity as not to be concern'd for a Man I must own myself oblig'd to—pray tell me truth.

SCANDAL. Faith, Madam, I wish telling a Lie would mend the matter. But this is no new effect of an unsuccessful Passion.

ANGELICA *(aside).* I know not what to think. Yet I shou'd be vext to have a trick put upon me. May I not see him?

SCANDAL. I'm afraid the Physician is not willing you shou'd see him yet. *Jeremy,* go in and inquire.

Exit Jeremy

ANGELICA *(aside).* Ha! I saw him wink and smile. I fancy 'tis a trick! I'll try.—I would disguise to all the World a Failing, which I must own to you. I fear my Happiness depends upon the recovery of *Valentine.* Therefore I conjure you, as you are his Friend, and as you have Compassion upon one fearful of Affliction, to tell me what I am to hope for,—I cannot speak.—But you may tell me; tell me, for you know what I wou'd ask.

SCANDAL. So, this is pretty plain.—Be not too much concern'd, Madam; I hope his Condition is not desperate: an Acknowledge of Love from you, perhaps, may work a Cure, as the fear of your Aversion occasion'd his Distemper.

ANGELICA *(aside).* Say you so; nay, then I'm convinc'd: and if I don't play Trick for Trick, may I never taste the Pleasure of Revenge.—Acknowledgment of Love! I find you have mistaken my Compassion, and think me guilty of a Weakness I am a Stranger to. But I have too much Sincerity to deceive you, and too much Charity to suffer him to be deluded with vain Hopes. Good Nature and Humanity oblige me to be concern'd for him; but to Love is neither in my Power nor Inclination; and if he can't be cur'd without I suck the Poison from his Wounds, I'm afraid he won't recover his Senses till I lose mine.

SCANDAL. Hey, brave Woman, i' faith.—Won't you see him then, if he desire it?

ANGELICA. What signify a Madman's Desires? Besides, 'twoud make me uneasy. If I don't see him, perhaps my Concern for him may lessen. If I forget him, 'tis no more than he has done by himself; and now the Surprise is over, methinks I am not half so sorry for him as I was.

SCANDAL. So, faith, good Nature works a-pace; you were confessing just now an Obligation to his Love.

ANGELICA. But I have consider'd that Passions are unreasonable and involuntary; if he loves, he can't help it; and if I don't love, I can't help it; no more than he can help his being a Man, or I my being a Woman; or no more than I can help my want of Inclination to stay longer here.—Come, *Jenny.*

Exit Angelica *and* Jenny.

SCANDAL. Humph! An admirable Composition, faith, this same Womankind.

Enter Jeremy.

JEREMY. What, is she gone, Sir?

SCANDAL. Gone! Why, she was never here, nor anywhere else; nor I don't know her if I see her, nor you neither.

JEREMY. Good lack! What's the matter now? Are any more of us to be mad? Why, Sir, my Master longs to see her, and is almost mad in good earnest with the Joyful News of her being here.

SCANDAL. We are all under a mistake. Ask no Questions, for I can't resolve you; but I'll inform your Master. In the mean time, if our Project succeed no better with his Father than it does with his Mistress, he may descend from his Exaltation of madness into the road of common Sense, and be content only to be made a Fool with other reasonable People. I hear Sir *Sampson;* you know your Cue. I'll to your Master.

Exit.

Enter Sir Sampson Legend *with a Lawyer.*

SIR SAMPSON. D'ye see, Mr. *Buckram,* here's the Paper sign'd with his own Hand.

BUCKRAM. Good, Sir. And the Conveyance is ready drawn in this Box, if he be ready to sign and seal.

SIR SAMPSON. Ready, body o' me, he must be ready; his Sham-sickness shan't excuse him.—O, here's his Scoundrel. Sirrah, where's your Master?

JEREMY. Ah, Sir, he's quite gone.

SIR SAMPSON. Gone! What, he is not dead?

JEREMY. No, Sir, not dead.

SIR SAMPSON. What, is he gone out of Town, run away, ha! Has he trick't me? Speak, Varlet.

JEREMY. No, no, Sir; he's safe enough, Sir, an he were but as sound, poor Gentleman. He is indeed here, Sir, and not here, Sir.

SIR SAMPSON. Hey day, Rascal, do you banter me? Sirrah, d'ye banter me? Speak Sirrah, where is he, for I will find him.

JEREMY. Would you could, Sir, for he has lost himself. Indeed, Sir, I have a most broke my Heart about him.—I can't refrain Tears when I think of him, Sir; I'm as melancholly for him as a Passing-Bell, Sir, or a Horse in a Pound.

SIR SAMPSON. A Pox confound your Similitudes, Sir. Speak to be understood, and tell me in plain Terms what the matter is with him, or I'll crack your Fool's Skull.

JEREMY. Ah, you've hit it, Sir; that's the matter with him, Sir; his Skull's crack'd, poor Gentleman; he's stark mad, Sir.

SIR SAMPSON. Mad!

BUCKRAM. What, is he *Non Compos?*

JEREMY. Quite *Non Compos,* Sir.

BUCKRAM. Why then all's obliterated, Sir *Sampson,* if he be *Non Compos mentis,* his Act and Deed will be of no effect; it is not good in Law.

SIR SAMPSON. Oons, I won't believe it; let me see him, Sir.—Mad! I'll make him find his Senses.

JEREMY. Mr. *Scandal* is with him, Sir; I'll knock at the Door.

Goes to the Scene, which opens and discovers Valentine *upon a Couch disorderly dress'd,* Scandal *by him.*

SIR SAMPSON. How now, what's here to do?–

VALENTINE *(starting).* Ha! who's that?

SCANDAL. For Heav'ns sake softly, Sir, and gently; don't provoke him.

VALENTINE. Answer me; Who is that? and that?

SIR SAMPSON. Gads bobs, does he not know me? Is he mischievous? I'll speak gently.–*Val, Val,* do'st thou not know me, Boy? Not know thy own Father, *Val!* I am thy own Father, and this is honest *Brief Buckram* the Lawyer.

VALENTINE. It may be so–I did not know you.–the World is full.–There are People that we do know, and People that we do not know; and yet the Sun shines upon all alike. There are Fathers that have many Children, and there are Children that have many Fathers.–'Tis strange! But I am Truth, and come to give the World the Lie.

SIR SAMPSON. Body o' me, I know not what to say to him.

VALENTINE. Why does that Lawyer wear black? Does he carry his Conscience withoutside?–Lawyer, what art thou? Dost thou know me?

BUCKRAM. O Lord, what must I say?–Yes, Sir.

VALENTINE. Thou liest, for I am Truth. 'Tis hard I cannot get a Livelihood amongst you. I have been sworn out of *Westminster-Hall* the first Day of every Term. Let me see–no matter how long. But I'll tell you one thing; it's a Question that would puzzle an Arithmetician if you should ask him: whether the Bible saves more Souls in *Westminster-Abby,* or damns more in *Westminster-Hall.* For my part, I am Truth, and can't tell; I have very few Acquaintance.

SIR SAMPSON. Body o' me, he talks sensibly in his madness.–Has he no Intervals?

161 *Scene:* inner stage, concealed by a curtain.
189 *Westminster Hall:* scene of the principal law courts.

JEREMY. Very short, Sir.

BUCKRAM. Sir, I can do you no Service while he's in this Condition; Here's your Paper, Sir. He may do me a mischief if I stay. The Conveyance is ready, Sir, if he recover his Senses.

Exit.

SIR SAMPSON. Hold, hold, don't you go yet.

SCANDAL. You'd better let him go, Sir, and send for him if there be occasion, for I fancy his Presence provokes him more.

VALENTINE. Is the Lawyer gone? 'tis well. Then we may drink about without going together by the Ears —heigh ho! What o'Clock is't? My Father here! Your Blessing, Sir?

SIR SAMPSON. He recovers. Bless thee, *Val*—how dost thou do, Boy?

VALENTINE. Thank you, Sir, pretty well. I have been a little out of Order. Won't you please to sit, Sir?

SIR SAMPSON. Aye, boy.—Come, thou shalt sit down by me.

VALENTINE. Sir, 'tis my Duty to wait.

SIR SAMPSON. No, no, come, come, sit you down, honest *Val*. How dost thou do? let me feel thy Pulse —Oh, pretty well now, *Val*. Body o'me, I was sorry to see thee indisposed; but I'm glad thou'rt better, honest *Val*.

VALENTINE. I thank you, Sir.

SCANDAL *(aside)*. Miracle! The Monster grows loving.

SIR SAMPSON. Let me feel thy Hand again, *Val*. It does not shake—I believe thou can'st write, *Val*: ha, boy? Thou can'st write thy Name, *Val*?—(*In Whisper to* Jeremy.) *Jeremy*, step and overtake Mr. *Buckram*, bid him make haste back with the Conveyance—quick —quick.

Exit Jeremy.

SCANDAL *(aside)*. That ever I shou'd suspect such a Heathen of any Remorse!

209 *going together by the Ears:* quarrelling.

SIR SAMPSON. Dost thou know this Paper, *Val*? I know thou'rt honest and wilt perform Articles.

Shows him the Paper, but holds it out of his reach.

VALENTINE. Pray let me see it, Sir. You hold it so far off that I can't tell whether I know it or no.

SIR SAMPSON. See it, boy? Aye aye, why, thou dost see it—'tis thy own Hand, *Val.* Why, let me see, I can read it as plain as can be: look you here. *(Reads.) The Condition of this Obligation*—Look you, as plain as can be, so it begins.—And then at the bottom, *As witness my Hand,* VALENTINE LEGEND, in great Letters. Why, 'tis as plain as the Nose in one's Face. What, are my Eyes better than thine? I believe I can read it farther off yet—let me see.

Stretches his Arm as far as he can.

VALENTINE. Will you please to let me hold it, Sir?

SIR SAMPSON. Let thee hold it, say'st thou? Aye, with all my Heart.—What matter is it who holds it? What need anybody hold it?—I'll put it up in my Pocket, *Val,* and then nobody need hold it. *(Puts the Paper in his Pocket.)* There *Val*: it's safe enough, Boy. But thou shalt have it as soon as thou hast set thy Hand to another Paper, little *Val.*

Re-enter Jeremy *with* Buckram.

VALENTINE. What, is my bad Genius here again! Oh no, 'tis the Lawyer with an itching Palm, and he's come to be scratch'd. My Nails are not long enough. —Let me have a Pair of Red-hot Tongs quickly, quickly, and you shall see me act St. *Dunstan,* and lead the Devil by the Nose.

BUCKRAM. O Lord, let me be gone; I'll not venture myself with a Madman.

Exit Buckram.

VALENTINE. Ha, ha, ha, you need not run so fast; Honesty will not overtake you.—Ha, ha, ha, the Rogue found me out to be in *Forma Pauperis* presently.

SIR SAMPSON. Oons! What a Vexation is here! I know not what to do, or say, nor which way to go.

271 *Forma Pauperis:* not liable for legal costs because of poverty.

VALENTINE. Who's that, that's out of his Way?—I am Truth, and can set him right. Hearkee, Friend, the straight Road is the worst way you can go. He that follows his Nose always will very often be led into a Stink. *Probatum est.* But what are you for? Religion or Politicks? There's a couple of Topics for you, no more like one another than Oil and Vinegar; and yet those two beaten together by a State-Cook make Sauce for the whole Nation.

SIR SAMPSON. What the Devil had I to do ever to beget Sons? Why did I ever marry?

VALENTINE. Because thou wert a Monster, old Boy: the two greatest Monsters in the World are a Man and a Woman. What's thy Opinion?

SIR SAMPSON. Why, my Opinion is that those two Monsters join'd together make yet a greater, that's a Man and his Wife.

VALENTINE. A ha! Old Truepenny, say'st thou so? Thou hast nick'd it—but it's wonderful strange, *Jeremy.*

JEREMY. What is, Sir?

VALENTINE. That Gray Hairs shou'd cover a Green Head—and I make a Fool of my Father.

Enter Foresight, Mrs. Foresight, *and* Mrs. Frail

VALENTINE. What's here! *Erra Pater*? or a bearded Sybil? If Prophecy comes, Truth must give place.
Exit with Jeremy.

FORESIGHT. What says he? What, did he prophesy? Ha, Sir *Sampson,* bless us! How are we?

SIR SAMPSON. Are we? A Pox o'your Prognostication. Why, we are Fools as we use to be. Oons, that you cou'd not foresee that the Moon would predominate, and my Son be mad.—Where's your Oppositions, your Trines, and your Quadrates?—What did your *Cardan* and your *Ptolomee* tell you? Your *Messahalah* and your *Longomontanus,* your Harmony of Chiromancy with Astrology. Ah! pox on't, that I that know the World, the Men and Manners, that don't believe

297 *Erra Pater:* fabulous astrologer whose name stood for an almanac.
307-8 *Cardan . . . Longomontanus:* an Italian and a Danish Renaissance scientist interested in astrology.

a Syllable in the Sky and Stars, and Sun and Almanacks and Trash, should be directed by a Dreamer, an Omen-hunter, and defer Business in Expectation of a lucky Hour, when, body o' me, there never was a lucky Hour after the first opportunity.

Exit Sir Sampson.

FORESIGHT. Ah, Sir *Sampson*, Heav'n help your Head! This is none of your lucky Hour; *Nemo omnibus horis sapit.* What, is he gone, and in contempt of Science! Ill Stars and unconvertible Ignorance attend him.

SCANDAL. You must excuse his Passion, Mr. *Foresight*, for he has been heartily vex'd. His Son is *Non compos mentis,* and thereby incapable of making any Conveyance in Law; so that all his measures are disappointed.

FORESIGHT. Ha! say you so?

MRS. FRAIL *(aside to* Mrs. Foresight). What, has my Sea-Lover lost his Anchor of Hope then?

MRS. FORESIGHT. Oh Sister, what will you do with him?

MRS. FRAIL. Do with him? Send him to Sea again in the next foul Weather.—He's us'd to an inconstant Element, and won't be surpris'd to see the Tide turn'd.

FORESIGHT. Wherein was I mistaken, not to forsee this?

Considers.

SCANDAL *(aside to* Mrs. Foresight). Madam, you and I can tell him something else that he did not foresee, and more particularly relating to his own Fortune.

MRS. FORESIGHT. What do you mean? I don't understand you.

SCANDAL. Hush, softly—the Pleasures of last Night, my Dear, too considerable to be forgot so soon.

MRS. FORESIGHT. Last Night! And what wou'd your Impudence infer from last night? Last Night was like the Night before, I think.

318 *Nemo omnibus horis sapit:* abbreviated from Pliny, *Nat. Hist.* VII, xl. 'What of the proverb that none among mortals is wise all the time?'

SCANDAL. S'death, do you make no difference between me and your Husband?

MRS. FORESIGHT. Not much—he's superstitious, and you are mad, in my opinion.

SCANDAL. You make me mad—You are not serious——Pray recollect yourself.

MRS. FORESIGHT. O yes, now I remember; you were very impertinent and impudent—and would have come to Bed to me.

SCANDAL. And did not?

MRS. FORESIGHT. Did not! With that face can you ask the Question?

SCANDAL. This I have heard of before, but never believ'd. I have been told she had that admirable quality of forgetting to a man's face in the morning that she had lain with him all night, and denying favours with more impudence than she cou'd grant 'em.—Madam, I'm your humble Servant, and honour you.—You look pretty well, Mr. *Foresight.* How did you rest last night?

FORESIGHT. Truly Mr. *Scandal,* I was so taken up with broken Dreams and distracted Visions that I remember little.

SCANDAL. 'Twas a very forgetting Night.—But would you not talk with *Valentine?* Perhaps you may understand him; I'm apt to believe there is something mysterious in his Discourses, and sometimes rather think him inspir'd than mad.

FORESIGHT. You speak with singular good Judgment, Mr. *Scandal,* truly. I am inclining to your *Turkish* opinion in this matter, and do reverance a man whom the vulgar think mad. Let us go in to him.

MRS. FRAIL. Sister, do you stay with them; I'll find out my Lover and give him his discharge, and come to you. O' my Conscience, here he comes.

Exeunt Foresight, Mrs. Foresight *and* Scandal.

Enter Ben.

BEN. All mad, I think. Flesh, I believe all the *Calentures* of the Sea are come ashore, for my part.

385 *Calentures:* tropical fever inducing delirium.

MRS. FRAIL. Mr. *Benjamin* in Choler!

BEN. No, I'm pleas'd well enough, now I have found you. Mess, I've had such a Hurricane upon your account yonder.

MRS. FRAIL. My account? Pray, what's the matter?

BEN. Why, Father came and found me squabbling with yon chitty-fac'd thing as he would have me marry—so he ask'd what was the matter. He ask'd in a surly sort of a way. (It seems Brother *Val* is gone mad, and so that put'n into a passion; but what did I know that; what's that to me?)—So he ask'd in a surly manner, and Gad I answer'd as surlily. What tho'f he be my Father, I an't bound Prentice to en: so faith; I told 'n in plain terms, if I were minded to marry, I'd marry to please myself, not him; and for the Young Woman that he provided for me, I thought it more fitting for her to learn her Sampler, and make Dirt-pies, than to look after a Husband; for my part I was none of her man.— I had another Voyage to make, let him take it as he will.

MRS. FRAIL. So then you intend to go to Sea again?

BEN. Nay, nay, my mind run upon you, but I wou'd not tell him so much.—So he said he'd make my heart ache, and if so be that he cou'd get a Woman to his mind, he'd marry himself. Gad, says I, an you play the fool and marry at these years, there's more danger of your head's aching than my heart. He was woundy angry when I gav'n that wipe. He had'nt a word to say, and so I left'n, and the Green Girl together. Mayhap the Bee may bite, and he'll marry her himself, with all my heart.

MRS. FRAIL. And were you this undutiful and graceless Wretch to your Father?

BEN. Then why was he graceless first? If I am undutiful and Graceless, why did he beget me so? I did not get myself.

MRS. FRAIL. O Impiety! How have I been mistaken! What an inhuman merciless Creature have I set my heart upon? O, I am happy to have discover'd the Shelves and Quicksands that lurk beneath that faithless smiling face.

BEN. Hey toss! What's the matter now? Why, you ben't angry, be you?

MRS. FRAIL. O, see me no more—for thou wert born amongst Rocks, suckl'd by Whales, cradled in a Tempest, and whistled to by Winds; and thou art come forth with Fins and Scales, and three rows of Teeth, a most outragious Fish of prey.

BEN. O Lord, O Lord, she's mad, poor Young Woman! Love has turn'd her senses, her Brain is quite overset. Well-a-day, how shall I do to set her to rights?

MRS. FRAIL. No, no, I am not mad, Monster; I am wise enough to find you out. Had'st thou the Impudence to aspire at being a Husband with that stubborn and disobedient temper?—You that know not how to submit to a Father, presume to have a sufficient stock of Duty to undergo a Wife? I should have been finely fobb'd indeed, very finely fobb'd.

BEN. Hearkee forsooth; if so be that you are in your right senses, d'ye see, for ought as I perceive I'm like to be finely fobb'd—if I have got anger here upon your account, and you are tack'd about already. What d'ye mean, after all your fair speeches, and stroking my Cheeks, and Kissing and Hugging, what, wou'd you sheer off so? Wou'd you, and leave me aground?

MRS. FRAIL. No, I'll leave you adrift, and go which way you will.

BEN. What, are you false-hearted then?

MRS. FRAIL. Only the Wind's chang'd.

BEN. More shame for you—the Wind's chang'd? It's an ill Wind blows nobody good. Mayhap I have good riddance on you, if these be your Tricks.—What d'ye mean all this while, to make a fool of me?

MRS. FRAIL. Any fool but a Husband.

BEN. Husband! Gad, I wou'd not be your Husband if you wou'd have me, now I know your mind, tho'f you had your weight in Gold and Jewels, and tho'f I lov'd you never so well.

MRS. FRAIL. Why, canst thou love, Porpoise?

BEN. No matter what I can do. Don't call Names—I don't love You so well as to bear that, whatever I did. I'm glad you shew yourself, Mistress: let them marry you as don't know you. Gad, I know you too well, by sad experience; I believe he that marries you will go to Sea in a Hen-peck'd Frigate. I believe that, Young Woman—and mayhap may come to an Anchor at *Cuckolds-point;* so there's a dash for you, take it as you will. Mayhap you may holla after me when I won't come to.

Exit.

MRS. FRAIL. Ha, ha, ha, no doubt on't.—

Sings.

My true Love is gone to Sea.—

Enter Mrs. Foresight.

O Sister, had you come a minute sooner, you would have seen the Resolution of a Lover. Honest *Tar* and I are parted; and with the same indifference that we met. O' my life, I am half vex'd at the insensibility of a Brute that I despis'd.

MRS. FORESIGHT. What then, he bore it most Heroically?

MRS. FRAIL. Most Tyranically, for you see he has got the start of me; and I, the poor forsaken Maid, am left complaining on the Shore. But I'll tell you a hint that he has given me: Sir *Sampson* is enrag'd, and talks desperately of commiting Matrimony himself.—If he has a mind to throw himself away, he can't do it more effectually than upon me, if we could bring it about.

MRS. FORESIGHT. Oh, hang him, old Fox, he's too cunning; besides he hates both you and me.—But I have a project in my head for you, and I have gone a good way towards it. I have almost made a Bargain with *Jeremy, Valentine's* man, to sell his Master to us.

MRS. FRAIL. Sell him, how?

MRS. FORESIGHT. *Valentine* raves upon *Angelica,* and took me for her, and *Jeremy* says will take anybody for her that he imposes on him. Now I have promis'd him Mountains, if in one of his mad fits he will bring you to him in her stead, and get you married together, and put to Bed together; and after Con-

473 *Cuckold's Point:* actual spot on the south side of the Thames at London, mentioned in numerous punning allusions.

summation, Girl, there's no revoking. And if he should recover his Senses, he'll be glad at least to make you a good Settlement.—Here they come. Stand aside a little, and tell me how you like the design.

Enter Valentine, Scandal, Foresight, *and* Jeremy.

SCANDAL. *(to Jeremy).* And have you given your Master a hint of their Plot upon him?

JEREMY. Yes, Sir; he says he'll favour it, and mistake her for *Angelica*.

SCANDAL. It may make sport.

FORESIGHT. Mercy on us!

VALENTINE. Husht—interrupt me not—I'll whisper Prediction to thee, and thou shalt Prophesy. I am Truth, and can teach thy Tongue a new Trick. I have told thee what's past, now I tell what's to come. Dost thou know what will happen tomorrow?—Answer me not, for I will tell thee. Tomorrow, Knaves will thrive thro' craft, and Fools thro' Fortune; and Honesty will go as it did, Frost-nip't in a Summer suit. Ask me Questions concerning tomorrow.

SCANDAL. Ask him, Mr. *Foresight*.

FORESIGHT. Pray, what will be done at Court?

VALENTINE. *Scandal* will tell you; I am Truth, I never come there.

FORESIGHT. In the City?

VALENTINE. Oh, Prayers will be said in empty Churches at the usual Hours. Yet you will see such Zealous Faces behind Counters as if religion were to be sold in every Shop. Oh, things will go methodically in the City; the Clocks will strike Twelve at Noon, and the Horn'd Herd Buzz in the Exchange at Two. Wives and Husbands will drive distinct Trades, and Care and Pleasure separately Occupy the Family. Coffee-Houses will be full of Smoke and Stratagem. And the cropt Prentice, that sweeps his Master's Shop in the morning, may, ten to one, dirty his Sheets before Night. But there are two things that you will see very strange; which are Wanton Wives, with their Legs at liberty, and Tame Cuckolds, with Chains about their Necks. But hold, I must examine you before I go further; you look suspiciously. Are you a Husband?

FORESIGHT. I am Married.

VALENTINE. Poor Creature! Is your Wife of *Covent-Garden* Parish?

FORESIGHT. No; St. *Martin's* in the Fields.

VALENTINE. Alas, poor Man; his Eyes are sunk, and his Hands shrivell'd; his Legs dwindl'd, and his back bow'd. Pray, pray, for a Metamorphosis. Change thy Shape, and shake off Age; get thee *Medea's* Kettle and be boil'd a-new, come forth with lab'ring *Callous* Hands, a Chine of Steel, and *Atlas'* Shoulders. Let *Taliacotius* trim the Calves of Twenty Chairmen, and make thee Pedestals to stand erect upon, and look Matrimony in the face. Ha, ha, ha! That a Man shou'd have a Stomach to a Wedding Supper, when the Pidgeons ought rather to be laid to his feet, ha, ha, ha!

FORESIGHT. His Frenzy is very high now, Mr. *Scandal.*

SCANDAL. I believe it is a Spring Tide.

FORESIGHT. Very likely truly; you understand these Matters.—Mr. *Scandal,* I shall be very glad to confer with you about these things which he has utter'd. His Sayings are very Mysterious and Hieroglyphical.

VALENTINE. Oh, why would *Angelica* 'be absent from my Eyes so long?

JEREMY. She's here, Sir.

MRS. FORESIGHT. Now, Sister.

MRS. FRAIL. O Lord, what must I say?

SCANDAL. Humour him, Madam, by all means.

VALENTINE. Where is she? Oh, I see her. She comes, like Riches, Health, and Liberty at once, to a

551 *Covent Garden:* notorious as a center of dissipation.
557 *Medea's Kettle:* in Ovid, *Metamorphoses,* viii, 251 ff, Medea prepares a potion restoring youth to Jason's father.
560 *Taliacotius:* celebrated Bolognese Renaissance surgeon.
564 *Pidgeons . . . laid to his feet:* a reputed cure for the plague.

despairing, starving, and abandon'd Wretch. Oh welcome, welcome.

MRS. FRAIL. How d'ye you, Sir? Can I serve you?

VALENTINE. Heark'ee, I have a Secret to tell you—*Endymion* and the Moon shall meet us upon Mount *Latmos,* and we'll be Marry'd in the dead of Night—but say not a word. *Hymen* shall put his Torch into a a dark Lanthorn, that it may be secret; and *Juno* shall give her *Peacock* Poppy-water, that he may fold his Ogling Tail, and *Argos's* hundred Eyes be shut, ha? Nobody shall know but *Jeremy.*

MRS. FRAIL. No, no, we'll keep it secret; it shall be done presently.

VALENTINE. The sooner the better.—*Jeremy,* come hither—closer—that one may overhear us. *Jeremy,* I can tell you News; *Angelica* is turn'd Nun, and I am turning Friar, and yet we'll Marry one another in spite of the Pope. Get me a Cowl and Beads that I may play my part, for she'll meet me Two Hours hence in black and white, and a long Veil to cover the Project, and we won't see one another's Faces till we have done something to be asham'd of; and then we'll blush once for all.

Enter Tattle, *and* Angelica.

JEREMY. I'll take care, and—

VALENTINE. Whisper.

ANGELICA. Nay, Mr. *Tattle,* If you make Love to me, you spoil my design, for I intended to make you my Confident.

TATTLE. But, Madam, to throw away your Person, such a Person! and such a Fortune, on a Madman!

ANGELICA. I never lov'd him till he was Mad; but don't tell anybody so.

SCANDAL. How's this! *Tattle* making Love to *Angelica!*

585 *Endymion:* shepherd with whom Luna fell in love as he slept on Mount Latmos.

588-590 *Juno . . . Argo's hundred eyes:* the hundred eyes of Argos, with which he spied on Jupiter for Juno, were placed by her in the tail of the peacock.

TATTLE. Tell, Madam! Alas, you don't know me. I have much ado to tell your Ladyship how long I have been in Love with you—but encourag'd by the impossibility of *Valentine's* making any more Addresses to you, I have ventur'd to declare the very inmost Passion of my Heart. Oh, Madam, look upon us both. There you see the ruins of a poor decay'd Creature; here, a compleat and lively Figure, with Youth and Health, and all his five Senses in perfection, Madam, and to all this, the most passionate Lover—

ANGELICA. O fie, for shame, hold your Tongue; a passionate Lover, and five Senses in perfection! When you are as Mad as *Valentine,* I'll believe you love me, and the maddest shall take me.

VALENTINE. It is enough. Ha! Who's here?

MRS. FRAIL *(to* Jeremy). O Lord, her coming will spoil all.

JEREMY. No, no, Madam, he won't know her. If he shou'd, I can persuade him.

VALENTINE. *Scandal,* who are all these? Foreigners? If they are, I'll tell you what I think. *(Whispers.)* Get away all the Company but *Angelica,* that I may discover my design to her.

SCANDAL. I will.—I have discover'd something of *Tattle* that is of a piece with Mrs. *Frail.* He Courts *Angelica.* If we cou'd contrive to couple 'em together —Heark'ee—.

Whisper.

MRS. FORESIGHT. He won't know you, Cousin; he knows nobody.

FORESIGHT. But he knows more than anybody. O Niece, he knows things past and to come, and all the profound Secrets of Time.

TATTLE. Look you, Mr. *Foresight,* it is not my way to make many words of Matters, and so I shan't say much,— But in short, d'ye see, I will hold you a Hundred Pound now, that I know more Secrets than he.

FORESIGHT. How! I cannot Read that knowledge in your Face, Mr. *Tattle.*—Pray, what do you know?

TATTLE. Why d'ye think I'll tell you, Sir! Read it in my Face? No, Sir, 'tis written in my Heart. And safer there, Sir, than Letters writ in Juice of Lemon, for no Fire can fetch it out. I am no blab, Sir.

VALENTINE *(to* Scandal*).* Acquaint *Jeremy* with it; he may easily bring it about. They are welcome, and I'll tell 'em so myself. What, do you look strange upon me?—Then I must be plain. *(Coming up to them.)* I am Truth, and hate an Old Acquaintance with a new Face.

Scandal *goes aside with* Jeremy.

TATTLE. Do you know me, *Valentine?*

VALENTINE. You? Who are you? No, I hope not.

TATTLE. I am *Jack Tattle,* your Friend.

VALENTINE. My Friend, what to do? I am no Married Man, and thou can'st not lie with my Wife; I am very poor, and thou can'st not borrow Money of me; then what Employment have I for a Friend?

TATTLE. Hah! A good open Speaker, and not to be trusted with a Secret.

ANGELICA. Do you know me, *Valentine?*

VALENTINE. O, very well.

ANGELICA. Who am I?

VALENTINE. You're a Woman—one to whom Heav'n gave Beauty when it grafted Roses on a Briar. You are the reflection of Heav'n in a Pond, and he that leaps at you is sunk. You are all white, a sheet of lovely spotless Paper, when you first are Born; but you are to be scrawl'd and blotted by every Goose's Quill. I know you; for I lov'd a Woman, and lov'd her so long that I found out a strange thing: I found out what a Woman was good for.

TATTLE. Aye, prithee, what's that?

VALENTINE. Why, to keep a Secret.

TATTLE. O Lord!

VALENTINE. O exceeding good to keep a Secret: for tho' she should tell, yet she is not to be believ'd.

TATTLE. Hah! good again, faith.

VALENTINE. I would have Musick—sing me the Song that I like.

SONG.

Set by Mr. *Finger.*

I tell thee, *Charmion,* could I Time retrieve,
And could again begin to Love and Live,
To you I should my earliest Off'ring give;
I know my Eyes would lead my Heart to you,
And I should all my Vows and Oaths renew,
But to be plain, I never would be true.

2.

For by our weak and weary Truth, I find,
Love hates to center in a Point assign'd,
But runs with Joy the Circle of the Mind.
Then never let us chain what should be free,
But for relief of either Sex agree,
Since Women love to change, and so do we.

No more, for I am melancholly.

Walks musing.

JEREMY *(to* Scandal). I'll do't, Sir.

SCANDAL. Mr. *Foresight,* we had best leave him. He may grow outragious, and do mischief.

FORESIGHT. I will be directed by you.

JEREMY *(to* Mrs. Frail). You'll meet, Madam; I'll take care everything shall be ready.

MRS. FRAIL. Thou shalt do what thou wilt, have what thou wilt; in short, I will deny thee nothing.

TATTLE *(to* Angelica). Madam, shall I wait upon you?

ANGELICA. No, I'll stay with him—Mr. *Scandal* will protect me. Aunt, Mr. *Tattle* desires you would give him leave to wait on you.

TATTLE. Pox on't, there's no coming off, now she has said that.—Madam, will you do me the Honour?

MRS. FORESIGHT. Mr. *Tattle* might have us'd less Ceremony.

698 *Mr. Finger:* Moravian composer resident in England; also set songs for Congreve's tragedy, *The Mourning Bride.*

SCANDAL. *Jeremy*, follow *Tattle.*

Exeunt Foresight, Mrs. Foresight, Tattle, Mrs. Frail, *and* Jeremy.

ANGELICA. Mr. *Scandal,* I only stay till my Maid comes, and because I had a Mind to be rid of Mr. *Tattle.*

SCANDAL. Madam, I am very glad that I overheard a better Reason, which you gave to Mr. *Tattle;* for his impertinence forc'd you to acknowledge a Kindness for *Valentine*, which you deny'd to all his Sufferings and my Solicitations. So I'll leave him to make use of the Discovery, and your Ladyship to the free Confession of your Inclinations.

ANGELICA. Oh Heavens! You won't leave me alone with a Madman?

SCANDAL. No, Madam; I only leave a Madman to his Remedy.

Exit Scandal.

VALENTINE. Madam, you need not be very much afraid, for I fancy I begin to come to myself.

ANGELICA *(aside).* Aye, but if I don't fit you, I'll be hang'd.

VALENTINE. You see what disguises Love makes us put on. Gods have been in counterfeited Shapes for the same Reason, and the Divine Part of me, my Mind, has worn this Mask of Madness, and this motly Livery, only as the Slave of Love, and Menial Creature of your Beauty.

ANGELICA. Mercy on me, how he talks! Poor *Valentine!*

VALENTINE. Nay, faith, now let us understand one another, Hypocrisy apart.—The Comedy draws toward an end, and let us think of leaving acting and be ourselves; and since you have lov'd me, you must own I have at length deserv'd you shou'd confess it.

ANGELICA *(sighs).* I would I had lov'd you—for Heaven knows I pity you; and could I have foreseen

750 *fit you:* find a fit punishment for you.

the sad Effects, I wou'd have striven; but that's too late.

Sighs.

VALENTINE. What sad Effects?—What's too late? My seeming Madness has deceiv'd my Father, and procur'd me time to think of means to reconcile me to him, and preserve the right of my Inheritance to his Estate, which otherwise by Articles I must this Morning have resign'd: and this I had inform'd you of today, but you were gone before I knew you had been here.

ANGELICA. How! I thought your love of me had caus'd this Transport in your Soul, which, it seems, you only counterfeited for mercenary Ends and sordid Interest.

VALENTINE. Nay, now you do me Wrong; for if any Interest was considered, it was yours, since I thought I wanted more than Love to make me worthy of you.

ANGELICA. Then you thought me mercenary.—But how am I deluded by this Interval of Sense, to reason with a Madman?

VALENTINE. Oh, 'tis barbarous to misunderstand me longer.

Enter Jeremy.

ANGELICA. O, here's a reasonable Creature.—Sure he will not have the Impudence to perserve.—Come, *Jeremy,* acknowledge your Trick, and confess your Master's Madness counterfeit.

JEREMY. Counterfeit, Madam! I'll maintain him to be as absolutely and substantially Mad, as any Freeholder in *Bethlehem;* nay, he's as Mad as any Projector, Fanatick, Chymist, Lover, or Poet in *Europe.*

VALENTINE. Sirrah, you lie; I am not Mad.

ANGELICA. Ha, ha, ha, you see he denies it.

JEREMY. O Lord, Madam, did you ever know any Madman Mad enough to own it?

796-7 *Freeholder in Bethlehem:* lunatic in the asylum of St. Mary of Bethlehem (Bedlam).
797 *Projector:* speculator.

VALENTINE. Sot, can't you apprehend?

ANGELICA. Why, he talk'd very sensibly just now.

JEREMY. Yes, Madam, He has Intervals: but you see he begins to look wild again now.

VALENTINE. Why you Thick-Skull'd Rascal, I tell you the Farce is done, and I will be Mad no longer.

Beats him.

ANGELICA. Ha, ha, ha, is he mad, or no, *Jeremy?*

JEREMY. Partly I think—for he does not know his Mind Two Hours. I'm sure I left him just now in a Humour to be mad, and I think I have not found him very quiet at the present.

One Knocks.

Who's there?

VALENTINE. Go see, you Sot. I'm very glad that I can move your Mirth, tho' not your Compassion.

Exit Jeremy.

ANGELICA. I did not think you had Apprehension enough to be exceptious: but Madmen show themselves most by over-pretending to a sound Understanding, as Drunken men do by over-acting Sobriety. I was half inclining to believe you, till I accidentally touch'd upon your tender Part; but now you have restor'd me to my former Opinion and Compassion.

Enter Jeremy.

JEREMY. Sir, your Father has sent to know if you are any better yet.—Will you please to be Mad, Sir, or how?

VALENTINE. Stupidity! You know the Penalty of all I'm worth must pay for the Confession of my Senses; I'm Mad, and will be Mad to everybody but this Lady.

JEREMY. So, just the very backside of Truth. But lying is a Figure in Speech that interlards the greatest part of my Conversation.—Madam, your Ladyship's Woman.

Goes to the Door.

Enter Jenny.

ANGELICA. Well, have you been there? Come hither.

JENNY *(aside to* Angelica). Yes, Madam, Sir *Sampson* will wait upon you presently.

VALENTINE. You are not leaving me in this Uncertainty?

ANGELICA. Wou'd anything but a Madman complain of Uncertainty? Uncertainty and Expectation are the Joys of Life. Security is an insipid thing, and the overtaking and possessing of a Wish discovers the Folly of the Chase. Never let us know one another better, for the Pleasure of a Masquerade is done when we come to show Faces. But I'll tell you two things before I leave you; I am not the Fool you take me for; and you are Mad and don't know it.

Exeunt Angelica *and* Jenny.

VALENTINE. From a Riddle you can expect nothing but a Riddle. There's my Instruction, and the Moral of my Lesson.

Re-enter Jeremy.

JEREMY. What, is the Lady gone again, Sir? I hope you understood one another before she went.

VALENTINE. Understood! She is harder to be understood than a Piece of *Ægyptian* Antiquity, or an *Irish* Manuscript; you may pore till you spoil your Eyes, and not improve your Knowledge.

JEREMY. I have heard 'em say, Sir, they read hard *Hebrew* Books backwards; maybe you begin to read at the wrong End.

VALENTINE. They say so of a Witches' Pray'r, and Dreams and Dutch Almanacks are to be understood by contraries. But there's Regularity and Method in that; she is a Medal without a Reverse or Inscription, for Indifference has both sides alike. Yet while she does not seem to hate me, I will pursue her, and know her if it be possible, in spite of the Opinion of my Satirical Friend, *Scandal,* who says,

That Women are like Tricks by sleight of Hand,
Which, to admire, we should not understand.

Exeunt.

ACT V. SCENE I.

A Room in Foresight's *House.*

Enter Angelica *and* Jenny

ANGELICA. Where is Sir *Sampson*? Did you not tell me he would be here before me?

JENNY. He's at the great Glass in the Dining-Room, Madam, setting his Cravat and Wig.

ANGELICA. How! I'm glad on't. If he has a mind I should like him, it's a sign he likes me; and that's more than half my Design.

JENNY. I hear him, Madam.

ANGELICA. Leave me, and d'ye hear, if *Valentine* shou'd come, or send, I am not to be spoken with.

Exit Jenny.

Enter Sir Sampson.

SIR SAMPSON. I have not been honour'd with the Commands of a fair Lady a great while—odd, Madam, you have reviv'd me—not since I was Five and Thirty.

ANGELICA. Why you have no great reason to complain, Sir *Sampson;* that is not long ago.

SIR SAMPSON. Zooks, but it is, Madam, a very great while, to a Man that admire a fine Woman as much as I do.

ANGELICA. You're an absolute Courtier, Sir *Sampson.*

SIR SAMPSON. Not at all, Madam; Odsbud you wrong me: I am not so old, neither, to be a bare Courtier, only a Man of Words. Odd, I have warm Blood about me yet; I can serve a Lady any way.—Come, come, let me tell you, you Women think a Man old too soon, faith and troth you do.—Come, don't despise Fifty; odd Fifty, in a hale Constitution, is no such contemptible Age.

ANGELICA. Fifty a contemptible Age! Not at all; a very fashionable Age I think. I assure you I know very considerable Beaus that set a good Face upon Fifty. Fifty! I have seen Fifty, in a side Box by Candle-light, out-blossom Five and Twenty.

SIR SAMPSON. O Pox, outsides, outsides; a pize take 'em, mere outsides. Hang your side-Box Beaus; no, I'm none of those, none of your forc'd Trees, that pretend to Blossom in the Fall, and Bud when they should bring forth Fruit. I am of a long-liv'd Race, and inherit Vigour; none of my Family married till Fifty, yet they begot Sons and Daughters till Fourscore. I am of your Patriarchs, I, a Branch of one of your *Antideluvian* Families, Fellows that the Flood could not wash away. Well, Madam, what are your Commands? Has any young Rogue affronted you, and shall I cut his Throat? or–

ANGELICA. No, Sir *Sampson,* I have no Quarrel upon my Hands; I have more Occasion for your Conduct than your Courage at this time. To tell you the Truth, I'm weary of living single, and want a Husband.

SIR SAMPSON. Odsbud, and 'tis pity you should. *(Aside.)* Odd, wou'd she wou'd like me; then I shou'd hamper my young Rogues; odd, wou'd she wou'd; faith and troth, she's devilish Handsome.–Madam, you deserve a good Husband, and 'twere pity you shou'd be thrown away upon any of these young idle Rogues about the Town. Odd, there's ne'er a young Fellow worth hanging–that is, a very young Fellow. Pize on 'em, they never think beforehand of anything; and if they commit Matrimony, 'tis as they commit Murder, out of a Frolick; and are ready to hang themselves, or to be hang'd by the Law, the next Morning.–Odso, have a care, Madam.

ANGELICA. Therefore I ask your Advice, Sir *Sampson:* I have Fortune enough to make any Man easy that I can like; If there were such a thing as a young agreeable Man, with a reasonable Stock of good Nature and Sense–for I would neither have an absolute Wit, nor a Fool.

SIR SAMPSON. Odd, you are hard to please, Madam; to find a young Fellow that is neither a Wit in his own Eye, nor a Fool in the Eye of the World, is a very hard Task. But, faith and troth, you speak very discreetly, for I hate both a Wit and a Fool.

ANGELICA. She that marries a Fool, Sir *Sampson,* commits the Reputation of her Honesty or Under-

35 *a pize:* a pox.

standing to the Censure of the World; and she that marries a very Witty Man, submits both to the Severity and insolent Conduct of her Husband. I should like a Man of Wit for a Lover, because I would have such a one in my Power; but I would no more be his Wife than his Enemy. For his Malice is not a more terrible Consequence of his Aversion, than his Jealousy is of his Love.

SIR SAMPSON. None of old *Foresight's* Sibyls ever utter'd such a Truth. Odsbud, you have won my Heart: I hate a Wit; I had a Son that was spoil'd among 'em; a good hopeful Lad, till he learn'd to be a Wit—and might have risen in the State. But, a pox on't, his Wit run him out of his Money, and now his Poverty has run him out of his Wits.

ANGELICA. Sir *Sampson*, as your Friend, I must tell you, you are very much abus'd in that Matter; he's no more Mad than you are.

SIR SAMPSON. How, Madam! Wou'd I cou'd prove it.

ANGELICA. I can tell you how that may be done.—But it is a thing that wou'd make me appear to be too much concern'd in your Affairs.

SIR SAMPSON *(aside)*. Odsbud, I believe she likes me.—Ah, Madam, all my Affairs are scarce worthy to be laid at your Feet; and I wish, Madam, they stood in a better Posture, that I might make a more becoming Offer to a Lady of your incomparable Beauty and Merit. If I had *Peru* in one Hand, and *Mexico* in t'other, and the *Eastern* Empire under my Feet, it would make me only a more glorious Victim to be offer'd at the Shrine of your Beauty.

ANGELICA. Bless me, Sir *Sampson*, what's the matter?

SIR SAMPSON. Odd, Madam, I love you—and if you wou'd take my Advice in a Husband—

ANGELICA. Hold, hold, Sir *Sampson*. I ask'd your Advice for a Husband, and you are giving me your Consent. I was indeed thinking to propose something like it in a Jest, to satisfy you about *Valentine:* for if a Match were seemingly carried on between you and me, it would oblige him to throw off his Disguise of Madness in Apprehension of losing me, for you know he has long pretended a Passion for me.

SIR SAMPSON. Gadzooks, a most ingenious Contrivance—if we were to go through with it. But why must the Match only be seemingly carried on? Odd, let it be a real Contract.

ANGELICA. O fie, Sir *Sampson,* what would the World say?

SIR SAMPSON. Say, they would say you were a wise Woman, and I a happy Man. Odd, Madam, I'll love you as long as I live, and leave you a good Jointure when I die.

ANGELICA. Aye, but that is not in your Power, Sir *Sampson;* for when *Valentine* confesses himself in his Senses, he must make over his Inheritance to his younger Brother.

SIR SAMPSON. Odd, you're cunning, a wary Baggage! Faith and Troth, I like you the better. But, I warrant you, I have a Proviso in the Obligation in favour of myself.—Body o'me, I have a Trick to turn the Settlement upon the Issue Male of our Two Bodies begotten. Odsbud, let us find Children, and I'll find an Estate.

ANGELICA. Will you? Well, do you find the Estate, and leave the t'other to me—

SIR SAMPSON. O Rogue! But I'll trust you. And will you consent? Is it a Match then?

ANGELICA. Let me consult my Lawyer concerning this Obligation; and if I find what you propose practicable, I'll give you my Answer.

SIR SAMPSON. With all my Heart. Come in with me, and I'll lend you the Bond. You shall consult your Lawyer, and I'll consult a Parson. Odzooks, I'm a young Man; odzooks, I'm a young Man, and I'll make it appear—odd, you're devilish Handsome; Faith and Troth, you're very Handsome, and I'm very Young, and very Lusty. Odsbud, Hussy, you know how to chuse, and so do I. Odd, I think we are very well met. Give me your Hand; odd, let me kiss it; 'tis as warm and as soft—as what?—odd, as t'other Hand—

give me t'other Hand, and I'll mumble 'em, and kiss 'em till they melt in my Mouth.

ANGELICA. Hold, Sir *Sampson.*–You're profuse of your Vigour before your time. You'll spend your Estate before you come to it.

SIR SAMPSON. No, no, only give you a Rent-roll of my Possessions–Ah, Baggage!–I warrant you, for little *Sampson.* Odd, *Sampson's* a very good Name for an able Fellow; your *Sampsons* were strong Dogs from the Beginning.

ANGELICA. Have a care, and don't over-act your Part. If you remember, the strongest *Sampson* of your Name pull'd an old House over his Head at last.

SIR SAMPSON. Say you so, Hussy? Come, let's go then. Odd, I long to be pulling down too, come away. Odso, here's somebody coming.

Exeunt.

Enter Tattle *and* Jeremy.

TATTLE. Is not that she, gone out just now?

JEREMY. Aye, Sir, she's just going to the Place of appointment. Ah Sir, if you are not very faithful and close in this Business, you'll certainly be the Death of a Person that has a most extraordinary Passion for your Honour's Service.

TATTLE. Aye, who's that?

JEREMY. Even my unworthy self, Sir. Sir, I have had an Appetite to be fed with your Commands a great while; and now, Sir, my former Master, having much troubled the Fountain of his Understanding, it is a very plausible Occasion for me to quench my Thirst at the Spring of your Bounty. I thought I could not recommend myself better to you, Sir, than by the delivery of a great Beauty and Fortune into your Arms, whom I have heard you Sigh for.

TATTLE. I'll make thy Fortune; say no more. Thou art a pretty Fellow, and can'st carry a Message to a Lady in a pretty soft kind of Phrase, and with a good persuading Accent.

JEREMY. Sir, I have the Seeds of Rhetorick and Oratory in my Head–I have been at *Cambridge.*

TATTLE. Aye, 'tis well enough for a Servant to be bred at an University, but the Education is a little too pedantic for a Gentleman. I hope you are secret in your Nature, private, close, ha?

JEREMY. O Sir, for that, Sir, 'tis my chief Talent; I'm as secret as the Head of *Nilus.*

TATTLE. Aye? Who's he, tho? A Privy Counsellor?

JEREMY *(aside).* O Ignorance! A cunning *Egyptian,* Sir, that with his Arms would over-run the Country, yet nobody could ever find out his Head-Quarters.

TATTLE. Close Dog! A good Whoremaster, I warrant him.—The time draws nigh, *Jeremy. Angelica* will be veil'd like a Nun, and I must be hooded like a Friar, ha, *Jeremy?*

JEREMY. Aye, Sir, hooded like a Hawk, to seize at first sight upon the Quarry. It is the Whim of my Master's Madness to be so dress'd; and she is so in Love with him, she'll comply with anything to please him. Poor Lady, I'm sure she'll have reason to pray for me, when she finds what a happy Exchange she has made between a Madman and so Accomplish'd a Gentleman.

TATTLE. Aye, faith, so she will, *Jeremy;* you're a good Friend to her, poor Creature.—I swear I do it hardly so much in consideration of myself, as Compassion to her.

JEREMY. 'Tis an Act of Charity, Sir, to save a fine Woman with Thirty Thousand Pound from throwing herself away.

TATTLE. So 'tis, faith. I might have sav'd several others in my time; but, i'Gad, I could never find in my Heart to Marry anybody before.

JEREMY. Well, Sir, I'll go and tell her my Master's coming, and meet you in half a quarter of an hour, with your Disguise, at your own Lodgings. You must talk a little madly; she won't distinguish the Tone of your Voice.

TATTLE. No, no, let me alone for a Counterfeit; I'll be ready for you.

Enter Miss Prue.

203 *Head of Nilus:* the sources of the Nile remained a mystery until the nineteenth century.

MISS PRUE. O Mr. *Tattle,* are you here! I'm glad I have found you; I have been looking up and down for you like anything, till I'm as tired as anything in the World.

TATTLE *(aside).* O Pox, how shall I get rid of this foolish Girl?

MISS PRUE. O, I have pure News; I can tell you pure News. I must not marry the Seaman now—my Father says so. Why won't you be my Husband? You say you love me, and you won't be my Husband. And I know you may be my Husband now if you please.

TATTLE. O fie, Miss; who told you so, Child?

MISS PRUE. Why, my Father—I told him that you lov'd me.

TATTLE. O fie, Miss, why did you do so? And who told you so, Child?

MISS PRUE. Who? Why you did; did not you?

TATTLE. O Pox, that was Yesterday, Miss; that was a great while ago, Child. I have been asleep since; slept a whole Night, and did not so much as dream of the matter.

MISS PRUE. Pshaw, O, but I dream't that it was so, tho.

TATTLE. Aye, but your Father will tell you that Dreams come by Contraries, Child.—O fie; what, we must not love one another now; pshaw, that would be a foolish thing indeed. 'Fie, fie, you're a Woman now, and must think of a new Man every Morning, and forget him every Night. No, no, to marry is to be a Child again, and play with the same Rattle always. O fie, marrying is a paw thing.

MISS PRUE. Well, but don't you love me as well as you did last Night, then?

TATTLE. No, no, Child, you would not have me.

MISS PRUE. No? Yes, but I would, though.

TATTLE. Pshaw, but I tell you, you would not. You forget you're a woman, and don't know your own mind.

268 *paw:* affected slang for 'improper'.

MISS PRUE. But here's my Father, and he knows my Mind.

Enter Foresight.

FORESIGHT. O, Mr. *Tattle,* your Servant. You are a close Man, but methinks your Love to my Daughter was a Secret I might have been trusted with—or had you a mind to try if I could discover it by my Art—hum, ha? I think there is something in your Physiognomy that has a resemblance of her; and the Girl is like me.

TATTLE. And so you wou'd infer that you and I are alike—*(Aside.)* what does the old Prig mean? I'll banter him, and laugh at him, and leave him.—I fancy you have a wrong Notion of Faces.

FORESIGHT. How? What? A wrong Notion! How so?

TATTLE. In the way of Art. I have some taking Features, not obvious to vulgar Eyes, that are Indications of a sudden turn of good Fortune in the Lottery of Wives, and promise a great Beauty and great Fortune reserved alone for me, by a private Intrigue of Destiny, kept secret from the piercing Eye of Perspicuity, from all Astrologers and the Stars themselves.

FORESIGHT. How! I will make it appear that what you say is impossible.

TATTLE. Sir, I beg your Pardon; I'm in haste—

FORESIGHT. For what?

TATTLE. To be married, Sir, married.

FORESIGHT. Aye, but pray take me along with you, Sir—

TATTLE. No, Sir; 'tis to be done privately. I never make Confidants.

FORESIGHT. Well; but my Consent, I mean. You won't marry my Daughter without my Consent?

TATTLE. Who I, Sir? I'm an absolute Stranger to you and your Daughter, Sir.

FORESIGHT. Hey day! What time of the Moon is this?

TATTLE. Very true, Sir, and desire to continue so. I have no more love for your Daughter than I have likeness of you; and I have a Secret in my Heart, which you wou'd be glad to know, and shan't know; and yet you shall know it too, and be sorry for't afterwards. I'd have you to know, Sir, that I am as knowing as the Stars, and as secret as the Night.—And I'm going to be Married just now, yet did not know of it half an Hour ago; and the Lady stays for me, and does not know of it yet.—There's a Mystery for you.—I know you love to unite Difficulties. Or, if you can't solve this, stay here a Quarter of an Hour, and I'll come and explain it to you.

Exit.

MISS PRUE. O Father, why will you let him go? Won't you make him be my Husband?

FORESIGHT. Mercy on us, what do these Lunacies portend? Alas! he's mad, Child, stark wild.

MISS PRUE. What, and must not I have e'er a Husband then? What, must I go to Bed to Nurse again, and be a Child as long as she's an old Woman? Indeed, but I won't: for now my Mind is set upon a Man, I will have a Man some way or other. Oh! methinks I'm sick when I think of a Man; and if I can't have one, I wou'd go to sleep all my Life, for when I'm awake, it makes me wish and long, and I don't know for what—and I'd rather be always a sleeping, than sick with thinking.

FORESIGHT. O fearful! I think the Girl's influenc'd too.—Hussy, you shall have a Rod.

MISS PRUE. A Fiddle of a Rod, I'll have a Husband; and if you won't get me one, I'll get one for myself: I'll marry our *Robin,* the Butler. He says he loves me, and he's a handsome Man, and shall be my Husband. I warrant he'll be my Husband and thank me too, for he told me so.

Enter Scandal, Mrs. Foresight, *and Nurse.*

FORESIGHT. Did he so?—I'll dispatch him for't presently. Rogue!—Oh, Nurse, come hither.

NURSE. What is your Worship's Pleasure?

FORESIGHT. Here, take your young Mistress, and lock her up presently, till farther Orders from me.

Not a Word Hussy—Do what I bid you; no Reply, away. And bid *Robbin* make ready to give an Account of his Plate and Linen; d'ye hear, be gone when I bid you.

Exeunt Nurse and Miss Prue.

MRS. FORESIGHT. What's the Matter, Husband?

FORESIGHT. 'Tis not convenient to tell you now.—Mr. *Scandal,* Heav'n keep us all in our Senses; I fear there is a contagious Frenzy abroad. How does *Valentine?*

SCANDAL. O, I hope he will do well again. I have a Message from him to your Niece *Angelica.*

FORESIGHT. I think she has not return'd since she went abroad with Sir *Sampson.*

Enter Ben.

MRS. FORESIGHT. Here's Mr. *Benjamin.* He can tell us if his Father be come Home.

BEN. Who, Father? Aye, he's come home with a Vengeance.

MRS. FORESIGHT. Why, what's the Matter?

BEN. Matter! Why, he's Mad.

FORESIGHT. Mercy on us, I was afraid of this.

BEN. And there's the handsome young Woman, she, as they say, Brother *Val* went mad for; she's mad too, I think.

FORESIGHT. O my poor Niece, is she gone too? Well, I shall run mad next.

MRS. FORESIGHT. Well, but how mad? How d'ye mean?

BEN. Nay, I'll give you leave to guess. I'll undertake to make a Voyage to *Antegoa*—no, hold, I mayn't say so neither—but I'll sail as far as *Ligorn* and back again, before you shall guess at the matter, and do nothing else; mess, you may take in all the Points of the Compass, and not hit right.

384 *Antegoa:* Antigua, in the Caribbean Sea.
385 *Ligorn:* Livorno, in English, Leghorn, on the north-west coast of Italy.

MRS. FORESIGHT. Your Experiment will take up a little too much time.

BEN. Why, then, I'll tell you: there's a new wedding upon the Stocks, and they two are a-going to be married to rights.

SCANDAL. Who?

BEN. Why Father and–the Young Woman. I can't hit of her Name.

SCANDAL. *Angelica?*

BEN. Aye, the same.

MRS. FORESIGHT. Sir *Sampson* and *Angelica,* impossible!

BEN. That may be–but I'm sure it is as I tell you.

SCANDAL. S'death it's a Jest. I can't believe it.

BEN. Look you, Friend, it's nothing to me, whether you believe it or no. What I say is true; d'ye see, they are married, or just going to be married, I know not which.

FORESIGHT. Well, but they are not Mad, that is, not Lunatic?

BEN. I don't know what you may call Madness, but she's mad for a Husband, and he's horn-mad, I think, or they'd ne'er make a Match together.–Here they come.

Enter Sir Sampson, Angelica, *with* Buckram.

SIR SAMPSON. Where is this old Soothsayer, this Uncle of mine elect? Aha, old *Foresight,* Uncle *Foresight,* wish me Joy, both as Uncle and Astrologer; here's a Conjunction that was not foretold in all your *Ephemeris.* The brightest Star in the blue Firmament –is shot from above, in a Jelly of Love, and so forth, and I'm Lord of the Ascendant. Odd, you're an old Fellow, *Foresight;* Uncle I mean, a very old Fellow, Uncle *Foresight;* and yet you shall live to dance at

418 *Ephemeris:* astronomical almanac.

418-9 *brightest Star . . . Jelly of Love:* misquoted by Sir Sampson from Dryden's heroic tragedy, *Tyrannic Love,* IV, i: 'And drop from above/ In a jelly of love!' The play was revived 1694. The brightest 'star' is the planet Venus.

my Wedding; faith and troth you shall. Odd, we'll have the Musick of the Spheres for thee, old *Lilly,* that we will, and thou shalt lead up a Dance in *Via Lactea.*

FORESIGHT. I'm Thunder-strook! You are not married to my Niece?

SIR SAMPSON. Not absolutely married, Uncle, but very near it; within a Kiss of the matter, as you see. *Kisses* Angelica.

ANGELICA. 'Tis very true indeed, Uncle; I hope you'll be my Father, and give me.

SIR SAMPSON. That he shall, or I'll burn his Globes. Body o'me, he shall be thy Father, I'll make him thy Father, and thou shalt make me a Father, and I'll make thee a Mother, and we'll beget Sons and Daughters enough to put the weekly Bills out of Countenance.

SCANDAL. Death and Hell! Where's *Valentine?* *Exit* Scandal.

MRS. FORESIGHT. This is so surprising—

SIR SAMPSON. How! What does my Aunt say? Surprising, Aunt? Not at all, for a young Couple to make a Match in Winter. Not at all—it's a Plot to undermine cold Weather, and destroy that Usurper of a Bed call'd a Warming-Pan.

MRS. FORESIGHT. I'm glad to hear you have so much Fire in you, Sir *Sampson.*

BEN. Mess, I fear his Fire's little better than Tinder; mayhap it will only serve to light up a Match for somebody else. The Young Woman's a handsome Young Woman, I can't deny it; but, Father, if I might be your Pilot in this Case, you should not marry her. It's just the same thing as if so be you should sail so far as the Straits without Provision.

SIR SAMPSON. Who gave you Authority to speak, Sirrah? To your Element, Fish; be mute, Fish, and to Sea; rule your Helm, Sirrah, don't direct me.

BEN. Well, well, take you care of your own Helm, or you mayn't keep your own Vessel steady.

425 *Via Lactea:* the Milky Way.
455 *Straits:* of Gibraltar.

SIR SAMPSON. Why you impudent Tarpaulin! Sirrah, do you bring your Forecastle Jests upon your Father? But I shall be even with you: I won't give you a Groat. Mr. *Buckram,* is the Conveyance so worded that nothing can possibly descend to this Scoundrel? I would not so much as have him have the Prospect of an Estate, tho' there were no way to come to it but by the *North-East Passage.*

BUCKRAM. Sir, it is drawn according to your Directions; there is not the least Cranny of the Law unstopt.

BEN. Lawyer, I believe there's many a Cranny and Leak unstopt in your Conscience. If so be that one had a Pump to your Bosom, I believe we shou'd discover a foul Hold. They say a Witch will sail in a Sieve, but I believe the Devil wou'd not venture aboard o' your Conscience. And that's for you.

SIR SAMPSON. Hold your Tongue, Sirrah. How now, who's there?

Enter Tattle *and* Mrs. Frail.

MRS. FRAIL. O, Sister, the most unlucky Accident!

MRS. FORESIGHT. What's the Matter?

TATTLE. O, the two most unfortunate poor Creatures in the World we are.

FORESIGHT. Bless us! How so?

MRS. FRAIL. Ah, Mr. *Tattle* and I, poor Mr. *Tattle* and I are—I can't speak it out.

TATTLE. Nor I—But poor Mrs. *Frail* and I are—

MRS. FRAIL. Married.

MRS. FORESIGHT. Married! How?

TATTLE. Suddenly— before we knew where we were— that Villain *Jeremy,* by help of Disguises, trickt us into one another.

FORESIGHT. Why, you told me just now you went hence in haste to be married.

ANGELICA. But I believe Mr. *Tattle* meant the Favour to me; I thank him.

468 *Northeast Passage:* the impossibly difficult sea route to the east, over the top of Norway and Siberia.

TATTLE. I did; as I hope to be sav'd, Madam, my Intentions were good. But this is the most cruel thing, to marry one does not know how, nor why, nor wherefore. The Devil take me if ever I was so much concern'd at anything in my Life.

ANGELICA. 'Tis very unhappy, if you don't care for one another.

TATTLE. The least in the World—that is, for my Part; I speak for myself. Gad, I never had the least thought of serious Kindness—I never lik'd anybody less in my Life. Poor Woman! Gad, I'm sorry for her too, for I have no reason to hate her neither; but I believe I shall lead her a damn'd sort of a Life.

MRS. FORESIGHT *(aside to* Mrs. Frail). He's better than no Husband at all, tho he's a Coxcomb.

MRS. FRAIL *(to her).* Aye, aye, it's well it's no worse.—Nay, for my part I always despised Mr. *Tattle* of all things; nothing but his being my Husband could have made me like him less.

TATTLE. Look you there, I thought as much. Pox on't, I wish we could keep it secret. Why, I don't believe any of this Company wou'd speak of it.

MRS. FRAIL. But, my Dear, that's impossible; the Parson and that Rogue *Jeremy* will publish it.

TATTLE. Aye, my Dear, so they will, as you say.

ANGELICA. O, you'll agree very well in a little time; Custom will make it easy to you.

TATTLE. Easy! Pox on't, I don't believe I shall sleep tonight.

SIR SAMPSON. Sleep, quotha! No! Why, you would not sleep o' your Wedding Night? I'm an older Fellow than you, and don't mean to sleep.

BEN. Why, there's another Match now, as tho'f a couple of Privateers were looking for a Prize, and should fall foul of one another. I'm sorry for the Young Man with all my Heart. Look you, Friend, if I may advise you—when she's going, for that you must expect; I have Experience of her—when she's going, let her go. For no *Matrimony* is tough enough to hold her, and if she can't drag her Anchor along with her, she'll break her Cable, I can tell you that. Who's here? the Madman?

Enter Valentine *dress'd,* Scandal, *and* Jeremy.

VALENTINE. No, here's the Fool; and if occasion be, I'll give it under my hand.

SIR SAMPSON. How now?

VALENTINE. Sir, I'm come to acknowledge my Errors, and ask your Pardon.

SIR SAMPSON. What, have you found your Senses at last then? In good time, Sir.

VALENTINE. You were abus'd, Sir; I never was Distracted.

FORESIGHT. How! Not Mad! Mr. *Scandal?*

SCANDAL. No really, Sir; I'm his Witness; it was all Counterfeit.

VALENTINE. I thought I had Reasons. But it was a poor Contrivance; the Effect has shown it such.

SIR SAMPSON. Contrivance, what, to cheat me? To cheat your Father! Sirrah, could you hope to prosper?

VALENTINE. Indeed, I thought, Sir, when the Father endeavoured to undo the Son, it was a reasonable return of Nature.

SIR SAMPSON. Very good, Sir! Mr. *Buckram,* are you ready?—Come, Sir, will you sign and seal?

VALENTINE. If you please, Sir; but first I would ask this Lady one Question.

SIR SAMPSON. Sir, you must ask my leave first. That Lady, no, Sir; you shall ask that Lady no Questions till you have ask'd her Blessing, Sir; that Lady is to be my Wife.

VALENTINE. I have heard as much, Sir, but I wou'd have it from her own Mouth.

SIR SAMPSON. That's as much as to say I lie, Sir, and you don't believe what I say.

VALENTINE. Pardon me, Sir. But I reflect that I very lately counterfeited Madness; I don't know but the Frolic may go round.

SIR SAMPSON. Come, Chuck, satisfy him, answer him.—Come, come, Mr. *Buckram,* the Pen and Ink.

BUCKRAM. Here it is, Sir, with the Deed; all is ready.

Valentine *goes to* Angelica.

ANGELICA. 'Tis true, you have a great while pretended Love to me; nay, what if you were sincere? Still you must pardon me, if I think my own Inclinations have a better Right to dispose of my Person, than yours.

SIR SAMPSON. Are you answer'd now, Sir?

VALENTINE. Yes, Sir.

SIR SAMPSON. Where's your Plot, Sir, and your Contrivance now, Sir? Will you sign, Sir? Come, will you sign and seal?

VALENTINE. With all my Heart, Sir.

SCANDAL. S'death, you are not mad, indeed, to ruin yourself?

VALENTINE. I have been disappointed of my only Hope; and he that loses hope may part with anything. I never valu'd Fortune but as it was subservient to my Pleasure; and my only Pleasure was to please this Lady. I have made many vain Attempts, and find at last that nothing but my Ruin can effect it: which, for that Reason, I will sign to—give me the Paper.

ANGELICA *(aside).* Generous *Valentine!*

BUCKRAM. Here is the Deed, Sir.

VALENTINE. But where is the Bond by which I am oblig'd to sign this?

BUCKRAM. Sir *Sampson,* you have it.

ANGELICA. No, I have it; and I'll use it as I would everything that is an Enemy to *Valentine.*

Tears the Paper.

SIR SAMPSON. How now!

VALENTINE. Ha!

ANGELICA *(to* Valentine*).* Had I the World to give you, it cou'd not make me worthy of so generous and faithful a Passion: here's my Hand, my Heart was always yours, and struggl'd very hard to make this utmost Trial of your Virtue.

VALENTINE. Between Pleasure and Amazement, I am lost—but on my Knees I take the Blessing.

SIR SAMPSON. Oons, what is the meaning of this?

BEN. Mess, here's the Wind chang'd again. Father, you and I may make a Voyage together now.

ANGELICA. Well, Sir *Sampson,* since I have played you a Trick, I'll advise you how you may avoid such another. Learn to be a good Father, or you'll never get a second Wife. I always lov'd your Son, and hated your unforgiving Nature. I was resolv'd to try him to the utmost; I have try'd you too, and know you both. You have not more Faults than he has Virtues; and 'tis hardly more Pleasure to me, that I can make him and myself happy, than that I can punish you.

VALENTINE. If my happiness cou'd receive Addition, this kind surprize would make it double.

SIR SAMPSON. Oons, you're a *Crocodile.*

FORESIGHT. Really, Sir *Sampson,* this is a sudden Eclipse—

SIR SAMPSON. You're an illiterate Fool, and I'm another, and the Stars are Liars; and if I had Breath enough, I'd curse them and you, myself and every-body. Oons—cully'd, bubbl'd, jilted, Woman-bobb'd at last.—I have not Patience.

Exit Sir Sampson

TATTLE. If the Gentleman is in this disorder for want of a Wife, I can spare him mine. *(To* Jeremy.) Oh, are you there, Sir? I'm indebted to you for my Happiness.

JEREMY. Sir, I ask you ten thousand Pardons; 'twas an errant mistake. You see, Sir, my Master was never mad, nor anything like it. Then how could it be otherwise?

VALENTINE. *Tattle,* I thank you; you would have interposed between me and Heav'n; but Providence laid Purgatory in your way. You have but Justice.

SCANDAL. I hear the Fiddles that Sir *Sampson* pro-vided for all his own Wedding; methinks 'tis pity they should not be employ'd when the Match is so much mended. *Valentine,* tho it be Morning, we may have a Dance.

VALENTINE. Anything, my Friend, everything that looks like Joy and Transport.

SCANDAL. Call 'em *Jeremy.*

ANGELICA. I have done dissembling now, *Valentine;* and if that Coldness which I have always worn before you should turn to an extreme Fondness, you must not suspect it.

VALENTINE. I'll prevent that suspicion—for I intend to doat on at that immoderate rate that your Fondness shall never distinguish itself enough to be taken notice of. If ever you seem to love too much, it must be only when I can't love enough.

ANGELICA. Have a care of large Promises; you know you are apt to run more in Debt than you are able to pay.

VALENTINE. Therefore, I yield my Body as your Prisoner, and make your best on't.

SCANDAL. The Musick stays for you.

Dance.

SCANDAL. Well, Madam, You have done exemplary Justice, in punishing an inhuman Father, and rewarding a faithful Lover; but there is a third good Work, which I in particular must thank you for; I was an Infidel to your Sex, and you have converted me.—For now I am convinc'd that all Women are not like Fortune, blind in bestowing Favours either on those who do not merit, or who do not want 'em.

ANGELICA. 'Tis an unreasonable Accusation that you lay upon our Sex: you tax us with Injustice, only to cover your own want of Merit. You would all have the Reward of Love, but few have the Constancy to stay till it becomes your due. Men are generally Hypocrites and Infidels; they pretend to worship, but have neither Zeal nor Faith. How few, like *Valentine,* would perserve even unto Martyrdom, and sacrifice their Interest to their Constancy! In admiring me, you misplace the Novelty.

The Miracle today is that we find
A Lover true, not that a Woman's kind.

Exeunt Omnes.

FINIS.

Epilogue

Spoken at the opening of the New House,

By Mrs. *Bracegirdle.*

Sure Providence at first design'd this Place
To be the Player's Refuge in distress;
For still in every Storm they all run hither,
As to a Shed that shields 'em from the Weather.
But thinking of this change which last befell us,
It's like what I have heard our Poets tell us:
For when behind our Scenes their Suits are pleading,
To help their Love, sometimes they show their Reading;
And wanting ready Cash to pay for Hearts,
They top their Learning on us, and their Parts.
Once of Philosophers they told us Stories,
Whom, as I think they call'd–*Py–Pythagories,*
I'm sure 'tis some such *Latin* Name they give 'em,
And we, who know no better, must believe 'em.
Now to these Men (say they) such Souls were given,
That after Death ne'er went to Hell, nor Heaven,
But liv'd, I know not how, in Beasts; and then,
When many Years were past, in Men again.
Methinks we *Players* resemble such a Soul,
That does from Bodies, we from Houses stroll.
Thus *Aristotle's* Soul, of old that was,
May now be damn'd to animate an Ass;
Or in this very House, for ought we know,
Is doing painful Penance in some *Beau;*
And this our Audience, which did once resort
To shining Theatres to see our Sport,
Now find us toss'd into a Tennis-Court.
These Walls but t'other Day were fill'd with Noise
Of Roaring Gamesters, and your *Damme Boys.*

1 *this Place:* a tennis court, converted into the new Lincoln's Inn Theatre.

Then bounding Balls and Rackets they encompass'd,
And now they're fill'd with Jests, and Flights, and Bombast!
I vow, I don't much like this Transmigration,
Strolling from Place to Place, by Circulation.
Grant Heaven, we don't return to our first Station.
I know not what these think, but for my Part,
I can't reflect without an aching Heart,
How we shou'd end in our Original, a Cart.
But we can't fear, since you're so good to save us,
That you have only set us up, to leave us.
Thus from the past, we hope for future Grace,
I beg it–
And some here know I have a begging Face.
Then pray continue this your kind behaviour,
For a clear Stage won't do, without your Favour.

38 *Cart:* from which early plays were performed by travelling actors; also used to carry condemned criminals to the gallows.
45 *clear Stage:* free of debts.

THE WAY OF THE WORLD

Introduction

In 1697, Congreve surpassed even the triumph of *Love for Love* with the reception of his tragedy, *The Mourning Bride*. In its dedication to Princess Anne, later Queen Anne, the author refers to an old problem which was stimulating increasing controversy—the question of morality in drama. He deplores the 'licentious Practice of the Modern Theatre', and insists that poets must instruct 'not alone by Precepts which persuade, but also by Examples which illustrate. Thus is Delight interwoven with Instruction; when not only Vertue is prescrib'd, but also represented.' Clearly, he hoped to protect himself from criticism by attaching a didactic, high-minded purpose to his drama. Whether or not his tragedy succeeded in elevating the moral tone of its audience, the dedication did not exempt its author from scathing denunciation a year later in Jeremy Collier's notorious *Short View of the Immorality and Profaneness of the English Stage*. Congreve lost his temper at this attack; his published defence is scarcely more moderate in tone than the fulminations against him, but, fortunately, he did not give up his intention to write another play. In fact, Collier may have done posterity a service by stimulating Congreve in his last and greatest display of comic genius, *The Way of the World*. Determined to bring out something on a level to silence hostile criticism, he polished his lines for months before allowing them on the boards. The dedication to the play contains a free admission that he wrote it with little regard for public taste, implying that his sole concern was to achieve his private artistic ideal. He also declared himself satisfied with its initial reception, although in fact the play had but moderate success at its opening in March 1700, despite the expert performance of Anne Bracegirdle as Millamant, and the enthusiasm of more sophisticated critics, headed as always by the loyal Dryden. The highly complicated plot and keen satire were both mentioned as obstacles to enjoyment, and the listeners could have detected very little direct, comforting resemblance to earlier comedies in this, Congreve's most original work. The play never achieved the success of *Love for Love* or *The Old Batchelour* in Congreve's lifetime, but he survived to see three revivals, in 1705, 1715, and most notably, in 1718, with Mrs. Oldfield much praised as Millamant. Its popularity grew steadily later in the eighteenth century, waned in the nineteenth along with all Restoration comedy, and had a rebirth in modern times with a revival by the Mermaid Society in 1904. Since that time, it has been fully appreciated and often performed, most notably recently in a 1969 production by the National Theatre in London, with Geraldine McEwan as Millamant, and Hazel Hughes an astonishing Lady Wishfort. Several separate editions of the play are available, including those by Kathleen Lynch for the Regents Restoration Drama Series, 1965, and by Brian Gibbons in a New Mermaids Dramabook, 1969.

THE

WAY OF THE WORLD,

A

COMEDY.

As it is ACTED at the

Theatre in Lincoln's-Inn-Fields

BY

His Majesty's Servants.

Written by Mr. CONGREVE.

---

* *Audire est Operæ pretium, procedere recte*
Qui mæchis non vultis—— Hor. Sat. 2. 1. I.
——Metuat doti deprensa.—— Ibid.

LONDON,

Printed for *Jacob Tonson,* within *Gray's-Inn-Gate* next *Gray's-Inn-Lane.* 1700.

'It is worth your while to listen, those of you who do not wish adulterers to be successful . . . When she is caught let her fear for the dowry.' (Horace, *Satires*, I, ii, 37-8, and 131.)

To the Right Honourable RALPH

Earl of Mountague, &c.*

My LORD,

Whether the World will arraign me of Vanity or not, that I have presum'd to Dedicate this Comedy to your Lordship, I am yet in doubt: Tho' it may be it is some degree of Vanity even to doubt of it. One who has at any time had the Honour of your Lordship's Conversation, cannot be suppos'd to think very meanly of that which he would prefer to your perusal; yet it were to incur the Imputation of too much Sufficiency to pretend to such a Merit as might abide the Test of your Lordship's Censure.

Whatever Value may be wanting to this Play, while yet it is mine, will be sufficiently made up to it when it is once become your Lordship's; and it is my Security that I cannot have overrated it more by my Dedication than your Lordship will dignify it by your Patronage.

That it succeeded on the Stage was almost beyond my Expectation; for but little of it was prepar'd for that general Taste which seems now to be predominant in the Palates of our Audience.

Those Characters which are meant to be ridiculous in most of our Comedies are of Fools so gross that, in my humble Opinion, they should rather disturb than divert the well-natur'd and reflecting part of an Audience; they are rather Objects of Charity than Contempt; and instead of moving our Mirth, they ought very often to excite our Compassion.

This Reflection mov'd me to design some Characters which should appear ridiculous not so much thro' a natural Folly (which is incorrigible, and therefore not proper for the Stage) as thro' an affected Wit; a Wit, which at the same time that it is affected, is also false. As there is some Difficulty in the formation of a Character of this Nature, so there is some Hazard which attends the progress of its Success upon the Stage. For many come to a Play so over-charg'd with Criticism that they very often let fly their Censure, when through their rashness they have mistaken their Aim. This I had occasion

* Ralph, Earl of Montague, Whig diplomat; entertained Congreve at his country house in Northants during the summer of 1699. His fashionable friends may have provided Congreve with hints for character types in the play.

lately to observe; for this Play had been Acted two or three Days, before some of these hasty Judges cou'd find the leisure to distinguish betwixt the Character of a *Witwoud* and a *Truewit.*†

I must beg your Lordship's Pardon for this Digression from the true Course of this Epistle; but that it may not seem altogether impertinent, I beg that I may plead the occasion of it in part of that Excuse of which I stand in need for recommending this Comedy to your Protection. It is only by the Countenance of your Lordship, and the *Few* so qualified, that such who write with Care and Pains can hope to be distinguish'd, for the Prostituted Name of *Poet* promiscuously levels all that bear it.

Terence, the most correct Writer in the World, had a *Scipio* and a *Lelius,* if not to assist him, at least to support him in his Reputation; and notwithstanding his extraordinary Merit, it may be their Countenance was not more than necessary.

The Purity of his Style, the Delicacy of his Turns, and the Justness of his Characters, were all of them Beauties which the greater part of his Audience were incapable of Tasting; some of the coarsest Strokes of *Plautus,* so severally censured by *Horace,* were more likely to affect the Multitude; such who come with expectation to laugh out the last Act of a Play, and are better entertained with two or three unseasonable Jests, than with the artful Solution of the *Fable.*

As *Terence* excell'd in his Performances, so had he great Advantages to encourage his Undertakings; for he built most on the Foundations of *Menander:* his Plots were generally modell'd, and his Characters ready drawn to his Hand. He copied *Menander;* and *Menander* had no less Light in the Formation of his Characters from the Observations of *Theophrastus,* of whom he was a Disciple; and *Theophrastus* it is known was not only the Disciple but the immediate Successor of *Aristotle,* the first and greatest Judge of Poetry. These were great Models to design by; and the further Advantage which *Terence* possess'd, towards giving his Plays the due Ornaments of Purity of Style, and Justness of Manners, was not less considerable from the freedom of Conversation which was permitted him with *Lelius* and *Scipio,*

† *Witwoud and a Truewit:* Congreve's character in the play contrasted with Jonson's Truewit in *Epicoene: or the Silent Woman* (1609).

two of the greatest and most polite Men of his Age. And indeed, the Privilege of such a Conversation is the only certain Means of attaining to the Perfection of Dialogue.

If it has happened in any part of this Comedy, that I have gain'd a Turn of Style, or Expression more Correct, or at least more Corrigible* than in those which I have formerly written, I must, with equal Pride and Gratitude, ascribe it to the Honour of your Lordship's admitting me into your Conversation, and that of a Society where everybody else was so well worthy of you, in your Retirement last Summer from the Town, for it was immediately after that this Comedy was written. If I have fail'd in my Performance, it is only to be regretted, where there were so many not inferior either to a *Scipio* or a *Lelius,* that there should be one wanting equal to the Capacity of a *Terence.*

If I am not mistaken, Poetry is almost the only Art which has not yet laid claim to your Lordship's Patronage. Architecture, and Painting, to the great Honour of our Country, have flourish'd under your Influence and Protection. In the mean time, Poetry, the eldest Sister of all Arts, and Parent of most, seems to have resign'd her Birth-right by having neglected to pay her Duty to your Lordship, and by permitting others of a later Extraction to prepossess that Place in your Esteem to which none can pretend a better Title. Poetry, in its nature, is sacred to the Good and Great; the relation between them is reciprocal, and they are ever propitious to it. It is the Privilege of Poetry to address to them, and it is their Prerogative alone to give it Protection.

This receiv'd Maxim is a general Apology for all Writers who Consecrate their Labours to great Men. But I could wish at this time that this Address were exempted from the common pretence of all Dedications; and that, as I can distinguish your Lordship even among the most Deserving, so this Offering might become remarkable by some particular Instance of Respect, which shou'd assure your Lordship that I am, with all due Sense of your extreme Worthiness and Humanity,

My LORD,

Your Lordship's most obedient
and most oblig'd humble Servant,

Will. Congreve.

* *corrigible:* capable of correction.

To Mr. *CONGREVE*, Occasion'd by his COMEDY Call'd the WAY *of the* WORLD.*

When Pleasure's falling to the low Delight,
In the vain Joys of the uncertain Sight;
No Sense of Wit when rude Spectators know,
But in distorted Gesture, Farce, and Show;
How could, great Author, your aspiring Mind
Dare to write only to the Few Refin'd?
Yet tho' that nice Ambition you pursue,
'Tis not in *Congreve's* Power to please but few.
Implicitly devoted to his Fame,
Well-dress'd Barbarians know his awful Name;
Though senseless they're of Mirth, but when they laugh,
As they feel Wine, but when, 'till drunk, they quaff.
　　On you, from Fate, a lavish Portion fell
In ev'ry way of Writing to excell.
Your Muse Applause to *Arabella* brings,
In Notes as sweet as *Arabella* sings.
Whene'er you draw an undissembled Woe,
With sweet Distress your Rural Numbers flow;
Pastora's the Complaint of ev'ry Swain,
Pastora still the Echo of the Plain!
Or if your Muse describe, with warming Force,
The wounded *Frenchman* falling from his Horse;
And her own *William* glorious in the Strife,
Bestowing on the prostrate Foe his Life;
You the great Act as gen'rously rehearse,
And all the *English* Fury's in your Verse.
By your selected Scenes, and handsome Choice,
Ennobled Comedy exalts her Voice;
Your check unjust Esteem and fond Desire,

* Commendatory verses first published in Congreve's *Collected Works*, 1710.

15 *Arabella:* reference to Congreve's pindaric ode, *On Mrs. Arabella Hunt, Singing.*

19 *Pastora:* Congreve's elegy, *The Mourning Muse of Alexis,* laments the death of Queen Mary, 1694, under the name of Pastora.

23 *William:* Congreve's *Pindarique Ode to the King, On His Taking Namur* celebrates William's victory of 1695.

And teach to Scorn, what else we should Admire;
The just Impression taught by you we bear,
The Player acts the World, the World the Player,
Whom still that World unjustly disesteems,
Tho' he, alone, professes what he seems.
But when your Muse assumes her Tragick Part,
She conquers and she reigns in ev'ry Heart;
To mourn with her Men cheat their private Woe,
And gen'rous Pity's all the Grief they know.
The Widow, who, impatient of Delay,
From the Town joys must mask it to the Play,
Joins with your *Mourning Bride's* resistless Moan,
And weeps a Loss she slighted, when her own.
You give us Torment, and you give us Ease,
And vary our Afflictions as you please.
Is not a Heart so kind as yours in Pain,
To load your Friends with Cares you only feign;
Your Friends in Grief, compos'd yourself, to leave?
But 'tis the only way you'll e'er deceive.
Then still, great Sir, your moving Pow'r employ,
To lull our Sorrow, and correct our Joy.

*R. STEELE**

Prologue,

Spoken by Mr. Betterton.*

Of those few Fools who with ill Stars are curs'd,
Sure scribbling Fools, call'd Poets, fare the worst;
For they're a sort of Fools which *Fortune* makes,
And after she has made 'em Fools, forsakes.
With *Nature's* Oafs 'tis quite a diff'rent Case,
For *Fortune* favours all her *Idiot-Race;*
In her own Nest the *Cuckoo-Eggs* we find,
O'er which she broods to hatch the *Changling-Kind.*
No Portion for her own she has to spare,

41 *Mourning Bride:* Congreve's highly successful tragedy, produced 1697.
* Sir Richard Steele (1672-1729), the famous Whig gazetteer, essayist, and playwright. His own comedies reflect the change of taste which influenced Congreve's early retirement from the theatre.
* The great actor, now well into his sixties, took the part of Fainall in the play.
5 *Oafs:* 'a changeling; a foolish child left by the fairies.' (Johnson, *Dictionary.*)
7 *Cuckoo:* notorious for laying its eggs in other birds' nests for them to hatch.

So much she doats on her adopted Care.
  Poets are Bubbles, by the Town drawn in,
Suffer'd at first some trifling Stakes to win;
But what unequal Hazards do they run!
Each time they write, they venture all they've won;
The 'Squire that's butter'd still, is sure to be undone.
This Author, heretofore, has found your Favour,
But pleads no Merit from his past Behaviour.
To build on that might prove a vain Presumption,
Should Grants to Poets made admit Resumption;
And in *Parnassus* he must lose his Seat,
If that be found a forefeited Estate.
  He owns, with Toil he wrought the following Scenes,
But, if they're naught ne'er spare him for his Pains;
Damn him the more; have no Commiseration
For Dulness on mature Deliberation.
He swears he'll not resent one hiss'd-off Scene,
Nor, like those peevish Wits, his Play maintain,
Who, to assert their Sense, your Taste arraign.
Some Plot we think he has, and some new Thought;
Some Humour too, no Farce; but that's a Fault.
Satire, he thinks, you ought not to expect;
For so Reform'd a Town who dares Correct?
To please, this time, has been his sole Pretence;
He'll not instruct, lest it should give Offence.
Should he by chance a Knave or Fool expose,
That hurts none here, sure here are none of those.
In short, our Play, shall (with your leave to show it)
Give you one Instance of a Passive Poet.
Who to your Judgments yields all Resignation;
So Save or Damn, after your own Discretion.

Dramatis Personæ

MEN

FAINALL, In Love with MRS. MARWOOD	Mr. Betterton
MIRABELL, In Love with MRS. MILLAMANT	Mr. Verbrugen
WITWOUD, Followers of MRS. MILLAMANT	Mr. Bowen
PETULANT, Followers of MRS. MILLAMANT	Mr. Bowman
SIR WILFULL WITWOUD, Half Brother to WITWOUD, and Nephew to LADY WISHFORT	Mr. Underhill
WAITWELL, Servant to MIRABELL	Mr. Bright

11 *Bubbles:* dupes.
15 *butter'd:* 'loaded with fulsome praise' *(OED);* here, persuaded to double his wager.

WOMEN

LADY WISHFORT, Enemy to MIRABELL, for having falsely pretended Love to her	Mrs. Leigh
*MRS. MILLAMANT, A fine Lady, Niece to LADY WISHFORT, and loves MIRABELL	Mrs. Bracegirdle
MRS. MARWOOD, Friend to MR. FAINALL, and likes MIRABELL	Mrs. Barry
MRS. FAINALL, Daughter to LADY WISHFORT, and Wife to FAINALL, formerly Friend to MIRABELL	Mrs. Bowman
FOIBLE, Woman to LADY WISHFORT	Mrs. Willis
MINCING, Woman to MRS. MILLAMANT	Mrs. Prince

Dancers, Footmen, *and* Attendants.

SCENE LONDON.

The Time equal to that of the Presentation.

THE WAY OF THE WORLD.

ACT I. SCENE I.

A Chocolate-house.

Mirabell *and* Fainall *Rising from Cards.* Betty *waiting.*

MIRABELL. You are a fortunate Man, Mr. *Fainall.*

FAINALL. Have we done?

MIRABELL. What you please. I'll play on to entertain you.

FAINALL. No, I'll give you your Revenge another time, when you are not so indifferent; you are thinking of something else now, and play too negligently. The Coldness of a losing Gamester lessens the Pleasure of the Winner. I'd no more play with a Man that slighted his ill Fortune than I'd make Love to a Woman who undervalu'd the Loss of her Reputation.

* The designation *Mrs.* was used at that time for both married and unmarried women.

MIRABELL. You have a Taste extremely delicate, and are for refining on your Pleasures.

FAINALL. Prithee, why so reserv'd? Something has put you out of Humour.

MIRABELL. Not at all. I happen to be grave today, and you are gay; that's all.

FAINALL. Confess, *Millamant* and you quarrell'd last Night after I left you; my fair Cousin has some Humours that wou'd tempt the patience of a Stoic. What, some Coxcomb came in and was well receiv'd by her, while you were by?

MIRABELL. *Witwoud* and *Petulant,* and what was worse, her Aunt, your Wife's Mother, my evil Genius; or to sum up all in her own Name, my old Lady *Wishfort* came in.

FAINALL. O there it is then! She has a lasting Passion for you, and with Reason.—What, then my Wife was there?

MIRABELL. Yes, and Mrs. *Marwood,* and three or four more whom I never saw before. Seeing me, they all put on their grave Faces, whisper'd one another; then complain'd aloud of the Vapours, and after fell into a profound Silence.

FAINALL. They had a mind to be rid of you.

MIRABELL. For which Reason I resolv'd not to stir. At last the good old Lady broke tho' her painful Taciturnity with an Invective against long Visits. I would not have understood her, but *Millamant* joining in the Argument, I rose and with a constrain'd Smile told her, I thought nothing was so easy as to know when a Visit began to be troublesome. She reddened, and I withdrew, without expecting her Reply.

FAINALL. You were to blame to resent what she spoke only in Compliance with her Aunt.

MIRABELL. She is more Mistress of herself than to be under the necessity of such a resignation.

43 *expecting:* waiting for.

FAINALL. What? tho' half her Fortune depends upon her marrying with my Lady's Approbation?

MIRABELL. I was then in such a Humour that I shou'd have been better pleas'd if she had been less discreet.

FAINALL. Now I remember, I wonder not they were weary of you; last Night was one of their Cabal-nights; they have 'em three times a Week, and meet by turns at one another's Apartments, where they come together like the Coroner's Inquest, to sit upon the murder'd Reputations of the Week. You and I are excluded; and it was once propos'd that all the Male Sex shou'd be excepted. But somebody mov'd that to avoid Scandal there might be one Man of the Community; upon which Motion *Witwoud* and *Petulant* were enroll'd Members.

MIRABELL. And who may have been the Foundress of this Sect? My Lady *Wishfort,* I warrant, who publishes her Detestation of Mankind, and full of the Vigour of Fifty five, declares for a Friend and *Ratafia,* and let posterity shift for itself, she'll breed no more.

FAINALL. The discovery of your sham Addresses to her, to conceal your Love to her Niece, has provok'd this Separation; had you dissembl'd better, Things might have continu'd in the state of Nature.

MIRABELL. I did as much as Man cou'd, with any reasonable Conscience; I proceeded to the very last Act of Flattery with her, and was guilty of a Song in her Commendation. Nay, I got a Friend to put her into a Lampoon, and complement her with the Imputation of an Affair with a young Fellow, which I carry'd so far that I told her the malicious Town took notice that she had grown fat of a sudden; and when she lay in of a Dropsy, persuaded her she was reported to be in Labour. The Devil's in't, if an old woman is to be flatter'd further, unless a Man shou'd endeavour downright personally to debauch her; and that my Virtue forbad me. But for the discovery of that Amour I am Indebted to your Friend, or your

55 *Cabal:* originally, a group of ministers engaged in a political plot.
68 *Ratafia:* liqueur flavoured with fruit stones.
82 *Dropsy:* disorder involving swelling from accumulation of fluid in the body.

Wife's Friend, Mrs. *Marwood.*

FAINALL. What should provoke her to be your Enemy, without she has made you Advances which you have slighted? Women do not easily forgive Omissions of that Nature.

MIRABELL. She was always civil to me till of late. I confess I am not one of those Coxcombs who are apt to interpret a Woman's good Manners to her Prejudice, and think that she who does not refuse 'em everything can refuse 'em nothing.

FAINALL. You are a gallant Man, *Mirabell;* and tho' you may have Cruelty enough not to satisfy a Lady's longing, you have too much Generosity not to be tender of her Honour. Yet you speak with an Indifference which seems to be affected, and confesses you are conscious of a Negligence.

MIRABELL. You pursue the Argument with a distrust that seems to be unaffected, and confesses you are conscious of a Concern for which the Lady is more indebted to you than is your Wife.

FAINALL. Fie, fie, Friend! If you grow Censorious I must leave you.—I'll look upon the Gamesters in the next Room.

MIRABELL. Who are they?

FAINALL. *Petulant* and *Witwoud. (To* Betty.) Bring me some Chocolate.

Exit.

MIRABELL. *Betty,* what says your Clock?

BETTY. Turn'd of the last Canonical Hour, Sir.

Exit.

MIRABELL. How pertinently the Jade answers me! (*Looking at his Watch.*) Ha? almost One o'clock! O, y'are come—

Enter a Servant.

116 *Canonical Hour:* between 8 a.m. and 3 p.m., the hours for legal marriage in church.

Well, is the grand Affair over? You have been something tedious.

SERVANT. Sir, here's such Coupling at *Pancras* that they stand behind one another, as 'twere in a Country Dance. Ours was the last Couple to lead up, and no hopes appearing of dispatch, besides the Parson growing hoarse, we were afraid his Lungs would have fail'd before it came to our turn; so we drove round to *Duke's Place,* and there they were riveted in a trice.

MIRABELL. So, so, you are sure they are Married.

SERVANT. Married and Bedded, Sir; I am Witness.

MIRABELL. Have you the Certificate?

SERVANT. Here it is, Sir.

MIRABELL. Has the Taylor brought *Waitwell's* clothes home, and the new Liveries?

SERVANT. Yes, Sir.

MIRABELL. That's well. Do you go home again, d'ye hear, and adjourn the Consummation till farther Order; bid *Waitwell* shake his Ears, and Dame *Partlet* rustle up her Feathers, and meet me at One o'Clock by *Rosamond's* Pond, that I may see her before she returns to her Lady; and as you tender your Ears, be secret.

Exit Servant.

Re-Enter Fainall.

FAINALL. Joy of your Success, *Mirabell;* you look pleas'd.

MIRABELL. Aye; I have been engag'd in a Matter of some sort of Mirth, which is not yet ripe for discovery. I am glad this is not a Cabal-night. I wonder, *Fainall,* that you who are Married, and of Consequence should be discreet, will suffer your Wife to be of such a Party.

124 *Pancras:* St Pancras, outside the city, where unlicensed marriages were performed.
130 *Duke's Place:* St James, in Duke Place, also performed illicit marriages.
141 *Partlet:* Pertelote, wife of Chanticleer the cock in the fable of *Reynard the Fox.*
143 *Rosamond's Pond:* well-known trysting place in south-west corner of St James's Park.

FAINALL. Faith, I am not Jealous. Besides, most who are engag'd are Women and Relations; and for the Men, they are of a Kind too Contemptible to give Scandal.

MIRABELL. I am of another Opinion. The greater the Coxcomb, always the more the Scandal; for a Woman who is not a Fool can have but one Reason for associating with a Man that is.

FAINALL. Are you Jealous as often as you see *Witwoud* entertain'd by *Millamant?*

MIRABELL. Of her Understanding I am, if not of her Person.

FAINALL. You do her wrong; for, to give her her Due, she has Wit.

MIRABELL. She has Beauty enough to make any Man think so, and Complaisance enough not to contradict him who shall tell her so.

FAINALL. For a passionate Lover, methinks you are a Man somewhat too discerning in the Failings of your Mistress.

MIRABELL. And for a discerning Man, somewhat too passionate a Lover; for I like her with all her Faults; nay, like her for her Faults. Her Follies are so natural, or so artful, that they become her; and those Affectations which in another Woman wou'd be odious, serve but to make her more agreeable. I'll tell thee, *Fainall,* she once us'd me with that Insolence, that in Revenge I took her to pieces, sifted her, and separated her Failings; I study'd 'em, and got 'em by rote. The Catalogue was so large that I was not without hopes one Day or other to hate her heartily: to which end I so us'd myself to think of 'em that at length, contrary to my Design and Expectation, they gave me every Hour less and less disturbance; 'till in a few Days it became habitual to me to remember 'em without being displeas'd. They are now grown as familiar to me as my own Frailties; and in all probability, in a little time longer I shall like 'em as well.

FAINALL. Marry her, marry her! Be half as well acquainted with her Charms as you are with her

Defects, and my Life on't, you are your own Man again.

MIRABELL. Say you so?

FAINALL. Aye, aye, I have Experience; I have a Wife, and so forth.

Enter Messenger.

MESSENGER. Is one Squire *Witwoud* here?

BETTY. Yes; what's your Business?

MESSENGER. I have a Letter for him, from his Brother Sir *Wilfull,* which I am charg'd to deliver into his own Hands.

Exit Messenger.

MIRABELL. What, is the Chief of that noble Family in Town, Sir *Wilfull Witwoud?*

FAINALL. He is expected today. Do you know him?

MIRABELL. I have seen him. He promises to be an extraordinary Person; I think you have the Honour to be related to him.

FAINALL. Yes; he is half Brother to this *Witwoud* by a former Wife, who was Sister to my Lady *Wishfort,* my Wife's Mother. If you marry *Millamant,* you must call Cousins too.

MIRABELL. I had rather be his Relation than his Acquaintance.

FAINALL. He comes to Town in order to Equip himself for Travel.

MIRABELL. For Travel! Why, the Man that I mean is above Forty.

FAINALL. No matter for that; 'tis for the Honour of *England,* that all *Europe* should know we have Blockheads of all Ages.

MIRABELL. I wonder there is not an Act of Parliament to save the Credit of the Nation, and prohibit the Exportation of Fools.

FAINALL. By no means, 'tis better as 'tis; 'tis better to Trade with a little Loss than to be quite eaten up with being overstock'd.

MIRABELL. Pray, are the Follies of this Knight-Errant and those of the Squire his Brother anything related?

FAINALL. Not at all; *Witwoud* grows by the Knight, like a Medlar grafted on a Crab. One will melt in your Mouth, and t'other set your Teeth on edge; one is all Pulp, and the other all Core.

MIRABELL. So one will be rotten before he be ripe, and the other will be rotten without ever being ripe at all.

FAINALL. Sir *Wilfull* is an odd mixture of Bashfulness and Obstinacy. But when he's drunk, he's as loving as the Monster in *The Tempest,* and much after the same manner. To give the t'other his due, he has something of good Nature and does not always want Wit.

MIRABELL. Not always; but as often as his Memory fails him, and his commonplace of Comparisons. He is a Fool with a good Memory and some few Scraps of other Folks' Wit. He is one whose Conversation can never be approv'd, yet it is now and then to be endur'd. He has indeed one good Quality; he is not exceptious; for he so passionately affects the Reputation of understanding Raillery that he will construe an Affront into a Jest, and call downright Rudeness and ill Language, Satire and Fire.

FAINALL. If you have a mind to finish his Picture, you have an opportunity to do it at full length. Behold the Original!

Enter Witwoud.

WITWOUD. Afford me your Compassion, my Dears! Pity me, *Fainall! Mirabell,* pity me!

MIRABELL. I do from my Soul.

FAINALL. Why, what's the Matter?

238 *Medlar:* a small fruit edible when over-ripe, unlike the crab-apple, which remains sour.
246 *Monster in* the Tempest: Syorax, in the popular Dryden-Davenant drastic revision of Shakespeare (1674).
251 *commonplace of Comparisons:* book used for jotting down metaphors to season conversation.
256 *exceptious:* apt to take exception.

WITWOUD. No Letters for me, *Betty?*

BETTY. Did the Messenger bring you one but now, Sir?

WITWOUD. Aye, but no other?

BETTY. No, Sir.

WITWOUD. That's hard, that's very hard.—A Messenger! a Mule, a Beast of Burden! He has brought me a Letter from the Fool my Brother, as heavy as a Panegyric in a Funeral Sermon, or a Copy of Commendatory Verses from one Poet to another. And what's worse, 'tis as sure a forerunner of the Author as an Epistle Dedicatory.

MIRABELL. A Fool, and your Brother, *Witwoud!*

WITWOUD. Aye, aye, my half Brother. My half Brother he is, no nearer, upon Honour.

MIRABELL. Then 'tis possible he may be but half a Fool.

WITWOUD. Good, good, *Mirabell le Drole!* Good, good, hang him, don't let's talk of him.—*Fainall,* how does your Lady? Gad, I say anything in the World to get this Fellow out of my Head. I beg Pardon that I shou'd ask a Man of Pleasure and the Town a Question at once so Foreign and Domestic. But I talk like an old Maid at a Marriage; I don't know what I say; but she's the best Woman in the World.

FAINALL. 'Tis well you don't know what you say, or else your Commendation wou'd go near to make me either vain or jealous.

WITWOUD. No Man in Town lives well with a Wife but *Fainall.* Your Judgment, *Mirabell?*

MIRABELL. You had better step and ask his Wife, if you wou'd be credibly inform'd.

WITWOUD. *Mirabell.*

MIRABELL. Aye.

WITWOUD. My Dear, I ask ten thousand Pardons;—Gad, I have forgot what I was going to say to you.

292 *best Woman in the World:* Mrs Fainall.

MIRABELL. I thank you heartily, heartily.

WITWOUD. No, but prithee excuse me; my Memory is such a Memory.

MIRABELL. Have a care of such Apologies, *Witwoud;* for I never knew a Fool but he affected to complain either of the Spleen or his Memory.

FAINALL. What have you done with *Petulant?*

WITWOUD. He's reckoning his Money—my Money it was. I have no Luck today.

FAINALL. You may allow him to win of you at Play, for you are sure to be too hard for him at Repartee; since you monopolize the Wit that is between you, the Fortune must be his of Course.

MIRABELL. I don't find that *Petulant* confesses the Superiority of Wit to be your Talent, *Witwoud.*

WITWOUD. Come, come, you are malicious now, and wou'd breed Debates. *Petulant's* my Friend, and a very honest Fellow, and a very pretty Fellow, and has a smattering—Faith and Troth, a pretty deal of an odd sort of a small Wit; nay, I'll do him Justice. I'm his Friend, I won't wrong him neither. And if he had but any Judgment in the World, he wou'd not be altogether contemptible. Come come, don't detract from the Merits of my Friend.

FAINALL. You don't take your Friend to be over-nicely bred?

WITWOUD. No, no, hang him, the Rogue has no Manners at all, that I must own. No more breeding than a Bum-baily, that I grant you.—'Tis Pity, faith; the Fellow has Fire and Life.

MIRABELL. What, Courage?

WITWOUD. Hum, faith, I don't know as to that; I can't say as to that.—Yes, faith, in a Controversy he'll contradict anybody.

MIRABELL. Tho' 'twere a Man whom he fear'd, or a Woman whom he lov'd.

332 *Bum-baily:* 'A bailiff of the meanest kind; one that is employed in arrests.' (Johnson, *Dictionary.*)

WITWOUD. Well, well, he does not always think before he speaks; we have all our Failings. You're too hard upon him, you are, faith. Let me excuse him; I can defend most of his Faults, except one or two; one he has, that's the Truth on't; if he were my Brother, I cou'd not acquit him.—That, indeed, I cou'd wish were otherwise.

MIRABELL. Aye, marry, what's that, *Witwoud?*

WITWOUD. O, pardon me!—Expose the Infirmities of my Friend?—No, my Dear, excuse me there.

FAINALL. What, I warrant he's unsincere, or 'tis some such Trifle.

WITWOUD. No, no, what if he be? 'Tis no matter for that; his Wit will excuse that. A Wit shou'd no more be sincere than a Woman constant; one argues a decay of Parts, as t'other of Beauty.

MIRABELL. May be you think him too positive?

WITWOUD. No, no, his being positive is an Incentive to Argument, and keeps up Conversation.

FAINALL. Too Illiterate?

WITWOUD. That! that's his Happiness; his want of Learning gives him the more opportunities to show his natural Parts.

MIRABELL. He wants Words.

WITWOUD. Aye, but I like him for that now; for his want of Words gives me the pleasure very often to explain his meaning.

FAINALL. He's Impudent.

WITWOUD. No, that's not it.

MIRABELL. Vain.

WITWOUD. No.

MIRABELL. What, he speaks unseasonable Truths sometimes, because he has not Wit enough to invent an Evasion?

WITWOUD. Truths! Ha, ha, ha! No, no, since you will have it,—I mean he never speaks Truth at all,—

355 *Parts:* abilities.

that's all. He will lie like a Chambermaid, or a Woman of Quality's Porter. Now, that is a Fault.

Enter Coachman.

COACHMAN. Is Master *Petulant* here, Mistress?

BETTY. Yes.

COACHMAN. Three Gentlewomen in the Coach would speak with him.

FAINALL. O brave *Petulant!* Three!

BETTY. I'll tell him.

COACHMAN. You must bring two Dishes of Chocolate and a Glass of Cinnamon-water.

Exit Betty. *and Coachman.*

WITWOUD. That should be for two fasting Strumpets, and a Bawd troubl'd with Wind. Now you may know what the three are.

MIRABELL. You are very free with your Friend's Acquaintance.

WITWOUD. Aye, aye, Friendship without Freedom is as dull as Love without Enjoyment, or Wine without Toasting. But to tell you a Secret, these are Trulls that he allows Coach-hire, and something more, by the Week, to call on him once a Day at publick Places.

MIRABELL. How!

WITWOUD. You shall see he won't go to 'em because there's no more Company here to take notice of him.—Why this is nothing to what he us'd to do; before he found out this way, I have known him call for himself.

FAINALL. Call for himself? What dost thou mean?

WITWOUD. Mean, why he wou'd slip you out of this Chocolate-house, just when you had been talking to him; as soon as your Back was turn'd—whip, he was gone! Then trip to his Lodging, clap on a Hood and Scarf and Mask, slap into a Hackney-Coach, and drive hither to the Door again in a trice, where he wou'd send in for himself; that I mean, call for himself, wait for himself, nay, and what's more, not finding himself, sometimes leave a Letter for himself.

386 *Cinnamon-water:* fortified hot spiced punch.

MIRABELL. I confess this is something extraordinary. —I believe he waits for himself now, he is so long a-coming. Oh! I ask his Pardon.

Enter Petulant.

BETTY. Sir, the Coach stays.

PETULANT. Well, well, I come.—'Sbud, a Man had as good be a profess'd Midwife as a profest Whoremaster, at this rate! To be knock'd up and rais'd at all Hours, and in all Places. Pox on 'em, I won't come!—D'ye hear, tell 'em I won't come. Let 'em snivel and cry their Hearts out.

FAINALL. You are very cruel, *Petulant.*

PETULANT. All's one, let it pass. I have a Humour to be cruel.

MIRABELL. I hope they are not Persons of Condition that you use at this rate.

PETULANT. Condition! Condition's a dry'd Fig, if I am not in Humour! By this Hand, if they were your—a—a—your What-d'ye-call-'ems themselves, they must wait or rub off, if I want Appetite.

MIRABELL. What-d'ye-call-'ems! What are they, *Witwoud?*

WITWOUD. Empresses, my Dear; by your What-d'ye-call-'ems he means Sultana Queens.

PETULANT. Ay, *Roxolanas.*

MIRABELL. Cry you Mercy!

FAINALL. *Witwoud* says they are—

PETULANT. What does he say th' are?

WITWOUD. I? Fine Ladies, I say.

PETULANT. Pass on, *Witwoud.*—Hearkee, by this Light his Relations: two Co-heiresses his Cousins, and an old Aunt that loves Caterwauling better than a Conventicle.

428 *Persons of Condition:* of high social rank.
438 *Roxolanas:* Turkish sultana in Davenant's *Siege of Rhodes* (1656).
446 *Conventicle:* clandestine assembly, usually of religious nonconformists.

WITWOUD. Ha, ha, ha! I had a Mind to see how the Rogue wou'd come off.—Ha, ha, ha! Gad, I can't be angry with him, if he said they were my Mother and my Sisters.

MIRABELL. No!

WITWOUD. No; the Rogue's Wit and Readiness of Invention charm me, Dear *Petulant!*

BETTY. They are gone, Sir, in great Anger.

PETULANT. Enough, let 'em trundle. Anger helps Complexion, saves Paint.

FAINALL. This Continence is all dissembled; this is in order to have something to brag of the next tme he makes Court to *Millamant,* and swear he has abandon'd the whole Sex for her Sake.

MIRABELL. Have you not left your impudent Pretensions there yet? I shall cut your Throat sometime or other, *Petulant,* about that Business.

PETULANT. Aye, aye, let that pass—There are other Throats to be cut—

MIRABELL. Meaning mine, Sir?

PETULANT. Not I—I mean nobody—I know nothing. But there are Uncles and Nephews in the World, and they may be Rivals—what then? All's one for that.

MIRABELL. How! hearkee *Petulant,* come hither. Explain, or I shall call your Interpreter.

PETULANT. Explain! I know nothing.—Why, you have an Uncle, have you not, lately come to Town, and lodges by my Lady *Wishfort's?*

MIRABELL. True.

PETULANT. Why, that's enough. You and he are not Friends; and if he shou'd marry and have a Child, you may be disinherited, ha?

MIRABELL. Where hast thou stumbled upon all this Truth?

PETULANT. All's one for that; why then, say I know something.

MIRABELL. Come, thou art an honest Fellow, *Petulant,* and shalt make Love to my Mistress, thou sha't, Faith. What hast thou heard of my Uncle?

PETULANT. I? Nothing I. If Throats are to be cut, let Swords clash! Snugs the Word; I shrug and am silent.

MIRABELL. O Raillery, Raillery. Come, I know thou art in the Women's Secrets. What, you're a Cabalist; I know you stayed at *Millamant's* last Night, after I went. Was there any mention made of my Uncle or me? Tell me. If thou hadst but good Nature equal to thy Wit, *Petulant, Tony Witwoud,* who is now thy Competitior in Fame, wou'd show as dim by thee as a dead Whiting's Eye by a Pearl of Orient; he wou'd no more be seen by thee than *Mercury* is by the Sun. Come, I'm sure thou wo't tell me.

PETULANT. If I do, will you grant me common Sense then, for the future?

MIRABELL. Faith, I'll do what I can for thee, and I'll pray that Heav'n may grant it thee in the meantime.

PETULANT. Well, hearkee.

FAINALL. *Petulant* and you both will find *Mirabell* as warm a Rival as a Lover.

WITWOUD. Pshaw! pshaw! That she laughs at *Petulant* is plain. And for my part, but that it is almost a Fashion to admire her, I shou'd—Hearkee, to tell you a Secret, but let it go no further; between Friends, I shall never break my Heart for her.

FAINALL. How!

WITWOUD. She's handsome; but she's a sort of an uncertain Woman.

FAINALL . I thought you had died for her.

WITWOUD. Umh—no—

FAINALL. She has Wit.

WITWOUD. 'Tis what she will hardly allow anybody else. Now, Demme, I shou'd hate that, if she were as handsome as *Cleopatra. Mirabell* is not so sure of her as he thinks for.

FAINALL. Why do you think so?

WITWOUD. We stayed pretty late there last Night, and heard something of an Uncle to *Mirabell*, who is lately come to Town,—and is between him and the best part of his Estate. *Mirabell* and he are at some distance, as my Lady *Wishfort* has been told; and you know she hates *Mirabell* worse than a Quaker hates a Parrot, or than a Fishmonger hates a hard Frost. Whether this Uncle has seen Mrs. *Millamant* or not, I cannot say; but there were Items of such a Treaty being in Embryo, and if it shou'd come to Life, poor *Mirabell* wou'd be in some sort unfortunately fobb'd, i'faith.

FAINALL. 'Tis impossible *Millamant* should hearken to it.

WITWOUD. Faith, my Dear, I can't tell; she's a Woman, and a kind of a Humorist.

MIRABELL. And this is the Sum of what you cou'd collect last Night?

PETULANT. The Quintessence. Maybe *Witwoud* knows more; he stay'd longer. Besides, they never mind him; they say anything before him.

MIRABELL. I thought you had been the greatest Favourite.

PETULANT. Ay, *tête à tête*, but not in publick, because I make Remarks.

MIRABELL. Do you?

PETULANT. Aye, aye, pox, I'm malicious, Man! Now he's soft you know; they are not in awe of him. The Fellow's well-bred; he's what you call a—what-d'ye-call-'em. A fine Gentleman, but he's silly withal.

MIRABELL. I thank you. I know as much as my Curiosity requires.—*Fainall*, are you for the *Mall*?

FAINALL. Aye, I'll take a turn before Dinner.

WITWOUD. Aye, we'll all walk in the Park; the Ladies talk'd of being there.

537 *Humorist:* given to whims.
553 *Mall:* fashionable promenade in St James's Park.

MIRABELL. I thought you were oblig'd to watch for your Brother Sir *Wilfull's* arrival.

WITWOUD. No, no, he comes to his Aunt's, my Lady *Wishfort.* Pox on him, I shall be troubled with him too; what shall I do with the Fool?

PETULANT. Beg him for his Estate, that I may beg you afterwards; and so have but one Trouble with you both.

WITWOUD. O rare *Petulant!* Thou art as quick as a Fire in a frosty Morning; thou shalt to the *Mall* with us, and we'll be very severe.

PETULANT. Enough, I'm in a Humour to be severe.

MIRABELL. Are you? Pray then walk by yourselves: let not us be accessary to your putting the Ladies out of Countenance with your senseless Ribaldry, which you roar out aloud as often as they pass by you; and when you have made a handsome Woman blush, then you think you have been severe.

PETULANT. What, what? Then let 'em either show their Innocence by not understanding what they hear, or else show their Discretion by not hearing what they would not be thought to understand.

MIRABELL. But hast not thou then Sense enough to know that thou ought'st to be most asham'd thyself, when thou hast put another out of Countenance?

PETULANT. Not I, by this Hand! I always take blushing either for a Sign of Guilt, or ill Breeding.

MIRABELL. I confess you ought to think so. You are in the right, that you may plead the error of your Judgment in defence of your Practice.

Where Modesty's ill Manners, 'tis but fit
That Impudence and Malice pass for Wit.

Exeunt.

ACT II. SCENE I.

St. James's Park.

Enter Mrs. Fainall *and* Mrs. Marwood.

MRS. FAINALL. Ay, ay, dear *Marwood,* if we will be happy, we must find the means in ourselves, and among ourselves. Men are ever in Extremes; either doating or averse. While they are Lovers, if they have Fire and Sense, their Jealousies are insupportable. And when they cease to Love, (we ought to think at least) they loath; they look upon us with Horror and Distaste; they meet us like the Ghosts of what we were, and as such, fly from us.

MRS. MARWOOD. True, 'tis an unhappy Circumstance of Life, that Love shou'd ever die before us; and that the Man so often shou'd out-live the Lover. But say what you will, 'tis better to be left than never to have been lov'd. To pass our Youth in dull Indifference, to refuse the Sweets of Life because they once must leave us, is as preposterous as to wish to have been born Old, because we one Day must be Old. For my part, my Youth may wear and waste, but it shall never rust in my Possession.

MRS. FAINALL. Then it seems you dissemble an Aversion to Mankind, only in compliance with my Mother's Humour.

MRS. MARWOOD. Certainly. To be free, I have no Taste of those insipid dry Discourses with which our Sex of force must entertain themselves, apart from Men. We may affect Endearments to each other, profess eternal Friendships, and seem to doat like Lovers; but 'tis not in our Natures long to persevere. Love will resume his Empire in our Breasts, and every Heart, or soon or late, receive and readmit him as its lawful Tyrant.

MRS. FAINALL. Bless me, how have I been deceiv'd! Why you profess a Libertine!

MRS. MARWOOD. You see my Friendship by my Freedom. Come, be as sincere, acknowledge that your Sentiments agree with mine.

MRS. FAINALL. Never!

MRS. MARWOOD. You hate Mankind?

MRS. FAINALL. Heartily, inveterately.

MRS. MARWOOD. Your Husband?

MRS. FAINALL. Most transcendantly; ay, tho' I say it, meritoriously.

MRS. MARWOOD. Give me your Hand upon it.

MRS. FAINALL. There.

MRS. MARWOOD. I join with you; what I have said has been to try you.

MRS. FAINALL. Is it possible? Dost thou hate those Vipers Men?

MRS. MARWOOD. I have done hating 'em, and am now come to despise 'em; the next thing I have to do is eternally to forget 'em.

MRS. FAINWALL. There spoke the Spirit of an *Amazon*, a *Penthesilea!*

MRS. MARWOOD. And yet I am thinking sometimes to carry my Aversion further.

MRS. FAINALL. How?

MRS. MARWOOD. Faith, by Marrying; if I cou'd but find one that lov'd me very well and would be thoroughly sensible of ill usage, I think I shou'd do myself the violence of undergoing the Ceremony.

MRS. FAINALL. You would not make him a Cuckold?

MRS. MARWOOD. No, but I'd make him believe I did, and that's as bad.

MRS. FAINALL. Why, had not you as good do it?

MRS. MARWOOD. Oh, if he shou'd ever discover it, he wou'd then know the worst, and be out of his Pain; but I wou'd have him ever to continue upon the Rack of Fear and Jealousy.

MRS. FAINALL . Ingenious Mischief? Wou'd thou wert married to *Mirabell*.

MRS. MARWOOD. Wou'd I were!

MRS. FAINALL. You change Colour.

MRS. MARWOOD. Because I hate him.

MRS. FAINALL. So do I; but I can hear him nam'd. But what Reason have you to hate him in particular?

53 ***Penthesilea:*** in classical mythology, queen of the Amazons, the nation of female warriors.

MRS. MARWOOD. I never lov'd him; he is, and always was, insufferably proud.

MRS. FAINALL. By the Reason you give for your Aversion, one wou'd think it dissembl'd; for you have laid a Fault to his Charge of which his Enemies must acquit him.

MRS. MARWOOD. Oh, then it seems you are one of his favourable Enemies. Methinks you look a little pale, and now you flush again.

MRS. FAINALL. Do I? I think I am a little sick o' the sudden.

MRS. MARWOOD. What ails you?

MRS. FAINALL. My Husband. Don't you see him? he turn'd short upon me unawares, and has almost overcome me.

Enter Fainall *and* Mirabell.

MRS. MARWOOD. Ha, ha, ha; he comes opportunely for you.

MRS. FAINALL. For you, for he has brought *Mirabell* with him.

FAINALL. My Dear.

MRS. FAINALL. My Soul.

FAINALL. You don't look well today, Child.

MRS. FAINALL. D'ye think so?

MIRABELL. He is the only Man that does, Madam.

MRS. FAINALL. The only Man that would tell me so at least; and the only Man from whom I could hear it without Mortification.

FAINALL. O my Dear, I am satisfy'd of your Tenderness; I know you cannot resent anything from me; especially what is an effect of my Concern.

MRS. FAINALL. Mr. *Mirabell,* my Mother interrupted you in a pleasant Relation last Night; I wou'd fain hear it out.

MIRABELL. The Persons concern'd in that Affair have yet a tolerable Reputation. –I am afraid Mr.

Fainall will be Censorious.

MRS. FAINALL. He has a Humour more prevailing than his Curiosity and will willingly dispence with the hearing of one scandalous Story, to avoid giving an occasion to make another by being seen to walk with his Wife. This way, Mr. *Mirabell,* and I dare promise you will oblige us both.

Exeunt Mrs. Fainall *and* Mirabell.

FAINALL. Excellent Creature! Well, sure if I shou'd live to be rid of my Wife, I shou'd be a miserable Man.

MRS. MARWOOD. Ay!

FAINALL. For having only that one Hope, the accomplishment of it, of Consequence, must put an end to all my hopes; and what a Wretch is he who must survive his hopes! Nothing remains when that Day comes but to sit down and weep like *Alexander,* when he wanted other Worlds to conquer.

MRS. MARWOOD. Will you not follow 'em?

FAINALL. Faith, I think not.

MRS. MARWOOD. Pray let us; I have a Reason.

FAINALL. You are not Jealous?

MRS. MARWOOD. Of whom?

FAINALL. Of *Mirabell.*

MRS. MARWOOD. If I am, is it inconsistent with my Love to you that I am tender of your Honour?

FAINALL. You wou'd intimate, then, as if there were a *fellow-feeling* between my Wife and Him.

MRS. MARWOOD. I think she does not hate him to that degree she wou'd be thought.

FAINALL. But he, I fear, is too Insensible.

MRS. MARWOOD. It may be you are deceiv'd.

FAINALL. It may be so. I do now begin to apprehend it.

MRS. MARWOOD. What?

FAINALL. That I have been deceiv'd Madam, and

128 *Alexander:* the Great, of Macedon.

you are false.

MRS. MARWOOD. That I am false! What mean you?

FAINALL. To let you know I see through all your little Arts.—Come, you both love him, and both have equally dissembl'd your Aversion. Your mutual Jealousies of one another have made you clash till you have both struck Fire. I have seen the warm Confession red'ning on your Cheeks and sparkling from your Eyes.

MRS. MARWOOD. You do me wrong.

FAINALL. I do not. 'Twas for my ease to oversee and wilfully neglect the gross advances made him by my Wife; that by permitting her to be engag'd, I might continue unsuspected in my Pleasures, and take you oftner to my Arms in full Security. But cou'd you think, because the nodding Husband would not wake, that e'er the watchful Lover slept?

MRS. MARWOOD. And wherewithal can you reproach me?

FAINALL. With Infidelity, with loving of another, with love of *Mirabell.*

MRS. MARWOOD. 'Tis false. I challenge you to show an Instance that can confirm your groundless Accusation. I hate him.

FAINALL. And wherefore do you hate him? He is Insensible, and your Resentment follows his Neglect. An Instance? The Injuries you have done him are a proof: your interposing in his Love. What cause had you to make Discoveries of his pretended Passion? To undeceive the credulous Aunt, and be the officious Obstacle of his Match with *Millamant?*

MRS. MARWOOD. My Obligations to my Lady urg'd me; I had profess'd a Friendship to her, and could not see her easy Nature so abus'd by that Dissembler.

FAINALL. What, was it Conscience then? Profess'd a Friendship! O the pious Friendships of the Female Sex!

MRS. MARWOOD. More tender, more sincere, and more enduring than all the vain and empty Vows of

158 *oversee:* overlook, ignore.

Men, whether professing Love to us, or mutual Faith to one another.

FAINALL. Ha, ha, ha! You are my Wife's Friend too.

MRS. MARWOOD. Shame and Ingratitude! Do you reproach me? You, you upbraid me? Have I been false to her, thro' strict Fidelity to you, and sacrific'd my Friendship to keep my Love inviolate? And have you the baseness to charge me with the Guilt, unmindful of the Merit! To you it shou'd be meritorious, that I have been vicious. And do you reflect that Guilt upon me, which should lie buried in your Bosom?

FAINALL. You misinterpret my Reproof. I meant but to remind you of the slight Account you once could make of strictest Ties, when set in Competition with your Love to me.

MRS. MARWOOD. 'Tis false; you urg'd it with deliberate Malice. 'Twas spoke in scorn, and I never will forgive it.

FAINALL. Your Guilt, not your Resentment, begets your Rage. If yet you lov'd, you could forgive a Jealousy; but you are stung to find you are discover'd.

MRS. MARWOOD. It shall be all discover'd. You too shall be discover'd; be sure you shall. I can but be expos'd. If I do it myself, I shall prevent your Baseness.

FAINALL. Why, what will you do?

MRS. MARWOOD. Disclose it to your Wife; own what has past between us.

FAINALL. Frenzy!

MRS. MARWOOD. By all my Wrongs I'll do't! I'll publish to the World the Injuries you have done me, both in my Fame and Fortune! With both I trusted you, you bankrupt in Honour, as indigent of Wealth.

FAINALL. Your Fame I have preserv'd. Your Fortune has been bestow'd as the prodigality of your Love would have it, in Pleasures which we both have shar'd. Yet had not you been false, I had e'er this repaid it. 'Tis true, had you permitted *Mirabell* with *Millamant* to have stoll'n their Marriage, my Lady had been incens'd beyond all means of reconcilement; *Millamant* had forfeited the Moiety of her Fortune, which then wou'd have descended to my Wife. And wherefore did I marry, but to make lawful Prize of a rich Widow's Wealth, and squander it on Love and you?

MRS. MARWOOD. Deceit and frivolous Pretence!

FAINALL. Death, am I not married? What's pretence? Am I not Imprison'd, Fetter'd? Have I not a Wife? Nay a Wife that was a Widow, a handsome Widow; and would be again a Widow, but that I have a Heart of Proof, and something of a Constitution to bustle thro' the ways of Wedlock and this World. Will you yet be reconcil'd to Truth and me?

MRS. MARWOOD. Impossible. Truth and you are inconsistent.—I hate you, and shall for ever.

FAINALL. For loving you?

MRS. MARWOOD. I loath the name of Love after such usage; and next to the Guilt with which you wou'd asperse me, I scorn you most. Farewell.

FAINALL. Nay, we must not part thus.

MRS. MARWOOD. Let me go.

FAINALL. Come, I'm sorry.

MRS. MARWOOD. I care not—Let me go—Break my Hands, do! I'd leave 'em to get loose.

FAINALL. I would not hurt you for the World. Have I no other Hold to keep you here?

MRS. MARWOOD. Well, I have deserv'd it all.

FAINALL. You know I love you.

MRS. MARWOOD. Poor dissembling!—Oh, that—well, it is not yet—

FAINALL. What? What is it not? What is it not yet? It is not yet too late—

MRS. MARWOOD. No, it is not yet too late—I have that Comfort.

FAINALL. It is to love another.

MRS. MARWOOD. But not to loath, detest, abhor Mankind, myself, and the whole treacherous World.

227 *Moiety:* half.

FAINALL. Nay, this is Extravagance. Come, I ask your Pardon.–No Tears.–I was to blame; I cou'd not love you and be easy in my Doubts.–Pray, forbear. I believe you; I'm convinc'd I've done you wrong, and any way, every way will make amends. I'll hate my Wife yet more, damn her! I'll part with her, rob her of all she's worth, and we'll retire somewhere, anywhere to another World. I'll marry thee; be pacify'd. –'Sdeath, they come; hide your Face, your Tears. You have a Mask; wear it a Moment. This way, this way. Be persuaded.

Exeunt.

Enter Mirabell *and* Mrs. Fainall.

MRS. FAINALL. They are here yet.

MIRABELL. They are turning into the other Walk.

MRS. FAINALL. While I only hated my Husband, I could bear to see him; but since I have despis'd him, he's too offensive.

MIRABELL. Oh, you should Hate with Prudence.

MRS. FAINALL. Yes, for I have Lov'd with Indiscretion.

MIRABELL. You shou'd have just so much disgust for your Husband as may be sufficient to make you relish your Lover.

MRS. FAINALL. You have been the cause that I have lov'd without Bounds, and wou'd you set Limits to that Aversion of which you have been the occasion? Why did you make me marry this Man?

MIRABELL. Why do we daily commit disagreeable and dangerous Actions? To save that Idol Reputation. If the familiarities of our Loves had produc'd that Consequence of which you were apprehensive, where could you have fix'd a Father's Name with Credit, but on a Husband? I knew *Fainall* to be a Man lavish of his Morals, an interested and professing Friend, a false and a designing Lover; yet one whose wit and outward fair Behaviour have gain'd a Reputation with the Town

272 *Mask:* still worn occasionally by ladies in public; gradually became associated with disreputable women, particularly at the theatre.
297 *interested and professing:* self-serving and hypocritical.

enough to make that Woman stand excus'd who has suffer'd herself to be won by his Addresses. A better Man ought not to have been sacrific'd to the Occasion; a worse had not answer'd to the Purpose. When you are weary of him, you know your Remedy.

MRS. FAINALL. I ought to stand in some degree of Credit with you, *Mirabell.*

MIRABELL. In Justice to you, I have made you privy to my whole Design, and put it in your Power to ruin or advance my Fortune.

MRS. FAINALL. Whom have you instructed to represent your pretended Uncle?

MIRABELL. *Waitwell,* my Servant.

MRS. FAINALL. He is an humble Servant to *Foible* my Mother's Woman, and may win her to your Interest.

MIRABELL. Care is taken for that. She is won and worn by this time. They were married this morning.

MRS. FAINALL. Who?

MIRABELL. *Waitwell* and *Foible.* I wou'd not tempt my Servant to betray me by trusting him too far. If your Mother, in hopes to ruin me, shou'd consent to marry my pretended Uncle, he might, like *Mosca* in the *Fox,* stand upon Terms; so I made him sure before-hand.

MRS. FAINALL. So if my poor Mother is caught in a Contract, you will discover the Imposture betimes, and release her by producing a Certificate of her Gallant's former Marriage.

MIRABELL. Yes, upon Condition she consent to my Marriage with her Niece, and surrender the Moiety of her Fortune in her Possession.

MRS. FAINALL. She talk'd last Night of endeavoring at a Match between *Millamant* and your Uncle.

MIRABELL. That was by *Foible's* Direction, and my Instruction, that she might seem to carry it more privately.

322-23 *Mosca in the Fox:* a trickster and parasite in Ben Jonson's *Volpone, or The Fox* (1606).

MRS. FAINALL. Well, I have an Opinion of your Success, for I believe my Lady will do anything to get a Husband; and when she has this, which you have provided for her, I suppose she will submit to anything to get rid of him.

MIRABELL. Yes, I think the good Lady wou'd marry anything that resembl'd a Man, tho' 'twere no more than what a Butler cou'd pinch out of a Napkin.

MRS. FAINALL. Female Frailty! We must all come to it, if we live to be Old and feel the craving of a false Appetite when the true is decay'd.

MIRABELL. An old Woman's Appetite is deprav'd like that of a Girl.—'Tis the Green Sickness of a second Childhood, and, like the faint Offer of a latter Spring, serves but to usher in the Fall, and withers in an affected Bloom.

MRS. FAINALL. Here's your Mistress.

Enter Mrs. Millamant, Witwoud, *and* Mincing.

MIRABELL. Here she comes, i'faith, full sail, with her Fan spread, and her Streamers out, and a shoal of Fools for Tenders.—Ha, no, I cry her Mercy.

MRS. FAINALL. I see but one poor empty Sculler, and he tows her Woman after him.

MIRABELL. You seem to be unattended, Madam. You us'd to have the *Beau-mond* Throng after you, and a Flock of gay, fine Perukes hovering round you.

WITWOUD. Like Moths about a Candle.—I had like to have lost my Comparison for want of Breath.

MILLAMANT. Oh, I have deny'd myself Airs today. I have walk'd as fast through the Crowd—

WITWOUD. As a Favourite in disgrace, and with as few Followers.

MILLAMANT. Dear Mr. *Witwoud,* truce with your Similitudes; for I am as sick of 'em—

349 *Green Sickness:* 'A disease of maids, so-called from the paleness which it produces.' (Johnson, *Dictionary.*)
357 *Tenders:* boats attending larger vessels.
362 *Perukes:* wigs.

WITWOUD. As a Physician of a good Air.—I cannot help it Madam, tho' 'tis against myself.

MILLAMANT. Yet again! *Mincing,* stand between me and his Wit.

WITWOUD. Do, Mrs. *Mincing,* like a Screen before a great Fire. I confess I do blaze today; I am too bright.

MRS. FAINALL. But dear *Millamant,* why were you so long?

MILLAMANT. Long, Lord, have I not made violent haste? I have ask'd every living Thing I met for you; I have enquir'd after you as after a new Fashion.

WITWOUD. Madam, truce with your Similitudes. No, you met her Husband, and did not ask him for her.

MIRABELL. By your leave, *Witwoud,* that were like enquiring after an old Fashion, to ask a Husband for his Wife.

WITWOUD. Hum, a hit, a hit, a palpable hit! I confess it.

MRS. FAINALL. You were dress'd before I came abroad.

MILLAMANT. Ay, that's true.—Oh, but then I had—*Mincing,* what had I? Why was I so long?

MINCING. O Mem, your Laship stayed to peruse a Pecquet of Letters.

MILLAMANT. Oh, ay, Letters—I had Letters—I am persecuted with Letters—I hate Letters. Nobody knows how to write Letters, and yet one has 'em, one does not know why. They serve one to pin up one's Hair.

WITWOUD. Is that the way? Pray Madam, do you pin up your Hair with all your Letters? I find I must keep Copies.

MILLAMANT. Only with those in Verse, Mr. *Witwoud.* I never pin up my Hair with Prose. I fancy one's Hair wou'd not curl if it were pinn'd up with Prose. I think I try'd once, *Mincing.*

388 a palpable hit: cf. Osric in *Hamlet,* V, ii, l. 292.

MINCING. O Mem, I shall never forget it.

MILLAMANT. Ay, poor *Mincing* tift and tift all the morning.

MINCING. 'Till I had the Cremp in my Fingers I'll vow, Mem. And all to no purpose. But when your Laship pins it up with Poetry, it sits so pleasant the next Day as anything, and is so pure and so crips.

WITWOUD. Indeed, so crips?

MINCING. You're such a Critick, Mr. *Witwoud.*

MILLAMANT. *Mirabell,* did not you take Exceptions last Night? Oh, ay, and went away.—Now I think on't, I'm angry.—No, now I think on't I'm pleas'd, for I believe I gave you some Pain.

MIRABELL. Does that please you?

MILLAMANT. Infinitely; I love to give Pain.

MIRABELL. You wou'd affect a Cruelty which is not in your Nature; your true Vanity is in the power of pleasing.

MILLAMANT. Oh, I ask your Pardon for that. One's Cruelty is one's Power, and when one parts with one's Cruelty, one parts with one's Power; and when one has parted with that, I fancy one's Old and Ugly.

MIRABELL. Ay, ay, suffer your Cruelty to ruin the object of your Power, to destroy your Lover—and then how vain, how lost a Thing you'll be! Nay, 'tis true: you are no longer handsome when you've lost your Lover; your Beauty dies upon the Instant. For Beauty is the Lover's Gift; 'tis he bestows your Charms, your Glass is all a Cheat. The Ugly and the Old, whom the Looking-glass mortifies, yet after Commendation can be flatter'd by it, and discover Beauties in it; for that reflects our Praises, rather than your Face.

MILLAMANT. O the Vanity of these Men! *Fainall,* d'ye hear him? If they did not commend us, we were not handsome! Now you must know they could not commend one, if one was not handsome. Beauty the Lover's Gift!—Lord, what is a Lover, that it can give?

409 *tift:* arranged.
415 *crips:* dialect for 'crisp'.

Why, one makes Lovers as fast as one pleases, and they live as long as one pleases, and they die as soon as one pleases; and then, if one pleases, one makes more.

WITWOUD. Very pretty. Why you make no more of making of Lovers, Madam, than of making so many Card-matches.

MILLAMANT. One no more owes one's Beauty to a Lover, than one's Wit to an Echo. They can but reflect what we look and say; vain empty Things if we are silent or unseen, and want a being.

MIRABELL. Yet to those two vain empty Things you owe two the greatest Pleasures of your Life.

MILLAMANT. How so?

MIRABELL. To your Lover you owe the pleasure of of hearing yourselves prais'd; and to an Echo the pleasure of hearing yourselves talk.

WITWOUD. But I know a Lady that loves talking so incessantly, she won't give an Echo fair play; she has that everlasting Rotation of Tongue, that an Echo must wait till she dies before it can catch her last Words.

MILLAMANT. O Fiction! *Fainall,* let us leave these Men.

MIRABELL (*aside to* Mrs. Fainall). Draw off *Witwoud.*

MRS. FAINALL. Immediately.—I have a Word or two for Mrs. *Witwoud.*

MIRABELL. I wou'd beg a little private Audience too—

Exit Witwoud *and* Mrs. Fainall

You had the Tyranny to deny me last Night, tho' you knew I came to impart a Secret to you that concern'd my Love.

MILLAMANT. You saw I was engag'd.

MIRABELL. Unkind! You had the leisure to entertain a Herd of Fools; Things who visit you from their

451 *Card-matches:* cardboard matches.

excessive Idleness, bestowing on your easiness that time which is the incumbrance of their Lives. How can you find delight in such Society? It is impossible they should admire you; they are not capable. Or if they were, it shou'd be to you as a Mortification; for sure, to please a Fool is some degree of Folly.

MILLAMANT. I please myself.—Besides, sometimes to converse with Fools is for my Health.

MIRABELL. Your Health! Is there a worse Disease than the Conversation of Fools?

MILLAMANT. Yes, the Vapours; Fools are Physicks for it, next to *Assa-fœtida.*

MIRABELL. You are not in a Course of Fools?

MILLAMANT. *Mirabell,* If you persist in this offensive Freedom, you'll displease me.—I think I must resolve, after all, not to have you; we shan't agree.

MIRABELL. Not in our Physick, it may be.

MILLAMANT. And yet our Distemper in all likelihood will be the same; for we shall be sick of one another. I shan't endure to be reprimanded nor instructed; 'tis so dull to act always by Advice, and so tedious to be told of one's Faults—I can't bear it. Well, I won't have you *Mirabell*—I'm resolv'd—I think —You may go. Ha, ha, ha! What wou'd you give that you cou'd help loving me?

MIRABELL. I would give something that you did not know I cou'd not help it.

MILLAMANT. Come, don't look grave then. Well, what do you say to me?

MIRABELL. I say that a Man may as soon make a Friend by his Wit, or a Fortune by his Honesty, as win a Woman with plain Dealing and Sincerity.

MILLAMANT. Sententious *Mirabell!* Prithee, don't look with that violent and inflexible wise Face, like *Solomon* at the dividing of the Child in an old Tapestry-hanging.

492 *Physicks:* remedies.
493 *Assa-foetida:* asafetida, a dried plant resin used here for smelling salts.
494 *Course of Fools:* using fools as medicine to effect a cure.
516-7 *Solomon . . . Tapestry-hanging:* a popular subject for illustration; see I *Kings,* III, 16-28.

MIRABELL. You are merry, Madam, but I wou'd persuade you for one Moment to be serious.

MILLAMANT. What, with that Face? No, if you keep your Countenance, 'tis impossible I shou'd hold mine. Well, after all, there is something very moving in a love-sick Face. Ha, ha, ha!—Well, I won't laugh; don't be peevish. Heigho! Now I'll be melancholly, as melancholly as a Watch-light. Well, *Mirabell*, if ever you will win me, woe me now.—Nay, if you are so tedious, fare you well; I see they are walking away.

MIRABELL. Can you not find in the variety of your Disposition one Moment—

MILLAMANT. To hear you tell me that *Foible's* married, and your Plot like to speed?—No.

MIRABELL. But how came you to know it?

MILLAMANT. Unless by the help of the Devil, you can't imagine; unless she shou'd tell me herself. Which of the two it may have been, I will leave you to consider; and when you have done thinking of that, think of me.

Exit.

MIRABELL. I have something more—Gone! Think of you? To think of a Whirlwind, tho' 'twere in a Whirlwind, were a Case of more steady Contemplation; a very tranquility of Mind and Mansion. A Fellow that loves in a Windmill has not a more whimsical Dwelling than the Heart of a Man that is lodg'd in a Woman. There is no Point of the Compass to which they cannot turn, and by which they are not turn'd; and by one as well as another, for Motion, not Method is their Occupation. To know this, and yet continue to be in Love, is to be made wise from the Dictates of Reason, and yet persevere to play the Fool by the force of Instinct.—Oh, here come my pair of Turtles. What, billing so sweetly? Is not *Valentine's* Day over with you yet?

Enter Waitwell *and* Foible.

Sirrah, *Waitwell,* why sure you think you were married for your own Recreation, and not for my Conveniency.

551 *turtles:* turtledoves.

WAITWELL. Your Pardon, Sir. With Submission, we have indeed been solacing in lawful Delights; but still with an Eye to Business, Sir. I have instructed her as well as I cou'd. If she can take your Directions as readily as my Instructions, Sir, your Affairs are in a prosperous way.

MIRABELL. Give you Joy, Mrs. *Foible.*

FOIBLE. O las, Sir, I'm so asham'd! I'm afraid my Lady has been in a thousand Inquietudes for me. But I protest, Sir, I made as much haste as I could.

WAITWELL. That she did indeed, Sir. It was my Fault that she did not make more.

MIRABELL. That I believe.

FOIBLE. But I told my Lady as you instructed me, Sir: that I had a prospect of seeing Sir *Rowland* your Uncle; and that I wou'd put her Ladyship's Picture in my Pocket to show him; which I'll be sure to say has made him so enamour'd of her Beauty that he burns with Impatience to lie at her Ladyship's Feet and worship the Original.

MIRABELL. Excellent *Foible!* Matrimony has made you eloquent in Love.

WAITWELL. I think she has profited, Sir; I think so.

FOIBLE. You have seen Madam *Millamant,* Sir?

MIRABELL. Yes.

FOIBLE. I told her, Sir, because I did not know that you might find an Opportunity; she had so much Company last Night.

MIRABELL. Your Diligence will merit more. In the meantime–

Gives Money.

FOIBLE. O dear Sir, your humble Servant!

WAITWELL. Spouse.

MIRABELL. Stand off, Sir, not a Penny!–Go on and prosper, *Foible;* the Lease shall be made good and the Farm stock'd, if we succeed.

FOIBLE. I don't question your Generosity, Sir; and you need not doubt of Success. If you have no more

Commands, Sir, I'll be gone; I'm sure my Lady is at her Toilet, and can't dress till I come. (*Looking out.*) O Dear, I'm sure that was Mrs. *Marwood* that went by in a Mask; if she has seen me with you I'm sure she'll tell my Lady. I'll make haste home and prevent her. Your Servant, Sir. B'w'y, *Waitwell.*

Exit Foible.

WAITWELL. Sir *Rowland,* if you please. The Jade's so pert upon her Preferment she forgets herself.

MIRABELL. Come Sir, will you endeavour to forget yourself, and transform into Sir *Rowland?*

WAITWELL. Why Sir, it will be impossible I shou'd remember myself.—Married, knighted, and attended all in one Day! 'Tis enough to make any Man forget Acquaintance and Familiarity with my former self, and fall from my Transformation to a Reformation into *Waitwell.* Nay, I shan't be quite the same *Waitwell,* neither—for, now I remember me, I am married and can't be my own Man again.

Ay there's the Grief; that's the sad change of Life;
To lose my Title, and yet keep my Wife.

Exeunt.

ACT III. Scene I.

A Room in Lady Wishfort's *House.*

Lady Wishfort *at her Toilet,* Peg *waiting.*

LADY WISHFORT. Merciful, no News of *Foible* yet?

PEG. No, Madam.

LADY WISHFORT. I have no more patience. If I have not fretted myself till I am pale again, there's no Veracity in me. Fetch me the Red—the Red, do you hear, Sweet-heart? An errant Ash colour, as I'm a Person. Look you how this Wench stirs! Why dost thou not fetch me a little Red? Did'st thou not hear me, Mopus?

PEG. The red *Ratifia* does your Ladyship mean, or the Cherry Brandy?

9 *Mopus:* dullard.

LADY WISHFORT. *Ratifia,* Fool? No, Fool. Not the *Ratifia,* Fool–Grant me patience! I mean the *Spanish* Paper, Idiot; Complexion, Darling. Paint, Paint, Paint; dost thou understand that, Changeling, dangling thy Hands like Bobbins before thee? Why dost thou not stir, Puppet? thou wooden Thing upon Wires!

PEG. Lord, Madam, your Ladyship is so impatient–I cannot come at the Paint, Madam; Mrs. *Foible* has lock'd it up, and carry'd the Key with her.

LADY WISHFORT. A Pox take you both–fetch me the Cherry Brandy then. (*Exit* Peg.) I'm as pale and as faint, I look like Mrs. Qualmsick, the Curate's Wife, that's always breeding.

Wench, come, come, Wench, what art thou doing? Sipping? Tasting? Save thee, dost thou not know the Bottle?

Enter Peg *with a Bottle and* China-*cup.*

PEG. Madam, I was looking for a Cup.

LADY WISHFORT. A Cup, save thee! and what a Cup hast thou brought! Dost thou take me for a *Fairy,* to drink out of an *Acorn?* Why didst thou not bring thy Thimble? Hast thou ne'er a Brass Thimble clinking in thy Pocket with a bit of Nutmeg? I warrant thee. Come, fill, fill! So–again. *(One Knocks.)* See who that is. Set down the Bottle first. Here, here, under the Table. What, wou'dst thou go with the Bottle in thy Hand like a Tapster? As I'm a Person, this Wench has liv'd in an Inn upon the Road before she came to me, like *Maritornes* the *Asturian* in *Don Quixote.* No *Foible* yet?

PEG. No, Madam; Mrs. *Marwood.*

LADY WISHFORT. Oh, *Marwood;* let her come in. Come in, good *Marwood.*

Enter Mrs. Marwood.

MRS. MARWOOD. I'm surpris'd to find your Ladyship in *dishabilie* at this time of day.

LADY WISHFORT. *Foible's* a lost Thing; has been abroad since Morning, and never heard of since.

13 *Spanish Paper:* used for applying rouge.

40 *Maritornes:* the innkeeper's daughter well-known on the London stage in Thomas D'Urfey's bawdy adaptation of Cervantes, *The Comical History of Don Quixote* (1694).

MRS. MARWOOD. I saw her but now, as I came mask'd through the Park, in Conference with *Mirabell.*

LADY WISHFORT. With *Mirabell!* You call my Blood into my Face with mentioning that Traitor. She durst not have the Confidence. I sent her to Negotiate an Affair in which, if I'm detected, I'm undone. If that wheadling Villain has wrought upon *Foible* to detect me, I'm ruin'd. O my dear Friend, I'm a Wretch of Wretches if I'm detected.

MRS. MARWOOD. O Madam, you cannot suspect Mrs. *Foible's* Integrity.

LADY WISHFORT. Oh, he carries Poison in his Tongue that wou'd corrupt Integrity itself. If she has given him an Oportunity, she has as good as put her Integrity into his Hands. Ah, dear *Marwood,* what's Integrity to an Opportunity?—Hark! I hear her. Go, you Thing, and send her in. (*Exit* Peg.) Dear Friend, retire into my Closet, that I may examine her with more freedom. You'll pardon me, dear Friend; I can make bold with you. There are Books over the Chimney—*Quarles* and *Pryn,* and the *Short View of the Stage,* with *Bunyan's* Works, to entertain you.

Exit Marwood.

Enter Foible.

O *Foible,* where hast thou been? What hast thou been doing?

FOIBLE. Madam, I have seen the Party.

LADY WISHFORT. But what hast thou done?

FOIBLE. Nay, 'tis your Ladyship has done, and are to do; I have only promis'd. But a Man so enamour'd—so transported! Well, here it is, all that is left; all that is not kiss'd away. Well, if worshipping of Pictures be a Sin, Poor Sir *Rowland,* I say.

LADY WISHFORT. The Miniature has been counted like. But hast thou not betray'd me, *Foible?* Hast

70 *Quarles and Pryn:* Francis Quarles, whose didactic religious poems, *Emblems* (1635), were often reprinted; William Prynne's *Histriomastix* (1633) attacked the stage.

70 *Short View of the Stage:* Jeremy Collier's notorious attack on the stage (1698), including Congreve's earlier plays.

71 *Bunyan's Works:* first printed in 1692, four years after the death of the Puritan author of *Pilgrim's Progress.*

thou not detected me to that faithless *Mirabell*? What had'st thou to do with him in the Park? Answer me, he has got nothing out of thee?

FOIBLE (*aside*). So, the Devil has been beforehand with me. What shall I say?—Alas, Madam, cou'd I help it, if I met that confident Thing? Was I in Fault? If you had heard how he us'd me, and all upon your Ladyship's Account, I'm sure you wou'd not suspect my Fidelity. Nay, if that had been the worst, I cou'd have born; but he had a Fling at your Ladyship too, and then I could not hold, but i'faith I gave him his own.

LADY WISHFORT. Me? What did the filthy Fellow say?

FOIBLE. O Madam, 'tis a shame to say what he said, with his Taunts and his Fleers, tossing up his Nose. "Humh!" says he. "What, you are a hatching some Plot," says he. "You are so early abroad, or Catering," says he. "Ferreting for some disbanded Officer, I warrant. Half-Pay is but thin Subsistance," says he. "Well, what Pension does your Lady propose? Let me see," says he. "What, she must come down pretty deep now, she's super-annuated," says he, "and—"

LADY WISHFORT. Ods my Life, I'll have him, I'll have him murder'd! I'll have him poison'd! Where does he eat? I'll marry a Drawer to have him poison'd in his Wine. I'll send for *Robin* from *Locket's* immediately.

FOIBLE. Poison him? Poisoning's too good for him. Starve him Madam, starve him; marry Sir *Rowland* and get him disinherited. Oh, you would bless yourself to hear what he said.

LADY WISHFORT. A Villain! "Superannuated!"

FOIBLE. "Humh," says he. "I hear you are laying Designs against me too," says he, "and Mrs. *Millamant* is to marry my Uncle" (he does not suspect a Word of your Ladyship); "but," says he, "I'll fit you for that, I warrant you," says he. "I'll hamper you for that," says he. "You and your old Frippery too," says he. "I'll handle you—"

111 *Locket's:* popular Charing Cross tavern.
123 *Frippery:* tattered, once-fine clothes.

LADY WISHFORT. Audacious Villain! "handle" me; wou'd he durst!—"Frippery? old Frippery!" Was there ever such a foul-mouth'd Fellow? I'll be married tomorrow; I'll be contracted tonight.

FOIBLE. The sooner the better, Madam.

LADY WISHFORT. Will Sir *Rowland* be here, say'st thou? When, *Foible?*

FOIBLE. Incontinently, Madam. No new Sheriff's Wife expects the return of her Husband after Knighthood with that Impatience in which Sir *Rowland* burns for the dear hour of kissing your Ladyship's Hands after Dinner.

LADY WISHFORT. "Frippery! Superannuated Frippery!" I'll Frippery the Villain; I'll reduce him to Frippery and Rags! A Tatterdemallion!—I hope to see him hung with Tatters, like a Long-Lane Penthouse or a Gibbet thief. A slander-mouth'd Railer! I warrant the Spendthrift Prodigal's in Debt as much as the Million Lottery, or the whole Court upon a Birthday. I'll spoil his Credit with his Taylor. Yes, he shall have my Niece with her Fortune, he shall.

FOIBLE. *He!* I hope to see him lodge in *Ludgate* first, and Angle into *Black Friers* for Brass Farthings with an old Mitten.

LADY WISHFORT. Ay dear *Foible;* thank thee for that dear *Foible.* He has put me out of all patience. I shall never recompose my Features to receive Sir *Rowland* with any Economy of Face. This Wretch has fretted me that I am absolutely decay'd. Look, *Foible.*

FOIBLE. Your Ladyship has frown'd a little too rashly, indeed, Madam. There are some Cracks discernable in the white Varnish.

LADY WISHFORT. Let me see the Glass.—Cracks, say'st thou? Why I am arrantly flea'd; I look like an

132 *incontinently:* 'immediately', a meaning obsolete by the mid-eighteenth century.

140 *Long-Lane Penthouse:* second-hand clothing stalls in Long Lane, West Smithfield.

143 *Million Lottery:* government lottery of 1694 attempting to raise a million pounds.

143 *Birthday:* of royalty.

146 *Ludgate:* debtors' prison in Blackfriars.

old peel'd Wall. Thou must repair me *Foible,* before Sir *Rowland* comes, or I shall never keep up to my Picture.

FOIBLE. I warrant you, Madam, a little Art once made your Picture like you; and now a little of the same Art must make you like your Picture. Your Picture must sit for you, Madam.

LADY WISHFORT. But art thou sure Sir *Rowland* will not fail to come? Or will 'a not fail when he does come? Will he be Importunate *Foible,* and push? For if he shou'd not be Importunate, I shall never break Decorums. I shall die with Confusion, if I am forc'd to advance.—Oh no, I can never advance! I shall swoon if he shou'd expect advances. No, I hope Sir *Rowland* is better bred than to put a Lady to the necessity of breaking her Forms. I won't be too coy neither. I won't give him despair—but a little Disdain is not amiss; a little Scorn is alluring.

FOIBLE. A little Scorn becomes your Ladyship.

LADY WISHFORT. Yes, but Tenderness becomes me best—a sort of a dyingness. You see that Picture has a sort of a—ha, *Foible?* A swimminess in the Eyes. Yes, I'll look so. My Niece affects it, but she wants Features. Is Sir *Rowland* handsome? Let my Toilet be remov'd—I'll dress above. I'll receive Sir *Rowland* here. Is he handsome? Don't answer me. I won't know; I'll be surpris'd. I'll be taken by Surprise.

FOIBLE. By Storm, Madam. Sir *Rowland's* a brisk Man.

LADY WISHFORT. Is he! Oh, then he'll importune, if he's a brisk Man. I shall save Decorums if Sir *Rowland* importunes. I have a mortal Terror at the apprehension of offending against Decorums. Nothing but Importunity can surmount Decorums. Oh, I'm glad he's a brisk Man. Let my Things be remov'd, good *Foible.*

Exit.

Enter Mrs. Fainall.

MRS. FAINALL. O *Foible,* I have been in a Fright, least I shou'd come too late! That Devil *Marwood* saw you in the Park with *Mirabell,* and I'm afraid will discover it to my Lady.

FOIBLE. Discover what, Madam?

MRS. FAINALL. Nay, nay, put not on that strange Face. I am privy to the whole Design, and know that *Waitwell*, to whom thou wert this morning Married, is to personate *Mirabell's* Uncle, and as such, winning my Lady, to involve her in those Difficulties from which *Mirabell* only must release her, by his making his Conditions to have my Cousin and her Fortune left to her own disposal.

FOIBLE. O dear Madam, I beg your Pardon. It was not my Confidence in your Ladyship that was deficient; but I thought the former good Correspondence between your Ladyship and Mr. *Mirabell* might have hinder'd his communicating this Secret.

MRS. FAINALL. Dear *Foible*, forget that.

FOIBLE. O dear Madam, Mr. *Mirabell* is such a sweet winning Gentleman,—but your Ladyship is the Pattern of Generosity. Sweet Lady, to be so good! Mr. *Mirabell* cannot choose but be grateful. I find your Ladyship has his Heart still. Now, Madam, I can safely tell your Ladyship our success. Mrs. *Marwood* had told my Lady, but I warrant I manag'd myself; I turn'd it all for the better. I told my Lady that Mr. *Mirabell* rail'd at her. I laid horrid Things to his charge, I'll vow; and my Lady is so incens'd, that she'll be contracted to Sir *Rowland* tonight, she says. I warrant I work'd her up, that he may have her for asking for, as they say of a *Welch* Maiden-head.

MRS. FAINALL. O rare *Foible!*

FOIBLE. Madam, I beg your Ladyship to acquaint Mr. *Mirabell* of his success. I wou'd be seen as little as possible to speak to him. Besides, I believe Madam *Marwood* watches me. She has a Month's mind, but I know Mr. *Mirabell* can't abide her. (*Enter Footman.*) *John*, remove my Lady's Toilet. Madam, your Servant. My Lady is so impatient, I fear she'll come for me if I stay.

234 *Month's mind:* 'Originally a religious celebration held a month from the day of a funeral, and hence (owing to a thing being kept well in memory) a strong desire.' (Summers)

MRS. FAINALL. I'll go with you up the back Stairs, lest I shou'd meet her.

Exeunt.

Enter Mrs. Marwood.

MRS. MARWOOD. Indeed Mrs. Engine, is it thus with you? Are you become a go-between of this Importance? Yes, I shall watch you. Why this Wench is the *Pass-par-tout,* a very Master-Key to everybody's strong-Box. My Friend *Fainall,* have you carried it so swimmingly? I thought there was something in it; but it seems it's over with you. Your loathing is not from a want of Appetite then, but from a Surfeit. Else you could never be so cool to fall from a Principal to be an Assistant; to procure for him! "A Pattern of Generosity," that I confess. Well, Mr. *Fainall,* you have met with your Match.—O Man, Man! Woman, Woman! The Devil's an Ass; if I were a Painter, I wou'd draw him like an Idiot, a Driveler, with a Bib and Bells. Man shou'd have his Head and Horns, and Woman the rest of him. Poor simple Fiend! "Madam *Marwood* has a Month's Mind, but he can't abide her." 'Twere better for him you had not been his Confessor in that Affair, without you cou'd have kept his Counsel closer. I shall not prove another Pattern of Generosity and stalk for him, till he takes his Stand to aim at a Fortune. He has not oblig'd me to that with those Excesses of himself; and now I'll have none of him. Here comes the good Lady, panting ripe; with a Heart full of Hope, and a Head full of Care, like any Chymist upon the Day of Projection.

Enter Lady Wishfort.

LADY WISHFORT. O dear *Marwood,* what shall I say for this rude forgetfulness? But my dear Friend is all Goodness.

MRS. MARWOOD. No Apologies, dear Madam. I have been very well entertained.

LADY WISHFORT. As I'm a Person, I am in a very Chaos to think I shou'd so forget myself.—But I have such an Olio of Affairs really I know not what to do.

268 *Day of Projection:* alchemist's final process in transforming base metal into precious.
277 *Olio:* muddle.

(Calls.) Foible! I expect my Nephew, Sir *Wilfull,* every moment too—why, *Foible!* He means to Travel for Improvement.

MRS. MARWOOD. Methinks Sir *Wilfull* should rather think of Marrying than Travelling at his Years. I hear he is turn'd of Forty.

LADY WISHFORT. Oh, he's in less Danger of being spoil'd by his Travels. I am against my Nephew's marrying too young. It will be time enough when he comes back and has acquir'd Discretion to choose for himself.

MRS. MARWOOD. Methinks Mrs. *Millamant* and he wou'd make a very fit Match. He may Travel afterwards. 'Tis a Thing very usual with young Gentlemen.

LADY WISHFORT. I promise you I have thought on't; and since 'tis your Judgment, I'll think on't again. I assure you I will; I value your Judgment extremely. On my Word, I'll propose it.

Enter Foible.

Come, come *Foible,* I had forgot my Nephew will be here before Dinner. I must make haste.

FOIBLE. Mr. *Witwoud* and Mr. *Petulant* are come to Dine with your Ladyship.

LADY WISHFORT. O Dear, I can't appear till I'm dress'd. Dear *Marwood,* shall I be free with you again, and beg you to entertain 'em? I'll make all imaginable haste. Dear Friend, excuse me.

Exit Lady Wishfort *and* Foible.

Enter Mrs. Millamant *and* Mincing.

MILLAMANT. Sure never anything was so Unbred as that odious Man!—*Marwood,* your Servant.

MRS. MARWOOD. You have a Colour; what's the matter?

MILLAMANT. That horrid Fellow *Petulant* has provok'd me into a Flame. I have broke my Fan—*Mincing,* lend me yours; is not all the Powder out of my Hair?

MRS. MARWOOD. No. What has he done?

MILLAMANT. Nay, he has done nothing; he has only talk'd—nay, he has said nothing neither; but he has contradicted everything that has been said. For my part, I thought *Witwoud* and he wou'd have quarrell'd.

MINCING. I vow Mem, I thought once they wou'd have fit.

MILLAMANT. Well, tis a lamentable thing, I'll swear, that one has not the liberty of choosing one's Acquaintance as one does one's Clothes.

MRS. MARWOOD. If we had the liberty, we shou'd be as weary of one Set of Acquaintance, tho' never so good, as we are of one Suit, tho' never so fine. A Fool and a *Doily* Stuff wou'd now and then find Days of Grace, and be worn for variety.

MILLAMANT. I could consent to wear 'em, if they wou'd wear alike, but Fools never wear out—they are such *Drap-du-Berry* Things! without one cou'd give 'em to one's Chambermaid after a day or two.

MRS. MARWOOD. 'Twere better so indeed. Or what think you of the Play-house? A fine gay glossy Fool shou'd be given there, like a new masking Habit, after the Masquerade is over, and we have done with the Disguise. For a Fool's Visit is always a Disguise, and never admitted by a Woman of Wit but to blind her Affair with a Lover of Sense. If you wou'd but appear bare-fac'd now, and own *Mirabell*, you might as easily put off *Petulant* and *Witwoud* as your Hood and Scarf. And indeed 'tis time, for the Town has found it; the secret is grown too big for the Pretence. 'Tis like Mrs. *Primly's* great Belly; she may lace it down before, but it burnishes on her Hips. Indeed, *Millamant*, you can no more conceal it than my Lady *Strammel* can her Face, that goodly Face, which in defiance of her Rhenish-wine Tea, will not be comprehended in a Mask.

322 *fit:* fought.
329 *Doily Stuff:* inexpensive woollen material.
333 *Drap-du-Berry:* heavy woollen cloth originally from Berry in France.
350 *Rhenish-wine Tea:* light Rhenish wine recommended for reducing diets.
350 *comprehended:* contained.

MILLAMANT. I'll take my Death, *Marwood,* you are more Censorious than a decay'd Beauty, or a discarded Toast; *Mincing,* tell the Men they may come up. My Aunt is not dressing; their Folly is less provoking than your Malice. (*Exit* Mincing.) "The Town has found it." What has it found? That *Mirabell* loves me is no more a Secret than it is a Secret that you discover'd it to my Aunt, or than the Reason why you discover'd it is a Secret.

MRS. MARWOOD. You are nettl'd.

MILLAMANT. You're mistaken. Ridiculous!

MRS. MARWOOD. Indeed my Dear, you'll tear another Fan if you don't mitigate those violent Airs.

MILLAMANT. O Silly! Ha, ha, ha! I cou'd laugh immoderately. Poor *Mirabell!* His Constancy to me has quite destroy'd his Complaisance for all the World beside. I swear, I never enjoin'd it him to be so coy. If I had the Vanity to think he wou'd obey me, I wou'd command him to show more Gallantry. 'Tis hardly well bred to be so particular on one Hand, and so insensible on the other. But I despair to prevail, and so let him follow his own way. Ha, ha, ha. Pardon me, dear Creature, I must laugh, ha, ha, ha, tho' I grant you 'tis a little barbarous. Ha, ha, ha!

MRS. MARWOOD. What pity 'tis, so much fine Raillery, and deliver'd with so significant Gesture, shou'd be so unhappily directed to miscarry.

MILLAMANT. Ha? Dear Creature, I ask your Pardon—I swear I did not mind you.

MRS. MARWOOD. Mr. *Mirabell* and you both may think it a Thing impossible, when I shall tell him by telling you—

MILLAMANT. O Dear, what? For it is the same thing if I hear it, ha, ha, ha.

MRS. MARWOOD. That I detest him, hate him, Madam.

MILLAMANT. O Madam, why so do I—And yet the Creature loves me, Ha, ha, ha. How can one forbear laughing to think of it. I am a Sybil if I am not amaz'd to think what he can see in me. I'll take my

Death, I think you are handsomer–and within a Year or two as young. If you cou'd but stay for me, I shou'd overtake you–but that cannot be. Well, that Thought makes me Melancholly.–Now I'll be sad.

MRS. MARWOOD. Your merry Note may be chang'd sooner than you think.

MILLAMANT. D'ye say so? Then I'm resolv'd I'll have a Song to keep up my Spirits.

Enter Mincing.

MINCING. The Gentlemen stay but to comb, Madam, and will wait on you.

MILLAMANT. Desire Mrs. ––, that is in the next Room to sing the Song I wou'd have learnt Yesterday. You shall hear it Madam–not that there's any great matter in it, but 'tis agreeable to my Humour.

Set by Mr. John Eccles, *and Sung by* Mrs. Hodgson.

SONG.

I.

Love's but the frailty of the Mind,
When 'tis not with Ambition join'd;
A sickly Flames, which, if not fed, expires;
And feeding, wasts in Self-consuming Fires.

II.

'Tis not to wound a wanton Boy
Or am'rous Youth, that gives the Joy;
But 'tis the Glory to have pierc'd a Swain,
For whom inferiour Beauties sigh'd in vain.

III.

Then I alone the the Conquest prize,
When I insult a Rival's Eyes;
If there's Delight in Love, 'tis when I see
That Heart Which others bleed for, bleed for me.

Enter Petulant *and* Witwoud.

MILLAMANT. Is your Animosity compos'd, Gentlemen?

WITWOUD. Raillery, Raillery, Madam; we have no Animosity. We hit off a little Wit now and then, but

401 *comb:* i.e. their wigs.
407 *John Eccles:* also responsible for incidental music for the play.

no Animosity. The falling out of Wits is like the falling out of Lovers; we agree in the main, like Treble and Base. Ha, *Petulant*?

PETULANT. Ay, in the main—but when I have a Humour to contradict.

WITWOUD. Ay, when he has a Humour to contradict, then I contradict too. What, I know my Cue. Then we contradict one another like two Battle-dores; for Contradictions beget one another like *Jews*.

PETULANT. If he says Black's Black, if I have a Humour to say 'tis Blue, let that pass; all's one for that. If I have a Humour to prove it, it must be granted.

WITWOUD. Not positively must—but it may, it may.

PETULANT. Yes, it positively must, upon Proof positive.

WITWOUD. Ay, upon Proof positive it must; but upon Proof presumptive it only may. That's a Logical Distinction now, Madam.

MRS. MARWOOD. I perceive your Debates are of Importance and very learnedly handl'd.

PETULANT. Importance is one Thing, and Learning's another; but a Debate's a Debate, that I assert.

WITWOUD. *Petulant's* an Enemy to Learning; he relies altogether on his Parts.

PETULANT. No, I'm no Enemy to Learning; it hurts not me.

MRS. MARWOOD. That's a Sign indeed it's no Enemy to you.

PETULANT. No, no, it's no Enemy to anybody but them that have it.

MILLAMANT. Well, an illiterate Man's my Aversion. I wonder at the Impudence of any Illiterate Man to offer to make Love.

WITWOUD. That I confess I wonder at too.

MILLAMANT. Ah! to marry an Ignorant that can hardly Read or Write.

PETULANT. Why shou'd a Man be ever the further from being married tho' he can't Read, any more than he is from being Hang'd? The Ordinary's paid for setting the *Psalm,* and the Parish-Priest for reading the Ceremony. And for the rest which is to follow in both Cases, a Man may do it without Book—so all's one for that.

MILLAMANT. D'ye hear the Creature? Lord, here's Company; I'll be gone.

Exeunt Millamant *and* Mincing.

WITWOUD. In the Name of *Bartlemew* and his Fair, what have we here?

MRS. MARWOOD. 'Tis your Brother, I fancy. Don't you know him?

WITWOOD. Not I.—Yes, I think it is he.—I've almost forgot him; I have not seen him since the Revolution.

Enter Sir Wilfull Witwoud *in a Country Riding Habit, and Servant to* Lady Wishfort.

SERVANT. Sir, my Lady's dressing. Here's Company, if you please to walk in, in the mean time.

SIR WILFULL. Dressing! What, it's but Morning here, I warrant with you, in *London;* we shou'd count it towards Afternoon in our Parts, down in *Shropshire.* Why then, belike my Aunt han't din'd yet—ha, Friend?

SERVANT. Your Aunt, Sir?

SIR WILFULL. My Aunt, Sir, yes my Aunt, Sir, and your Lady, Sir; your Lady is my Aunt, Sir.—Why, what, do'st thou not know me, Friend? Why then send Somebody here that does. How long hast thou liv'd with thy Lady, Fellow, ha?

SERVANT. A Week, Sir; longer than anybody in the House, except my Lady's Woman.

SIR WILFULL. Why then, belike thou dost not know thy Lady if thou see'st her, ha, Friend?

468 *The Ordinary:* the Newgate chaplain who ministered to condemned prisoners.

476 *Bartlemew:* the annual fair, full of curiosities, held in August on the Feast of St Bartholomew.

481 *Revolution:* the Glorious Revolution of 1688.

SERVANT. Why truly, Sir, I cannot safely swear to her Face in a Morning, before she is dress'd. 'Tis like I may give a shrewd guess at her by this time.

SIR WILFULL. Well, prithee try what thou can'st do; if thou can'st not guess, enquire her out, do'st hear Fellow? And tell her, her Nephew, Sir *Wilfull Witwoud,* is in the House.

SERVANT. I shall, Sir.

SIR WILFULL. Hold ye, hear me, Friend; a Word with you in your Ear. Prithee who are these Gallants?

SERVANT. Really Sir, I can't tell; here come so many here, 'tis hard to know 'em all.

Exit Servant.

SIR WILFULL. Oons, this Fellow knows less than a Starling; I don't think 'a knows his own Name.

MRS. MARWOOD. Mr. *Witwoud,* your Brother is not behindhand in forgetfulness; I fancy he has forgot you too.

WITWOUD. I hope so.—The Devil take him that remembers first, I say.

SIR WILFUL. Save you, Gentlemen and Lady.

MRS. MARWOOD. For shame, Mr. *Witwoud;* why won't you speak to him?—And you, Sir.

WITWOUD. *Petulant,* speak.

PETULANT. And you, Sir.

SIR WILFULL. No Offence, I hope.

Salutes Mrs. Marwood.

MRS. MARWOOD. No sure, Sir.

WITWOUD. This is a vile Dog; I see that already. No Offence! Ha, ha, ha! To him, to him, *Petulant;* smoke him.

PETULANT. It seems as if you had come a Journey, Sir, hem, hem.

Surveying him round.

SIR WILFULL. Very likely, Sir, that it may seem so.

529 *smoke him:* make him ridiculous.

PETULANT. No Offence, I hope, Sir.

WITWOUD. Smoke the Boots, the Boots, *Petulant,* the Boots. Ha, ha, ha!

SIR WILFULL. Maybe not, Sir; thereafter as 'tis meant, Sir.

PETULANT. Sir, I presume upon the Information of your Boots.

SIR WILFULL. Why, 'tis like you may, Sir. If you are not satisfy'd with the Information of my Boots, Sir, if you will step to the Stable, you may enquire further of my Horse, Sir.

PETULANT. Your Horse, Sir! Your Horse is an Ass, Sir!

SIR WILFULL. Do you speak by way of Offence, Sir?

MRS. MARWOOD. The Gentleman's merry, that's all, Sir. *(Aside.)* 'Slife, we shall have a Quarrel betwixt an Horse and an Ass, before they find one another out. *(Aloud.)* You must not take any Thing amiss from your Friends, Sir. You are among your Friends here, tho' it may be you don't know it. If I am not mistaken, you are Sir *Wilfull Witwoud.*

SIR WILFULL. Right Lady; I am Sir *Wilfull Witwoud,* so I write myself; no offence to anybody, I hope; and Nephew to the Lady *Wishfort* of this Mansion.

MRS. MARWOOD. Don't you know this Gentleman, Sir?

SIR WILFULL. Hum! What, sure 'tis not—yea, by'r Lady, but 'tis. 'Sheart, I know not whether 'tis or no—yea but 'tis, by the *Rekin.* Brother *Anthony!* What *Tony,* i'faith! What, do'st thou not know me? By'r Lady, nor I thee, thou art so becravated, and beperriwig'd.—'Sheart, why do'st not speak? Art thou o'erjoy'd?

WITWOUD. Odso, Brother, is it you? Your Servant, Brother.

SIR WILFULL. Your Servant! Why, yours, Sir. Your Servant again, 'Sheart, and your Friend and Servant

563 *Rekin:* The Wrekin, a conspicuous hill in Shropshire.

to that, and a *(Puff.)* and a flapdragon for your Service, Sir! and a Hare's Foot, and a Hare's Scut for your Service, Sir, an you be so cold and so courtly!

WITWOUD. No offence, I hope, Brother.

SIR WILFULL. 'Sheart, Sir, but there is, and much offence! A pox, is this your Inns o' Court breeding, not to know your Friends and your Relations, your Elders, and your Betters?

WITWOUD. Why, Brother *Wilfull* of *Salop*, you may be as short as a *Shrewsbury* Cake, if you please. But I tell you 'tis not modish to know Relations in Town. You think you're in the Country, where great lubberly Brothers slabber and kiss one another when they meet, like a Call of Serjeants.—'Tis not the fashion here; 'tis not indeed, dear Brother.

SIR WILFULL. The Fashion's a Fool; and you're a Fop, dear Brother. 'Sheart, I've suspected this.—By'r Lady I conjectur'd you were a Fop, since you began to change the Style of your Letters, and write in a scrap of Paper gilt round the Edges, no broader than a *Subpœna*. I might expect this when you left off "Honour'd Brother," and "hoping you are in good Health," and so forth, to begin with a "Rat me, Knight, I'm so sick of a last Night's debauch"—Ods heart, and then tell a familiar Tale of a Cock and a Bull, and a Whore and a Bottle, and so conclude. You cou'd write News before you were out of your Time, when you liv'd with honest *Pumple Nose* the Attorney of *Furnival's* Inn; you cou'd intreat to be remember'd then to your Friends round the *Rekin*. We cou'd have Gazettes then, and *Dawk's* Letter, and the weekly Bill, 'till of late Days.

PETULANT. 'Slife, *Witwoud*, were you ever an Attorney's Clerk? Of the Family of the *Furnivals*? Ha, ha, ha!

572 *Flapdragon:* 'A play in which they catch raisins out of burning brandy, and, extinguishing them by closing the mouth, eat them.' (Johnson, *Dictionary*.) Also, a case of venereal disease.
573 *Scut:* tail.
580 *Salop:* Shropshire, its county seat Shrewsbury.
585 *Call of Serjeants:* ceremony of admitting sergeants-at-law to the rank of barrister.
602 *Dawk's Letter:* weekly paper, begun 1696, printed to resemble a hand-written letter.
603 *weekly Bill:* list of deaths in London.

WITWOUD. Ay, ay, but that was for a while, not long, not long. Pshaw, I was not in my own Power then; an Orphan, and this Fellow was my Guardian. Ay, ay, I was glad to consent to that Man to come to *London;* he had the disposal of me then. If I had not agreed to that, I might have been bound Prentice to a Felt maker in *Shrewsbury;* this Fellow wou'd have bound me to a Maker of Felts.

SIR WILFULL. 'Sheart, and better than to be bound to a Maker of Fops, where, I suppose, you have serv'd your Time; and now you may set up for yourself.

MRS. MARWOOD. You intend to Travel, Sir, as I'm inform'd.

SIR WILFULL. Belike I may, Madam. I may chance to sail upon the salt Seas, if my Mind hold.

PETULANT. And the Wind serve.

SIR WILFULL. Serve or not serve, I shan't ask License of you, Sir; nor the Weather-Cock your Companion. I direct my Discourse to the Lady, Sir. 'Tis like my Aunt may have told you, Madam. Yes, I have settl'd my Concerns, I may say now, and am minded to see Foreign Parts. If and how that the Peace holds, whereby, that is, Taxes abate.

MRS. MARWOOD. I thought you had design'd for *France* at all Adventures.

SIR WILFULL. I can't tell that; 'tis like I may, and 'tis like I may not. I am somewhat dainty in making a Resolution, because when I make it I keep it. I don't stand shill I, shall I, then; if I say't, I'll do't. But I have Thoughts to tarry a small matter in Town, to learn somewhat of your Lingo first, before I cross the Seas. I'd gladly have a spice of your *French,* as they say, whereby to hold discourse in Foreign Countries.

MRS. MARWOOD. Here is an Academy in Town for that use.

SIR WILFULL. There is? 'Tis like there may.

MRS. MARWOOD. No doubt you will return very much improv'd.

628 *Peace:* the Peace of Ryswick (1697), a temporary lull in the incessant wars between Louis XIV of France and most of the rest of Europe.

WITWOUD. Yes, refin'd, like a *Dutch* Skipper from a Whale-fishing.

Enter Lady Wishfort *and* Fainall

LADY WISHFORT. Nephew, you are welcome.

SIR WILFULL. Aunt, your Servant.

FAINALL. Sir *Wilfull,* your most faithful Servant.

SIR WILFULL. Cousin *Fainall,* give me your Hand.

LADY WISHFORT. Cousin *Witwoud,* your Servant; Mr. *Petulant,* your Servant.—Nephew, you are welcome again. Will you drink anything after your Journey, Nephew, before you eat? Dinner's almost ready.

SIR WILFULL. I'm very well, I thank you, Aunt; however, I thank you for your courteous Offer. 'Sheart, I was afraid you wou'd have been in the fashion too, and have remember'd to have forgot your Relations. Here's your Cousin *Tony;* belike I mayn't call him Brother for fear of offence.

LADY WISHFORT. O he's a Rallier, Nephew—my Cousin's a Wit, and your great Wits always rally their best Friends to choose. When you have been abroad, Nephew, you'll understand Raillery better.

Fainall *and* Mrs. Marwood *talk a-part.*

SIR WILFULL. Why then let him hold his Tongue in the meantime, and rail when that day comes.

Enter Mincing.

MINCING. Mem, I come to acquaint your Laship that Dinner is impatient.

SIR WILFULL. Impatient? Why then belike it won't stay 'till I pull off my Boots. Sweetheart, can you help me to a pair of Slippers? My Man's with his Horses, I warrant.

LADY WISHFORT. Fie, fie, Nephew, you wou'd not pull off your Boots here. Go down into the Hall; dinner shall stay for you.—My Nephew's a little un-

663 *Rallier:* an indulger in raillery.
665 *to choose:* by choice.

bred; you'll pardon him, Madam. Gentlemen, will you walk? *Marwood?*

MRS. MARWOOD. I'll follow you, Madam, before Sir *Wilfull* is ready.

Manent Mrs. Marwood *and* Fainall.

FAINALL. Why then, *Foible's* a Bawd, an Errant, Rank, Matchmaking Bawd! And I it seems am a Husband, a Rank Husband; and my Wife a very Errant, Rank Wife,—all in *the Way of the World.* 'Sdeath, to be an Anticipated Cuckold, a Cuckold in Embryo! Sure I was born with budding Antlers like a young Satyr, or a Citizen's Child. 'Sdeath to be Out-Witted, to be Out-Jilted,—Out-Matrimony'd! If I had kept my speed like a Stag, 'twere somewhat; but to crawl after, with my Horns, like a Snail, and out-strip'd by my Wife—'tis Scurvy Wedlock.

MRS. MARWOOD. Then shake it off. You have often wish'd for an opportunity to part, and now you have it. But first prevent their Plot; the half of *Millamant's* Fortune is too Considerable to be parted with, to a Foe, to *Mirabell.*

FAINALL. Damn him! that had been mine—had you made that fond discovery. That had been forfeited, had they been Married. My Wife had added Lustre to my Horns by that Increase of fortune; I cou'd have worn 'em tipt with Gold, tho' my forehead had been furnish'd like a Deputy-Lieutenant's Hall.

MRS. MARWOOD. They may prove a Cap of Maintenance to you still, if you can away with your Wife. And she's no worse than when you had her—I dare swear she had given up her Game before she was Marry'd.

FAINALL. Hum! That may be. She might throw up her Cards; but I'll be hang'd if she did not put Pam in her Pocket.

691 *Citizen's Child:* the 'citizen' in trade in the city was often thought to be cuckolded by gentlemen of leisure.

702 *fond:* foolish.

706 *Deputy-Lieutenant's Hall:* its walls covered with antlers.

707-8 *Cap of Maintenance:* in Heraldry, a cap with two points like horns appearing on the eschutcheon of certain families; hence, a symbol of dignity.

708 *away with:* endure.

713 *Pam:* knave of clubs, highest trump in the game of Loo.

MRS. MARWOOD. You Married her to keep you; and if you can contrive to have her keep you better than you expected, why should you not keep her longer than you intended?

FAINALL. The means, the means.

MRS. MARWOOD. Discover to my Lady your Wife's conduct; threaten to part with her. My Lady loves her, and will come to any Composition to save her reputation. Take the opportunity of breaking it, just upon the discovery of this imposture. My Lady will be enraged beyond bounds, and Sacrifice Niece and Fortune and all at that Conjuncture. And let me alone to keep her warm; if she should flag in her part, I will not fail to prompt her.

FAINALL. Faith, this has an appearance.

MRS. MARWOOD. I'm sorry I hinted to my Lady to endeavour a match between *Millamant* and Sir *Wilfull;* that may be an Obstacle.

FAINALL. Oh, for that matter leave me to manage him; I'll disable him for that. He will drink like a *Dane;* after dinner, I'll set his hand in.

MRS. MARWOOD. Well, how do you stand affected toward your Lady?

FAINALL. Why, faith, I'm thinking of it. Let me see —I am married already, so that's over. My Wife has played the Jade with me; well, that's over too. I never lov'd her, or if I had, why that wou'd have been over too by this time. Jealous of her I cannot be, for I am certain; so there's an end of Jealousie. Weary of her I am, and shall be. No, there's no end of that; no, no, that were too much to hope. Thus far concerning my repose; now for my Reputation. As to my own, I married not for it; so that's out of the Question. And as to my part in my Wife's—why she had parted with hers before; so bringing none to me, she can take none from me. 'Tis against all rule of Play that I should lose to one who has not wherewithal to stake.

MRS. MARWOOD. Besides, you forget, Marriage is honourable.

FAINALL. Hum! Faith, and that's well thought on. Marriage is honourable as you say; and if so, wherefore should Cuckoldom be a discredit, being deriv'd from so honourable a Root?

MRS. MARWOOD. Nay I know not; if the Root be honourable, why not the Branches?

FAINALL. So, so; why this point's clear.—Well, how do we proceed?

MRS. MARWOOD. I will contrive a Letter which shall be deliver'd to my Lady at the time when that Rascal who is to act Sir *Rowland* is with her. It shall come as from an unknown hand—for the less I appear to know of the truth, the better I can play the Incendiary. Besides, I would not have *Foible* provok'd if I cou'd help it, because you know she knows some passages. Nay, I expect all will come out; but let the Mine be sprung first, and then I care not if I'm discover'd.

FAINALL. If the worst come to the worst, I'll turn my Wife to Grass. I have already a deed of Settlement of the best part of her Estate, which I wheadl'd out of her; and that you shall partake at least.

MRS. MARWOOD. I hope you are convinc'd that I hate *Mirabell* now; you'll be no more Jealous?

FAINALL. Jealous, no—by this Kiss. Let Husbands be Jealous; but let the Lover still believe. Or if he doubt, let it be only to endear his pleasure and prepare the Joy that follows, when he proves his Mistress true. But let Husbands' doubts convert to endless Jealousie; or if they belief, let it corrupt to Superstition and blind Credulity. I am single, and will herd no more with 'em. True, I wear the badge, but I'll disown the Order. And since I take my leave of 'em, I care not if I leave 'em a common Motto to their common Crest.

All Husbands must or pain or shame endure,
The Wise too jealous are, Fools too secure.

Exeunt.

759 *Branches:* i.e. of a cuckold's horns.

ACT IV. Scene I.

Scene Continues.

Enter Lady Wishfort *and* Foible.

LADY WISHFORT. Is Sir *Rowland* coming, say'st thou, *Foible?* and are things in Order?

FOIBLE. Yes, *Madam.* I have put Wax-Lights in the Sconces, and plac'd the Floormen in a Row in the Hall, in their best Liveries, with the Coachman and Postilion to fill up the Equipage.

LADY WISHFORT. Have you pullvill'd the Coachman and Postilion, that they may not stink of the Stable when Sir *Rowland* comes by?

FOIBLE. Yes, Madam.

LADY WISHFORT. And are the Dancers and the Musick ready, that he may be entertain'd in all points with Correspondence to his Passion?

FOIBLE. All is ready, *Madam.*

LADY WISHFORT. And—well—and how do I look. *Foible?*

FOIBLE. Most killing well, *Madam.*

LADY WISHFORT. Well, and how shall I receive him? In what figure shall I give his Heart the first Impression? There is a great deal in the first Impression. Shall I sit? No, I won't sit—I'll walk; ay, I'll walk from the door upon his entrance, and then turn full upon him. No, that will be too sudden. I'll lie—ay, I'll lie down. I'll receive him in my little dressing Room; there's a Couch—yes, yes, I'll give the first Impression on a Couch. I won't lie neither, but loll and lean upon one Elbow, with one Foot a little dangling off, jogging in a thoughtful way. Yes, and then as soon as he appears, start, ay, start and be surpris'd, and rise to meet him in a pretty disorder. Yes—oh, nothing is more alluring than a Levee from a Couch in some Confusion. It shows the Foot to advantage, and furnishes with Blushes and re-composing Airs beyond Comparison. Hark! There's a Coach.

FOIBLE. 'Tis he, *Madam.*

7 *pulvill'd:* 'To sprinkle with perfumes in powder.' (Johnson, *Dictionary.*)

LADY WISHFORT. O dear, has my *Nephew* made his Addresses to *Millamant?* I order'd him.

FOIBLE. Sir *Wilfull* is set in to Drinking, *Madam,* in the Parlour.

LADY WISHFORT. Ods my life, I'll send him to her. Call her down, *Foible;* bring her hither. I'll send him as I go. When they are together, then come to me, *Foible,* that I may not be too long alone with Sir *Rowland.*

Exit.

Enter Mrs. Millamant, *and* Mrs. Fainall.

FOIBLE. *Madam,* I stay'd here to tell your Ladyship that Mr. *Mirabell* has waited this half hour for an Opportunity to talk with you, tho' my Lady's Orders were to leave you and Sir *Wilfull* together. Shall I tell Mr. *Mirabell* that you are at leisure?

MILLAMANT. No—what would the dear Man have? I am thoughtful, and would amuse myself; bid him come another time.

There never yet was Woman made,
Nor shall, but to be curs'd.

Repeating and Walking about.

That's hard!

MRS. FAINALL. You are very fond of Sir *John Suckling* today, *Millamant,* and the *Poets.*

MILLAMANT. He? Ay, and filthy Verses; so I am.

FOIBLE. Sir *Wilfull* is coming, *Madam.* Shall I send Mr. *Mirabell* away?

MILLAMANT. Ay, if you please, *Foible,* send him away—or send him hither; just as you will, dear *Foible.* I think I'll see him; shall I? Ay, let the Wretch come.

Thyrsis a Youth of the Inspir'd train—

Repeating.

Dear *Fainall,* Entertain Sir *Wilfull.* Thou hast Philosophy to undergo a Fool; thou art Married and hast Patience. I would confer with my own Thoughts.

55 *There never yet,* etc.: opening of a lyric by Sir John Suckling (1609-1642). See his *Works,* ed. W. Carew Hazlitt, Vol. I, p. 19.

68 *Thyrsis,* etc.: opening of *The Story of Phoebus and Daphne, Applied,* by Edmund Waller (1606-1687), in *Waller's Poems,* ed. G. Thorn-Drury, I, p. 52.

MRS. FAINALL. I am oblig'd to you, that you would make me your Proxy in this Affair; but I have business of my own.

Enter Sir Wilfull.

O *Sir Wilfull,* you are come at the Critical Instant. There's your Mistress up to the Ears in Love and Contemplation; pursue your Point, now or never.

SIR WILFULL. Yes; my Aunt would have it so. I would gladly have been encouraged with a Bottle or two, because I'm somewhat wary at first, before I am acquainted. But I hope, after a time, I shall break my mind—that is, upon further acquaintance. So for the present, Cousin, I'll take my leave. If so be you'll be so kind to make my Excuse, I'll return to my Company—

This while Millamant *walks about Repeating to herself.*

MRS. FAINALL. Oh, fie, Sir *Wilfull!* What, you must not be Daunted.

SIR WILFULL. Daunted! No, that's not it. It is not so much for that—for if so be that I set on't, I'll do't. But only for the present; 'tis sufficient till further acquaintance, that's all—your Servant.

MRS. FAINALL. Nay, I'll swear you shall never lose so favourable an opportunity, if I can help it. I'll leave you together and lock the Door.

Exit.

SIR WILFULL. Nay, nay Cousin—I have forgot my Gloves. What d'ye do? 'Shart, 'a has lock'd the Door indeed, I think. Nay, Cousin *Fainall,* open the Door! Pshaw, what a Vixon trick is this? Nay, now 'a has seen me too. Cousin, I made bold to pass thro' as it were. I think this Door's inchanted—.

MILLAMANT *(repeating).*

I prithee spare me, gentle Boy,
Press me no more for that slight Toy.

SIR WILFULL. Anan? Cousin, your Servant.

MILLAMANT. *That foolish Trifle of a Heart*—Sir *Wilfull!*

106 *I prithee spare me,* etc.: Suckling, *Works,* Vol. I, p. 22. Millamant continues to quote the poem in her next two speeches.

SIR WILFULL. Yes—your Servant. No offence I hope, Cousin.

MILLAMANT *(repeating)*.

I swear it will not do its part,
Tho' thou do'st thine, employ'st the Power and Art.

Natural, easy *Suckling!*

SIR WILFULL. Anan? *Suckling?* No such Suckling neither, Cousin, nor Stripling; I thank Heav'n, I'm no Minor.

MILLAMANT. Ah Rustic! ruder than *Gothick.*

SIR WILFULL. Well, well, I shall understand your *Lingo* one of these days, Cousin; in the meanwhile, I must answer in plain English.

MILLAMANT. Have you any business with me, Sir *Wilfull?*

SIR WILFULL. Not at present, Cousin.—Yes, I made bold to see, to come and know if that how you were dispos'd to fetch a walk this Evening; if so be that I might not be troublesome, I wou'd have sought a walk with you.

MILLAMANT. A walk? What then?

SIR WILFULL. Nay, nothing—only for the walk's sake, that's all.

MILLAMANT. I Nauseate walking; 'tis a Country diversion. I loath the Country and everything that relates to it.

SIR WILFULL. Indeed! Hah! Look ye, look ye, you do? Nay, 'tis like you may. Here are choice of Pastimes here in Town, as Plays and the like; that must be confess'd indeed.

MILLAMANT. *Ah l' etourdie!* I hate the Town too.

SIR WILFULL. Dear Heart, that's much. Hah! that you shou'd hate 'em both! Hah! 'tis like you may; there are some can't relish the Town, and others can't

116 *easy Suckling:* 'Suckling's easie Pen'; cf. Earl of Rochester, *Satyr* (1685) in *The Collected Works of John Wilmot, Earl of Rochester,* ed. John Hayward (1926), p. 79 (Davis).
141 *Ah l'etourdie:* 'Oh, the stupid fellow.'

away with the Country. Tis like you may be one of those, Cousin.

MILLAMANT. Ha, ha, ha! Yes, 'tis like I may—You have nothing further to say to me?

SIR WILFULL. Not at present, Cousin.—'Tis like when I have an Opportunity to be more private. I may break my mind in some measure. I conjecture you partly guess—however, that's as time shall try; but spare to speak and spare to speed, as they say.

MILLAMANT. If it is of no great Importance, Sir *Wilfull*, you will oblige me to leave me; I have just now a little business.—

SIR WILFULL. Enough, enough, Cousin; yes, yes, all a case—when you're dispos'd, when you're dispos'd. Now's as well as another time; and another time as well as now. All's one for that. Yes, yes, if your Concerns call you, there's no haste; it will keep cold, as they say. Cousin, your Servant.—I think this door's lock'd.

MILLAMANT. You may go this way, Sir.

SIR WILFULL. Your Servant; then with your leave I'll return to my Company.

Exit.

MILLAMANT. Ay, ay; ha, ha, ha!

Like Phœbus *sung the no less am'rous Boy.*

Enter Mirabell.

MIRABELL. —*Like* Daphne *she as lovely and as Coy.* Do you lock yourself up from me, to make my search more Curious? Or is this pretty Artifice Contriv'd to Signify that here the Chase must end and my pursuit be Crown'd, for you can fly no further?

MILLAMANT. Vanity! No—I'll fly and be follow'd to the last moment. Tho' I am upon the very Verge of Matrimony, I expect you shou'd solicit me as much as if I were wavering at the grate of a Monastery, with one foot over the threshold. I'll be solicited to the very last, nay, and afterwards.

MIRABELL. What, after the last?

169 *Like Phoebus . . . and as coy:* 11. 3-4 of the Waller poem above.

MILLAMANT. Oh, I should think I was poor and had nothing to bestow, if I were reduc'd to an inglorious Ease and free'd from the agreeable Fatigues of Solicitation.

MIRABELL. But do not you know that when favours are conferr'd upon instant and tedious Solicitation, that they diminish in their value, and that both the giver loses the grace, and the receiver lessens his Pleasure?

MILLAMANT. It may be in things of common Application, but never sure in Love. Oh, I hate a Lover that can dare to think he draws a moment's air independent on the Bounty of his Mistress. There is not so impudent a thing in Nature as the saucy look of an assured Man, confident of Success. The Pedantick Arrogance of a very Husband has not so Pragmatical an Air. Ah! I'll never marry, unless I am first made sure of my Will and Pleasure.

MIRABELL. Wou'd you have 'em both before Marriage? Or will you be contented with the first now, and stay for the other till after grace?

MILLAMANT. Ah, don't be Impertinent! My dear Liberty, shall I leave thee? My faithful Solitude, my darling Contemplation, must I bid you then adieu? ay-h adieu, my morning thoughts, agreeable wakings, indolent slumbers, all ye *douceurs, ye Someils du Matin,* adieu.—I can't do't, 'tis more than Impossible. Positively *Mirabell,* I'll lie a-bed in a morning as long as I please.

MIRABELL. Then I'll get up in a morning as early as I please.

MILLAMANT. Ah! Idle Creature, get up when you will—and d'ye hear, I won't be call'd Names after I'm married; positively I won't be call'd Names.

MIRABELL. Names!

MILLAMANT. Ay, as Wife, Spouse, My Dear, Joy, Jewel, Love, Sweetheart and the rest of that nauseous Cant in which Men and their Wives are so fulsomely familiar; I shall never bear that.—Good *Mirabell,* don't let us be familiar or fond, nor kiss before folks, like

207 *ye douceurs, ye Someils du Matin:* 'ye sweet pleasures, ye morning snoozes.'

my Lady *Fadler* and Sir *Francis;* nor go to *Hyde Park* together the first *Sunday* in a new Chariot, to provoke Eyes and Whispers, and then never to be seen there together again, as if we were proud of one another the first Week, and asham'd of one another for ever after. Let us never visit together, nor go to a Play together; but let us be very strange and well bred; let us be as strange as if we had been married a great while, and as well bred as if we were not married at all.

MIRABELL. Have you any more Conditions to offer? Hitherto your demands are pretty reasonable.

MILLAMANT. Trifles!–As liberty to pay and receive visits to and from whom I please; to write and receive Letters, without Interrogatories or wry Faces on your part. To wear what I please, and choose Conversation with regard only to my own taste; to have no obligation upon me to converse with Wits that I don't like, because they are your acquaintance, or to be intimate with Fools, because they may be your Relations. Come to Dinner when I please; dine in my dressing room when I'm out of humour, without giving a reason. To have my Closet Inviolate; to be sole Empress of my Tea-table, which you must never presume to approach without first asking leave. And lastly, wherever I am, you shall always knock at the door before you come in. These Articles subscrib'd, if I continue to endure you a little longer, I may by degrees dwindle into a Wife.

MIRABELL. Your bill of fare is something advanc'd in this latter account. Well, have I Liberty to offer Conditions, that when you are dwindl'd into a Wife, I may not be beyond Measure enlarg'd into a Husband?

MILLAMANT. You have free leave. Propose your utmost; speak and spare not.

MIRABELL. I thank you. *Inprimis* then, I covenant that your acquaintance be general; that you admit no sworn Confident, or Intimate of your own Sex; no she-friend to screen her affairs under your Countenance and tempt you to make trial of a Mutual Secrecy. No Decoy-Duck to wheadle you a *fop, scrambling* to

222 *Lady Fadler:* 'To faddle: to trifle; to toy; to play. A low word.' (Johnson, *Dictionary*).

the Play in a Mask; then bring you home in a pretended fright, when you think you shall be found out—and rail at me for missing the Play, and disappointing the Frolick which you had to pick me up and prove my Constancy.

MILLAMANT. Detestable *Inprimis!* I go to the Play in a Mask!

MIRABELL. *Item,* I article, that you continue to like your own Face, as long as I shall. And while it passes Current with me, that you endeavour not to new Coin it. To which end, together with all Vizards for the day, I prohibit all Masks for the Night, made of oil'd skins and I know not what—Hog's-bones, Hare's-gall, Pig-water, and the marrow of a roasted Cat. In short, I forbid all Commerce with the Gentlewoman in *what-de-call-it*-Court. *Item,* I shut my doors against all Bauds with Baskets, and penny-worths of *Muslin, China, Fans, Atlases, &c.—Item,* when you shall be Breeding—

MILLAMANT. Ah! Name is not.

MIRABELL. Which may be presum'd, with a blessing on our endeavours—

MILLAMANT. Odious endeavours!

MIRABELL. I denounce against all strait-Lacing, Squeezing for a Shape, till you mold my boy's head like a Sugar-loaf; and instead of a Man-child, make me the Father to a crooked billet. Lastly, to the Dominion of the *Tea-Table* I submit—but with *proviso* that you exceed not in your province, but restrain yourself to native and simple *Tea-Table* drinks, as *Tea, Chocolate* and *Coffee.* As likewise to genuine and authoriz'd *Tea-Table* talk, such as mending of Fashions, spoiling Reputations, railing at absent Friends, and so forth; but that on no account you encroach upon the men's prerogative, and presume to drink healths, or toast fellows; for prevention of which, I banish all *Foreign Forces,* all Auxiliaries to the *Tea-Table,* as *Orange-Brandy,* all *Anniseed, Cinamon, Citron* and *Barbado's-Waters,* together with *Ratifia* and the most

274 *Pig-water:* animal urine was often used as a complexion aid.
279 *Atlases:* 'Silk-satin manufactured in the East.' (OED)
299 *Orange-Brandy . . . Clary:* all fortified, highly intoxicating drinks.

noble Spirit of *Clary.* But for *Cowslip-Wine, Poppy-Water* and all *Dormitives,* those I allow.—These *proviso's* admitted, in other things I may prove a tractable and complying Husband.

MILLAMANT. O horrid *proviso's!* filthy strong Waters! I toast fellows, odious Men! I hate your odious proviso's.

MIRABELL. Then we're agreed. Shall I kiss your hand upon the Contract? And here comes one to be a witness to the Sealing of the Deed.

Enter Mrs. Fainall.

MILLAMANT. *Fainall,* what shall I do? Shall I have him? I think I must have him.

MRS. FAINALL. Ay, ay, take him, take him; what shou'd you do?

MILLAMANT. Well then—I'll take my death I'm in a horrid fright. *Fainall,* I shall never say it. Well—I think—I'll endure you.

MRS. FAINALL. Fie, fie, have him, have him, and tell him so in plain terms; for I am sure you have a mind to him.

MILLAMANT. Are you? I think I have; and the horrid Man looks as if he thought so too. Well, you ridiculous thing you, I'll have you.—I won't be kiss'd, nor I won't be thank'd. Here, kiss my hand tho'. So, hold your tongue now, and don't say a word.

MRS. FAINALL. *Mirabell,* there's a Necessity for your obedience; you have neither time to talk nor stay. My Mother is coming; and, in my Conscience, if she should see you wou'd fall into fits, and maybe not recover time enough to return to Sir *Rowland,* who as *Foible* tells me, is in a fair way to succeed. Therefore spare your Extacies for another occasion, and slip down the back-stairs, where *Foible* waits to consult you.

MILLAMANT. Ay, go, go. In the meantime I suppose you have said something to please me.

MIRABELL. I am all Obedience.

Exit Mirabell.

302 *Dormitives:* sleeping potions.

MRS. FAINALL. Yonder Sir *Wilfull's* Drunk, and so noisy that my Mother has been forc'd to leave Sir *Rowland* to appease him; but he answers her only with Singing and Drinking. What they have done by this time I know not, but *Petulant* and he were upon quarrelling as I came by.

MILLAMANT. Well, If *Mirabell* shou'd not make a good Husband, I am a lost thing; for I find I love him violently.

MRS. FAINALL. So it seems, when you mind not what's said to you. If you doubt him, you had best take up with Sir *Wilfull*.

MILLAMANT. How can you name that superannuated Lubber? foh!

Enter Witwoud *from drinking.*

MRS. FAINALL. So, is the fray made up, that you have left 'em?

WITWOUD. Left 'em? I cou'd stay no longer. I have laugh'd like ten Christnings—I am tipsy with laughing. If I had stayed any longer I shou'd have burst; I must have been let out and piec'd in the sides like an unsiz'd Camlet. Yes, yes, the fray is compos'd; my Lady came in like a *Noli prosequi and* stop't their proceedings.

MILLAMANT. What was the dispute?

WITWOUD. That's the Jest; there was no dispute. They cou'd neither of 'em speak for rage, and so fell a sputt'ring at one another like two roasting Apples.

Enter Petulant *Drunk.*

Now *Petulant*? All's over, all's well? Gad, my head begins to whim it about—why dost thou not speak? Thou art both as drunk and as mute as a Fish.

PETULANT. Look you, Mrs. *Millamant*, if you can love me, dear Nymph, say it—and that's the Conclusion. Pass on, or pass off, that's all.

361 *unsiz'd Camlet:* unstiffened satin fabric from the East.
362 *Noli prosequi:* legal entry indicating the end of a suit in court.

WITWOUD. Thou hast utter'd *Volumes, Folios,* in less than *Decimo Sexto,* my Dear *Lacedemonian.* Sirrah *Petulant,* thou art an Epitomizer of words.

PETULANT. *Witwoud,* you are an anihilator of sense.

WITWOUD. Thou art a retailer of Phrases, and dost deal in Remnants of Remnants, like a maker of Pincushions; thou art in truth (Metaphorically speaking) a speaker of shorthand.

PETULANT. Thou art (without a figure) just one half of an Ass, and *Baldwin* yonder, thy half Brother, is the rest. A *Gemini* of Asses split would make just four of you.

WITWOUD. Thou dost bite, my dear Mustard-seed; kiss me for that.

PETULANT. Stand off! I'll kiss no more Males. I have kiss'd your *twin* yonder in a humour of reconcilation, till he (*hiccup*) rises upon my stomack like a Radish.

MILLAMANT. Eh, filthy creature—what was the quarrel?

PETULANT. There was no quarrel—there might have been a quarrel.

WITWOUD. If there had been words enow between 'em to have express'd provocation, they had gone together by the Ears like a pair of Castanets.

PETULANT. You were the Quarrel.

MILLAMANT. Me!

PETULANT. If I have a humour to Quarrel, I can make less matters conclude Premises. If you are not handsome, what then, if I have a humour to prove it? If I shall have my Reward, say so; if not, fight for your Face the next time yourself—I'll go sleep.

WITWOUD. Do, rap thyself up like a *Wood-louse* and dream Revenge; and hear me, if thou canst learn to write by tomorrow Morning, pen me a Challenge. I'll carry it for thee.

376 *Decimo Sexto:* a small book, one-eighth the size of a folio.
376 *Lacedemonian:* Spartan; given to few words.
384 *Baldwin:* the ass in the beast-epic *Reynard the Fox,* reprinted 1694.

PETULANT. Carry your Mistress's *Monkey* a *Spider!* Go flea Dogs, and read Romances! I'll go to bed to my Maid.

Exit.

MRS. FAINALL. He's horridly drunk. How came you all in this pickle?

WITWOUD. A plot, a plot, to get rid of the Knight! – Your Husband's advice, but he sneak'd off.

Enter Lady Wishfort *and* Sir Wilfull *drunk.*

LADY WISHFORT. Out upon't, out upon't, at years of Discretion, and comport yourself at this Rantipole rate!

SIR WILFULL. No Offence, Aunt.

LADY WISHFORT. Offence? As I'm a Person, I'm asham'd of you.--Fogh! how you stink of Wine! D'ye think my Niece will ever endure such a *Borachio!* you're an absolute *Borachio.*

SIR WILFULL. *Borachio!*

LADY WISHFORT. At a time when you shou'd commence an Amour, and put your best foot foremost–

SIR WILFULL. 'Sheart, an you grutch me your Liquor, make a Bill. Give me more drink, and take my Purse.

(*Sings*).

Prithee fill me the Glass
Till it laugh in my Face,
With Ale that is Potent and Mellow,
He that Whines for a Lass
Is an Ignorant Ass,
For a *Bumper* has not its Fellow.

but if you wou'd have me marry my Cousin, say the Word, and I'll do't. *Wilfull* will do't, that's the Word –*Wilfull* will do't; that's my Crest. My Motto I have forgot.

LADY WISHFORT. My Nephew's a little overtaken, Cousin–but 'tis with drinking your Health. O' my Word you are oblig'd to him.

420 *Rantipole:* 'Wild; roving; rakish.' (Johnson, *Dictionary.*)
424 *Borachio:* goatskin wine bottle; hence, a drunkard.
429 *grutch:* dialect for 'grudge'.

SIR WILFULL. *In vino veritas* Aunt. If I drunk your Health today Cousin, I am a *Borachio.* But if you have a Mind to be marry'd, say the Word, and send for the Piper; *Wilfull* will do't. If not, dust it away, and let's have t'other round– *Tony!* Ods-heart, where's *Tony? Tony's* an honest fellow, but he spits after a Bumper, and that's a Fault.

(Sings.)

We'll drink, and we'll never ha' done, Boys,
Put the glass then around with the Sun, Boys;
Let *Apollo's* Example invite us;
For he's drunk every Night,
And that makes him so bright,
That he's able next Morning to light us.

the Sun's a good Pimple, an honest Soaker; he has a Cellar at your *Antipodes.* If I travel, Aunt, I touch at your *Antipodes*–your *Antipodes* are a good rascally sort of topsy-turvy Fellows. If I had a Bumper, I'd stand upon my Head and drink a Health to 'em. A Match or no Match, Cousin with the hard Name? Aunt, *Wilfull* will do't. If she has her Maidenhead, let her look to't; if she has not, let her keep her own Counsel in the meantime, and cry out at the nine Month's end.

MILLAMANT. Your Pardon, Madam, I can stay no longer.–Sir *Wilfull* grows very powerful. Egh, how he smells! I shall be overcome if I stay. Come, Cousin.

Exeunt Millamant *and* Mrs. Fainall.

LADY WISHFORT. Smells! He would poison a Tallow-Chandler and his Family! Beastly Creature, I know not what to do with him. Travel, quoth 'a! Ay, travel, travel, get thee gone, get thee but far enough, to the *Saracens* or the *Tartars* or the *Turks,* for thou are not fit to live in a Christian Commonwealth, thou beastly Pagan.

SIR WILFULL. *Turks,* no; no *Turks,* Aunt: your *Turks* are Infidels, and believe not in the Grape. Your *Mahometan,* your *Mussulman,* is a dry Stinkard–no Offence, Aunt. My Map says that your *Turk* is not

460 *good Pimple:* boon companion.
461 *Antipodes:* opposite side of the earth, and its inhabitants.
475 *Tallow-Chandler:* maker and seller of tallow candles, a smelly occupation.

so honest a Man as your Christian. I cannot find by the Map that your *Mufti* is Orthodox—whereby it is a plain Case that Orthodox is a hard Word, Aunt, and (*hiccup*) Greek for Claret.

(*Sings.*)

To drink is a Christian Diversion,
Unknown to the *Turk* and the *Persian*:
Let *Mahometan* Fools
Live by Heathenish Rules,
And be damn'd over Tea-Cups and Coffee!
But let British Lads sing,
Crown a Health to the King,
And a Fig for your *Sultan* and *Sophy!*

Ah, *Tony!*

Enter Foible, *and whispers* Lady Wishfort.

LADY WISHFORT. Sir *Rowland* impatient? Good lack! What shall I do with this beastly Tumbril?—Go lie down and sleep, you Sot, or as I'm a person, I'll have you bastinado'd with Broom-sticks. Call up the Wenches.

Exit Foible.

SIR WILFULL. Ahey! Wenches, where are the Wenches?

LADY WISHFORT. Dear Cousin *Witwoud,* get him away, and you will bind me to you inviolably. I have an Affair of moment that invades me with some precipitation. You will oblige me to all Futurity.

WITWOUD. Come, Knight. Pox on him, I don't know what to say to him.—Will you go to a Cock-match?

SIR WILFULL. With a Wench, *Tony?* Is she a shake-bag, Sirrah? Let me bite your Cheek for that.

WITWOUD. Horrible! He has a breath like a *Bagpipe!* —Ay, ay, come, will you March, my *Salopian?*

SIR WILFULL. Lead on, little *Tony*—I'll follow thee, my *Anthony,* My *Tantony.* Sirrah, thou sha't be my

486 *Mufti:* Moslem religious teacher.
497 *Sophy:* a Persian ruling dynasty; the Emperor of Persia.
514-5 *shake-bag:* large game cock, originally shaken out of a bag into the fighting ring.
519 *Anthony:* St Anthony, patron saint of swineherds, often portrayed accompanied by a pig.

Tantony, and I'll be thy *Pig.*
—and a fig for your *Sultan* and *Sophy.*
Exit Singing with Witwoud.

LADY WISHFORT. This will never do. It will never make a Match—at least before he has been abroad.

Enter Waitwell, *disguis'd as* Sir Rowland

Dear Sir *Rowland,* I am Confounded with Confusion at the Retrospection of my own rudeness! I have more pardons to ask than the *Pope* distributes in the Year of Jubilee. But I hope where there is likely to be so near an alliance, we may unbend the severity of *Decorum* and dispense with a little Ceremony.

WAITWELL. My Impatience, *Madam,* is the effect of my transport; and till I have the possession of your adorable Person, I am tantaliz'd on a rack, and do but hang, *Madam,* on the tenter of Expectation.

LADY WISHFORT. You have Excess of gallantry, Sir *Rowland,* and press things to a Conclusion with a most prevailing Vehemence. But a day or two for decency of Marriage—

WAITWELL. For decency of Funeral, *Madam!* The delay will break my heart—or, if that should fail, I shall be Poison'd. My *Nephew* will get an inkling of my Designs and Poison me; and I wou'd willingly starve him before I die; I wou'd gladly go out of the World with that Satisfaction.—That wou'd be some Comfort to me, If I cou'd but live so long as to be reveng'd on that Unnatural *Viper.*

LADY WISHFORT. Is he so Unnatural, say you? Truly I wou'd contribute much both to the saving of your Life and the accomplishment of your revenge. —Not that I respect myself, tho' he has been a perfidious wretch to me.

WAITWELL. Perfidious to you!

LADY WISHFORT. O Sir *Rowland,* the hours that he has dy'd away at my Feet, the Tears that he has shed, the Oaths that he has sworn, the Palpitations that he

529 *Year of Jubilee:* a celebration held normally every quarter-century, in which the Pope grants special remissions of penance for sin.

has felt, the Trances, and the Tremblings, the Ardors and the Ecstacies, the Kneelings and the Risings, the Heart-heavings and the Hand-gripings, the Pangs and the Pathetick Regards of his protesting Eyes! Oh, no memory can Register!

WAITWELL. What, my Rival! Is the Rebel my Rival? 'A dies.

LADY WISHFORT. No, don't kill him at once Sir *Rowland;* starve him gradually, inch by inch.

WAITWELL. I'll do't. In three weeks he shall be barefoot; in a month out at knees with begging an Alms. —He shall starve upward and upward, till he has nothing living but his head, and then go out in a stink like a Candle's end upon a Save-all.

LADY WISHFORT. Well, Sir *Rowland,* you have the way. You are no Novice in the Labyrinth of Love; you have the Clue.—But as I am a person, Sir *Rowland,* You must not attribute my yielding to any sinister appetite, or Indigestion of Widow-hood; nor impute my Complacency to any Lethargy of Continence. I hope you do not think me prone to any iteration of Nuptials.

WAITWELL. Far be it from me—

LADY WISHFORT. If you do, I protest I must recede, or think that I have made a prostitution of decorums; but in the Vehemence of Compassion, and to save the life of a Person of so much Importance—

WAITWELL. I esteem it so—

LADY WISHFORT.. Or else you wrong my Condescension—

WAITWELL. I do not, I do not!

LADY WISHFORT. Indeed you do.

WAITWELL. I do not, fair shrine of Virtue!

LADY WISHFORT. If you think the least scruple of Carnality was an Ingredient—

570 *Save-all:* candlestick pin supporting candle-ends so that they may burn completely.

WAITWELL. Dear *Madam*, no. You are all *Camphire* and *Frankincense*, all *Chastity* and *Odour*.

LADY WISHFORT. Or that—

Enter Foible.

FOIBLE. *Madam*, the Dancers are ready, and there's one with a Letter, who must deliver it into your own hands.

LADY WISHFORT. Sir *Rowland*, will you give me leave? Think favourably, judge candidly, and conclude you have found a Person who wou'd suffer racks in honour's cause, dear Sir *Rowland*, and will wait on you incessantly.

Exit.

WAITWELL. Fie, fie! What a Slavery have I undergone! Spouse, hast thou any *Cordial*?—I want *Spirits*.

FOIBLE. What a washy Rogue art thou, to pant thus for a quarter of an hour's lying and swearing to a fine Lady!

WAITWELL. Oh, she is the *Antidote* to desire! Spouse, thou will't fare the worse for't. I shall have no appetite to iteration of Nuptials this eight-and-forty Hours.—By this hand I'd rather be a *Chair-man* in the *Dog-days* than Act Sir *Rowland* till this time to morrow.

Enter Lady Wishfort *with a Letter.*

LADY WISHFORT. Call in the *Dancers*. Sir *Rowland*, we'll sit if you please, and see the Entertainment.

Dance.

Now, with your permission Sir *Rowland*, I will peruse my Letter. I wou'd open it in your presence, because I wou'd not make you Uneasy. If it shou'd make you Uneasy, I wou'd burn it.—Speak, if it does. But you may see by the Superscription it is like a Woman's hand.

FOIBLE *(to him)*. By Heaven! Mrs. *Marwood's;* I know it, My heart aches—get it from her.

592 *Camphire:* camphor, whose pungent odour was supposed to lessen sexual desire.

613-4 *Chair-man in the Dog-days:* carry a sedan chair during the hottest part of the summer.

WAITWELL. A Woman's hand? No, *Madam,* that's no Woman's hand; I see that already. That's somebody whose throat must be cut.

LADY WISHFORT. Nay, Sir *Rowland,* since you give me a proof of your Passion by your Jealousy, I promise you'll make you a return, by a frank Communication. You shall see it—we'll open it together. Look you here.

(*Reads.*) – Madam, *tho' unknown to you* (Look you there; 'tis from nobody that I know)—*I have that honour for your Character, that I think myself oblig'd to let you know you are abus'd. He who pretends to be Sir* Rowland *is a cheat and a Rascal—*

Oh Heavens! what's this?

FOIBLE. Unfortunate! All's ruin'd.

WAITWELL. How, how, Let me see, let me see—*(Reading.) A Rascal, and disguis'd and suborn'd for that imposture.*—O villainy, O villainy!—*by the Contrivance of—*

LADY WISHFORT. I shall faint, I shall die, I shall die, oh!

FOIBLE (*to him*). Say 'tis your Nephew's hand—quickly—his plot, swear, swear it!

WAITWELL. Here's a Villain! *Madam,* don't you perceive it, don't you see it?

LADY WISHFORT. Too well, too well! I have seen too much.

WAITWELL. I told you at first I knew the hand. A Woman's hand? The Rascal writes a sort of a large hand, your *Roman* hand. I saw there was a throat to be cut presently. If he were my Son, as he is my Nephew, I'd Pistol him!

FOIBLE. O Treachery! But are you sure, Sir *Rowland,* it is his writing?

WAITWELL. Sure? Am I here? Do I live? Do I love this Pearl of *India?* I have twenty Letters in my Pocket from him in the same Character.

656 *Roman hand:* round, bold lettering, as in ancient Roman inscriptions.

LADY WISHFORT. How!

FOIBLE. Oh, what luck it is, Sir *Rowland,* that you were present at this Juncture! This was the business that brought Mr. *Mirabell* disguis'd to *Madam Millamant* this Afternoon. I thought something was contriving, when he stole by me and would have hid his face.

LADY WISHFORT. How, how!—I heard the Villain was in the house indeed, and now I remember, my *Niece* went away abruptly, when Sir *Wilfull* was to have made his addresses.

FOIBLE. Then, then, *Madam,* Mr. *Mirabell* waited for her in her Chamber, but I wou'd not tell your Ladyship to discompose you when you were to receive Sir *Rowland.*

WAITWELL. Enough, his date is short.

FOIBLE. No, good Sir *Rowland,* don't incur the Law.

WAITWELL. Law? I care not for Law. I can but die, and 'tis in a good cause.—My Lady shall be satisfied of my Truth and Innocence, tho' it cost me my life.

LADY WISHFORT. No, dear Sir *Rowland,* don't fight; if you shou'd be kill'd I must never show my face, or hang'd. Oh, Consider my Reputation, Sir *Rowland!* No, you shan't fight.—I'll go in and Examine my *Niece;* I'll make her Confess. I conjure you, Sir *Rowland,* by all your love, not to fight.

WAITWELL. I am Charm'd *Madam;* I obey. But some proof you must let me give you; I'll go for a black box which contains the Writings of my whole Estate, and deliver that into your hands.

LADY WISHFORT. Ay, dear Sir *Rowland,* that will be some Comfort; bring the black box.

WAITWELL. And may I presume to bring a Contract to be sign'd this Night? May I hope so far?

LADY WISHFORT. Bring what you will; but come alive, pray come alive. O this is a happy discovery!

WAITWELL. Dead or Alive I'll come—and married we will be in spite of treachery. Ay, and get an Heir that shall defeat the last remaining glimpse of hope in my abandon'd *Nephew.* Come, my Buxom Widow.

Ere long you shall Substantial Proof receive
That I'm an Arrant Knight–

FOIBLE. Or Arrant Knave.

Exeunt.

ACT V. Scene I.

Scene Continues.

Lady Wishfort *and* Foible.

LADY WISHFORT. Out of my house, out of my house, thou *Viper!* thou *Serpent,* that I have foster'd! Thou bosom traitress that I rais'd from nothing–begone, begone, begone, go, go! That I took from washing of old Gauze and weaving of dead Hair, with a bleak blue Nose, over a Chafing-dish of starv'd Embers, and dining behind a Traverse Rag, in a shop no bigger than a Bird-cage–go, go, starve again, do, do.

FOIBLE. Dear *Madam,* I'll beg pardon on my knees.

LADY WISHFORT. Away, out, out, go set up for yourself again! Do, drive a Trade, do, with your three penny-worth of small Ware, flaunting upon a Packthread, under a Brandy-seller's Bulk, or against a dead Wall by a Ballad-monger. Go, hang out an old *Frisoneer-gorget,* with a yard of Yellow *Colberteen* again. Do; an old gnaw'd *Mask,* two rowes of *Pins* and a *Child's Fiddle; a Glass Necklace* with the Beads broken, and a *Quilted Night-cap* with one Ear. Go, go, drive a trade! These were your *Commodities,* you treacherous Trull! This was your *Merchandise* you dealt in when I took you into my house, plac'd you next myself, and made you Governante of my whole Family. You have forgot this, have you, now you have feather'd your Nest?

FOIBLE. No, no, dear *Madam.* Do but hear me; have but a Moment's patience–I'll Confess all. Mr. *Mirabell* seduc'd me; I am not the first that he has wheedl'd with his dissembling Tongue. Your Ladyship's own

704 *Arrant Knight . . . arrant Knave:* wandering knight . . . unmitigated rascal.
7 *Traverse Rag:* tattered curtain.
13 *Bulk:* merchant's stall.
15 *Frisoneer-gorget:* neckcloth of rough Frisian material.
15 *Colberteen:* cheap French lace.

Wisdom has been deluded by him; then how shou'd I, a poor Ignorant, defend myself? O *Madam,* if you knew but what he promis'd me, and how he assur'd me your Ladyship shou'd come to no damage! Or else the Wealth of the *Indies* shou'd not have brib'd me to conspire against so good, so sweet, so kind a Lady as you have been to me.

LADY WISHFUL. "No damage?" What, to betray me, to marry me to a Cast-servingman? To make me a receptacle, an Hospital for a decay'd Pimp? "No damage?" O thou frontless Impudence, more than a big-belly'd Actress.

FOIBLE. Pray do hear me *Madam;* he cou'd not marry your Ladyship, *Madam.*—No indeed; his Marriage was to have been void in Law, for he was married to me first, to secure your Ladyship. He cou'd not have bedded your Ladyship; for if he had Consummated with your Ladyship, he must have run the risque of the Law and been put upon his *Clergy.*—Yes indeed; I enquir'd of the Law in that case before I wou'd meddle or make.

LADY WISHFORT. What, then I have been your Property, have I? I have been convenient to you it seems! While you were Catering for *Mirabell,* I have been Broker for you? What, have you made a passive Bawd of me? This exceeds all Precedent; I am brought to fine uses, to become a botcher of second-hand Marriages between *Abigails* and *Andrews!* I'll couple you! Yes, I'll baste you together, you and your *Philander.* I'll *Duke's-Place* you, as I'm a Person! Your Turtle is in Custody already; you shall coo in the same Cage, if there be Constable or Warrant in the Parish.

Exit.

FOIBLE. Oh, that ever I was born! Oh, that I was ever married!—A Bride! ay, I shall be a *Bridewell-*

47 *put upon his Clergy:* clergy, and other educated men could claim exemption from trial by a secular court.
49 *meddle or make:* proverbial for interfere in another's business.
55 *botcher:* mender.
56 *Abigails and Andrews:* generic names for waiting-women and men-servants, from characters in Beaumont and Fletcher's *The Scornful Lady* (1616), and Fletcher's *The Elder Brother* (1637).
58 *Duke's-Place:* where the marriage took place. See note to Act I, l. 130.
64 *Bridewell-Bride:* Bridewell, the women's house of correction.

Bride! Oh!

Enter Mrs. Fainall.

MRS. FAINALL. Poor *Foible,* what's the matter?

FOIBLE. *O Madam,* my Lady's gone for a Constable; I shall be had to a Justice, and put to *Bridewell* to beat Hemp. Poor *Waitwell's* gone to prison already.

MRS. FAINALL. Have a good heart, *Foible; Mirabell's* gone to give security for him. This is all *Marwood's* and my Husband's doing.

FOIBLE. Yes, yes, I know it, *Madam;* she was in my Lady's Closet, and over-heard all that you said to me before Dinner. She sent the Letter to my Lady; and that missing Effect, Mr. *Fainall* laid this Plot to arrest *Waitwell* when he pretended to go for the Papers; and in the meantime Mrs. *Marwood* declar'd all to my Lady.

MRS FAINALL. Was there no mention made of me in the Letter?—My Mother does not suspect my being in the Confederacy? I fancy *Marwood* has not told her, tho' she has told my husband.

FOIBLE. Yes, *Madam,* but my Lady did not see that part. We stifl'd the Letter before she read so far. Has that mischievous Devil told Mr. *Fainall* of your Ladyship then?

MRS. FAINALL. Ay, all's out, my Affair with *Mirabell,* everything discover'd. This is the last day of our living together; that's my Comfort.

FOIBLE. Indeed *Madam,* and so 'tis a Comfort if you knew all.—He has been even with your Ladyship; which I cou'd have told you long enough since, but I love to keep Peace and Quietness by my good will. I had rather bring friends together than set 'em at distance. But Mrs. *Marwood* and he are nearer related than ever their Parents thought for.

MRS. FAINALL. Say'st thou so, *Foible?* Can'st thou prove this?

FOIBLE. I can take my Oath of it, *Madam;* so can Mrs. *Mincing.* We have had many a fair word from Madam *Marwood,* to conceal something that pass'd in our Chamber one Evening when you were at *Hyde-*

Park and we were thought to have gone a-walking; but we went up unawares, tho' we were sworn to secrecy too. Madam *Marwood* took a Book and swore us upon it, but it was but a Book of Verses and Poems. —So as long as it was not a Bible-Oath, we may break it with a safe Conscience.

MRS. FAINALL. This discovery is the most opportune thing I cou'd wish. Now, *Mincing*?

Enter Mincing.

MINCING. My Lady wou'd speak with Mrs. *Foible*, Mem. Mr. *Mirabell* is with her; he has set your Spouse at liberty, Mrs. *Foible*, and wou'd have you hide yourself in my Lady's Closet till my old Lady's anger is abated. O, my old Lady is in a perilous passion at something Mr. *Fainall* has said. He swears, and my old Lady cries. There's a fearful Hurricane, I vow. He says, Mem, how that he'll have my Lady's Fortune made over to him, or he'll be divorc'd.

MRS. FAINALL. Does your Lady and *Mirabell* know that?

MINCING. Yes, Mem; they have sent me to see if Sir *Wilfull* be sober, and to bring him to them. My Lady is resolv'd to have him, I think, rather than loose such a vast Sum as six thousand Pound. Oh, come Mrs. *Foible*; I hear my old Lady.

MRS. FAINALL. *Foible*, you must tell *Mincing* that she must prepare to vouch when I call her.

FOIBLE. Yes, yes, Madam.

MINCING. O yes, Mem, I'll vouch anything for your Ladyship's service, be what it will.

Exeunt Mincing *and* Foible.

Enter Lady Wishfort *and* Marwood.

LADY WISHFORT. O my dear Friend, how can I enumerate the benefits that I have receiv'd from your goodness? To you I owe the timely discovery of the false vows of *Mirabell*; to you the Detection of the Imposter Sir *Rowland*. And now you are become an Intercessor with my Son-in-Law, to save the Honour of my House, and compound for the frailties of my Daughter. Well, Friend, you are enough to reconcile me to the bad World, or else I wou'd retire to Desarts and Solitudes, and feed harmless Sheep by *Groves* and *Purling Streams.* Dear *Marwood,* let us leave the World, and retire by ourselves and be *Shepherdesses.*

MRS. MARWOOD. Let us first dispatch the affair in hand, Madam. We shall have leisure to think of Retirement afterwards. Here is one who is concern'd in the treaty.

LADY WISHFORT. O Daughter, Daughter, is it possible thou should'st be my Child, Bone of my Bone, and Flesh of my Flesh, and, as I may say, another Me, and yet transgress the most minute Particle of severe Virtue? Is it possible you should lean aside to Iniquity, who have been Cast in the direct Mold of Virtue? I have not only been a Mold, but a Pattern for you, and a Model for you, after you were brought into the World.

MRS. FAINALL. I don't understand your Ladyship.

LADY WISHFORT. Not understand? Why, have you not been naught? Have you not been sophisticated? Not understand? Here I am ruin'd to compound for your *Caprices* and your *Cuckoldoms.* I must pawn my *Plate* and my *Jewels,* and ruin my Niece, and all little enough—

MRS FAINALL. I am wrong'd and abus'd, and so are you. 'Tis a false accusation, as false as *Hell,* as false as your Friend there, ay, or your Friend's Friend, my false Husband.

MRS. MARWOOD. My Friend, Mrs. *Fainall?* Your Husband my Friend? What do you mean?

MRS. FAINALL. I know what I mean Madam, and so do you; and so shall the World at a time convenient.

MRS. MARWOOD. I am sorry to see you so passionate, Madam. More Temper wou'd look more like Innocence. But I have done. I am sorry my Zeal to serve your Ladyship and family shou'd admit of Misconstruction, or make me liable to affronts. You will par-

164 *naught:* wicked.
164 *sophisticated:* 'Corrupted with something spurious.' (Johnson, *Dictionary.)*
178 *Temper:* temperateness.

don me, Madam, if I meddle no more with an affair in which I am not personally concern'd.

LADY WISHFORT. O dear Friend, I am so asham'd that you should meet with such returns!—You ought to ask Pardon on your Knees, ungrateful Creature; she deserves more from you than all your life can accomplish—don't leave me destitute in this Perplexity! No, stick to me, my good Genius.

MRS. FAINALL. I tell you, Madam, you're abus'd.—Stick to you? Ay, like a *Leach,* to suck your best Blood; she'll drop off when she's full. Madam, you shan't pawn a *Bodkin,* nor part with a *Brass Counter* in Composition for me. I defy 'em all. Let 'em prove their aspersions; I know my own innocence, and dare stand a trial.

Exit.

LADY WISHFORT. Why, if she shou'd be innocent, if she shou'd be wrong'd after all, ha? I don't know what to think—and, I promise you, her Education has been unexceptionable. I may say it; for I chiefly made it my own Care to initiate her very Infancy in the Rudiments of Virtue and to impress upon her tender Years a Young *Odium* and *Aversion* to the very sight of Men. Ay, Friend, she wou'd ha' shriek'd if she had but seen a Man, till she was in her Teens. As I'm a Person 'tis true. She was never suffer'd to play with a Male-Child, tho' but in Coats; nay, her very Babies were of the *Feminine Gender.* Oh, she never look'd a Man in the Face but her own Father, or the Chaplain, and him we made a shift to put upon her for a Woman, by the help of his long Garments and his sleek face, till she was going in her fifteen.

MRS. MARWOOD. 'Twas much she shou'd be deceiv'd so long.

LADY WISHFORT. I warrant you, or she wou'd never have born to have been Catechiz'd by him; and have heard his long lectures against Singing and Dancing, and such Debaucheries, and going to filthy *Plays,* and Profane *Musick-meetings,* where the lewd Trebles squeek nothing but Bawdy, and the Bases roar *Blasphemy.* Oh, she wou'd have swooned at the sight or

193 *Bodkin:* large needle.
208 *Babies:* dolls.

name of an obscene Play-Book! And can I think after all this, that my Daughter can be naught? What, a Whore? and thought it excommunication to set her foot within the door of a Play-house! O my dear friend, I can't believe it, no, no! As she says, let him prove it, let him prove it.

MRS. MARWOOD. Prove it Madam? What, and have your name prostituted in a publick Court? Yours and your Daughter's reputation worry'd at the Bar by a pack of bawling Lawyers? To be ushered in with an Oyez of Scandal, and have your Case open'd by an old fumbling Leacher in a Quoif like a Man-Midwife; to bring your Daughter's Infamy to light; to be a Theme for legal Punsters and Quiblers by the Statute, and become a Jest against a Rule of Court, where there is no precedent for a Jest in any record, not even in *Doomsday Book;* to discompose the gravity of the Bench, and provoke naughty Interrogatories in more naughty *Law Latin,* while the good Judge, tickl'd with the proceeding, simpers under a grey Beard, and fidges off and on his Cushion as if he had swallow'd *Cantharides,* or sat upon *Cow-Itch!*

LADY WISHFORT. Oh, 'tis very hard!

MRS. MARWOOD. And then to have my Young *Revellers* of the *Temple* take Notes, like Prentices at a *Conventicle;* and after, talk it all over again in Commons, or before Drawers in an *Eating-house.*

LADY WISHFORT. Worse and worse!

MRS. MARWOOD. Nay, this is nothing; if it wou'd end here, 'twere well. But it must after this be consign'd by the Short-hand Writers to the publick Press; and from thence be transferr'd to the Hands, nay into the Throats and Lungs of Hawkers, with Voices more Licentious than the loud *Flounder-man's* or the *Woman* that crys *Grey pease.* And this you must hear till you are stunn'd; nay, you must hear nothing else for some days.

234 *Quoif:* white cap worn at that time by lawyers.
244 *Cantharides:* diuretic medicine reputed to be an aphrodisiac.
244 *Cow-Itch:* cowage, a tropical vine with barbed pods causing severe itching.
247-8 *Prentices at a Conventicle:* apprentices were sometimes expected to take notes for their employers on sermons preached at meetinghouses.
248-9 *in Commons:* in a collegiate dining hall.

LADY WISHFORT. Oh, 'tis insupportable. No, no, dear Friend; make it up, make it up; ay, ay, I'll compound. I'll give up all, myself and my all, my Niece and her all,—anything, everything for Composition.

MRS. MARWOOD. Nay Madam, I advise nothing. I only lay before you as a Friend the Inconveniencies which perhaps you have overseen. Here comes Mr. *Fainall.* If he will be satisfi'd to huddle up all in Silence, I shall be glad. You must think I would rather congratulate than condole with you.

Enter Fainall.

LADY WISHFUL. Ay, ay, I do not doubt it, dear *Marwood;* no, no, I do not doubt it.

FAINALL. Well, Madam, I have suffer'd myself to be overcome by the Importunity of this Lady your Friend, and am content you shall enjoy your own proper Estate during Life, on condition you oblige yourself never to marry, under such penalty as I think convenient.

LADY WISHFORT. Never to marry?

FAINALL. No more Sir *Rowlands*—the next Imposture may not be so timely detected.

MRS. MARWOOD. That condition, I dare answer, my Lady will consent to without difficulity; she has already but too much experienc'd the perfidiousness of Men. Besides, Madam, when we retire to our pastoral Solitude, we shall bid adieu to all other Thoughts.

LADY WISHFORT. Ay, that's true; but in Case of Necessity, as of Health, or some such Emergency—

FAINALL. Oh, if you are prescrib'd Marriage, you shall be consider'd; I will only reserve to myself the Power to chuse for you. If your Physick be wholesome, it matters not who is your Apothecary. Next, my Wife shall settle on me the remainder of her Fortune not made over already, and for her Maintenance depend entirely on my Discretion.

LADY WISHFORT. This is most inhumanly Savage, exceeding the Barbarity of a *Muscovite* Husband.

FAINALL. I learn'd it from his *Czarish* Majesty's Retinue, in a Winter Evening's Conference over Brandy and Pepper, amongst other secrets of Matrimony and Policy, as they are at present Practis'd in the *Northern* Hemisphere. But this must be agreed unto, and that positively. Lastly, I will be endow'd, in right of my Wife, with that six thousand Pound which is the Moiety of Mrs. *Millamant's* Fortune in your Possession; and which she has forfeited (as will appear by the last Will and Testament of your deceas'd Husband, Sir *Jonathan Wishfort*) by her disobedience in contracting herself against your Consent or Knowledge, and by refusing the offer'd Match with Sir *Wilfull Witwoud,* which you, like a careful Aunt, had provided for her.

LADY WISHFORT. My Nephew was *non Compos,* and cou'd not make his Addresses.

FAINALL. I come to make demands.—I'll hear no objections.

LADY WISHFORT. You will grant me time to consider?

FAINALL. Yes, while the Instrument is drawing, to which you must set your Hand till more sufficient Deeds can be perfected; which I will take care shall be done with all possible speed. In the meanwhile, I will go for the said Instrument, and till my return, you may balance this Matter in your own Discretion. *Exit* Fainall.

LADY WISHFORT. This Insolence is beyond all Precedent, all Parallel; must I be subject to this merciless Villain?

MRS. MARWOOD. 'Tis severe indeed, *Madam,* that you shou'd smart for your Daughter's wantonness.

LADY WISHFORT. 'Twas against my Consent that she Married this Barbarian, but she wou'd have him, tho' her Year was not out.—Ah! her first Husband, my Son *Languish,* would not have carry'd it thus. Well, that was my Choice, this is hers; she is match'd now

299 *Czarish Majesty's Retinue:* the visit of Peter the Great to London in 1697 stimulated great interest in Muscovy.
335 *Son:* son-in-law.

with a Witness. I shall be mad! Dear Friend, is there no Comfort for me? Must I live to be confiscated at this Rebel-rate?—Here come two more of my *Egyptian* Plagues too.

Enter Millamant *and* Sir Wilfull.

SIR WILFUL. Aunt, your Servant.

LADY WISHFORT. Out *Caterpillar,* Call not me Aunt! I know thee not!

SIR WILFUL. I confess I have been a little in disguise, as they say. 'Sheart! and I'm sorry for't. What wou'd you have? I hope I committed no Offence, Aunt,—and if I did, I am willing to make satisfaction; and what can a man say fairer? If I have broke anything, I'll pay for't, an it cost a Pound. And so let that content for what's past, and make no more words. For what's to come, to pleasure you I'm willing to marry my Cousin. So pray let's all be Friends, she and I are agreed upon the matter before a Witness.

LADY WISHFORT. How's this, dear Niece? Have I any comfort? Can this be true?

MILLAMANT. I am content to be a Sacrifice to your repose, Madam; and to convince you that I had no hand in the Plot, as you were misinform'd, I have laid my commands on *Mirabell* to come in Person, and be a Witness that I give my hand to this flower of *Knighthood;* and for the Contract that past between *Mirabell* and me, I have oblig'd him to make a Resignation of it, in your Ladyship's presence. He is without, and waits your leave for admittance.

LADY WISHFORT. Well, I'll swear I am something reviv'd at this Testimony of your Obedience; but I cannot admit that Traitor. I fear I cannot fortify myself to support his appearance. He is as terrible to me as a *Gorgon;* if I see him, I fear I shall turn to Stone, petrify incessantly.

MILLAMANT. If you disoblige him, he may resent your refusal and insist upon the contract still. Then 'tis the last time he will be offense to you.

337 *with a Witness:* effectually, bindingly.
339-40 *Egyptian Plagues:* the ten plagues of Egypt in *Exodus,* VII-XII.

LADY WISHFORT. Are you sure it will be the last time?—If I were sure of that!—Shall I never see him again?

MILLAMANT. Sir *Wilfull,* you and he are to travel together, are you not?

SIR WILFULL. 'Sheart, the Gentleman's a civil Gentleman, Aunt; let him come in. Why, we are sworn Brothers and fellow Travellers.—We are to be *Pylades* and *Orestes,* he and I. He is to be my Interpreter in foreign Parts. He has been Over-seas already; and with proviso that I marry my Cousin will cross 'em once again, only to bear me Company. 'Sheart, I'll call him in.—An I set on't once, he shall come in; and see who'll hinder him.

MRS. MARWOOD. This is precious Fooling, if it wou'd pass; but I'll know the bottom of it.

LADY WISHFORT. O dear *Marwood,* you are not going?

MARWOOD. Not far, Madam; I'll return immediately. *Exit.*

Re-enter Sir Wilfull *and* Mirabell.

SIR WILFULL. Look up Man, I'll stand by you; 'sbud an she do frown, she can't kill you; besides, hearkee, she dare not frown desperately, because her face is none of her own; 'Sheart, an she shou'd, her forehead wou'd wrinkle like the Coat of a Cream-cheese, but mum for that, fellow Traveller.

MIRABELL. If a deep sense of the many Injuries I have offer'd to so good a Lady, with a sincere remorse and a hearty Contrition, can but obtain the least glance of Compassion I am too Happy.—Ah Madam, there was a time—but let it be forgotten. I confess I have deservedly forfeited the high Place I once held, of sighing at your Feet. Nay, kill me not by turning from me in disdain, I come not to plead for favour; nay, not for Pardon. I am a Suppliant only for your pity.—I am going where I never shall behold you more.

SIR WILFULL. How, fellow Traveller! You shall go by yourself then.

382-3 Pylades and Orestes: Plyades, devoted friend and guide to Orestes, son of Agamemnon and Clytemnestra.

MIRABELL. Let me be pitied first, and afterwards forgotten, I ask no more.

SIR WILFULL. By'r Lady, a very reasonable request, and will cost you nothing, Aunt. Come, come, Forgive and Forget, Aunt; why you must, an you are a Christian.

MIRABELL. Consider, Madam, in reality you cou'd not receive much prejudice; it was an innocent device; tho' I confess it had a Face of guiltiness. It was at most an Artifice which Love contriv'd, and errours which Love produces have ever been accounted *Venial.* At least think it is Punishment enough that I have lost what in my heart I hold most dear, that to your cruel Indignation I have offer'd up this Beauty, and with her my Peace and Quiet; nay, all my hopes of future Comfort.

SIR WILFULL. An he does not move me, wou'd I might never be *o' the Quorum!* An it were not as good a deed as to drink, to give her to him again, I wou'd I might never take Shipping. Aunt, if you don't forgive quickly, I shall melt, I can tell you that. My contract went no further than a little Mouth-Glue, and that's hardly dry; one doleful Sigh more from my fellow Traveller, and 'tis dissolv'd.

LADY WISHFORT. Well, *Nephew,* upon your account—ah, he has a false insinuating Tongue! Well Sir, I will stifle my just resentment at my Nephew's request. I will endeavour what I can to forget, but on *proviso* that you resign the Contract with my Niece Immediately.

MIRABELL. It is in Writing, and with Papers of Concern; but I have sent my Servant for it, and will deliver it to you, with all acknowledgments for your transcendent goodness.

LADY WISHFORT *(apart).* Oh, he has *Witch-craft* in his Eyes and Tongue! When I did not see him, I cou'd have brib'd a Villain to his Assassination; but his appearance rakes the *Embers* which have so long lain smother'd in my Breast.

Enter Fainall *and* Mrs. Marwood.

431 *o' the Quorum:* one of the body of county Justices of the Peace.

FAINALL. Your date of deliberation, *Madam*, is expir'd. Here is the Instrument; are you prepar'd to sign?

LADY WISHFORT. If I were prepar'd, I am not impowr'd. My Niece exerts a lawful claim, having Match'd herself by my direction to Sir *Wilfull.*

FAINALL. That sham is too gross to pass on me, tho 'tis impos'd on you, Madam.

MILLAMANT. Sir, I have given my consent.

MIRABELL. And, Sir, I have resign'd my pretensions.

SIR WILFULL. And, Sir, I assert my right; and will maintain it in defiance of you, Sir, and of your Instrument. 'Sheart an you talk of an Instrument, Sir, I have an old *Fox* by my Thigh shall hack your Instrument of *Ram Vellum* to shreds, Sir. It shall not be sufficient for a *Mittimus* or a *Taylor's* measure. Therefore withdraw your Instrument, Sir, or by'r Lady, I shall draw mine.

LADY WISHFORT. Hold, Nephew, hold.

MILLAMANT. Good Sir *Wilfull,* respite your valour.

FAINALL. Indeed? Are you provided of a Guard, with your single Beef-eater there? But I'm prepar'd for you, and insist upon my first proposal. You shall submit your own Estate to my management, and absolutely make over my Wife's to my sole use, as pursuant to the Purport and Tenor of this other Covenant. (*To* Mrs. Millamant.) I suppose, Madam, your Consent is not requisite in this Case; nor, Mr. *Mirabell,* your resignation; nor, Sir *Wilfull,* your right. You may draw your *Fox* if you please, Sir, and make a *Bear-Garden* flourish somewhere else, for here it will not avail. This, my Lady *Wishfort*, must be subscrib'd, or your darling Daughter's turn'd adrift, like a leaky hulk to sink or swim, as she and the Current of this lewd Town can agree.

467 *old Fox:* common term for sword.
468 *Ram Vellum:* sheepskin parchment.
469 *Mittimus:* warrant for imprisonment.
469 *Taylor's measure:* parchment was often used in taking measurements for clothing.

LADY WISHFORT. Is there no means, no Remedy, to stop my ruin? Ungrateful Wretch! dost thou not owe thy being, thy subsistance, to my Daughter's Fortune?

FAINALL. I'll answer you when I have the rest of it in my possession.

MIRABELL. But that you wou'd not accept of a Remedy from my hands—I own I have not deserv'd you shou'd owe any Obligation to me; or else perhaps I cou'd advise—

LADY WISHFORT. Oh, what? what? to save me and my Child from Ruin, from Want, I'll forgive all that's past; nay I'll consent to anything to come, to be deliver'd from this Tyranny.

MIRABELL. Ay, Madam; but that is too late, my reward is intercepted. You have dispos'd of her who only cou'd have made me a Compensation for all my Services. But be it as it may, I am resolv'd I'll serve you; you shall not be wrong'd in this *Savage* manner.

LADY WISHFORT. How! Dear Mr. *Mirabell,* can you be so generous at last? But it is not possible. *Hearkee,* I'll break my Nephew's Match; you shall have my Niece yet, and all her fortune, if you can but save me from this imminent danger.

MIRABELL. Will you? I take you at your word. I ask no more. I must have leave for two Criminals to appear.

LADY WISHFORT. Ay, ay, anybody, anybody.

MIRABELL. *Foible* is one, and a Penitent.

Enter Mrs. Fainall, Foible, *and* Mincing.

MRS. MARWOOD *(to* Fainall). O my shame! (Mirabell *and* Lady Wishfort *go to* Mrs. Fainall *and* Foible.) These corrupt things are bought and brought hither to expose me.

FAINALL. It if must all come out, why let 'em know it; 'tis but *the Way of the World.* That shall not urge me to relinquish or abate one tittle of my Terms; no, I will insist the more.

FOIBLE. Yes indeed, Madam; I'll take my Bible-oath of it.

MINCING. And so will I, Mem.

LADY WISHFORT. *O Marwood, Marwood,* art thou false? my friend deceive me? Hast thou been a wicked accomplice with that profligate man?

MRS. MARWOOD. Have you so much Ingratitude and Injustice, to give credit against your Friend to the Aspersions of two such Mercenary Trulls?

MINCING. "Mercenary," Mem? I scorn your words. 'Tis true we found you and Mr. *Fainall* in the Blue garret; by the same token, you swore us to Secrecy upon *Messalina's* Poems. "Mercenary?" No, if we wou'd have been Mercenary, we shou'd have held our Tongues; you wou'd have brib'd us sufficiently.

FAINALL. Go, you are an Insignificant thing. Well, what are you the better for this? Is this Mr. *Mirabell's* Expedient? I'll be put off no longer. You thing that was a Wife shall smart for this. I will not leave thee where-withall to hide thy Shame; your Body shall be naked as your Reputation.

MRS. FAINALL. I despise you and defy your Malice! You have aspers'd me wrongfully. I have prov'd your falsehood. Go you and your treacherous—I will not name it, but starve together—perish!

FAINALL. Not while you are worth a Groat, indeed, my dear. Madam, I'll be fool'd no longer.

LADY WISHFORT. Ah, Mr. *Mirabell,* this is small comfort, the detection of this affair.

MIRABELL. Oh, in good time. Your leave for the other Offender and Penitent to apear, Madam.

Enter Waitwell *with a Box of Writings.*

LADY WISHFORT. O Sir *Rowland!*—Well, Rascal?

WAITWELL. What your Ladyship pleases. I have brought the black box at last, Madam.

MIRABELL. Give it me. Madam, you remember your promise.

LADY WISHFORT. Ay, dear Sir.

539 *Messalina's Poems:* Mincing may mean either 'Miscellany Poems', or some anonymous collection of obscene lyrics, attributed to Messalina, dissolute wife of the Roman Emperor Claudius.

MIRABELL. Where are the Gentlemen?

WAITWELL. At hand Sir, rubbing their Eyes; just risen from Sleep.

FAINALL. 'Sdeath, what's this to me? I'll not wait your private concerns.

Enter Petulant *and* Witwoud.

PETULANT. How now? What's the matter? Who's hand's out?

WITWOUD. Heyday! what, are you all got together, like Players at the end of the last Act?

MIRABELL. You may remember, Gentlemen, I once requested your hands as Witnesses to a certain Parchment.

WITWOUD. Ay, I do, my hand I remember.—*Petulant* set his Mark.

MIRABELL. You wrong him; his name is fairly written, as shall appear. You do not remember, Gentlemen, anything of what that Parchment contain'd? *(Undoing the Box.)*

WITWOUD. No.

PETULANT. Not I. I writ. I read nothing.

MIRABELL. Very well; now you shall know. Madam, your promise.

LADY WISHFORT. Ay, ay, Sir, upon my honour.

MIRABELL. Mr. *Fainall,* it is now time that you shou'd know that your Lady, while she was at her own disposal, and before you had by your Insinuations wheedl'd her out of a pretended Settlement of the greatest part of her fortune—

FAINALL. Sir! pretended!

MIRABELL. Yes, Sir. I say that this Lady while a Widow, having it seems receiv'd some Cautions respecting your Inconstancy and Tyranny of temper, which from her own partial Opinion and Fondness of you, she cou'd never have suspected—she did, I say, by the wholesome advice of Friends and of Sages learned in the Laws of this Land, deliver this same as her

Act and Deed to me in trust, and to the uses within mention'd. You may read if you please—*(Holding out the Parchment.)* tho' perhaps what is inscrib'd on the back may serve your occasions.

FAINALL. Very likely, Sir. What's here? Damnation! *(Reads.) A deed of Conveyance of the whole Estate real of* Arabella Languish, *Widow, in trust to* Edward Mirabell. Confusion!

MIRABELL. Even so, Sir; 'tis *the Way of the World,* Sir, of the Widows of the World. I suppose this Deed may bear an elder Date than what you have obtain'd from your Lady.

FAINALL. Perfidious Fiend! then thus I'll be reveng'd. —*(Offers to run at Mrs.* Fainall.*)*

SIR WILFULL. Hold, Sir, Now you may make your *Bear-Garden* flourish somewhere else, Sir.

FAINALL. *Mirabell,* You shall hear of this, Sir; be sure you shall. Let me pass, *Oaf!*

Exit.

MRS. FAINALL. Madam, you seem to stifle your Resentment; you had better give it Vent.

MRS. MARWOOD. Yes, it shall have Vent—and to your Confusion, or I'll perish in the attempt.

Exit.

LADY WISHFORT. O Daughter, Daughter, 'tis plain thou hast inherited thy Mother's prudence.

MRS. FAINALL. Thank Mr. *Mirabell,* a cautious Friend, to whose advice all is owing.

LADY WISHFORT. Well, Mr. *Mirabell,* you have kept your promise, and I must perform mine. First, I pardon, for your sake, Sir *Rowland* there, and *Foible.* The next thing is to break the Matter to my Nephew, and how to do that—

MIRABELL. For that, Madam, give yourself no trouble; let me have your Consent. Sir *Wilfull* is my Friend; he has had compassion upon Lovers and generously engag'd a Volunteer in this Action, for our Service, and now designs to prosecute his Travel's.

SIR WILFULL. 'Sheart Aunt, I have no mind to marry. My Cousin's a Fine Lady, and the Gentleman loves her, and she loves him, and they deserve one another; my resolution is to see Foreign Parts. I have set on't—and when I'm set on't, I must do't. And if these two Gentlemen wou'd travel too, I think they may be spar'd.

PETULANT. For my part, I say little; I think things are best off or on.

WITWOUD. I' Gad, I understand nothing of the matter; I'm in a maze yet, like a *Dog* in a *Dancing School.*

LADY WISHFORT. Well Sir, take her, and with her all the Joy I can give you.

MILLAMANT. Why does not the man take me? Wou'd you have me give myself to you over again.

MIRABELL. Ay, and over and over again; for I wou'd have you as often as possibly I can. *(Kisses her hand.)* Well, heav'n grant I love you not too well; that's all my fear.

SIR WILFULL. 'Sheart, you'll have him time enough to toy after you're married; or if you will toy now, let us have a Dance in the meantime, that we who are not Lovers may have some other employment besides looking on.

MIRABELL. With all my heart, dear Sir *Wilfull.* What shall we do for Musick?

FOIBLE. O Sir, some that were provided for Sir *Rowland's* Entertainment are yet within Call.

A Dance.

LADY WISHFORT. As I am a person I can hold out no longer. I have wasted my spirits so today already that I am ready to sink under the fatigue; and I cannot but have some fears upon me yet that my Son *Fainall* will pursue some desperate Course.

MIRABELL. Madam, disquiet not yourself on that account. To my knowledge his Circumstances are such, he must of force comply. For my part, I will Contribute all that in me lies to a Reunion. *(To Mrs.* Fainall.*)*

673 *Son:* son-in-law.

In the meantime, Madam let me before these Witnesses restore to you this deed of trust. It may be a means, well manag'd, to make you live easily together.

From hence let those be warn'd, who mean to wed,
Lest mutual Falsehood stain the Bridal-Bed;
For each Deceiver to his Cost may find,
That Marriage Frauds too oft are paid in kind.

Exeunt Omnes.

Epilogue.

Spoken by Mrs. Bracegirdle.

After our *Epilogue* this Crowd dismisses,
I'm thinking how this Play'll be pull'd to Pieces.
But pray consider ere you doom its fall,
How hard a thing 'twould be to please you all.
There are some Criticks so with Spleen diseas'd,
They scarcely come inclining to be Pleas'd;
And sure he must have more than mortal Skill,
Who pleases anyone against his Will.
Then, all bad Poets we are sure are Foes,
And how their Number's swell'd the Town well knows;
In shoals I've mark'd 'em judging in the Pit;
Tho' they're on no pretence for Judgment fit,
But that they have been Damn'd for want of wit.
Since when, they, by their own offences taught,
Set up for Spies on Plays, and finding Fault.
Others there are whose Malice we'd prevent;
Such who watch Plays with scurrilous intent
To mark out who by *Characters* are meant.
And tho' no perfect likeness they can Trace,
Yet each pretends to know the *Copy'd Face.*
These with false Glosses feed their own Ill-nature,
And turn to *Libel,* what was meant a *Satire.*
May such malicious *Fops* this Fortune find,
To think themselves alone the *Fools* design'd;
If any are so arrogantly Vain,
To think they *singly* can support a *Scene,*
And furnish *Fool* enough to entertain.
For well the Learn'd and the Judicious know,
That *Satire* scorns to stoop so meanly low
As any *one abstracted Fop* to shew.
For, as when Painters form a matchless Face,

They from each *Fair One* catch some different Grace,
And shining Features in one Portrait blend,
To which no single Beauty must pretend;
So Poets oft do in one Piece expose
Whole *Belles Assemblées* of *Cocquettes* and *Beaux*.

FINIS.